Communication in Education

Richard A. Fiordo

Editor

Detselig Enterprises Ltd.

Calgary, Alberta

Richard A. Fiordo

University of Calgary
Calgary, Alberta, Canada

Canadian Cataloguing in Publication Data

Main entry under title:

Communication in Education

ISBN 1-55059-003-0

1. Communication in education.   2.
Interpersonal communication.   I. Fiordo,
Richard A.
LB2806.C64 1989   371.1'022   C89-091198-3

371.1022 C734f

Communication in education

© 1990 by Detselig Enterprises Ltd.
P.O. Box G 399
Calgary, Alberta, Canada T3A 2G3

Printed in Canada   SAN 115-0324   ISBN 1-55059-0003-0

Preface

This book was designed to apply communication studies to the training of teachers and instructors generally. An interdisciplinary approach was used. The book emphasizes communication studies in relation to educators and instructors in several fields. The educators may be in a training program at a university, already working in a school, or working in a training department in government or business. The book addresses readers interested in educational and instructional communication. Whether the readers are undergraduate students, graduate students, or practioners in an educational or informational field, the writings have clarity and depth sufficient to satisfy the interests of its readers.

If instructional communication outside the field of education is the primary concern, the writings in this book will be able to guide readers not majoring in education toward the beneficial acquisition of information. Readers outside education who would benefit from improving their instructional and informative skills include social workers, nurses, clergy, lawyers, doctors, managers, counselors, administrators, and those working to advance their grasp of educational communication.

Many books in communication attain clarity without depth or depth without clarity. The purpose of some communication books is to introduce readers to the subject area of communication. The purpose of other texts is to assume introductions have been made and then treat special subject areas of communication with sophistication. Both types of communication books may attain their ends. The present book introduces readers interested in educational communication to general topics in the field of communication and education; it also develops selected special topics. The contributions to this book were designed to meet the general and special needs of introducing material and developing it. Since footnotes and references abound in the writings, readers are encouraged to investigate the sources of the contributors scholarship.

The material presented in Part A provides the textual core of curriculum for the field of communication. An overview of communication principles and research are related to the field of education. The content has been adjusted to address the concerns of the classroom teacher; the concerns pertain to communication in general and educational communication in particular. The material puts theory into practice and practice into theory. Based on research and experience, the content is practical. Educators interested in advancing communication competence constitute the primary audience for Part A of this book; communication students interested in education constitute the secondary audience; and people in general concerned about communication used for instructional purposes constitute the tertiary audience.

Section one provides an overview of communication with an emphasis on interpersonal and intrapersonal dimensions. Section two presents information on professional codes, interpersonal values, and social standards: that is, what is of value, what to pursue and abandon, and how to judge and relate. Section three details material on gender and intercultural issues in educational communication. Section four explains the organizational concepts and principles that apply to communication within educational systems and communities: that is, how communication functions in the organizational context of a school. Section five provides information on verbal and nonverbal communication pertinent to educational settings, and chapter six elucidates (for teachers who are neither technicians nor technological) the essentials of educational communication mediated especially through the unfolding of electronic communications technologies.

Part B serves to amplify portions of the content of Part A. Some instructors may wish to use the chapters in Part B to supplement the material in Part A; others may wish to use the material for optional reading.

These chapters cover special communication topics that are related to the core materials in Part A. Part B is designed to be used for classroom discussion or integrated with the core curriculum found in Part A; it has the additional capacity to be utilized to illustrate research methods – statistical, interpretive, critical, historical, and discourse analysis; and it may thereby serve to illuninate the special content and method related to communication.

Contents

Verbal and Nonverbal Communication

Educational Communications Technology

Part B: Selected Readings

Contributors

Joe Ayres, Ph.D., Professor, Department of Communications, Washington State University.

John Beames, M.A., Teacher, Calgary Public School District.

Robert Chester, Ph.D., Associate Professor, Department of Language Education, The University of British Columbia.

Howard Cotrell, M.S., Associate Professor, Instructional Media Center, Bowling Green State University.

Joseph DeVito, Ph.D., Professor, Department of Communications, Hunter College – CUNY.

Ray Fenton, Ph.D., Researcher, Assessment and Evaluation, Anchorage School District, Alaska.

Richard Fiordo, Ph.D., Department of Teacher Education and Supervision, The University of Calgary.

John Friesen, Ph.D., Professor, Department of Educational Policy and Administrative Studies, The University of Calgary.

Vic Grossi, Ph.D., Director, Calgary Outreach Services, Alberta.

Lynne Hughes, M.A., Instructor, Effective Writing Program, The University of Calgary.

William Hunter, Ph.D., Educational Technology Unit, The University of Calgary.

Tom Jones, Ph.D., Assistant Professor, Department of Educational Psychology, The University of Calgary.

Madeline Keaveney, Ph.D., Professor, Department of Communication, University of California – Chico.

Paul Licker, Ph.D., Associate Professor, Faculty of Management, The University of Calgary.

John Leipzig, Ph.D., Associate Professor, Department of Speech and Drama, University of Alaska – Fairbanks.

Kathleen Mahoney, LL.M., Associate Professor, Faculty of Law, The University of Calgary.

Suzanne McCorkle, Ph.D., Associate Professor, Department of Communication, Boise State University.

Neal Muhtadi, M.A., Associate Superintendent of Schools, Abbotsford School District, B.C.

Doug Nancarrow, Ph.D., Professor, Communication Arts, Alaska Pacific University, Anchorage.

Frank Oliva, Ph.D., Dean, Faculty of Education, The University of Calgary.

James Owen, Professor, Department of Communication, University of Nevada – Reno.

Erv Schieman, Ph.D., Associate Professor, Department of Curriculum and Instruction, The University of Calgary.

Ronald Sept, Ph.D., Assistant Professor, Graduate Program in Communication Studies, The University of Calgary.

LeRoy Travis, Ph.D., Associate Professor, Department of Educational Psychology and Special Education, The University of British Columbia.

Claudio Violato, Ph.D., Associate Professor, Department of Teacher Education and Supervision, The University of Calgary.

Richard Weaver II, Ph.D., Professor, Department of Communication, Bowling Green State University.

Acknowledgments

My special thanks are extended to my family for their patience and help during the development of this book. For their suggestions on the form and content of the manuscript, I thank Marilyn Stratton, Cynthia Fiordo, Claudio Violato, Ted Giles, Madeline Keaveney and Erv Schieman. For their technical assistance, I thank Doug Dau, Elaine Henry, and Heber Jones. For their secretarial assistance, I thank Doreen de Souza and Dolores Clarkson. For their professional efficiency and humane cooperation, I thank all the contributing authors. My lifelong thanks go to my junior high school son, Nicolin, and all those who encourage human communication to advance beyond the trivial, the deceitful, the vindictive, and the unproductive.

Appreciation is expressed for permission to reprint the following article: *Communication Reports,* "Interpersonal Surrogates and Communication Theory (A Behavioral View)" by James L. Owen in Vol. 2, No. 1, Winter 1989, pp 48-51.

Detselig Enterprises Ltd. appreciates the financial assistance for its 1990 publishing program from

Alberta Foundation for the Literary Arts
Canada Council
Department of Communications
Alberta Culture

Part A

Core Communication Curriculum

Do not imagine that the exploration
ends, that she has yielded all her mystery
or that the may you hold
cancels further discovery

. . . .

I mean the moment when it seems most plain
is the moment when you must begin again.

From "The Discovery," Gwendolyn Macewen

Section One

Interpersonal and Intrapersonal Communication

1

Overview

Richard A. Fiordo

In a chapter on "Pedagogic Communication" in a book entitled *Human Communication,* the Spanish philosopher Jose Luis Aranguren maintains that the family constitutes the first school of communication. While it constitutes the first school of "tension, toleration, discussion, integration, adoption and disagreement," the family also provides the first school of non-communication and its accompaniments of disintegration, broken relationships, "divorce, desertion and serious quarrels." In modern schools, "as in the family and other informal educational structures," integration and disintegration create tension. Fluctuation between being communicative and being uncommunicative creates tension.

Aranguren calls attention to two major directions in the style of teaching (or, educational communication). One direction reveals the suitability of the teacher and the other reveals the unsuitability. The suitable teacher practices quick and direct communication, is accessible, is ready to provide information, directs studies, makes suggestions, advises, and does research with students. The unsuitable teacher executes educational duties in a "purely formal way" and through aloofness inhibits communication with students.[1] With a leaning toward suitability, the writings in this textbook address both directions. Suitable communication, in short, is an integrating force.

This chapter of the book will survey fundamentals of communication studies in application to the field of education and will cover terms, concepts, and principles from communication applicable to teachers and future teachers in schools in the North American milieu.

3

Models

Numerous models of human communication exist. Many models appropriate to educational communication exist as well.[2] The educational communication model presented here is sufficiently broad and abstract enough to include the organizational and interpersonal contexts of educational communication discussed throughout this textbook. It will also serve to meet the general interest level of education students studying communication. Figure 1 presents a model that is not highly technical yet covers communication components applicable to interpersonal communication in education.

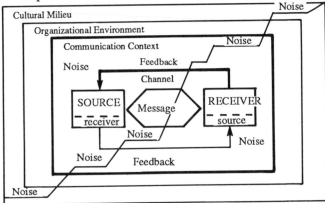

Figure 1: Interpersonal Model of Communication

Applied to the classroom, a specific model follows in Figure 2:

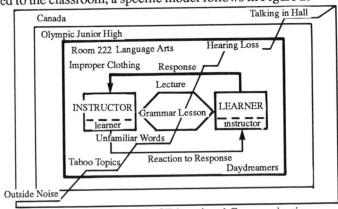

Figure 2. Applied Model of Educational Communication

The *cultural milieu* refers to the legal, provincial, or national setting in which we communicate. The *organizational environment* is the school in which we communicate. The *educational communication* context refers to the classroom in which we communicate and includes the history we have with each group of students on a daily and semesterly basis. It is the place and time that binds teacher with students for the daily pedagogical tasks of the term. We can, in fact, delineate additional contexts: one for the school district, another for the nation, and so on. To differentiate distant situational influences from close situational influence, we selected the three terms of milieu, environment, and context. There is no need to adhere to these divisions. They are mere conveniences.

Within the educational communication context, where the immediate action of communication is to be found, a *source* initiates a *message* and sends it to a *receiver* (or receivers) through a *channel* of communication. The receiver then returns the message to the source through *feedback* that is *nonverbal* to *verbal*. The role of source and receiver is interchangeable. The source may become a receiver, and a receiver may become a source. The model shows this through capital and small letters.

As teachers we serve primarily as sources but secondarily as receivers. The reverse is true of our students. They may serve primarily as receivers but secondarily as sources. The ratio of being a source to being a receiver in a classroom would vary according to many factors. The style of instruction, for example, would see one teacher as being 51% source, a second teacher as being 67% source, and a third teacher as being 95% source. The percentages might correspond crudely to *laissez faire, democratic,* and *authoritarian* styles of teaching: where control as a source is comparatively low for the laissez faire style, comparatively high for the authoritarian style, and somewhere in between for the democratic style.

Further, the model shows *noise* slashing through all the components. Noise refers to the interference and distortion present in any effort to communicate. The noise may be in the channel, the message, the communicators and their roles as sources and receivers, the context (or environment or milieu), and even in the feedback. Whenever we try to get an idea or feeling across to someone, we face noise. What is clear to us confuses others. What is acceptable to us offends others. What we intend with kindness may be construed as malice. While noise erodes communication and may eventuate in a *communication breakdown* (or the termination of communication), it does not go unchecked. One countermeasure to noise is redundancy (or repeating and varying a message). Noise, also, has a positive side – especially in education; it tells us how and where we are failing to teach.[3] The model combines the notions of communication as a transactional process with communication as the creation of meaning.[4] It assumes that communication involves active and meaningful participation between communicators. Sources and receivers negotiate meaning in a context with interference.

Educational communication has the restriction of aiming to instruct and manage classroom behavior. Educational communication tries to gain comprehension of subject matter and acceptance of conduct appropriate for learning. The differentiated end, in other words, of educational communication is learning: primarily of goals we target broadly (math, science, social studies, etc.) as well as specifically (factoring equations, osmosis, racism, etc.).

Each component of the communication model has meaning to the interacting communicators. A source may like spoken communication but may not like written communication. A receiver may appreciate a lecture linked to a slide show more than a lecture linked to a blackboard. A teacher (source) may prefer students (receivers) in middle school to those in high school. One group of students may favor a friendly teacher to a task master; another group may favor a task master to a friendly teacher. Others may want both. In other words, communication entails a content component and a relational component. We communicate about various subjects or topics, but we also communicate status and role and power distinctions.[5] Although each component has meaning and significance to the communicators, the range of meaning varies between communicators.

The source then is the initiator of a message. The receiver is the reactor to the message. The receiver actively participates in interpreting the message rather than passively absorbing it. The channel is the vehicle by which the message reaches one or more of the five senses of the communicators. In teaching, speech would be the primary channel. The contexts generally refer to the external conditions under which messages are transacted. Feedback applies to the response of a receiver to a message. It monitors, corrects, regulates, and appraises the effort of a source to get the desired response from the receiver. Feedback is signalled from receivers to sources through applause or boos, nods or frowns, attention or inattention, supportive comments or criticisms, and technical problems or successes in the use of media (e.g., overhead projectors, slides, etc.) during the source's presentation. It is verbal when words are used and nonverbal when other cues are used – gesture, facial expression, nearness, contact, pausing, tone of voice, silence, clothing, and any other signal that occurs in addition to (or in the absence of) words.

The message itself is the idea put into a code. Usually, in a classroom, the code will be a natural language: for example, English or French. The source encodes the idea or feeling (that is, says it in English or French) and the receiver decodes it (that is, deciphers the English or French). The message, however, in spoken communication, which is the most common mode of classroom teaching, may also be nonverbal. A well placed glance, a cough, a smile, a frown, and a pounding of a gavel exemplify nonverbal messages. Noise interference crosses all the components. Static on a telephone line, snow on a television picture, shouting in a classroom, a lawn being cut outside a classroom in session, a denasal voice, bizarre clothing, distracting cologne, a foreign language, unfamiliar words, an accent, an unpreferred age, inadequate knowledge, and any of a thousand other barriers constitute examples of noise. In school, what blocks our efforts to have students learn constitutes noise. Noise is always present, ever threatening to rain on the instructional parade. While it cannot be eliminated once and for all, it can be contained. Reducing noise in the communication must be your educational challenge. Ignore it and noise will destroy instruction. Once again, in this text, to communicate is to affect especially with intent through signs and language.[6] To teach (or practice educational communication) is to influence learning, especially by design, through signs and language.

Types of Communication

There are various types of communication – intrapersonal, interpersonal, public, mediated, organizational, intercultural, and mass. This text presents applied educational perspectives on these types of communication with the exception of mass communication which deals with messages mediated through television, newspapers, billboards, movies, and other channels aimed at comparatively large audiences. While mass communication functions to educate or teach, the practice of communication in the schools is our primary concern.[7]

Let us begin with a glance at *intrapersonal communication* which takes place within each of us as we talk to ourselves, rehearse, take the role of others, and come to see ourselves – as Tibetan Buddhists say - with all our joys and sorrows, hopes and disappointments, kindnesses and cruelties, loves and lusts, and angelic and devilish aspects. Intrapersonal communication is seen as the operational base for all the other types.[8] If we ignore Socrates' advice to know ourselves, we are like personae in a play rather than real people talking. *Interpersonal communication,* applies to people in dyads (twos), triads (threes), and small groups (usually four to eight) transacting messages and meaning. The communication may be mediated (as with telephones) or unmediated (as with face-to-face situations).[9] Small group communication is sometimes placed apart from interpersonal – committees, therapy groups, interest groups,and school clubs frequently fall into this category. Small group texts and research on small group are prolific and subsequently may warrant separate status.[10] In our general treatment of educational communication, small group is included in interpersonal.

Public communication refers to the sending of messages to an audience. Public communication generally refers to messages sent predominantly one way from a speaker to a group of listeners – a public. Public speaking exemplifies public communication. When a television station broadcasts a speech, the public communication overlaps with mass communication. When the public becomes familiar, public communication overlaps with interpersonal.[11] Sermons and lectures may lean toward mass communication when mediated via radio and may lean toward interpersonal when unmediated in front of a small audience. In teaching, we lean toward the interpersonal type usually in what may be called one-to-group, one-to-many, or teacher-class communication.[12]

Organizational communication refers to messages transacted within, from, and to an organization. The Oliva chapter discusses this area. School boards and schools would be such organizations. Teachers, administrators, students, librarians, secretaries, counsellors, coaches, school bus drivers, police, nurses, janitors, teacher aides, and parents may function in varying degrees within it. *Intercultural communication* applies to sending and receiving messages between organizations and individuals from different cultures, societies, or countries.[13] The Friesen chapter details this area. In Canadian schools, a teacher raised in Japan teaching science, three students who are Peigan taking social studies, a counsellor trained in Scotland, and a librarian from Kenya, would create conditions for intercultural or cross-cultural communication. Some would extend intercultural communication to subgroups as well.[14] To students in a class at an orphanage, a young offenders centre, or a school for the deaf, intercultural communication would also be applicable.

Finally, *mediated communication* pertains to the use of various technologies to mediate the sending and receiving of meaning and messages. The Schieman, Jones, and Hunter chapters address mediated technological communication. Included in this type would be all communication media from overhead projectors to interactive videodiscs, from school intercoms to electronic mail, and telecommunication devices for the deaf to educational microcomputers. Wherever low-tech or high-tech communication devices serve as the channel, mediated communication is in effect.[15]

(Notes for the first four chapters are located at the end of chapter four.)

2

The Learning Leaning

Richard A. Fiordo

The Learning Leaning

In educational communication, learning should be the primary effect (goal) sought. The learning, interest, bias, preoccupation, preference, or restriction of educational communication involves learning as the primary result sought. Learning is the primary, but not the exclusive, consequence of education. Other effects may be amusement, influence, and acculturation. Traditional speech studies examined purposes of speaking: that is, speaking to instruct, to entertain, and to amuse.[16]

The focus on effects, rather than intention, forces us to unduly give more weight to this leaning. We may want laughs and get them, want attitude change and get it; but we must dwell in education especially on wanting students to learn and getting them to learn. Thus, effects and intentions are seen here as primary and secondary concerns. What we want our students to learn and what they learn are not usually the same. We may want them to attain a certain score on a science test. Yet, they score less than our dream.

By focusing on intention, we may decide our efforts were worthwhile even though the ends of education were not attained. While this too may be an acceptable procedure, it does not give us adequate interpretation of the results. Our intention in writing the chapters of this textbook is to assist education students to improve their practice of communication, especially as it occurs in the schools, a decent goal indeed.

The educational bias of communication does not ignore diverse communication effects; it simply emphasizes learning as the primarily desirable effect. The students may laugh, change their thinking or behavior, and even modify their cultural conditioning in addition to learning. But, learn they must. Learning and its verification through results directs us, as teachers, to focus on actual accomplishments rather than the goals.

A comedian must focus on getting us to listen and laugh. A salesperson must focus on getting us to buy a Rainbow vacuum cleaner. A teacher must focus on getting us to learn something. When Peggy on the T.V. show "Married with Children" advises her neighbor, Marcy, never to let her husband enjoy food at home or he will never take her out for dinner, we may laugh as well as modify an attitude and learn something about the popular treatment (or mistreatment) of women. When Roseanne Barr gets us laughing at ourselves and our times, clearly she may also instruct us on folly and wisdom as well as change our attitudes or behavior on current affairs. When aerobic champions sell us memberships in their aerobic studios, they also serve to entertain us for a sweaty hour and instruct us on proper training and diet. However, should the entertainers focus more on instructing us than on amusing us, their ratings will drop. If salespeople focus more on instructing than on selling, their earnings will drop. Teachers may get a few laughs and even convince students they must join the debate team if true education is to be achieved. Yet, teachers must teach, or their evaluations will drop.

With learning as our leaning, we do not ignore other intentions and effects of communication. We simply make sure we lean toward learning as much as circumstances permit. We seek the effect of learning (purpose of instruction) primarily and the effects of humor (purpose of entertainment) and attitude or behavior change (purpose of persuasion) secondarily.

Meaning and Educational Communication

Meaning has two aspects for our purposes: signification and significance. When we struggle to express what we mean, we signify or symbolize an idea and we assign importance or value to our idea. Each word or symbol we use will have signification that denotes, designates, or points to something. "Sheltie" signifies a breed of dogs. "Feminism" signifies "organized activity on behalf of women's rights and interests." Dictionary definitions tend to be significations or denotations. The signification may be concrete and a part of the empirical world, such as the signification of the word "Sheltie," or the signification may be abstract and a part of the ideational world, such as the signification of the word "feminism." Each word we use will also have significance that connotes, suggests, evaluates, and prescribes favorable feelings and approach behavior.[17] "Sheltie" may have a positive significance and favorable associations of a family's four-legged friend or negative significance and unfavorable associations of a snapping, nervous, pesty, four-legged nuisance. "Feminism" too may have positive significance and favorable associations of women liberating themselves from the chains of masculine enslavement or negative associations of women wanting rights without responsibilities, freedom without duty, and advancement without qualifications.

As we speak before our classes, the words mean nothing if they are only recorded in a dictionary. Meanings operate in the students in our classes. Our students have (or lack) meanings for words. Meanings are in our students, not in the words per se. If we use unfamiliar words in class without explanation and definition, the meanings may not be clear from the context of the word use. We must select words, especially key ones, with signification and significance in mind. If we do not, learning suffers.

Tetragrammaton is a word well known to some, unfamiliar to others. To use such a word in a general class of Canadian students would likely earn us quizzical looks. Its signification and significance would be missing. Reasonably, we would introduce the term and then define it. However, if we know in our classes we have several Biblically oriented students, the likelihood is that they would have accurate signification of this term and favorable significance. Do you have signification for this term? Do you have significance for this term? If you have significance, is it positive or negative – or, perhaps, neutral?

Signification and significance change. Words known and valued today may be forgotten and devalued tomorrow. Our meanings for words fluctuate. They grow and shrink in signification or in significance. Figure 3 shows what is meant.

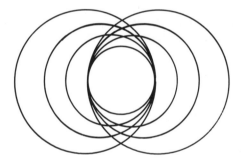

Figure 3: Meaning Fluctuations

Some terms grow in signification, others in significance. Some shrink in signification and grow in significance. "Lassie," the T.V. superdog, may over time grow in significance yet shrink or remain the same in signification, whereas "autism" over the years may shrink in significance yet grow or remain the same in signification. "Lassie" may, in other words, connote more and denote less, while "autism" may connote less and denote more. Controversial words may develop in this manner. "Homosexuality" may at first be high in significance but low in signification. Once we study homosexuality, the significance may shrink and the signification may grow. Sacred words may grow in both directions. If *satori* is studied, signification may grow through our acquisition of knowledge, significance through respect and benefits gained.

Other words may shrink in both signification and significance.[18] A word like "mugwump," for example, may lose both.

In a classroom, we might apply this principle and test our students' changes in meaning. We might have them read the same poem for two months and note how signification and significance have changed. Remember this. We mean. Our students mean. We learn meaning. What is signified and valued at a given time is the meaning from which we instruct. We have meanings that may be changed. As teachers, we aim to change meaning constructively and intelligently.

Levels of Abstraction in Educational Communication

Recounting a theme from Alfred Korzybski, founder of general semantics, Bois emphasizes that Korzybski held that his major effort in general semantics (or, the study of the relationships among language, thought and action) was to "bring about self-realization through a *general consciousness of abstracting.[19]* So important is abstracting in human communication that Johnson claims the "abuse of the process of abstracting gives us an array of symptoms of personal and social maladjustments."[20] Despite its communicative value, the levels and process of abstraction may sometimes be covered in a paragraph or two in a basic communication textbook. While we will write more than two paragraphs, we will not even approach the extensive worth of this concept. Korzybski wrote at least two hundred pages on it; Bois wrote at least forty pages on it.

In this context, *abstraction (abstracting or abstract)* refers to the process through symbolization of leaving out details, that usually proceeds from lower to higher levels, and is personally projective – that is, we project our perceptual biases outside our nervous systems and see the personally biased projections as real.[21] When we abstract, with interest or bias we "select from among the characteristics of the total ongoing world of processes" whatever is "within our capacity to observe with out unaided senses or with instruments." We ignore or cannot locate an "immensity of characteristics."[22] One test advised for determining abstraction levels produced through the activity of symbolization lies in whether the words (or symbols generally) may be referred to *lower* levels of abstraction rather than to *higher* levels. Hayakawa warns that high-level abstraction is commonly exploited in our society to "befuddle people." Besides, "*all we know are abstractions*" from concrete experience. As a safeguard, he counsels us to look to lower levels of abstraction to ground ourselves in the world of extensional (roughly empirical) experience. High abstraction causes us to get lost in the intensional (roughly mental).[23]

In application, abstraction can be seen in words, paragraphs, chapters, and even whole books that are predominantly at one level of abstraction. Details may abound or be sparse. High-level abstracting means word choices (or habits) have been made with terms that are general instead of concrete and paragraphs that neither analyze nor detail a subject matter. Low-level abstracting means word choices (or habits) that have been made with terms that are concrete instead of general and paragraphs that provide analysis and detail of a subject matter.[24]

If we stay at high-level or low-level abstracting almost always, we use language inadequately and we are guilty of *dead-level abstracting*. When we use language adequately, we "progress from description to higher levels of abstraction by clear and orderly stages, and return to description and to non-verbal demonstration as the needs of evaluation and communication require."[25] Borrowing from Hayakawa's favorite cow, Bessie, the upward and downward path of abstracting becomes visible. There is the *process level* of the cow Bessie known to science: atoms, electrons, et cetera. Then there is the cow we experience through our unaided senses. At this level many of the details known at the level as Bessie are abstracted or left-out. This is the object level of Bessie. Then we come to the first verbal level of the cow "Bessie." "Bessie" is the name for the object level cow. The unique cow we have in our corral. After "Bessie" we have the higher verbal level of "cow." We leave out more details now with each rung of the ladder we climb in abstracting from the process level. After "cow," we may choose "livestock." After "livestock," we may have "farm assets." After "farm assets," we may have "asset." And, after "asset," we may have "wealth."[26] To demonstrate an alternative upward way in abstracting, we might abstract from "cow" to "animal" to "life forms" and to "being." What we abstract and how we do so is again guided by personal interest usually conditioned by societal preferences. Specifics are lost in high-level abstracting; categories are unattained in low-level abstracting. Both have their place in educational communication. Figure 4 clarifies the levels.

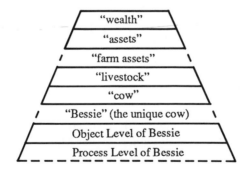

Figure 4: Figure Title

In teaching, the dreaded dead zone of abstraction is dead-level abstracting. *Dead* is the key term here. We should not abstract within a narrow range of levels. Relating dead-level abstracting to dull speaking, Johnson explains that "speakers are dull because either they seldom rise above the level of detailed description" or "seldom descend to the level of description." Consequently they leave us "with the disappointment that comes from having got nothing when presumably something had been promised." The low-level speaker fails to tell us what to do with the details provided while the high-level speaker keeps us from understanding what is being discussed. Relating abstracting to interesting speech, Johnson says the "secret of being an interesting speaker does not lie very largely in choosing interesting subjects." Rather, "it lies, in the main, in the manner of directing the listener's reaction to the subject." The speakers we find interesting usually climb and descend the levels of abstraction systematically. The speakers who restrict themselves within a range of abstraction levels – for example, between "Bessie" and "cow" or between "wealth" and "asset" – offend us regardless of the topic.[27]

Looking at two written selections, the living use of abstraction – that is, moving from higher to lower and lower to higher rhythmically – will be clear. Writing in *Thinking to Some Purpose,* the philosopher L. Susan Stebbing demonstrates her rhetorical wave action between the higher and lower levels of abstraction as she discusses "Democracy and Freedom of Mind":

> We (i.e., *you* or *I* and *you* and any *I*) cannot each of us make our own investigations with regard to the vast majority of the problems upon which we are called to make decisions. I (Susan Stebbing) must rely upon the expert knowledge of the physician when I am sick; I must rely upon Bradshaw when I want to know what trains are available to take me from King's Cross to St. Andrews, and so on. Frequently I am forced to say: 'This person's testimony is reliable'; 'that newspaper's report is to be trusted'. I am forced to say this; if my belief in the reliability of the testimony is false, then I am not free to decide. If such information as I have is not to be trusted, then I lack freedom of decision. For this reason, those who control the press have power to control our minds with regards to our thinking about 'all public transaction'. A controlled press is an obstacle to democracy, an obstacle that is the more dangerous in proportion as we are unaware of our lack of freedom[28].

This learned and eloquent philosopher utilizes higher and lower levels of abstracting to get us to learn something in an interesting manner. Would it not be edifying to have Stebbing's account of the way the Western press reported the "massacre" in Tiananmen Square in Beijing or the Columbian war with the drug lords?

The effective use of the levels of abstraction can be demonstrated from another angle as well. The philosopher Charles Morris gives a detailed account, a summary account of a paragraph, and a short statement of what he calls Ways to Live. These will be discussed later with respect to values. We will demonstrate abstraction at two levels – the summary and the statement, that is, lower and higher levels of abstraction respectively. Discussing a lifestyle he refers to as Way 8, Morris describes it in a middle range of abstraction in a summary paragraph:

Enjoyment should be the keynote of life. Not the hectic search for intense and exciting pleasures, but the enjoyment of the simple and easily obtainable pleasures: the pleasures of just existing, of savory food, of comfortable surroundings, of talking with friends, of rest and relaxation. A home that is warm and comfortable, chairs and a bed that are soft, a kitchen well stocked with food, a door open to the entrance of friends – this is the place to live. Body at ease, relaxed, calm in its movement, not hurried, breath slow, willing to nod and to rest, grateful to the world that is its food – so should the body be. Driving ambition and the fanaticism of ascetic ideals are the signs of discontented people who have lost the capacity to float in the stream of simple, carefree, wholesome enjoyment.[29]

In statement form, Way 8 becomes: "live with wholesome, carefree enjoyment"[30]. In popular song and through T-shirt philosophers, we get a version of Way 8 in the lines: "Don't worry. Be happy." The abstraction of the paragraph from the writing is valid and clear. The abstraction from the paragraph to the statement is valid and clear. Even its vernacular alternative would suffice as an abstraction.

We must keep in mind that the level of abstraction necessary for education and that level preferred by students may conflict. We may choose a middle range, such as the paragraphic account of Way 8. However, some students may call for the chapter with details and others the slogan level. Teachers and professors get criticized when they say too much – a slogan is requested but a chapter arrives. Finding the level of abstraction appropriate to the needs of our listeners and learners becomes our challenge as communicators and teachers. If a Calgarian is asked by a tourist how to get to the Olympic Oval, the response may range from a highly abstract gesture of pointing in a direction to a detailed step-by-step account. What level of abstraction might you select?

3

Teachers and Students –
Sources and Receivers

Richard A. Fiordo

Addressing The Class

As we instruct our students in our subject area, we must also monitor their behavior. In teacher-to-class (one-to-many or stand-up) speaking, the lesson may be a blend of monologue and dialogue. Monologue refers to one-way verbal communication; dialogue refers to two-way verbal communication. The DeVito chapter of this book discusses dialogue in terms of teaching interpersonally. Lectures would lean toward monologue and discussion toward dialogue.[31]

Given the role of nonverbal signals from a class and a teacher during instruction, classroom instruction would lean toward monological or dialogical communication in most cases. Figure 5 illustrates this.

Monologue · · · · · · · · · · · Dialogue
Lecture · · · · · · · · · · · Discussion

One-Way · · · · · · · · · · · Two-Way

Figure 5

Our instruction may have elements of both. The leaning encouraged for the schools would be usually toward dialogue and occasionally toward monologue. Since a *conversational* mode of speech continues to be endorsed by public speaking scholars,[32] dialogue would be conversational. The aim of the conversational style is for your "listeners to feel that you are *talking with them* – not performing for them, lecturing to them, or demonstrating your beautiful oral communication skills."[33]

The method endorsed here as best suited for teaching is the *extemporaneous method*. When we address our class, we may do so "without any advance preparation." This would constitute impromptu speaking. We may read a lecture "from a complete, prepared text." This constitutes a *manuscript speech*. When we memorize the lecture and deliver it, we have a *memorized speech*. While all of these may have places in educational communication, the *extemporaneous speech* (lesson or lecture) is the most commonly used and practicable for daily presentations to classes. In the extemporaneous presentation, we (1) prepare it thoroughly, (2) use a simple outline or notes for reference while speaking, and (3) rehearse the speech aloud and to ourselves in cognitive silence.[34] Ayres discusses this point further in a later chapter along with speaking anxiety. The use of instructional communication aids will be discussed in Schieman's chapter.

When presenting an extemporaneous lesson to a class, regardless of our learned and organized rhetorical manners, our students may engage in trivial pursuits – passing notes, throwing paper, whispering, doodling, daydreaming, and similar distractions. They still must learn through us, distractions or not. In addition to instructing students on some subject, order must also be maintained. We may miss some of their misdoings, see some but not comment on them, and some misconduct may be detected and corrected through comments. At least these three levels can be discernible in our classes. Figure 6 illustrates these three levels of behavior.

Figure 6

Insofar as we stay alert, we detect wrongdoings. Insofar as we articulate remedies quickly and accurately, we correct the deficiencies and excesses in classroom conduct. If we see and correct misbehavior continuously, we maintain order in the classroom. If we miss 60% of the misdeeds and correct but 5% of those we catch, we lose control of the classroom.

To monitor and judge ourselves, we could refer to Performance Criteria used through many practicums for student teachers.

Depending on the special effects sought and the specific circumstances, the criteria for judging classroom instruction and educational communication in general abound. These are but two sets of performance criteria in a list longer than the over two thousand year history of the subject.

Listening in the Classroom

In a general sense, *listening* refers to "making an effort to hear and understand a speaker's statement."[35] In the classroom, *listening* may apply to teachers and students exerting themselves to hear (receive or decode) and understand one another's verbal and nonverbal messages. While both messages are vital to comprehension, the traditional emphasis has been on verbal statements. Listening is a complex communication perspective in itself. For an extensive account of listening, Wolvin and Coakley's *Listening* is recommended. Our failure to listen results in our failure to learn.[36]

Reporting on classroom research on listening, Wolvin and Coakley conclude "listening is a major vehicle for learning in the classroom" and "the main channel of classroom instruction." In one study, elementary students spent 54% of their time listening to the teacher. In another study, high school students spent 66% of their time listening to the teacher. In a third study, while college women spent 42% of their "daily communication time listening," 82% of the college students who took part in the study judged listening as "equal to or more important than reading as a factor contributing to academic success in college." In a fourth study, college students spent 52.5% of their "total verbal communication time listening," 17.3% reading, 16.3% speaking, and 13.9% writing.[37]

Important as listening may be, we may still abuse it when we teach. Diogenes taught that we have two ears and one mouth in order to listen twice as much as we speak. When we choose to speak far more than we listen, we might be seen by others as having small ears and a large mouth:

When we choose to listen far more than we speak, we might be seen by others as way having big ears and a small mouth:

Are you either extreme? If not, what would your ear-mouth proportions be? Draw your own picture here:

This wisdom applies especially to teaching. Teacher and students must listen to one another and carefully use the feedback to improve the conditions for learning. When designing our lessons, we can take listening into account as an educational tactic. Since students have to hear us, we may prepare our instructional materials with their reactions in mind. We can decide to include or exclude materials on the grounds that our pupils may not receive certain information favorably at a certain time of the week or may not comprehend other information at a certain time in the semester. We analyze our audience as listeners. What will they listen to, and what will they ignore? What will get them to attend and what will produce daydreaming? We anticipate the effects our lesson will have on our listening students. We also anticipate duration, intensity, and frequency of listening in our class of listeners. Some will pay full attention to us throughout the day everyday. Audience analysis in a classroom, as with a public, is listener (or better, listening, as in Who is listening?) analysis. We must anticipate our students' backgrounds, knowledge, and understanding of the subject. It is also necessary for us to watch how our listeners are reacting as *we present* our lesson. We must develop skills at interpreting reactions from a class. If they seem bored, confused, or puzzled, we must improve the situation. We may do so by adjusting ourselves, the instructional media, the students, and the classroom to allow for learning to take place. We must also be careful to prevent our students' reactions from irritating or distracting us. Since our students' enthusiasm on our subject may pale next to ours, we must persevere to create interest and involve them – that is, get them to listen.[38]

We analyze those students who listen, those who do not, and those who listen sometimes. When we find out who is not listening, we may investigate how we can get them to listen, and thus contribute to their own learning. We may have to modify our environment, reduce noise, improve our speaking mannerisms, change our choice of topics, vary our use of instructional media, and so forth. Our students may have to hone their listening skills by developing their vocabularies, by concentrating, by remaining open to new ideas, by maintaining an objective mind, by following the lesson, by observing their teacher, by putting themselves in their teacher's place, by taking functional notes, by compensating for petty flaws in a teacher's delivery, by *preparing* to ask questions about the lesson, and by asking questions about the lesson when appropriate.[39]

As teachers and students, we must note obstacles to educational listening. We may: (1) dismiss a subject as uninteresting, (2) avoid listening to difficult material, (3) allow physical surroundings and physical appearance and speaking style to distract us, (4) be too critical, (5) fake attention, (6) listen to only one part of a message, (7) allow loaded language (snarls and purr words, for example) to upset us into blocking the message, (8) waste the advantage of thought speed over speech speed,[40] (9) allow our biases and prejudices to minimize or block or distort one another's meaning. We have obstacles to listening, but do we have remedies?

Hunt and Eadie use Nichols' polarized characteristics of the Good Listener Style and the Poor Listener Style. The Good Listener Style is characterized as being: alert, responsive, patient, not interruptive, empathic, interested, understanding, caring, attending, other-centred, curious, evaluative, unemotional, and not distracted. The Poor Listener Style is characterized as being: inattentive, defensive, impatient, interrupting, disinterested, insensitive, self-centred, uncaring, quick to judge, distracted, apathetic, and emotional.[41] As teachers, we might convert these into lists and check off each side after each class to see which way we lean. When we tally our score at the end of the day and week, we can determine whether our week has embodied mostly the good or the poor listening style. We can then take steps to continue in our good listening style or mend our poor listening style.

Other suggestions useful to teachers for remedying listening problems entail: listening with a purpose, assessing the speaker's purpose, listening defensively, determining to whom the speaker is talking,[42] paraphrasing the speaker while she is speaking to retain ideas rather than fragments of words, offering feedback to the speaker while he is speaking, suspending favorable or unfavorable judgments until the speaker has uttered the entire thought, observing nonverbal signals in relation to verbal ones to catch conflict or harmony between the speaker's content and delivery (that is, the speaker's insincerity may be revealed through contradictory gestures),[43] avoiding counterarguments to a message until we have heard it, checking our understanding with the speaker periodically, assessing the significance of what is being said, probing to assure ourselves we fully understand the speaker, encouraging the speaker to say more to make sure she has presented her ideas fully,[44] and receiving the speaker's message before passing judgment.[45]

Regardless of what we teach, we should teach listening principles and skills.

We should practice these principles and skills as well. In this way we transact and negotiate better conditions for relating interpersonally. In conclusion, in light of our diverse listening purposes and roles and circumstances in the schools, we would benefit from a listening orientation in our communication. And, the listening orientation would be especially helpful if it employed these effective listening keys: attention, concentration, sensory keenness, understanding, sensitivity, empathy, and evaluation.[46] By our listening (or lack of it), we will be approachable (or not).

Questioning in the Classroom

"There is no more important process in education than asking questions," writes Vasile and Mintz. Furthermore, we should never be "too embarrassed to ask questions."[47] As teachers, we must ask questions and encourage our students to ask them as well. There are numerous taxonomies of questions and questioning,[48] but only one system will be treated here. The system is based on the leading question and is called the SEA system. The meaning of this will follow soon.

Burke declares: "All questions are leading questions." Questions do "not have to be 'leading questions' in the obvious sense." This is the angle from which classroom questions and questioning is approached in this writing. Burke adds, implicit in a perspective are "two kinds of questions: (1) what to look for, and why; (2) how, when and where to look for it."[49] In a related, if not identical sense, we propose the SEA system of question. Its roots are semiotic; that is, it functions in our semiotic world of signs, symbols, language, words, processes of symbolizations, and histories of signification. In short, what appears to be a straightforward question may be leading; what appears to be a single question is a multiple question; what is apparently a straightforward question today proves to be a leading one tomorrow; and what appears to be a straightforward question in one set of circumstances becomes a leading question under another set of circumstances.

The motive for treating all questions as being, to some extent leading, is humane. We fool and hurt ourselves (and others) less when we do not pretend our questions are merely straightforward. A student complains to us that on one day we asked how her brother was feeling and on the next day the brother was sent to the coach's office because she said he was in great shape. If he were in great shape, why was he not at wrestling practice?

This "leading" view of questions is the SEA orientation. SEA is an acronym for suggestion, expectation, and assumption.[50] Through a High-SEA question, we lead our students through explicit or implicit meaning that suggests, expects, and assumes a response. High-SEA questions may be humane or cruel. When humanely employed, our questions guide students to a truth dialectically; when cruelly employed, our questions incriminate students eristically (the terms dialectically and eristically are defined in the section "Debate in

Education"). Since a classroom is not an interrogating room at a police station nor a cross-examination session in a courtroom, our questions should be designed to edify maximally and damage minimally. Questions, of course, range from High-SEA to Low-SEA.

Inarguably, Low-SEA questions would loosely and crudely be counterparts to so-called straightforward, direct, or straight questions. If we define artificially the questioning period as a ten minute stretch with no antecedent conditions and no consequent conditions (that is, no history and future for the participants but only a here and now), the classification of so-called direct questions would increase considerably. We believe it would do so at the expense of ourselves and our students. When a student is asked the apparently direct question of "What is the capitol of Prince Edward Island?" and offers the answer "Yellowknife," our response may show whether the question was leading (High-SEA) or direct (Low-SEA). If we request "Please try again," our question was likely a Low-SEA question. However, if we grumble "You never study your geography!" our question was likely a leadingly and punitively High-SEA question. High-SEA questions surprise students through demonstrating their erring ways. Traditionally, this was called by several names: loaded question, leading question, trick question, fallacy of false question, to fallacy of many questions.[51] High-SEA questions have their use in the dialectical pursuit of Socratic truth. Edification is the goal here. High-SEA questions, however, also have their use in the eristic pursuit of error. The goal here is showing others how wrong they are. Victory and humiliation replaces enlightenment and respect.

Typical High-SEA questions include: Have you stopped beating up your brother? Have you stopped cheating on exams? Do you still store liquor in your locker? How did you get away with vandalizing the VCR in the library? All of these High-SEA questions assume or expect or suggest an affirmative answer to a prior question or questions; they assume or expect or suggest the same answer applied to the masked question or questions as well as the apparent question.[52] In other words, you have beaten your brother up, but have you stopped? You never said you did, and the questioner never established that you did. You have cheated on exams, but have you stopped? You never said you cheated on exams, and the questioner never established that you did. You have stored liquor in your locker, but have you discontinued this practice? You never said you stored liquor in your locker, and the questioner never established that you did. Finally, you have vandalized the VCR and gotten away with it, but how did you do so? You never said you vandalized the VCR and never said you escaped detection or punishment, and the questioner never established that you did either. We must make sure the assumptions are converted into established facts before answering. High-SEA torpedoes are dangerous. We must navigate carefully when they are launched.

When High-SEA questions are posed in class, even when done with humor, they produce tension and anxiety to the wary and incrimination to the unwary.

Classroom questions at Low-SEA would be generally more suitable, even though High-SEA questions may have a place in class. With our orientation being that all questions *lead* us to some extent, we choose to be led or not. We have power over the question. The question does not trick us. We are in a state of *semper paratus* – always prepared. We want the advantage of reason and kindness, and we want our students to have it too.

Daily questioning in Low-Sea would be so-called direct questions. While no prior answers to questions need be assumed, we dare to answer the question. We knowingly risk it: knowingly because all questions lead, even the simplest. When we ask in English, "What time is it?" we assume the respondent knows how to tell time and has access to a clock and is willing to give us the time and speaks English. A lot of assumptions for an apparently so-called simple and straightforward question. How many additional assumptions can you find in the four questions at High-SEA cited earlier?

Low-SEA classroom questions would typically be the following: What were the conditions surrounding the Louis Riel rebellion? Where were the 1988 Winter Olympic Games held? Who is the Prime Minister of Canada? What is the area of a rectangle having a length of four meters and a width of ten meters? When did Manitoba join Confederation? And the list goes on.

Whether questions lean toward High-SEA or Low-SEA, they may have two kernel forms – open and closed. *Open questions* imply an unlimited response while closed questions imply a limited response.[53] Objective tests use, for the most part, closed questions – for example, true or false, yes or no, fill-ins and multiple choice. We have a limited range of reaction imposed on us by the question: Is Toronto the capital of New Brunswick? Yes or no? Is Margaret Thatcher an NDP? Yes or no? Is Simon Fraser University in Saskatchewan, California, New South Wales, Bavaria, or none of these areas? All of these are closed questions; they have restricted answers. Essay tests would typically ask open questions. What will be the economic consequences of the new tax on luxury cars? What are the cultural implications of the Old Man River Dam being built? How does the current recession affect teachers' benefits and salaries in Alberta? The responses to these questions are unrestricted unless indicated so: for example, "Please tell us in 500 words or less."

When we ask mostly open questions, we encourage our students to think, research, organize, and express their views. When time permits, this form of question meets the need. When time is limited, we may have to turn to closed questions. Closed questions also serve to elicit specific and concrete information. Time alone is not the only criterion, of course, for using open over closed or closed over open questions. What we want from our students and what is necessary to test them adequately in a subject area constitute additional reasons for using one form over the other.

The employment of High-SEA and Low-SEA in open and closed forms also apply to communication with colleagues, administrators, parents, and people in general. Although we cannot venture into these worthy directions here, we can alert you to the principles of questioning applying elsewhere. As Burke has noted, a sound approach to questioning asks what to look for and why. The SEA system provides for these questions. An approach to questioning should also ask how, when and where to look. The SEA system provides for these questions as well. We look for the depth of SEA in the question to protect ourselves and help our students. We also know how to ask certain questions as well as when and where.

For a detailed account of questioning see Fiordo's "The Semiotic SEA of Questioning" where patterns or formats of questioning are also discussed.[54] For cross-examination techniques of questioning, argumentation and debate texts can be consulted[55] or a regional debate society, such as, the Alberta Debate and Speech Association in Edmonton.

Empirical studies of questioning in the classroom may contribute considerably to improving our teaching. Brophy and Good found teachers reveal preferences through questioning. Who we ask, how frequently we ask them, how long we give them to answer, and how critical we are of their answers reveals preferences we have for students. They also found we call on our "good" students more often than others. We allow "good" students to speak more than others. We give "good" students more help than less favored ones if the answer provided is not exactly correct. If recognized at all, less favored students are simply corrected if they provide a faulty answer. On the other hand, our students play a role in the degree to which we recognize them. Some students may speak frequently in class, talk to us after class, chat with us during office hours, and show concern about their assignments. Others may not emerge without us coaxing them.[56] The result is a function of the two sides transacting (or failing to transact) their interests.

Seiler, Schuelke, and Lieb-Brilhart report a study by Moyer that found that 40% of the teachers studied asked ambiguous questions or questions that had ambiguity in their construction.[57] This may be true especially for questions with several ideas present. The SEA method addresses ambiguity directly. The way we react to questions was studied by Gage and Berliner: how long we wait, whether we give positive or negative feedback to a student's answers, and whether we restructure the response provided by a student.[58] Rowe suggests we wait at least three seconds for our students to respond to our questions. Most of us, she claims, react within one second. A one second *wait time* is simply too short. As we increase our wait time to three or more seconds, we get more volunteered responses, fewer failures to answer, longer responses from our students, more appropriate responses from them and others.[59] Gall estimates that approximately 60% of our questions ask our students to recall facts, around 20% ask our students to reflect, and about 20% are procedural.[60] Daines concluded that classroom questioning practices fail to promote reflective thinking and reduce the desire of class members to listen to a classmate's answer.[61] Communication suffers and so does learning. Hargreaves found open questions produced erratic responses and thereby increased the teacher's risk in managing the class.[62] Brophy and Good concluded we may use closed questions more frequently to manage our classes with a control greater than open questions allow.[63] Teachers must model effective questioning for their students to imitate.[64] We must take into account not only the joys of producing reflection in our students, but also the demands of managing their conduct during our class. Both concerns are real and respectable. Since we will likely continue to question, we should diversify our production of questions to meet the multiple demands school life puts upon us and our students.[65]

Feedback in Education

In describing her communicative relationship with her audience, the expressive female wrestler known as "Mt. Fiji," makes frequent reference to feedback. She is wise, for feedback is a tough term to wrestle with and pin. Attesting to its complexity, Fisher treats feedback as response, reinforcement, internal servomechanism, and social process.[66] Furthermore, he says "any thorough discussion of feedback would be book-length in itself." So, indeed, "Mt. Fiji" is wise or she has read the learned Fisher's text or both. Due to the practical concerns of teachers, we will touch on all four of Fisher's categories for feedback. In principle, however, we will side with the notion of feedback as social interactions involving feedback loops that counteract or correct deviation from the status quo or encourage or accelerate disturbances in a status quo. Hence, feedback loops from teacher to student to teacher or in any other triadic sequence of members of a school where one communication loops back to the initiator and the cycle repeats.[67]

Types of Feedback

In education, feedback in its kernel form might best refer to the verbal and nonverbal response we get from listeners. With respect to desirable expectations, feedback may allow us to recognize our class is favorable to our lessons by three criteria of response: (1) responsiveness, (2) over-responsiveness, or (3) under-responsiveness. These criteria contrast with a class behaving unresponsively or belligerently. We would usually worry less about responsive classes than we would about unresponsive or hostile classes. We would be happy with responsive classes – that is, classes that give us what we like. When the class deviates from our favored expectation, we become concerned. As the class moves great distances from our expectations, our concerns inflate to problems. In Canada, a favorable response might be to have nods of approval with thanks after a class. To be favorably over-responsive, our classes might applaud or shriek or whistle as they would at a Bruce Springsteen or Madonna concert. To be favorable yet under-responsive, our classes might simply be present with low expressiveness and no complaints. Unresponsive students might simply be present while belligerent ones might complain or rebel.

In short, feedback is crucial to our teaching success. If we make efficient use of it, we increase our chance of becoming successful teachers. If you ignore your teeth, a dentist advertises, they will go away. If you ignore feedback from your students, they too will go away – some will withdraw from your class (if possible) and others will withdraw into daydreams to overcome their classroom misery.

In human communication and specifically in educational communication, we obtain feedback ranging from negative to positive and usually in varying amounts. Circumstantially, feedback ranging from audience responsiveness to unresponsiveness becomes negative to positive. Negative feedback tells us to "cut back, slow down, discontinue"; positive feedback tells us to "increase, maintain, keep going."[68] Subsequently, feedback is positive when it praises and negative when it blames.[69]

Feedback may be classified also as *immediate or delayed, direct or indirect, verbal or nonverbal, zero to free,* and *congruent or incongruent.* Although we will mention these other aspects of feedback, we will stress the positive and negative aspects. As teachers we must respond to and give negative and positive feedback. We must notice nonverbal feedback (positive and negative) such as fidgeting before the bell rings or during a test, smiles, sitting close to our desk, yawning, etc., as well as verbal feedback, such as praise ("You make music fun, Ms. Hughes") and blame ("Your social studies lesson was dull, Mr. Jones"). We must also give nonverbal feedback that is negative (stern glances, frowns, etc.) and that is positive (smiles, applause, etc.) as well as verbal feedback that is negative ("You are committing too many fouls during the hockey game, John") and that is positive ("Your chemistry project truly impressed me, Kathleen").

Generally, educators encourage positive feedback and discourage negative feedback, whether the feedback is verbal or nonverbal. *Positive* feedback rewards and informs students for the conduct that is appropriate and desired; *negative* feedback "simply punishes undesirable behavior but does not inform about appropriate, desired behavior." Students may be unable to manage negative feedback from teachers sufficiently; and, teachers may not realize how unproductive their negative feedback can be to disobedient students. While there is evidence in support of the benefits of positive feedback, positive feedback need not always be beneficial. For example, positive feedback (especially when excessive in its use and marginal in its appropriateness) can promote complacency. In class, when we interact with students seeking approval, we will get more positive feedback from them than if we do not seek their approval. In seeking the approval, we use some nonverbal cues more than others: namely, we smile, nod, gesture, modify our timing, and alter our distance. Positive feedback typically – but not always - elicits the outcomes we desire while negative feedback typically – but not always - elicits outcomes we do not desire.[70] Approval and feedback will be discussed next after we examine the other aspects of feedback briefly: immediate and delayed, direct and indirect, verbal and nonverbal, zero and free, and congruent and incongruent.

Feedback allows us, if we dare, to learn whether our students have understood us and are obeying us. Feedback lets us know whether we have made sense to our class and are in charge of our pupils. If we have made sense and are in charge, we have established a common ground for our communication. We are sharing with our class varying degrees of comprehension and acceptance of ourselves, our subject matter, and our rules of educational conduct.

To determine whether we have established a common ground, we may look to feedback broadly first and then analytically. When we analyze feedback, we may discover the specific reasons for having (or not having) established a common ground. *Immediate feedback* refers to responses we obtain from our lesson either instantaneously or very soon after. *Delayed feedback* refers to responses we obtain eventually, but not soon relative to the demands of the situation. We expected a response in ten seconds but got it in a minute. We expected a response in an hour but got it after a week and so on. In a class, immediate feedback would be a prompt answer to a question or a quick response to a request; delayed feedback would be a tardy reaction to a request for a parental signature on a school form or taking a week to return examinations.

Direct feedback points to : (1) responding to a message with nothing intervening and (2) responding in a manner that is not roundabout. *Indirect feedback* points to: (1) responding to a message through someone else and (2) responding in a roundabout manner. In a school, direct feedback would be demonstrated by a principal telling a teacher with frankness that she is not pleased with him; indirect feedback would be shown through a teacher contacting a parent under the guise of ordering coffee and donuts for parents at the next open house as a means to inform the parent eventually of his daughter's misconduct in class.

Verbal feedback means words are the mode of response. Whether spoken or written, language (English, French, German, Ukrainian, Bengali, Bulgarian, Arabic, Mandarin, Luo, Cree, etc.) serves as the response. *Nonverbal feedback* means all those responses which are not a linguistic code – that is, a language per se. Nonverbal responses include the following: kinesics, haptics, proxemics, vocalics, chronemics, physical appearance, environment, and artifacts.[71] Anything planned or spontaneous, from a wink to a pinch or a hug to a slap, constitute nonverbal feedback. Morris believed nonverbal communication was usually a function of language.[72] We understand many gestures and facial expressions – those culturally prescribed such as finger pointing as well as those that occur ideosyncratically such as nervous habits (or nervantics)[73] – through language. Language allows us to forecast and interpret most nonverbals, whether accurately or not. Although estimates that nonverbal communication carries up to 93% of the meaning between two people talking may be faulty, "people rely heavily on nonverbal cues to express themselves and to interpret the communicative activity of others." Often, "nonverbal cues actually carry more weight than verbal ones."[74] As feedback when face-to-face, we cannot avoid nonverbal feedback. Figure 9 is a simple illustration of this.

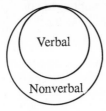

Figure 9

Although we may stop talking when communicating interpersonally, we do not stop signalling nonverbally. Our physical appearance, movement, eye contact, etc., are ongoing. Our words are not. When we speak, in addition to the semantic and syntactic meaning available through words and sentences, we also hear stress, tone, pitch, juncture, rate, volume, quality, and even dialect and idiolect. Clearly, nonverbal feedback is valuable.

In a classroom, verbal feedback would constitute the answer to this question: What is the capital of Nova Scotia? The student's reply of "Halifax" makes up the verbal feedback; but, numerous other cues that were not a part of the language response itself accompany the verbal feedback. These signals would constitute the nonverbal feedback: the answer may have been spoken in polite tones while looking out the window by a Caucasion girl with black hair and green eyes, wearing country and western clothes, about 160 centimeters tall, speaking rapidly in a modulated voice with an accent common to Christchurch, New Zealand.

Zero feedback would apply to a restriction in a school where a channel of communication is blocked. For example, a principal may only allow a grievance pertaining to a teacher from a student to reach his office if the student first files the grievance with a school counsellor and then the school's vice-principal. Thus, a zero feedback condition prevails until (and unless) the hurdles the student has before her have been overcome. Free feedback would apply to the removal of barriers in a school to a channel that has been blocked. For example, a principal may have an open-door policy in her school regarding grievances students have about teachers. If a student wants to complain, the situation permits the feedback loop to the principal to be free. The hurdles are lowered or even removed allowing for the free flow of feedback. Two-way communication supplants one-way.[75]

Zero and *free* feedback are directions rather than attainments. Unless the circumstances are contrived, zero and free feedback are unlikely. However, this can be said of the other dichotomies as well. How pure is positive feedback? Does the negative never work its way into a cheer? As with the other dichotomies (but perhaps more conspicuously so), zero and free feedback involves a predominant direction. Feedback, in other words, leans toward zero – and conceivably attains it – or toward being free – and conceivably attains it. In school settings, the absence of feedback can function as negative nonverbal feedback. Nonetheless, if zero feedback applies to conditions that maximally restrict the loops in our responses and if free feedback applies to conditions that minimally restrict the loops in our responses, then zero and free feedback become a workable notion.

The final classification of feedback treated here will be *congruous* and *incongruous*. This classification is derived from Fisher's account of feedback as a social interaction process that is simultaneous and complementary[76] and Wilmot's account of relational intricacies in dyadic communication.[77] Feedback to Fisher is a circular series of events which look back to the start. It is repeatable and predictable with regularity. It involves "an initial comment, a response to that comment, and reaction to the response."[78] Wilmot's discussion of paradox provides the contrary ingredient: "Paradoxes occur when a communication is self-contradictory."[79] The predictability and regularity of feedback deviates.

Feedback is, thus, congruous when it supplies us with what we expect. It is socially symmetrical, conformable, appropriate, sociable, logical, conventional, and complementary in terms of what we say and do in conversation. The congruous feedback loop gives us a social norm when we interact. Feedback is incongruous when it does not supply us with a social norm when we interact. Although a feedback loop prevails, the loop may be socially uncomplementary, unconventional, illogical, unsociable, inappropriate, and asymmetrical. While congruous feedback provides us with a perspective by congruity, incongruous feedback provides us with a perspective by incongruity.[80]

In a school setting, congruous feedback would be any remarks or gestures that are within a latitude of social acceptability. For example, a teacher may ask a student: Explain how a study of the religions of the world might benefit you even if you are an athiest? When the student responds with original or textbook comments germane to the question, the feedback is congruent.

Incongruous feedback in schools might assume protean manifestations. Some incongruous forms of feedback might circumstantially include: paradoxical responses, humor, answering questions with questions (how Socratic!), non-sequiturs, absurdities, witticisms, irrelevancies, imbecilities, double-binds and other modes of incongruity that might occur in school.

Examples of incongruous feedback abound. Wilmot cites the following paradoxes. Modified for educational settings, as incongruous feedback to a student, a teacher may say: "I want you to disagree with everything I say." A coach may say to an aspiring sychronized swimmer: "Don't think about synchronized swimming." One student may say to an unconscionable classmate: "I always lie."[81]

Consider also the incongruity of the feedback in this story. A teacher of religious studies has a student who discusses matters of religion with him daily and intensely during a school term. The teacher grows confident that this student is well read on these matters and has thought out religious problems well ahead of others in that class. On the final exam, the teacher asks: "Religion – why?" The student replies: "Because." And, the teacher in this case reciprocates the incongruous student response of one word with an incongruous "A" grade.

Or, a teacher has returned from a sabbatical taken in Japan at a Zen monastery. At a luncheon, the principal asks him to say something kind on behalf of a retiring faculty member. The teacher replies at the luncheon: "To Mr. Murphy, may you die of old age and then your children and then your grandchildren." How much astonishment might such praise cause? Clearly, although it is well-wishing that people die in their order of birth at an old age, the circumstances may not accommodate such incongruous insightfulness.

Another example of incongruous feedback comes from Rodney Dangerfield in the movie *Back to School*. He is trying to get a date with an instructor played by Sally Kellerman. Paraphrasing the lines, he asks her for a date on different days. She repeats she is sorry, but she has class on the dates he proposes: "I'm sorry, but I have class." He replies: "Well, then, when you don't have any class, call me." Rodney's feedback is humorously incongruous.

We will end this discussion with the incongruous feedback required of a double-bind communication – simply, a contradictory message where oftentimes the verbal signal contradicts the nonverbal. Drawing from a familiar Zen lesson where a Zen master holds a stick over a student's head and declares: "If you say this stick is real I will strike you with it. If you say this stick is not real I will strike you with it. If you don't say anything, I will strike you with it." Covering the logical options, the Zen master demands feedback. Congruous feedback would likely earn the student a rap on the head. However, if the student is clever enough to provide incongruous feedback, no rap on the head would follow. Many of us would congruently earn a rap on the head. Some of us would escape the Zen master's wrath through the incongruent and pragmatic feedback of grabbing the master's stick, "thereby breaking out of the confining conditions set by the Zen master."[82]

Can you think of other examples of incongruous feedback that use wit, non-sequiturs, and so on? When would you use incongruous feedback to your detriment and when to your benefit? Do you see incongruous feedback as positive, negative, or both?

Feedback for Teachers

Turning to feedback used for the benefit of teachers, we will examine how feedback can help us and hurt us. When we seek specific types of feedback, we must design our message to produce the response we desire. If we want our students to have a favorable response to us, we must present them with messages constructed to gain their approval. We may work toward gaining the approval of our students in numerous ways. The way focused on here is interpersonal attractiveness. Similarity is important for interpersonal attractiveness. If our students identify with us, usually one or more of the following aspects of similarity will be operating namely similar needs, similar attitudes, or similar personalities. To the extent that our students see these qualities in us, they see us as "stable, sincere, and warm."[83] As Burke says, insofar as others identify our ways and words with theirs, they feel one with us and are open to influence from us.[84] The feedback from students we would experience under these favorable conditions might provide us with the students' conduct that is maximally productive and minimally disruptive.

The style we use to communicate also contributes to our attractiveness and subsequent prolific output from our students. The style that Norton and Pettigrew found most attractive was described as dominant and open.[85] A dominant and open style of instructional communication suggests confidence. The confidence may have been the result of praise, rewards, reinforcement, and positive feedback generally.[86] To get positive ratings from our students, according to a study by Eagley and Chaiken, as teachers we can utilize praise and insult strategically. If we prefer feedback from our students that is supportive, we may say praiseworthy things about their attitudes, needs and personalities in order to identify these praiseworthy comments with our own attitudes, needs, and personalities. Incidentally and inarguably, the praise should be deserved to maintain ethical proceedings with our classes. This study found that students receiving praise from a speaker judged the speaker attractive. When insult was used, the speaker was judged unattractive. In short, pleasant things are uttered by attractive people, but unpleasant things are uttered by unattractive people.[87] Paraphrasing an old song, using this diplomatic approach to teaching we are home on the range where seldom is heard a discouraging word.

If we see high ratings from our students this caution should be kept in mind. In the practice of teaching, if we cannot or will not delete all derogation of students, we can certainly with disciplined effort express more praise of them than blame. It may not only be practical for our ratings to soar, but sharing praise and hoarding blame may meet our humane ends as well. We can share and celibrate what is positive with our students, and we can also hoard and mourn what is negative with our students. If students associate ugly people with the saying of ugly things, in our beautification of classroom instruction campaign we may give ourselves a facelift by making pleasant comments.

If this kindly practice were applied to a classroom, it would reflect Boucher and Osgood's findings on the Pollyanna Hypothesis. This hypothesis suggests a universal human leaning toward employing positive words more often and easily under more diverse circumstances than employing negative words. The language of children was found to have higher frequency and diversity in the use of positive words than in the use of negative words. Although this tendency decreases as children grow into adults, the pattern prevails into adult language.[88] If the Pollyanna Hypothesis is valid and reliable, we may deduce that the use of positive words would contribute to our interpersonal attractiveness and eventually to positive feedback from our students. The positive feedback may be direct and immediate or indirect and delayed. We gamble on good manners in abiding by the Pollyanna Hypothesis. When we surrender to the temptation to use snarl words (those that express negative feelings) over purr words (those that express positive feelings)[89] in our classroom, we tilt the Pollyanna scale toward negativity. When our purr words triumph, we tilt the Pollyanna scale in the direction of its tendency toward positive words. Thus, we have some control over our feedback from students, and the responses we want to create in our students can be influenced through these positive procedures.

So whenever we wish to help ourselves by helping our students with their positive options, we may praise their favorite hockey team, compliment them on their good manners during a school visit to the provincial capitol, and endorse their healthy need (or desire) to win the provincial championship in volleyball. We may also discuss topics that are both educational and pleasant whenever we can. If we must discuss unpleasant topics, such as the holocaust of WWII, we may stress the courage and strength of the survivors instead of the ugliness of their oppressors. We can also use words our students judge favorably over those they judge unfavorably. If "awesome" is a well received, descriptive term this semester, why should we not avoid it in class? If profane words are not well received, why should we use them in class? Whenever we have a choice between a favorably received word and one that is not, except for the deliberate educational shock value of employing some exotic words, why should we use negative words in class when so many positive words are available?

We may decide on occasion that negative words and criticism of student attitudes is required. If our general classroom climate is negative and insulting, the serious grievance we have will suffer leveling (the tendency to minimize differences) rather than appreciate sharpening (the tendency to maximize differences[90] by our students. We blur distinctions in our primary instructional style of communication when we fail to polarize negative and positive words as well as complements and criticisms. By clearly separating these features of instructional communication, our students see what we accept and reject in classroom life.

Feedback as Correction

Misbehavior may receive negative feedback in a classroom. The feedback may punish or announce punishment. It may require restitution. However, punishment may dispirit students, be costly, and even be destructive. Our students may not learn nor want to learn as a result of continual negative feedback. So, rather than punish students for misconduct, we urge that rewards be removed as the less destructive form of correction.

Time-out procedures isolate the disruptive student. Five to fifteen minutes of loneliness usually suffices to contain the misbehavior as long as the student recognizes this as unrewarding. In the case of more troublesome conduct, suspension from school becomes the feedback. Our students' misconduct results in a student being sent home for a designated period. About one in every 500 students will require this response.

In addition to time-out and suspension procedures which remove rewards for some time, response cost techniques remove amounts of reward. For example, a class may fine members who use obscenities in class. The students receive negative feedback through consequences arbitrarily designed, logically arranged, and naturally occuring.

An arbitrary consequence would be an arbitrary decision that Caroline and Ralph cannot sit next to each other any more due to their reciprocal disruptiveness. A logical consequence would involve rules: If you shove while in line to get ahead, you go to the end of the line. A natural consequence entails the pressure of reality or natural flow of events without our intervention. We allow the events following our students' actions to produce what they will. Natural shocks may be one unrewarding sequence. For example, we may warn: if you use a straight chair as a rocker, you may fall on the floor. Or, if you get a reputation for stealing, no one will trust you, and you will be the first to be blamed.

Overcorrection is the last form of negative feedback discussed here. We require through it our student to "restore the disrupted situation to a better state than existed before the disruption." In practice, overreaction may be used in this way. If students litter in the lunch room, they would have to clean up what they littered as well as what others littered. Overcorrection requires students to practice appropriate behavior.[91]

Would you provide feedback of the types just mentioned? Which would you provide as feedback? Which type might be most beneficial to you as classroom teachers?

Debate in Education

The Socratic *dialectic* refers to the art of conversing about a subject from every conceivable point of view through questions and answers that proceed toward what is true.[92] In contrast, *eristic* refers to the art of refuting an opponent in order to win rather than determine what is true.[93] Dialectics is still healthy in the modern form of argumentation,[94] and eristic too is doing well in the modern form of cross-examination.[95] These ancient and modern forms of verbal clash are subsumed here under *debate*.

Debate teams in schools can be found throughout Canada and the United States. The dialectic and eristic arts are found within debate in one form or another. Minnick advises us to use familiar terms.[96] Since debate has the broadest currency with the public and in the schools, debate will be our star. Adapting the views of debate scholars to education, when we debate, we argue opposite sides of a proposition (question or resolution) usually to sway the listeners toward our position.[97] That is, when we debate, we argue for opposing sides of a conflict to obtain a decision for one side or the other.[98] "Debate," in brief,"is the vehicle for an argument," just as an automobile provides but one means of transportation. Just as we can travel by airplane and train as well as by automobiles, we can argue in a discussion or in a conversation as well as in a debate.[99] However, debate serves as the most convenient forum for the performance of argumentation.[100] Since debaters expose conflicting ideas to the scrutiny of an audience (or judge) and encourage listeners to make objective decisions, debate becomes a valuable means for promoting democracy and for educating us all. Debate is especially useful in a classroom because it competitively leads to rational choices on issues. The debaters must meet the demands of their opponents' arguments while satisfying a classroom of critical members.[101] Through the use of debate as an instructional method, students and teachers learn how to enhance their capacities to obtain the approval of their listeners.[102] Students and teachers also learn how to back their ideas through a sound argument – that is, "a line of reasoning, with evidence, in support of a conclusion."[103]

During the 1988-89 school year, Canadians heard the leaders of the three major parties in their televised debate. Clash was the norm and goal. Canadians also heard at least portions of the televised *Solidarnosc* (Solidarity) debates in Poland. And, the U.S. Presidential race was also an arena for public debate. In the 1988-89 school year, debate was on the air and in the air not only in the national and international circles but in academic circles as well. The President of the Alberta Debate and Speech Association, John Baty, enjoyed seeing his team win national and world debate championships. In schools throughout Canada, debators contested formally within and between schools. And, finally, informally in classrooms everywhere to some extent, debate served as the method of instruction.

The general treatment of debate in this limited piece should not preclude potential teachers from pursuing debate as an educational tool as well as a tool for democracy, making decisions, thinking critically, appealing to decision makers, and so on. Rather, since attention has been drawn to the glories of debate as a mode of learning, debate should be investigated further for classroom use. The model for classroom use we provide is borrowed from parliamentary debate and adapted with few restraints to the classroom. Parliamentary debate serves to suggest, not prescribe, classroom applications.

Teachers and students involved in parliamentary debate should review parliamentary procedure.[104] While some maintain parliamentary procedure is but common sense with justice and courtesy added, "this is not quite accurate" because parliamentary procedure is a "collection of historical precedents and modern adaptations which sometimes cannot be rationally explained." The filibuster illustrates this point. Although procedures "operate within a democratic framework," rules may be used to "prevent democracy rather than to assure it."[105]

In Canada, the Speaker of the House presides over the debates in the House. A teacher may function as the Speaker of the Class. A guest teacher, respected student, administrator, or qualified parent may also serve as Speaker. The classroom may be arranged similar to the layout of the Legislature. The Speaker of the Class may be positioned at the front of the class with the students taking seats opposite one another on either side of the Speaker depending on their sympathies on the resolution – that is, the motion or proposition of policy scheduled for debate.

Under parliamentary procedures, classroom debaters may act "as members of a legislative assembly considering propositions of policy." The class may also debate propositions of fact and value. Debaters representing "Government members sit to the right of the Speaker" and propose propositions of policy as well as propositions of fact and value. "Debaters representing the Opposition sit on the Speaker's left" and attack the proposition of the Government debaters. The Speaker of the Class maintains order. Motions to censure the Speaker are out of order. Procedural rulings by the Speaker are final. The Speaker may not debate but may vote to break a tie. The Speaker must call on Members (i.e., debaters) from each side alternately. Debaters must show the Speaker respect. To preserve dignity and objectivity, debaters may address and refer to one another and the Speaker in the third person: for example, "Ms. Speaker," "The Leader of the Opposition," and the like. Debaters should not use offensive language nor repeat language or conduct for which the Speaker has reprimanded them. The debaters may heckle "as long as it is pertinent, humorous, brief and infrequent." Wit may be tolerated. Debaters have the right to insist the rules of debate be observed. They may rise on a "Point of Privilege," for instance, when "misquoted, misrepresented, or slandered."[106] Whatever facility the Speaker and Members of the Class have with parliamentary procedure may be applied at their discretion. The students and teacher may know debate and procedures well and so treat them with rigor; they may be neophytes at both and treat debate and procedures as guidelines. As long as learning through debate is taking place, educational communication is attained.

Although we lack room to discuss debate strategies, we must make room for a discussion of propositions. Whether parliament serves as the educational model for classroom debating or an informal structure of a proponent and opponent, propositions dictate what is debated and what evidence must be marshalled to support a case.

Even though policy debating is the norm in parliamentary debate and much academic debate, value and non-policy debate are gaining in some circles.[107] A classroom allows for three traditional propositions to be debated: fact, value, and policy.[108] Depending on the diverse interests of the class, all three have relevance. *A proposition of fact* asserts a "relationship between two things" and can be supported through objective verification independent of subjective feelings. The linking verb frequently signals a proposition of fact. An example would be: "Education majors *are* capable of passing an advanced college course in testing and measuring." *A proposition of value* asserts that "something is good, bad, right, wrong, better than, worse than, etc." and may depend on "subjective feelings and evaluations." A value term frequently signals a proposition of value. An example would be: "Education majors would *benefit* from an advanced college course in testing and measurement." *A proposition of policy* demands that "something be *done*. It calls for more than a fact or a feeling; it calls for action. Since it is based on "subpropositions of both fact and value," a proposition of fact is the most sophisticated and requires the most elaborate support to be understood and accepted by an audience.[109] The word *should* frequently signals propositions of policy. An example would be: "Education majors should be required to take an advanced college course in testing and measurement."

For classroom debates, we suggest the propositions be controversial and be stated as simple sentences with one subject and one predicate. The proposition of fact describes something. The proposition of value appraises something. And, the proposition of policy prescribes something. When the sentence is declarative, we have a proposition of fact, value, or policy. When the sentence is interrogative, we have a question of fact, value, or policy. We must practice formulating these three to minimize seepage from one to another. In everyday discourse, one proposition (or question) may blend elements of the other two. The result would be semantic confusion. An example of such confusion is: "Schools and colleges in Canada and the United States do a terrible job in training their teachers and should be drastically cut in funding as a punishment." As we debate semantically careless propositions or pursue semantically careless questions, the result is a communicative version of *koyaanisqatsi* – that is, a disharmony that calls for harmony.

Furthermore, we may want to employ a question rather than a proposition with our class to encourage inquiry more than advocacy. Or we may want to employ a *proposition* rather than a question with our class to encourage advocacy more than inquiry. Both questions and propositions polarize an audience in degree. However, questions may produce less polarization than the proposition since a proposition asserts and a question asks. Debate will serve productively in either case. When might you ask a question of fact, value, or policy? When a proposition? And, with what likely effects? You must someday decide for the educational welfare of your pupils, but you still have time to debate it.

Only the basic elements of debate will be mentioned here. Numerous texts on debate are readily available. The introductory text of *Advocacy and Opposition* by Karyn Rybacki and Donald Rybacki[110] would assist any teacher enthusiastic about debate as an instructional tool for the classroom or as a tool for making controversial decisions at school meetings.

When we debate, we choose to "reason rather than impose our will by force." The duties or responsibilities we as debaters take upon ourselves define our burdens (or obligations) of argument to our audience.[111] When we argue to *change* beliefs or practice pertaining to facts, values, or policies, we function as *advocates*. Those who argue to keep things the same or to reject the change the advocates support function as *opponents*. The debate takes place on a figurative ground of existing beliefs or practices. The ground represents the *status quo* or the way things are now.

Presumption is held by those who occupy this ground at the start of the debate. Presumption may be *artificial,* for example, when a defendant is presumed innocent until guilt or liability is demonstrated. Presumption may also be natural – for example, "derived from existing institutions, practices, customs, values, or interpretations of reality." Presumption rests with what is being challenged. Opponents of the advocated change have the presumption. Natural presumption resides in whatever point of view the audience of the debate holds.

The *burden of proof* refers to our obligation or responsibility as advocates to contest the presumption with reasoning and evidence sufficient to challenge the presumption and justify a change. When we advocate a change and offer support sufficient to justify changing a belief or practice "on the face of it" or "at first sight," we have presented a *prima facie case* which may succeed temporarily or permanently in suspending presumption.[112] The opponents have the *burden of refutation* once we present an acceptable case. After hearing opposing arguments, as advocates we must address legitimate refutations. We have the burden then of rebuttal.[113] As skillful advocates, we anticipate which methods of refutation and refutative arguments will be used in response to our opponents. That is, as advocates we must plan rebuttal blocs into our strategy for change.[114] While advocates of change must advance through the oppositions, the opponents of change must clash on points we make. Note that the burden of refutation and the burden of rebuttal shifts between the two sides. Sometimes these burdens are used synonymously. When they are differentiated, *refutation* refers to the attacking the other debaters intent on destroying their case by demonstrating its errors and inadequacies. *Rebuttal* refers to rebuilding a case after an attack or to defending a case from attack.[115]

In a sequence of debaters, then, the advocates have the burden of proof while their opponents have the presumption. When the advocates present a prima facie case, the opponents have the burden of refutation. While this may be called the burden of rebuttal,[116] it may also be called the burden of refutation.[117] We side with refutation in this sequential account. After having their case attacked, the advocates have the burden of rebuttal. From here on, the burdens of refutation and rebuttal shift between the advocates and their opponents.

There are many ways to classify arguments. The arguments we present in a debate may be comparatively sound or fallacious. Whatever the proportion of sound to specious arguments may be, we may use one or more of these selected types of arguments and their tests: (1) argument by example with these tests: Are the examples typical? Have a sufficient number of examples been examined? Are negative instances adequately accounted for?; (2) argument by analogy with these tests: Are the compared cases alike in all essential regards? Are the compared characteristics accurately described?; (3) argument by cause and its tests are: Is the association between the alleged cause and effect consistent, strong, in a regular time sequence, and coherent? Will intervening factors interfere with expected cause and effect relationships? Is the cause sufficient to bring about the effect? Will the cause result in other unspecified effects?; and (4) argument from sign with these tests: Have sufficient signs been presented? Are conflicting signs adequately considered?[118]

A detailed account of types of arguments and their tests based on the model of argument advocated by Stephen Toulmin[119] is available in Rieke and Sillar's Argumentation.[120] As teachers any number of questions may be used to challenge arguments. Several have been given. What additional questions might we ask an advocate or opponent?

4

Conflict Management

Richard A. Fiordo

Conflict Management in Educational Settings

Conflict at the interpersonal level has its healthy moments. Not all conflict should be avoided. Indeed, some conflict should be sought. Not all conflict, however, is productive. Some is unproductive and even counterproductive. Nonetheless, a classroom need not be a clash-room. To welcome conflict that is productive is not to invite disaster.[121] While to many people conflict means only quarrelling or fighting that is counterproductive, we can conflict with positive results. Besides, conflict is inevitable if we want innovation or improvement in a standard or practice.[122]

When a conflict surfaces in a school or classroom, we have options other than waiting for a solution akin to a classical Greek tragedy's *deus ex machina.* We must nip unproductive conflict in the bud when and where it occurs as soon as circumstances permit.[123] We may win the assistance of others, yet we may have to pursue a solution alone if no one else joins us. Riding on some famous lines, when facing imminent and unproductive conflict that screams for a solution, we must ask: If not us, who? If not now, when? If not here, where?

We must settle the conflict here and now, but we have options. We can determine whether the conflict emerges from the intrapersonal, interpersonal, organizational, or technological level of communication.[124] We can look carefully at our notion of conflict in school and classroom communication. Applied to education, from the authoritative text by Hocker and Wilmot entitled *Interpersonal Conflict,* we derive this clearly useful notion of conflict in communication: conflict is an expressed struggle between at least two interdependent parties (e.g., a teacher and administrator, a student and teacher, a teacher's association and a Minister of Education, and the like) who perceive incompatible goals, scarce rewards, and interference from the other party in achieving their goals (e.g. one interest group wants to secure provincial funding for a debate club while another interest group wants to secure funding for updated instructional media and both groups sabotage the efforts of one another). Once the conflict is *expressed*, it enters the realm of communication.[125] Analyzing this notion of conflict gives us directions to pursue in solving or resolving conflicts that surface.

Numerous approaches to escalating and de-escalating conflict have been researched. Limited space will permit us to look at several principle approaches deemed useful to the field of education. When conflicts emerge between teachers, teachers and administrators, or teachers and students, face-saving is crucial. *Face-saving* refers to the concern for how we appear to others during the expressed conflict and the effects this will have on future relationships; in other words, in face-saving or saving face we protect or repair our image. That others may have embarrassed us and not allowed us to face-save may lead to conflict. When we fear losing ground during a quarrel or ignore and avoid problematic conflicts, we may confront next an escalated conflict.[126] Managing the conflict becomes then a major challenge.

Other conflicts may grow out of our unwillingness to admit our aggression and anxiety with respect to our students or colleagues. As we admit to our unsavory ways, we may manage our conflicts rather than suppress, ignore, or avoid them.[127] We may also confront conflicts we face with two uncooperative cliques in a classroom by creating *distributive* and *integrative* conditions for the two warring groups. In a distributive situation one group wins at the expense of the other, as in a Nintendo game or a debate or a labor-management negotiation. In an integrative situation the groups discover ways to allow both sides to benefit, and in working jointly on a jigsaw puzzle or a class project or a school competition between different classes.[128]

Although the distributive or competitive approach works under some conditions, the preferred approach is the integrative or collaborative approach. For the classroom and school, the collaborative method of conflict management is endorsed due to its stress on maximizing gains for conflicting parties and joint problem solving. As treatments for conflicts, figuratively speaking, competitive treatments assume we must maximize our gains and the others' losses since the pie is small. Collaborative treatments assume the pie will grow as we work with rather than against the other party.[129] In a sense, we give the party in conflict with us the privilege of cutting the pie, and the other gives us the privilege of taking the first piece.

Moreover, when a conflict surfaces, a collaborative style of managing conflict practices (1) separates the people from the problem and attacks the problem not the people, (2) focuses on interests underlying positions rather than on positions to be defended, (3) generates a variety of possibilities before deciding what to do, (4) insists that the result be based on some objective or external standard of fairness that will apply justly to both parties in the conflict.

The following may serve as grounds for fair standards: "market value, precedent, scientific judgment, professional standards, efficiency, costs, what a court would decide, moral standards, equal treatment, and reciprocity."[130] Without objective standards acceptable to both parties, the conflict risks becoming a battle of wills and whimsies – both counterproductive.

There are other methods available for managing conflict. When we cannot resolve a conflict on our own, we may have a third party intervene.[131] This might be another teacher, a vice-principal, or an arbitrator from the teachers' association. Since communication creates and reflects conflict, communication itself becomes the vehicle for managing conflict productively or otherwise.[132] A third party may serve as that vehicle for productive conflict management if we have failed in our attempts. An informal group or an ad hoc committee may also serve as the vehicle for productive conflict management.

Mowrer, a learning theorist and psychotherapist, encouraged tensions to be resolved by changing ourselves, others, and our surroundings[133] Likewise parties to conflict have these options: try to change the other party, try to alter the conflict conditions, and change our own behavior.[134] To reduce conflicts, we may change the conditions under which we work by making resources available to one another. For example, if a staff of teachers has equal (but meagre) allotments of time on calculators and wordprocessors, those needing calculators more than wordprocessors may (with willing colleagues in order to avoid conflict) exchange their wordprocessor time for calculator time. We may change our communication habits to reduce conflicts. Instead of avoiding all dealings with staff who are in conflict with us, we may conduct business through memos or telecommunications media.[135] We change ourselves. The exchange of calculator and wordprocessor time along with the use of an alternative channel of communication may relax the other party.

Once the conflict has surfaced, we may change our conflict style and ask our opponents to change theirs. By unfreezing our conflict style, whether it is reliance on tabling a motion or gunnysacking or backstabbing, we increase our repertoire for managing conflict. If we lack humor for reducing conflict, we may use humor as a relief.[136] As we unfreeze our style, we adapt to the unique features of the conflict thereby increasing our potential to manage the conflict productively. Since both parties to a conflict have power, neither has the option of not using it. We may choose to use our power destructively or constructively. So, if some teachers control resources (such as money, equipment, and facilities) and some have interpersonal contacts in the network of a school district (for example, knowing key administrators and liaisons between schools), the power currencies may be exchanged because one group of teachers needs contacts and the other group needs resources.[137] Subsequently, the potential conflict becomes harmony. However, if no swapping of power currencies were possible, a conflict might ensue.

Productively managing conflict may also take the form of noting features that may increase risk in communication: gender differences, multicultural differences, religious differences, linguistic differences, value differences, rhetorical differences,[138] differences in training (trained incapacities being blocked through selective perception and biased scanning that results from professional training in one area and not another – e. g., biology instead of art or business),[139] differences in sexual preference, and any other differences that may make a difference (i.e., produce conflict that is handled destructively or unproductively).[140] If our students see us as sexists or racists, conflicts may emerge in time – whether we are or not. If we have values from a bygone generation, conflicts may emerge – whether we impose these values on them or not. If we announce to our colleagues sexual preferences inconsistent with the norm for sexual preference at our school, conflicts may emerge – whether we like it or not. If we have a style of writing business letters that is inappropriate, conflict may emerge – whether we deserve it or not. For example, if a vice-principal received a complaint about a veteran teacher with a fine teaching record and responded harshly to the teacher in a letter, the harshness may create conflicts on various grounds: ethical, professional, personal, legal, and so on. Especially if the grounds for the charges by the vice-principal were unfounded, the teacher and the vice-principal would face a conflict. Whether the conflict escalates (productively or not) or de-escalates (productively or not) depends on the communicative choices each makes. What might you do as the teacher? What might you do as the vice-principal? The risks are high. Self-disclosures may hurt more than help the situation. Hidden areas and blind spots may be communicated. Unknown areas of hostility may surface. Confrontation may benefit both parties, but it may not. Again, the choice would be difficult. We all face such matters in the profession of teaching. How successfully we manage our conflicts constitutes an ever-present concern. How do you think you will fare?

Notes

[1]J. L. Aranguren, *Human Communication* (Toronto: Mc Graw-Hill, 1967), 161-163 and 174-175. For an alternative yet similar view of the "transforming teacher," see: Marilyn Ferguson, *The Aquarian Conspiracy: Personal and Social Transformation in the 1980s*(Los Angeles: J. P. Tarcher, 1980), 292-293.

[2]Ernest G. Bormann, *Communication Theory* (Toronto: Holt, Rinehart, and Winston, 1980); Stephen W. Littlejohn, *Theories of Human Communication*, 2nd ed. (Belmont: Wadsworth, 1983); *The Interpersonal Communication Book*, 5th ed. (New York: Harper & Row, 1989, 26-30. And, Alton Barbour and Alvin A. Goldberg, *Interpersonal Communication: Teaching Strategies and Resources* (Urbana: Eric and New York: SCA, 1974).

[3]Jerrold E. Kemp and Don C. Smellie, *Planning, Producing, and Using Instructional Media*, 6th ed. (New York: Harper & Row, 1989), 15; Ann L. Darling, "Signalling Non-Comprehensions in the Classroom: Toward a Descriptive Typology," *Communication Education*, *38*:1 (January 1989), 35-38; and K. Cerulo, "What's Wrong With This Picture? Enhancing Communication Through Disorder," *Communication Research*, *15*:1 (February 1988) 94-98.

[4]John Fiske, *An Introduction to Communication Studies*; Dean C. Barnlund, *Interpersonal Communication* (Boston: Houghton Mifflin, 1968), 6; and Andrew D. Wolvin and Carolyn G. Coakley, *Listening*, 2nd ed. (Dubuque: Wm. C. Brown, 1985), 38.

[5]Paul Watzlawick, Janet H. Beavin, & Don D. Jackson, *Pragmatics of Human Communication: A Study of Interactional Patterns, Pathologies, and Paradoxes* (New York: Norton, 1967); and Joseph A. DeVito, *The Interpersonal Communication Book*, 5th ed. (New York: Harper & Row, 1989), 26-30.

[6]David K. Berlo, *The Process of Communication: An Introduction to Theory and Practice* (Toronto: Holt, Rinehart and Winston, 1960), 12; Frank E. X. Dance and Carl E. Larson, *Speech Communication: Concepts and Behavior* (Toronto: Holt, Rinehart and Winston, 1972), 7-13; and Frank E. X. Dance and Carl E. Larson, *The Functions of Human Communication* (Toronto: Holt, Rinehart and Winston, 1976). For the language aspect, see Thomas A. Sebeok, "On a High Horse," *Semiotica*, *67*: (1987), 141-145.

[7]Please see, Samuel L. Becker, *Discovering Mass Communication* 2nd ed. (Glenview: Scott, Foresman, 1983).

[8]William D. Brooks and Robert W. Heath, *Speech Communication*, 6th ed. (Dubuque: Wm. C. Brown, 1989), 15.

[9]Seppo Sneck, *Assessment of Chronography in Finnish-English Telephone Conversation: An Attempt at a Computer Analysis* (Jyvaskyla: University of Jyvaskyla, Department of English, 1987).

[10]Beatrice G. Schultz, *Communicating in the Small Group: Theory and Practice* New York: Harper and Row, 1989); Raymond Ross, *Small Groups in Organizational Settings* (Englewood Cliffs: Prentice-Hall, 1989; and Brooks and Heath, *Speech Communication*, 16.

[11]Joe Ayres and Janice Miller, *Effective Public Speaking*, 2nd ed. (Dubuque: Wm. C. Brown, 1986); Ron R. Allen and Ray McKerrow, *The Pragmatics of Public*

Communication, 3rd ed. (Dubuque: Kendal/Hunt, 1985).

[12]Marie Hockmuth Nichols, a specialist in the area of public communication, used to allude to classroom communication and stand-up speaking as well as the terms listed.

[13]William B. Gudykunst and Young Yun Kim, *Communicating With Strangers: An Approach to Intercultural Communication* (New York: Random House, 1984), 14-15.

[14]Larry A. Samovar, Richard E. Porter, and Memi C. Jain, *Understanding Intercultural Communication* (Belmont: Wadsworth, 1981), 4-18.

[15]Ronald E. Rice, ed., *Communication, Research, and Technology* (Beverly Hills: SAGE, 1984); Frank Greenwood, Mary M. Greenwood, and Robert E. Harding, *Business Telecommunications: Data Communications in the Information Age* (Dubuque: Wm. C. Brown, 1988); and Craig N. Locatis and Francis D. Atkinson, *Media and Technology for Education and Training* (Toronto: Charles E. Merrill, 1984).

[16]Richard A. Katula, *Principles and Patterns of Public Speaking* (Belmont: Wadsworth, 1987), 65-66; Richard Fiordo, "Teaching: Education Through Communication," *The Journal of Educational Thought*, *12*:1 (April 1978), 1-2. See also, Jack Martin, *Mastering Instruction* (Toronto: Allyn and Bacon, 1983), 31: Educational communication or "instruction may be defined as any purposeful activity on the part of a teacher that is responsible for changing another person's behavioral, cognitive, affective, and/or perceptual repertoire." Learning, as effects, may refer to "any change in an individual's behavioral, cognitive, affective, and/or perceptual repertoire."

[17]Charles Morris, *Signification and Significance: A Study in the Relations of Signs and Values* (Cambridge: M.I.T. Press, 1964), 26-28; for alternative views see: Poecke Luc Van, "Denotation/Connotation and Verbal/Non-Verbal Communication," *Semiotica, 71*: (1988), 125-151 as well as A. Jappy, "Beauty: Sign-Systems That Work," *Kodikas/Code ARS Semiotica, 8*: (1985), 111-119.

[18]Charles E. Osgood, George J. Suci, and Percy H. Tannenbaum, *The Measurement of Meaning* (Urbana: University of Illinois Press, 1957): Rollo Handy, *The Measurement of Values: Behavioral Science and Philosophical Approaches* (St. Louis: Warren H. Green, 1970).

[19]J. Samuel Bois, *The Art of Awareness*, 3rd ed. (Dubuque: Wm. C. Brown, 1978), 75.

[20]Wendell Johnson, *People in Quandaries* (New York: Harper & Row, 1946), 167-168.

[21]Ibid., 151.

[22]Bois, 80.

[23]S.I. Hayakawa, *Language in Thought and Action*, 3rd ed. (Chicago: Harcourt, Brace & World,), 185-90.

[24]Johnson, 270-276.

[25]Ibid., 270.

[26]Hayakawa, 179. Note that Hayakawa is criticized by Bois for failing to emphasize the differences between the process and object and between the object and words: *Art of Awareness*, 84.

[27]Johnson, 278.

[28]L. Susan Stebbing, *Thinking to Some Purpose* (Middlesex: Penguin, 1952), 241-242.

[29]Reproduced in Richard Fiordo, *Charles Morris and the Criticism of Discourse* (Bloomington: Indiana University and Lisse: The Peter De Ridder Press, 1977), Appendix B. See also, Charles Morris, *Varieties of Human Value* (Chicago: University of Chicago Press, 1932).

[30]Fiordo, 154.

[31]Reuel L. Howe, *The Miracle of Dialogue* (New York: The Seabury Press, 1963); John Stewart, ed., *Bridges Not Walls: A Book About Interpersonal Communication*, 4th ed. (New York: Random House, 1986).

[32]Katula, 7-8.

[33]Brooks and Heath, 224.

[34]Robert C. Jeffrey and Owen Peterson, *Speech: A Basic Text*, 3rd ed. (New York: Harper & Row, 1989), 167-172.

[35]Albert J. Vasile and Harold K. Minty, *Speak with Confidence: A Practical Guide*, 5th ed. (Boston: Scott, Foresman, 1989), 375.

[36]Wolvin and Coakley, 1-6.

[37]Ibid., 7 & 8.

[38]Jeffrey and Peterson, 20-21.

[39]Vasile and Mintz, 67-70.

[40]Philip Emmert and Victoria J. L. Emmert, *Interpersonal Communication* (Dubuque: Wm. C. Brown, 1984), 185-191.

[41]Gary T. Hunt and William F. Eadie, *Interviewing: A Communication Approach* (Toronto: Holt, Rinehart and Winston, 1987), 84.

[42] Wolvin and Coakley, 311.

[43]Katula, 34-36.

[44]Hunt and Eadie, 83-85.

[45]Jeffrey and Peterson, 21.

[46]Wolvin and Coakley, 319.

[47]Vasile and Minty, 70.

[48]Richard Fiordo, "The Semiotic SEA of Questioning," *Semiotica*, *73*: 1/2 (1989), 25-41.

[49]Kenneth Burke, *The Philosophy of Literary Form: Studies in Symbolic Action*, rev. ed. (New York: Vintage Books, 1957), 57.

[50]Fiordo, "Semiotic SEA,"

[51]S. Morris Engel, *With Good Reason: An Introduction to Informal Fallacies* (New York: St. Martin's Press, 1976), 82.

[52]Ibid., 83.

53 Charles J. Stewart and William B. Cash, Jr., *Interviewing: Principles and Practice*, 5th ed. (Dubuque: Wm. C. Brown, 1988), 59-62.

[54]Fiordo, "Semiotic SEA," 34-39.

[55]Joseph Corcoran, *An Introduction to Non-Policy Debating* (Dubuque: Kendall/Hunt, 1988); Stephen Wood and John Midgley, eds., *Prima Facie: A Guide to Value Debate* (Dubuque: Kendall/Hunt, 1986); and James M. Copeland, *Cross-*

Examination in Debate (Lincolnwood: National Textbook Company, 1988).

[56]J. Brophy and T. Good, *Teacher-Student Relationships: Causes and Consequences* (New York: Holt, Rinehart and Winston, 1974), 25-40.

[57]William J. Seiler, L. David Schuelke, and Barbara Lieb-Brilhart, *Communication for the Contemporary Classroom* (Toronto: Holt, Rinehart and Winston, 1984), 127.

[58]N. L. Gage and David C. Berliner, *Educational Psychology*, 2nd ed. (Boston: Houghton Mifflin, 1979), 62-70.

[59]Mary B. Rowe, "Wait Time: Slowing Down May Be a Way of Speeding Up," *Journal of Teacher Education*, (January/February 1986), 43-48.

[60]Meredith D. Gall, "Synthesis of Research on Teachers' Questioning," *Educational Leadership, 42*: 3 (1986), 40-46.

[61]Delva Daines, "Are Teachers Asking Higher Level Questions?" *Education, 6*:4, 368-374.

[62]David H. Hargreaves, "Teachers' Questions: Open, Closed and Half Open," *Educational Research, 26*:1 (1984), 46-50.

[63]J. Brophy and T. Good, "Teacher Behavior and Student Achievement." *Handbook of Research on Teaching*, 3rd ed. (New York: MacMillan, 1986), 328-370.

[64]Francis P. Hunkins, "Helping Students Ask Their Own Questions," *Social Education* (April 1985), 293-296; For another perspective, see: Ann L. Darling, "Signalling Non-Comprehension in the Classroom: Toward a Descriptive Typology," *Communication Education, 38*:1 (January 1989), 34-40.

[65]A portion of this research was contributed through a graduate paper. I would like to thank Nancy A. Pelkey for her enthusiastic review of literature on questioning in the classroom.

[66]B. Aubrey Fisher, *Perspectives on Human Communication* (New York: Macmillan, 1978), 285 & 293-295.

[67]Ibid., 293-295.

[68]Stephen W. Littlehohn, *Theories of Human Communication*, 2nd ed. (Belmont: Wadsworth, 1983), 35.

[69]Fisher, 297.

[70]Judee K. Burgoon, David B. Buller, and W. Gill Woodall, *Nonverbal Communication: The Unspoken Dialogue* (New York: Harper & Row, 1989), 454-456; see also, Scott Jacobs, "Language" and Judee K. Burgoon,"Nonverbal Signals" in Mark L. Knapp and Gerald R. Miller, eds., *Handbook of Interpersonal Communication* (Beverly Hills: Sage, 1985), 313-390. The Knapp and Miller text is the most thoroughly researched one known to me. I recommend it to serious students of communication.

[71]Burgoon, Buller, and Woodall, 35-150.

[72]Charles Morris, *Signs, Language, and Behavior* (New York: Braziller, 1955), 46-49; see also, Fiordo, *Charles Morris and Discourse*, 69-70 on postlanguage signs.

[73]Winston L. Brembeck and William S. Howell, *Persuasion: A Means of Social Influence*, 2nd ed. (Englewood Cliffs: Prentice-Hall, 1976), 210-211.

[74]Burgoon, Buller, and Woodall, 4.

[75]Fisher, 286-287.

[76]Ibid., 293-297.

[77]William W. Wilmot, *Dyadic Communication* 3rd ed. (New York: Random House, 1987), 158-162.

[78]Fisher, 294 and 298.

[79]Wilmot, 158.

[80]Kenneth Burke, *Perspectives by Incongruity*, edited by Stanley E. Hyman (Bloomington: Indiana University Press, 1964), 94-99.

[81]Wilmot, 161.

[82]Ibid., 163-164.

[83]Victoria O'Donnell and June Kable, *Persuasion: An Interactive Dependency Approach* (New York: Random House, 1982), 121.

[84]Kenneth Burke, *A Rhetoric of Motives* (Berkeley: University of California Press, 1969), 55-59.

[85]R. W. Norton and L. S. Pettigrew, "Communicator Style as an Effective Determinant of Attraction," *Communication Research, 4*:2 (1977), 257-282.

[86]O'Donnell and Kable, 121-122. See also, J. Gorham, "The Relationship Between Verbal Teacher Immediacy Behaviors and Student Learning," *Communication Education, 37*:1 (1988), 40-52.

[87]A. H. Eagley and S. Chaiken, "An attribution Analysis of the Effect of Communicator Characteristics on Opinion Change: The Case for Communicator Attractiveness," *Journal of Personality and Social Psychology 32*: 2 (1975) 136-144. See also, R. L. Duran, and L. Kelly, "The Influence of Communicative Competence on Perceived Task, Social, and Physical Attraction," *Communication Quarterly 36*:1 (Winter 1988), 41-49.

[88]Jerry Boucher and Charles E. Osgood, "The Pollyanna Hypothesis," *Journal of Verbal Learning and Verbal Behavior, 8*:1 (1969), 1-8. For an extensive listing of connotative studies, see: Pamela M. Maier, "The Use of the Semantic Differential in Speech Communication: An Annotated Bibliography," Unpublished Paper, Northwest Communication Association Conference, April, 1988.

[89]Hayakawa, 43-46.

[90]Charles G. Morris, *Psychology: An Introduction*, 3rd ed. (Englewood Cliffs: Prentice-Hall, 1979), 616 and 621.

[91]Harvey F. Clarizio, *Toward Positive Classroom Discipline*, 3rd ed. (Toronto: John Wiley and Sons, 1980), 129-151.

[92]William S. Sahakian, *Systems of Ethics and Value Theory* (New York: Philosophical Library, 1963), 159.

[93]James Benjamin, "Eristic, Dialectic, and Rhetoric," *Communication Quarterly*, 31 (1983), 21-26.

[94]Norbert Gutenberg, "Argumentation and Dialectical Logic" and P.J. van den Houen, "The External Justification of a Dialectical Consensus" in Frans H. van Eemeren, Rob Grootendorst, J. Anthony Blair, and Charles A. Willard, eds., *Argumentation Perspectives and Approaches, Pragmatics and Discourse Analysis* (Dordrecht-Holland: Foris Publications, 1987), 397-403 and 364-371; Richard Fiordo, Six Theories of Dialectics and their Relation to Human Communication," *Canadian Speech Communication Journal, 9*:9 (1977), 107-118; and J. Anthony Blair and Ralph H. Johnson, "Argumentation as Dialectical," *Argumentation, 1*:1 (1987), 41-56.

[95]Copeland, *Cross-Examination*; Benjamin, "Eristic."

[96]Wayne C. Minnick, *The Art of Persuasion*, 2nd ed. (Boston: Houghton Mifflin, 1968), 103.

[97]Ronald Lee and Karen K. Lee, *Arguing Persuasively* (New York: Longman, 1989), 225.

[98]Michael Pfau, David A. Thomas, and Walter Ulrich, *Debate and Argument: A Systems Approach to Advocacy* (Glenview: Scott, Foresman, 1987), 4.

[99]Russell T. Church and Charles Wilbanks, *Values and Policies in Controversy: An Introduction to Argumentation and Debate* (Scottsdale: Gorsuch Scarisbrick, 1986), 10 & 6.

[100]Lee and Lee, 224.

[101]Church and Wilbanks, 2.

[102]F. H. van Eemeren, R. Grootendorst, and T. Kruiger, *The Study of Argumentation* (New York: Irvington, 1984), 6.

[103]Abne M. Eisenberg and Joseph A. Ilardo, *Argument: A Guide to Formal and Informal Debate*, 2nd ed. (Englewood Cliffs: Prentice-Hall, 1980), 2.

[104]Wayne Tingley, "Organization of a Model Parliament," in *Speech and Debate: A Resource Booklet* (Edmonton: ACCESS Alberta, 1982), 53; for a comparison with British procedure in debating, see: J. Rodden, "British University Debating: A Reappraisal," *Communication Education*, *34*:4 (October 1985), 308-317.

[105]Richard Murphy, "Parliamentary Procedure for the Ordinary Citizen," in Harold Barrett, ed., *Rhetoric of the People* (Amsterdam: Rodopi, 1974), 63, 71, and 77.

[106]Tingley, 57-58.

[107]See Corcoran's *Non-Policy Debating* and Wood and Midgley's *Prima Facie*.

[108]Richard Fiordo, "Propositions of Fact, Value, and Policy: A Semiotic Augmentation of Argumentation," in J. Robert Cox, Malcolm O. Sillars, and Gregg B. Walker, eds., *Argument and Social Practice*: Proceedings of the Fourth *SCA/AFA Conference on Argumentation* (Annandale: Speech Communication Association, 1985), 100-108.

[109]Eisenberg and Illardo, 31-32.

[110]Karyn C. Rybacki and Donald J. Rybacki, *Advocacy and Opposition: An Introduction to Argumentation* (Englewood Cliffs: Prentice-Hall, 1986).

[111]Lee and Lee, 29.

[112]Rybacki and Rybacki, 17-23.

[113]Lee and Lee, 33.

[114]George W. Ziegelmueller and Charles A. Dause, *Argumentation: Inquiry and Advocacy* (Englewood Cliffs: Prentice-Hall, 1975), 205-206.

[115]Donald W. Klopf, *Coaching and Directing Forensics* (Lincolnwood: National Textbook, 1985), 97 & 167.

[116]Eisenberg and Ilardo, 30. James J. Murphy and Jon M. Ericson, *The Debater's Guide* (New York: Bobbs-Merril, 1961), 30.

[117]Klopf, 167.

[118]Ziegelmueller and Dause, 113-120.

[119]Stephen Toulmin, Richard Rieke, and Allan Janik, *An Introduction to*

Reasoning, 2d ed. (New York: Macmillan, 1984).

[120]Richard D. Rieke and Malcolm O. Sillars, *Argumentation and the Decision Making Process*, 2nd ed. (Glenview: Scott, Foresman, 1984), 66-86.

[121]Joyce L. Hocker and William W. Wilmot, *Interpersonal Conflict*, 2nd ed. (Dubuque: Wm C. Brown, 1985), 32.

[122]Bobby Patton, Kim Giffin, and Eleanor Nyquist Patton, *Decision-Making: Group Interaction*, 3rd ed. (New York: Harper & Row, 1989), 117.

[123]Joseph P. Folger and Marshall S. Poole, *Working Through Conflict: A Communication Perspective* (Glenview: Scott, Foresman, 1984), 169.

[124]Fred E. Jandt and Mark Hare, *Instruction in Conflict Resolution* (Urbana: Eric and Leesburg Pike: SCA, 1976), 3-4.

[125]Hocker and Wilmot, 23.

[126]Folger and Poole, 51.

[127]Gerald M. Goldhaber, *Organizational Communication*, 4th ed. (Dubuque: Wm. C. Brown, 1986), 299.

[128]Patton, Giffin, and Patton, 120-121.

[129]Hocker and Wilmot, 121.

[130]R. Fisher and W. Ury, *Getting to Yes: Negotiating Agreement Without Giving In.* (Boston: Houghton Mifflin, 1981), 88-98.

[131]Folger and Poole, 184-188.

[132]Hocker and Wilmot, 20.

[133]Richard Fiordo, "Integrity Training: A Moral Code and Method for Moral Education," *The Journal of Educational Thought*, *15*:1 (April 1981), 47-60.

[134]Hocker & Wilmot, 157-158.

[135]See Rice's *The New Media* or Greenwood, Greenwood, and Harding's *Business Telecommunications*.

[136]Joseph A. DeVito, *Human Communication: The Basic Course* (New York: Harper & Row, 1988), 237; V. C. Downs, M. Javidi, and J. F. Nussbaum, "An Analysis of Teachers' Verbal Communication Within the College Classroom: Use of Humor, Self-Disclosure, and Narratives," *Communication Education*, *37*:4 (1988), 127-140; and, M. Javidi, V. C. Downs, and J. F. Nussbaum, "A Comparative Analysis of Teachers' Use of Dramatic Style Behaviors at Higher and Secondary Educational Levels," *Communication Education*, *37*:4 (October 1988), 278-287.

[137]Hocker and Wilmot, 63-64 and 72-73. See also, David D. Burns, *Intimate Connections* (New York: Morrow, 1985). Burns explains the Johnny Carson Technique which is highly applicable to conflict management. It involves diverting attention from ourselves to others through paraphrase, inquiry, and support of their comments.

[138]Deborah Borisoff and David A. Victor, *Conflict Management: A Communication Skills Approach* (Englewood Cliffs: Prentice-Hall, 1989), 165-180.

[139]Folger and Poole, 65.

[140]For example, see: Constance C. Staley and Jerry L. Cohen, "Communicator Style and Social Style: Similarities and Differences Between the Sexes," *Communication Quarterly*, *36*:3 (Summer 1988), 192-201; D. Canary, E. Cunningham, and M. Codey, "Goal Types, Gender, and Locus of Control in Managing Interpersonal Conflict," *Communication Research*, *15*:4 (August 1988), 426-446; J. Gorham, D.

Kelly, and J. McCroskey, "The Affinity-Seeking of Classroom Teachers: A Second Perspective," *Communication Quarterly*, 37:1 (Winter 1989), 16-26; P. Yelsma, "Functional Conflict Management in Effective Marital Adjustment," *Communication Quarterly*, 32:1 (Winter 1984), 56-61; and J.K. Alberto, "An Analysis of Couples Conversational Complaints," *Communication Monographs*, 55:2 (June 1988), 184-197.

5

Intrapersonal Communication in Education

Richard L. Weaver II and *Howard W. Cotrell*

It is easier for teachers *not* to be concerned about intrapersonal communication. It is easier because it involves the processing of messages that happens *within* individuals, and teachers may wonder, "How in the world are we supposed to 'tap into' what happens *within* our students?" It is easier because it may occur at conscious *and* non-conscious levels, and teachers may ask, "What business do I have dealing with the non-conscious?" It is easier, too, because teachers can examine, test, and grade overt communication, like public speeches and reports, but, they would be correct in questioning, "Why encourage and promote a process that cannot be easily examined, tested, or graded – much less observed?"[1]

In this chapter we make a case for teaching intrapersonal communication techniques – or ways people have for generating internal messages. Actually, our goal is to discuss different techniques. The case, we feel, is made by their ease of use, their variety and applicability, and their potential value. That these techniques are valuable and worthwhile will be revealed as the techniques are explained. We will briefly discuss six: 1) self-talk, 2) intrapersonal feedback, 3) self-monitoring, 4) imaging, 5) *imagio* as a means for stimulating creativity, and 6) transpersonal communication. We do not suggest that these are all the possible techniques. They are, however, among the more common.[2]

Just by looking at the list of six techniques it is clear that these are not techniques normally discussed (or taught) in classrooms. Also, from looking at the list, it is clear the topics are not content or discipline specific; they relate to *any* content or discipline. Our contention is that the techniques are important because they not only are personal and direct but because they license the kind of behavior that frees the imagination, unleashes intuition, generates assumptions, and allows people to explore their mind in creative, free floating, speculative, unconventional, and informal ways.[3] They are, indeed, techniques

53

educators need to know.

Self-Talk

In their book on *Intrapersonal Communication Processes*, Charles Roberts and Kittie Watson, the editors, begin their introduction with the comment:

> "The term 'intrapersonal communication' first appeared in the communication literature a little over a quarter of a century ago. At that time, the focus on intrapersonal communication was almost exclusively, 'self-talk.' The primary intrapersonal communication process discussed was that of talking out loud to yourself."[4]

Since that time, the focus of researchers in intrapersonal communication has become truly multi-faceted. Along the way, too, "self-talk" has evolved to mean all talk – internal (silent) or external (out loud) – people engage in *with themselves*. The popularity of the two books by Shad Helmstetter, *What to Say When You Talk to Your Self* (Pocket Books, 1986) and *The Self-Talk Solution* (Pocket Books, 1987), popularized self-talk in corporate offices, churches, backyards, and grade-school classrooms. For those unable to generate original self-talk, Helmstetter provides the words, phrases, and scripts for dealing with family and relationships, fitness and health, job, career management, mental tune-ups, solving problems, getting organized, getting things done, and for successful living.

If our goal, as teachers, is "to ensure that students will *want* to continue and will *be able* to continue" their education (once they leave our classroom),[5] then we must prepare them with means for self-management, self-direction, and self-education – with the emphasis, in each case, on *self*. Although in charge of student selves for but a short time, we must then relax and step aside knowing that we have done everything to nurture and prepare students for life beyond the classroom and for life beyond our own personal facilitation.

Self-talk allows students to give *themselves* directions, thoughts, and images that will help guide their action. Teachers need to 1) give students license to engage in it, and 2) guide it in productive, positive directions. License comes from mentioning it, providing examples (perhaps, personal ones) of its use, and suggesting ways it can be done. When it is talked about, it begins to create its own environment. That is, students help create scripts, share scripts, modify the scripts of others, and enjoy sharing results of script usage outside the classroom.

Guidance comes from making specific suggestions of possible self-talk words, phrases, or images – the program students are to follow (or adapt). No program, no action! The programming is designed to create beliefs, the beliefs help determine student attitudes. Attitudes create feelings, and the feelings determine student *actions*.[6] The actions then create success or failure. Self-talk gets students moving, encourages them to think differently, and may change the way they look at problems.

Use of self-talk requires repetition, practice, and listening on the part of users. Students must be encouraged to repeat scripts – much the same way they learn the words to rock music or television advertisements. They must be encouraged to take time during the day to repeat them often, whether this occurs first thing in the morning, when driving the car, during exercise, meditation, or relaxation, or just before going to sleep at night. And, too, they need to be encouraged to *listen* to the script. That is, they must become aware of everything they are saying to themselves for it to make an impression.

In the following space we offer some suggestions – mere hints of possibilities. It should be clear that any of these can be changed to fit various situations. Also, students should be encouraged to write them in words *they* feel comfortable using. Our goal here as authors, is simply to provide some samples to show what self-talk scripts look like.[7]

To help students set goals in a course: Have them write out specific goals; give them possibilities such as:

I will learn to write clear paragraphs.
I will learn to properly conjugate each verb.
I will learn all formulas.
I will learn how to construct effective outlines.

Then, teachers can encourage them to write: My goals are specific. I review them daily. I act on them. I will achieve them.

Teachers can set daily goals, weekly or monthly goals, or goals for an entire semester or course. By setting clear, specific goals (or learning objectives), teachers give students direction. When completed, they provide closure. If they are numerous, short-range, and achieveable, students feel like they are gaining something; they feel like they are getting results; and, when successful, they feel like they are being rewarded. Closure, or accomplishment, is a form of reward. Going over the goals with students, rehearsing the self-talk publicly, helps reinforce and underscore its purpose, nature, and effectiveness.

There are numerous possibilities for creating self-talk. Before a particularly challenging assignment, the self-talk could be programmed: "I have courage. I will meet this challenge with confidence knowing that I have the energy to endure and the determination to succeed." When students seem to be down on themselves, depressed, or especially tired, the self-talk could read: "I build my enthusiasm by keeping my interest level high! The more interested I become in anything I do, the more enthusiasm I have. The more enthusiasm I have, the more energy I create." If an assignment needs to be organized in some way, it could be organized for students in a general way through self-talk: "I organize my thoughts. I assess the situation. I look for alternatives and different approaches. I select the proper course of action. I make the right decision. I record my thoughts and actions." For a report before the class: "In every opportunity I have to communicate with others, I am decisive, direct, warmly received – and effective!"

Self-talk, as discussed above, is not the only way it is used. Because of Helmstetter's books, it is, perhaps, the most popular. Two other dimensions can also be mentioned to students as ways to nurture and develop the process: 1) internal dialogue (or imagined interactions) and 2) the internal adviser. Because of space limitations, our discussions of each of these will be brief.

Internal dialogue, or imagined interactions, occurs when people create other characters with whom they internally converse; they imagine themselves talking to others. We suggest to students, for example, the importance of creating situations internally before they occur: a conflict with a parent, spouse, or relationship partner, a job or an appraisal interview, or a confrontation with a friend or teacher. In these situations – especially where the potential for stress or loss of face is high – students play out a variety of scenarios to better prepare them for what might happen in the actual situations.

In their article on ". . . Imagined Interactions," Honeycutt, Zagacki, and Edwards tell us that imagined interactions occur daily. "Most involve," they write, "actors in conversation with significant others, such as family members, close friends, intimates, or work partners." [8] The unique thing in internal dialogue is how students can envision participation in discourse, anticipate responses, and even assume others' roles. Honeycutt, Zagacki, and Edwards suggest "that imagined interactions *can* help individuals predict a future event" [italics ours] (p. 169).

The internal adviser is another dimension of self-talk. Both the authors of this chapter often have had vivid experiences of their mentors while in college giving them advice and counsel internally, long after the actual mentoring experience had terminated. We call this residual mentoring. Sometimes the internal adviser experience can be like Freud's superego – that part of the psyche which controls, at an unconscious level, the impulses of the id. Sometimes it can be like an internal voice that guides and directs. It might be a father, mother, teacher, or even a member of the clergy. Sometimes, too, it can be, simply, our own subconscious helping us select proper choices, make correct decisions, or resolve problems in everyone's best interests.

Intrapersonal Feedback

How often do you think teachers receive papers from students, hear student reports, or assess student projects and wonder, "How could the students be so far off base?" "How could they have wandered so far astray?" To help students achieve greater accuracy, we need to encourage intrapersonal feedback – internal messages they construct to respond to the other messages they create. Many students think that once away from the classroom and from the teacher's presence, they operate in a vacuum, with no give-and-take, no possibility to ask questions – no feedback. Intrapersonal feedback is a tool that helps people adapt and adjust their communications with others. It is helpful in keeping people spontaneous and flexible – and yet, on target.

When we, as authors of this chapter, began to discover that the kinds of concerns we had with our own writing, were the same as those concerns later expressed by critics of our writing, we realized that we had a powerful tool for growth and improvement. If we could just be patient, disciplined, and sensitive enough to listen to our own feedback, it was useful. This realization gave us power because it gave us credibility. Our *own* ideas were sufficient not just to guide our actions, but to adjust, correct, and improve them as well. Our point in discussing this is that it was this discovery that activated and validated the process. It can be taught as an intrapersonal communication technique.

There are several things teachers can do to encourage intrapersonal feedback. First, they can cite their own experiences with it. Where has their own corrective, intrapersonal feedback helped improve products they created? Second, they can begin the process by offering students specific criteria to use in their intrapersonal feedback. For example, they can supply checklists to use before submitting assignments. They can give them the exact criteria by which the assignment will be evaluated. In one of our courses, the evaluation forms used to assess all assignments are provided to students in a workbook they purchase for the course. The advantage is that they always know what the criteria are; they can look ahead to discover them; and they can plan ahead based on them. The advantage for teachers is that they seldom hear the excuse, "I didn't know what to do." The key is to get students to use these forms themselves before an assignment is either completed or, perhaps, at all stages in assignment preparation and development. The main reason students do not do assignments correctly is that they are not given sufficient direction. But that does not mean that all direction throughout an assignment or project must come from the teacher! Intrapersonal communication helps students become more independent, self-sufficient, and self-confident.

There may be a third way to stimulate intrapersonal feedback as well. Encourage the questioning process. Get students to be their *own* audience or critic. Questions like the following will help:

Would *I* want to read this paper?
Does this paper live up to *my* own personal standards?
Would *I* be pleased with this report, speech, project, or assignment?
Does this make sense *to me*?
Is *this* the best way *I* can express this idea or concept?

There is no doubt that some students will answer all of these questions "Yes" without really applying proper standards. We would suggest, however, that many students have never even asked the questions. We are trying to get them to engage in the process; we are not always able to control the results of the process!

Self-Monitoring

Self-monitoring is much like self-talk and intrapersonal feedback. It is the process of warning, reminding, or checking on ourselves. There are two aspects of self-monitoring that relate to intrapersonal communication for teachers. The first relates to systematic sensitization; the second to self-evaluation and self-assessment.

"Systematic sensitization is a method for constructing incremental steps that will move the [learner] closer to a desired image."[9] We simply break large goals into a number of subsidiary smaller goals each of which, when successfully completed, moves us a step closer (systematically) to the large goal. Sensitization occurs as students are exposed to each of the levels or steps in the process and, finally, to the large goal. We explain the concept to students, and then we develop systematic sensitization sequences (S.S.S.'s) for them, as models, in a variety of contexts. In public-speaking we have developed them to help students in seeking content, organizing ideas, presenting speeches, and overcoming fear. In interpersonal communication, we have them for developing trust, striving for confidence, managing conflict, and achieving assertiveness. In personal situations, we have developed them for overcoming worry, becoming more successful, eliminating loneliness, and striving for personal excellence. One of our most effective uses involves breaking down assignments or projects into smaller, more manageable steps. We then place deadlines for the accomplishment of each of the steps. This helps students pace themselves in their working through projects or assignments and reduces stress. A generic S.S.S. for a major paper might look like this:

Completed Paper

9. Submit the final, polished manuscript.

8. Read, evaluate, and correct first (rough) draft.

7. Write the first (or rought) draft.

6. Prepare a prospectus or complete outline.

5. Narrow the topic, if necessary, and rewrite thesis.

4. Do a literature review and computer search.

3. Develop a tentative thesis, central idea, or hypothesis.

2. Read broadly, widely, and in-depth on the topic.

1. Secure a broad topic area or area of interest.

Begin Work on the Paper

We construct S.S.S.'s in a stair-step configuration from bottom to top. This helps emphasize the necessity of completing one step before moving on to the next just as people traverse a staircase. It also underscores the need to work from a foundation or ground-floor level. In addition, it keeps the goal ahead or above us as we work. Symbolically, it seems to be both a workable and important configuration.

Self-monitoring is an important aspect of the process. At each step, people need to assess their progress and reward themselves if successful. Because an S.S.S. can be composed of any number of steps, growth (or successful progress toward the final goal) lends itself to self-monitoring – trying to discover how I'm doing! Sometimes the self-monitoring brings people to the realization that they need to break the S.S.S. into smaller increments, or that some steps need to be changed, perhaps eliminated, altogether. We have found that if the large goals are kept small, and the number of steps is also kept small (ten or less, if possible), the S.S.S. is not as likely to be as overwhelming to students as when the goals appear to be out of reach and the steps so numerous that completion appears impossible.

The second part of self-monitoring involves self-evaluation and self-assessment. This is not particularly new. But if the process of self-assessment is a regular and integral part of courses, students become accustomed to doing it. There are numerous ways to encourage it. Students can be asked to prepare an informal essay assessing their work at any point. They could be given a formal evaluation form to use. They could be asked for an oral assessment during a scheduled office visit.

Several years ago, the authors of this chapter developed a unique method called "the half-sheet response" that can be used in classes of any size and at any time to gather student self-assessments.[10] They ask students to take out a half-sheet of paper and to record their impression or assessment on that. It is turned in and read by the teacher. The best responses can be shared anonymously at the next class meeting. If students are responding on half-sheets on a daily basis, and challenged to think like this often (to make self-assessments and self-evaluations regularly), self-monitoring is more likely to become part of their behavior. We use half-sheets in classes of 150-175 students to take attendance, give quizzes, conduct surveys, gather student examples and anecdotes, to elicit on-going responses to the activities we conduct, as well as to elicit frequent self-assessments and self-evaluations on behaviors or criteria discussed in class.

Simple questions can be used to trigger self-assessment responses. Some of these might include:

How do you think you did?

How would you assess someone else who performed like you did?

How did *you* do on these criteria? (Criteria are written on the chalk board or handed out to students.)

How did you feel in this assignment?

How did this activity (or assignment) make you feel?

Imaging

Akhter Ahsen states that the eidetic (or unusually vivid) image is "a material picture in the mind which can be scanned by the person as he [or she] would scan a real current event in his [or her] environment. . . ."[11] Simply think of images as vivid mental pictures. The point here is that the creation of mental pictures is an intrapersonal-communication process over which teachers can have some control.

The mental laboratory has often been overlooked as a workspace. We show movies and videos; we take students on field trips; we use pictures and slides; how often do we stimulate students to use their *own* mind to create the picture? In another place we explained seven methods that can be used to stimulate mental images.[12] They include examples and illustrations, instructional aids, trigger words, exercises and activities, daydreams and fantasies, organization features (ways to get students to interact with the information being presented,[13] and giving instructions. Imagery instructions refer to statements that direct people to visualize the information or concepts to be learned.[14]

There is another use of imaging, too, that ties in to self-concept enhancement.[15] It offers another use of systematic sensitization. To put imaging to work, students or teachers need to decide on the kind of image they want to project, or how they want others to see them. In the construction of an S.S.S., this image becomes the large goal. This image needs to be clear, specific, and vivid so that they can subdivide it. They need to ask, what steps are necessary for me to move from where I am right now (the present or status quo) to acquisition or assumption of that image?

In this case, however, much of the developmental portion of the S.S.S. can come from feedback and self-observation. Feedback can come from open-ended course evaluations, or students can be asked, specifically, to write about the image that you (the teacher) presents in the classroom. They could even be asked to make suggestions for improvement. Most students *willingly* comply! These suggestions can be modified and then organized and structured into an S.S.S.. Feedback also can come from the use of videotapes of classroom behavior. Yet another way is to solicit the help of a colleague, friend, or trained instructional developer.[16]

What is the likely reward if individuals can complete an S.S.S. of this nature. Weaver and Cotrell summarize J.S. Bois:

> "Imaging, because of its powerful potential, can affect the self at various levels. At the electrochemical level it can reduce the neuronal activity associated with fear. At the self-moving level, it can affect the control of movements such as hands, legs, and head. At the feeling level, it can affect [imagers'] needs and drives, wants and fears, hopes and ambitions. At the thinking level, it can affect their speaking, listening, asking and answering questions, decision making, and strategy formulation."[17]

Imagio as a Means for Stimulating Creativity

In our article on *"Imagio:* Precursor to *Inventio,"* we make a case for the role that imagery, visualization, imagination – and all other related inner activities that occur prior to any external activities – play in idea creation.[18] All of these techniques – imagery, visualization, imagination, and any other internal processes that play a part in idea creation – will be grouped under the term *imagio* in this section. *Imagio,* then, represents a variety of intrapersonal techniques that aid individuals in creating ideas.

There are distinct advantages for teachers to focus specifically on the *imagio* aspect of the idea-conception process. We will focus on five of these advantages. These advantages relate to the stimulation of creativity in students – that is, teachers' ability to encourage, or motivate, students to be inventive and productive.

The first advantage of focusing on *imagio* is that it provides an opportunity to approach the unknown. It offers a source of power, control, and pleasure not limited by tradition, reality, or external people or conditions. We are dealing with things that go on in students' heads! It is not limited by space, time, or circumstances.[19]

The second advantage is that focusing on *imagio* allows a separation from verbal representations. Emphasis on the verbal inhibits work with ideas simply because words are restrictive. Their well-defined and already-learned meanings confine us to categories and ways of responding that are already present in each of us. They blind us to alternatives other than our current response patterns. Researchers in this area suggest that verbal processes are characterized by a higher degree of sequential constraint which limits memory capacity, flexibility, and speed in thinking.[20] It was a group of Russian researchers who found that *imagio* occupies a major role in the search space of problem solvers whereas verbal processes are more important in the terminating phases of problem solving.[21]

The third advantage for teachers to stress the role of *imagio* in idea creation is that it enlarges the universe by uncovering new dimensions. It licenses free association and mental construction. It helps people overcome some of the mental blocks outlined by Roger von Oech: looking for one right answer, trying to be logical, following the rules, having to be practical, avoiding ambiguity, being fearful of making mistakes or being wrong, avoiding any kind of playfulness with ideas, narrowing the focus or limiting the viewpoint too early, being foolish, or believing we are not creative.[22] *Imagio* sanctions behavior that allows people to see situations in a wide variety of ways and explodes their tunnel vision. *Imagio* opens a panorama of ideas and fresh perspectives.[23]

The fourth advantage of stressing *imagio* involves spatial manipulation. Stephen Michael Kosslyn claims that we can use *imagio* as a "simulation" of possible and impossible transformations in the world.[24] Three often-cited examples of using the results of imagined spatial relations and transformations come from the field of science:

> "Friedrich Kekule's image of the structure of the benzene molecule and James Watt's visualization of the mechanism of the condensing steam engine. Einstein remarked that he arrived at the theory of relativity by 'visualizing . . . effects, consequences, and possibilities, through more or less clear images which can be 'voluntarily' reproduced and combined.'"[25]

The final advantage of stressing *imagio* is that images have a strong tendency to activate both the affective and motivational system. In the creation and development of ideas, the entire emotional backdrop of ideas can be represented. Also, images can serve motivationally to push us toward or away from certain ideas. J. Melvin Witmer claims that because *imagio* can give rise to feelings, as they are attached to created ideas and images, they can serve as motivational directives.[26]

Images can serve as a source of energy and as a well-spring for motivation because the emotions move, stir, and excite us to action. They are the raw material, according to Witmer, that constitutes the energy that underlies people's beliefs, attitudes, and values.[27] *Imagio* has been used in the laboratory to enhance students' cognitive abilities including memory, problem-solving, and reading comprehension.[28]

In another place, we have written about developing creativity in the classroom.[29] In that essay we suggested that developing creativity first depends upon creating the proper, supportive, encouraging, and spontaneous atmosphere. Second, we suggested ways for generating ideas such as brainstorming, goading and challenging, and allowing time for intense concentration. Third, we offered ways for focusing on the content of the course. We mentioned using improvisation, simulations, field study, creative dramatics, role playing, case studies, and exercises and games that call for emotional or sensory recall to help students get involved with the content. Finally, we encouraged instructors to apply the content of the course in creative ways to the real world. Relating concepts, principles, and ideas to the students' current and future frames of reference shows students how course content can be transferred. To encourage, share, and extend these applications takes creativity beyond classroom walls. It is clear that along with an emphasis on the *imagio* dimension of intrapersonal communication processes, the above criteria for encouraging creativity are also relevant and important. They may, indeed, be catalysts.

Transpersonal Communication

We hesitate to mention and develop this area of intrapersonal communication simply because of the likelihood of raising unwarranted fears about the mystical, psychic, or spiritual and the possibility that these associations will be tied to intrapersonal communication in general. "The term 'transpersonal,'" according to Beverly-Colleene Galyean, "means to go beyond the ordinary physical-emotional way of viewing oneself and the world, and to recognize as valid mystical, psychic, and spiritual dimensions as well."[30] Our reason for mentioning it is simply to offer readers a wide variety of techniques as well as to indicate the breadth of the intrapersonal-communication domain. Any fears about the mystical, psychic, or spiritual should be tied to the transpersonal domain of intrapersonal communication alone. It should be clear at the outset that the area of the transpersonal is just one area of the intrapersonal domain; we do not suggest that it needs to be or should be taught. Teachers must make these decisions based on the specific learning objectives or teaching outcomes desired.

In his article, "Imaging and Creativity: An Integrating Perspective," Vaune Ainsworth-Land labelled the transpersonal dimension "fourth-order creativity" or an "ultimate form of relatedness."[31] He referred to it as "cosmic conscious-ness." It involves the recognition of the divine or the ultimate wisdom of life. It is the process of seeing oneself as part of a larger reality.

We are not suggesting that all teachers will be comfortable working in transpersonal dimensions. Often, it is an awareness and consciousness of the dimension in one's own life that allows teachers to bring this awareness to their students. They then lead students "in imagery activities designed to activate profound levels of consciousness."[32] Galyean describes the nature of some of these intrapersonal experiences:

> "Symbols such as 'light,' 'fire,' 'gold,' 'wise persons,' and 'voyages to moun-tain tops, skies, and castles,' are often included in these images. Talking with personal guides, archetypal figures, and communicating with spiritual symbols such as crosses, mandalas, religious books, and gold crowns sometimes induces transpersonal awareness. Students are not only interested in exploring transpersonal consciousness, but often relate personal stories pointing to their own spiritual lives."[33]

It should be clear that the goal here is to "target inner awareness and expanded intellectual performance."[34] Our concern is that "spiritual" not be confused with "religious." Some imagery of this nature can be overtly reli-gious; however, just because such religious images are evoked does not mean the major focus of transpersonal communication is, indeed, religious.

Great literature or experiencing major works of Middle Age and Renais-sance art or music may stimulate or produce transpersonal awareness or even a mystic vision. Such vision may be infused with deep feeling such as horror, ecstasy, or desolation. The purpose is to enable students to break through the limits of conscious perception. It has been noted that "the mystical is the source of all true science."[35] Once such vision can be experienced, some believe that people take on an "enormously greater capacity for learning and living."[36]

Summary

The area of intrapersonal communication has the potential of generating much teacher interest. From our experiences in teaching, we have found that the main reason it creates student interest and awareness is because it *involves* students. We are dealing here with mental processes that engage students actively and dramatically. Also, although we have no direct evidence to prove it, it is likely to benefit learning. Part of this is because the techniques are personal and direct for students; part is because they tend to be different than what normally occurs in classrooms; and part, too, is because some of the techniques involve visualization, and it has been shown that information that can be represented in visual terms "is comprehended and remembered better."[37]

You may wonder what can be done now that you are familiar with the intrapersonal techniques. Because of their variety and uniqueness, they can be handled by teachers in many different ways. We do not suggest that any one way is best. We have found, however, that (for us) the best way to handle all of them (or any one of them) is to use some or all of the following guidelines:

1. Talk about the technique(s) with students. Explain the essentials. Then adapt the technique(s) or apply it(them) to the course content or to the specific learning objective(s).

2. Provide a model. Show students how *you* use the technique(s) or some of the results likely to accrue from its(their) use. Give personal examples when possible.

3. Give examples of others using the technique(s). Keep a file of examples of others using it(them), and share these examples when appropriate (like during the explanation).

4. Give clear and specific directions to students in technique use. Make the use of any technique a specific assignment for students. Then gather clear and specific results through written or oral responses. Or have students keep a journal. Journals lend themselves well to recording intrapersonal-communication experiences.

5. Assign readings on the techniques. We have tried to include some beginning readings as footnotes with this chapter. These footnotes will lead readers to other articles and books. Keep a file of useful supplementary sources that can be assigned or recommended as additional resources.

6. Discuss responses and results in class. Share experiences. Provide support and encouragement for students' insights and activities. Because they are sharing intrapersonal experiences, sharing may be considered, by some, as high-risk self-disclosure. A supportive, non-evaluative, open atmosphere is important to encourage such disclosures.

We have briefly discussed self-talk, intrapersonal feedback, self-monitoring, imaging, *imagio* as a means for stimulating creativity, and transpersonal communication as intrapersonal-communication techniques. Many of these work well when used in combination. These are ways individuals have for stimulating, nurturing, and maintaining the processing of messages that happen within them as they attempt to understand themselves and their environment.[38] In the words of William James, "The greatest revolution of our generation is the discovery that human beings, by changing the inner attitudes of their minds, can change the outer aspects of their lives."[39] Awareness is the first step toward change. As Socrates said, "The unreflected life isn't worth living." That is why intrapersonal communication has an important place in the classroom and why, too, these techniques are what educators need to know.

Notes

[1]Our definition of intrapersonal communication relies heavily on that provided by Charles Roberts, Renee Edwards, and Larry Barker, *Intrapersonal Communication Processes* (Scottsdale, AZ: Gorsuch Scarisbrick, Publishers, 1987), p. 2. Their definition, for your reference is: "All of the physiological and psychological processing of messages that happens within individuals at conscious and non-conscious levels as they attempt to understand themselves and their environment."

[2]We have not considered the process of listening as an intrapersonal technique. Those interested in listening as an intrapersonal process should consult Charles V. Roberts and Kittie W. Watson, eds., *Intrapersonal Communication Processes: Original Essays* (New Orleans, LA: Spectra, 1989), especially Part VI, "Listening As Intrapersonal Processing," pp. 505-569. There are numerous and excellent textbooks available on listening.

[3]See Richard L. Weaver II, Marcia L. Bailey, and Howard W. Cotrell, "*Imagio*: Precursor to *Inventio*." In Roberts and Watson, eds., *Intrapersonal Communication Processes . . .*, p. 15.

[4]Roberts and Watson, eds., *Intrapersonal Communication Processes . . .*, p. ix.

[5]Wayne C. Booth, *The Vocation of a Teacher: Rhetorical Occasions, 1967-1988* (Chicago: The University of Chicago Press, 1988), p. 213.

[6]Shad Helmstetter, *The Self-Talk Solution* (New York: Pocket Books, 1987), p. 51.

[7]The authors suggest consulting Helmstetter's books for hundreds of other possibilities. Most of his possibilities can be re-written to accommodate different circumstances. The examples we cite in this chapter have been adapted from Helmstetter's suggestions.

[8]James M. Honeycutt, Kenneth S. Zagacki, and Renee Edwards, "Intrapersonal Communication, Social Cognition, and Imagined Interactions." In Roberts and Watson, eds., *Intrapersonal Communication Processes . . .*, pp. 166-184.

[9]Richard L. Weaver II and Howard W. Cotrell, "Using Interactive Images in the Lecture Hall," *Educational Horizons* (The official publication of Pi Lambda Theta) 64:4 (Summer 1986), p. 183, citing the same authors, "Imaging Can Increase Self Concept and Lecturing Effectiveness," *Education, 105* (Spring 1985), pp. 264-270. Our use of the phrase "systematic sensitization" came about as a response to "systematic desensitization" which involves behavior modification generally related to

negative behaviors (e.g., communication apprehension). Our goal was to coin a similar phrase that had no negative connotations.

[10]Richard L. Weaver II and Howard W. Cotrell, "Mental Aerobics: The Half-Sheet Response," *Innovative Higher Education, 10* (December 1985), pp. 23-31.

[11]Akhter Ahsen, "Eidetics: An Overview," *Journal of Mental Imagery, 1* (1977), p. 5.

[12]Richard L. Weaver II, Howard W. Cotrell, and Thomas A. Michel, "Imaging: A Technique for Effective Lecturing," *Journal of Mental Imagery, 9*:4 (1985), pp. 91-108.

[13]Sondra M. Napell, "Updating the Lecture," *Journal of Teacher Education, 29* (1978), pp. 53-56.

[14]K. L. Alesandrini, "Imagery-eliciting Strategies and Meaningful Learning," *Journal of Mental Imagery, 6* (1982), pp. 125-140.

[15]Richard L. Weaver II and Howard W. Cotrell, "Imaging Can Increase Self Concept and Lecturing Effectiveness," *Education, 105*: 3 (Spring 1985), pp. 264-270.

[16]The reader is referred to our article on faculty dynamation. See Richard L. Weaver II, Darrell G. Mullins, Howard W. Cotrell, and Thomas A. Michel, "Faculty Dynamation: Guided Empowerment," *Innovative Higher Education, 14*:2 (1989), (in press).

[17]Weaver and Cotrell, "Imaging Can Increase Self-Concept . . .," p. 268, citing J. S. Bois, *The Art of Awareness*, 3rd ed. (Dubuque, IA: Wm. C. Brown, 1978).

[18]See Weaver, Bailey, and Cotrell, "*Imagio*: Precursor to *Inventio*," in Roberts and Watson, eds. *Intrapersonal Communication Processes . . .*, pp. 4-27. See especially pp. 19-22.

[19]See J. Melvin Witmer and Mark E. Young, *Pathways to Personal Growth: Developing A Sense of Worth and Competence* (Muncie, IN: Accelerated Development Inc., 1985), p. 214.

[20]G. Kaufman, and T. Helstrup, "Mental Imagery and Problem Solving: Implications for the Educational Press." In A. A. Sheikh and K. S. Sheikh, eds. *Imagery in Education: Imagery In the Educational Process* (Farmingdale, NY: Baywood Publishing Company, 1985), pp. 113-144.

[21]U.P. Zinchenko, U. M. Munipov, and V. M. Gordon, "The Study of Visual Thinking," *Voprosy Psikhologii, 2* (1973), pp. 3-14.

[22]Roger von Oech, *A Whack On the Side of the Head: How to Unlock Your Mind for Innovation* (New York: Warner Books, 1983).

[23]Weaver, Bailey, and Cotrell, "*Imagio*: Precursor to *Inventio*." In Roberts and Watson, eds., *Intrapersonal Communication Processes . . .*, p. 20. The authors cite J. Melvin Witmer, *Pathways to Personal Growth*, p. 233.

[24]Stephen Michael Kosslyn, *Image and Mind* (Cambridge, MA: Harvard University Press, 1980), p. 456.

[25]Weaver, Bailey, and Cotrell, "*Imagio*: Precurson to *Inventio*." In Roberts and Watson, eds., *Intrapersonal Communication Processes . . .*, p. 21. The authors cite L.A. Cooper and R.N. Shepherd, "Turning Something Over in the Mind," *Scientific American, 251* (1984), pp. 106-114.

[26]J. Melvin Witmer, *Pathways to Personal Growth*, p. 73.

[27]Witmer, *Pathways* . . ., p. 73.

[28]A. Paivio, *Imagery and Verbal Processes* (New York: Holt, Rinehart and Winston, 1971). See also W. Rohwer, "Images and Pictures in Children's Learning: Research Results and Instructional Implications." In H. Reese (Chm.), "Imagery in Children's Learning: A Symposium," *Psychological Bulletin, 73* 1970), pp. 393-403.

[29]Richard L. Weaver II, "Kindling the Creative Spark," *Iowa Journal of Speech Communication, 11* (Fall 1979), pp. 24-31.

[30]Beverly-Colleene Galyean, "Guided Imagery in the Curriculum," *Educational Leadership, 40*:6 (March 1983), pp. 54-58.

[31]Vaune Ainsworth-Land, "Imaging and Creativity: An Integrating Perspective," *The Journal of Creative Behavior, 16*:1 (First Quarter 1982), p. 17.

[32]Galyean, "Guided Imagery . . .," p. 57.

[33]Galyean, "Guided Imagery . . .," p. 57.

[34]Galyean, "Guided Imagery . . .," p. 57.

[35]Ainsworth-Land, "Imaging and Creativity . . .," p. 18. Land cited Albert Einstein as the source of this quote. Albert Einstein, *The World As I See It*. (London, 1935).

[36]Land, "Imaging and Creativity . . .," p. 19. He cited R.M. Bucke, *Cosmic Consciousness*, 18th ed. (New York: Dutton, 1901), p. 1956.

[37]R.N. Haber, "The Power of Visual Perceiving," *Journal of Mental Imagery, 27* (1978), pp. 153-158.

[38]Roberts, Edwards, and Barker, *Intrapersonal Communication Processes*, p. 2.

[39]Arnold A. Hutschnecker, *Hope: The Dynamics of Self-Fulfillment* (New York: Pocket Books (A division of Simon and Schuster), 1981), p. 252.

6

Interpersonal Surrogates and Communication Theory
(A Behavioral View)

James L. Owen

Most of the evidence about communication phenomena lies outside the boundaries of our skin. It consists of what we do and say and of conditions outside us that contribute to our doing or saying it. In developing theories of human communication, some stay close to this evidence and make it the focus of their subject matter. Others, however, move well beyond the observed facts. Specifically, they take evidence of interpersonal processes and translate this evidence into corresponding surrogates which are placed inside us. Quite often, the surrogates are then assumed to play a causal role and are employed as explanatory devices.

Take, for example, the notion of an internal "self concept." We are sometimes told that "a speaker develops a self concept based on what that individual has observed and been told about his or her activities as a speaker." But the only evidence points to the developing behavior and to the contribution of conditions located in our external environment. We stay closer to the facts when we simply say that "a speaker is changed in what he or she says and does based on what that individual has observed and been told about his or her speaking activities."

For those who convert interpersonal processes into an internal surrogate, it is often the case that the next step is to employ the surrogate as an explanatory device. This move is made in the statement, "a person may avoid speech activities *due* to a poor self concept." But an internal "self concept" cannot explain anything; rather, it is a term requiring explanation. Even if we did possess something on the order of a controlling self concept, we would still have to return to conditions in the environment to explain its origins.

A particularly popular surrogate is the metaphorical "attitude." Some uses of the term, of course, point to conditions actually observed. For example, we describe the attitude of a ship when we say that is "listing toward starboard." In the context of human behavior we sometimes say that a person has a particular attitude when all we mean is that – based on what a person has said and done – he or she appears to be "leaning toward a particular position." The mistake is made when the observable evidence is translated into an internal "condition" or "state" which is then employed as an explanatory device. This move is made when the manager says, "He is doing a poor job *because* of his attitude."

Some interpersonal surrogates, such as the metaphor of the "mental map," suggest that our total environment must be translated into things going on inside of us. From this view it is reasoned that as a speaker has contacts with a listener, "impressions" are made and formulated into a "mental map." The mental map is then "consulted" as a guide for future responding to that listener. What the evidence simply indicates, however, is that speakers and listeners have particular kinds of contact with each other and are changed by them. The notion of a mental map does not get us any closer to the processes actually involved in producing these changes.

In preparing a speech the evidence is that we "process" and "store" information in the sense that we take certain kinds of actions on the environment. That is, we *sort* through data, *select* and *file* pieces of evidence, and *organize* materials into separate categories. In order to have pertinent information available at a later date, we *prepare* notes, *underline* important passages, and *rehearse* and *edit* what we have prepared.

All of these overt activities also have their hypothetical surrogates. But there is no evidence that we employ an internal "decoder," plug into an internal "value system," or scan internal "memory banks" in order to "assign meanings." Even if we did these kinds of things we would have to return to the environment in order to explain them.

What is seen, of course, can be described in different paradigmatic ways. Further, a clarifying metaphor can be generated for each paradigm. But nothing is gained by inventing explanatory metaphors that convert interpersonal processes into things going on inside us. Metaphors also have a legitimate place in practical everyday conversation; they provide a convenient shorthand description of things actually observed. For example, as the professional astronomer interacts with his young daughter, he may find it convenient to talk about the "rising" and "setting" sun. In the role of a professional, however, the talk of both astronomers and communication theorists must get closer to the known facts.

We often say that the essence of our subject matter is the *process* involved in *codetermining* each other's behavior. But there is no reason to couch this process in vague and general terms, and to place it inside us. We get explicit about the ways in which we codetermine each other's behavior when we observe the historical activities of a language community as it provides the individual with repertories of communication behavior, and when we look at the activities of an individual as he or she employs these repertories to change other members of the language community. We keep abreast of this process by maintaining a focus on the occasion for current speaker messages, the topography of those messages, their effects on a listener, listener-provided consequences directed at the speaker, and the effects of these consequences on future speaker messages in similar settings.

At some distant point the neurologist (who is trained to study real nervous systems) will be able to show how these codetermining activities result in certain structural and functional changes in our brain. In the meantime, we can make considerable progress by simply focusing on the historical, contextual, and behavioral features of our interactions. Internal surrogates may give the *feeling* that one is dealing with things going on within the "mind," or that one is getting at a "deeper" level of analysis. At best, however, hypothetical surrogates simply duplicate those things that we have already learned by observing what is going on between us and how we are affected by them.

A small amount of evidence about communication phenomena does lie within the boundaries of our skin. This evidence consists of introspectively observed behaviors such as thought (verbal behavior), feelings (as with pain), images (as in a dream), and consciousness (as when someone makes us aware of something by asking a question about it). While these behaviors are not simultaneously observable by two or more people, we all experience and report such things as *thinking* through a problem, *considering* strategies, and *making* plans. We also *feel* disposed to say or do something and *imagine* how things might turn out. Further, we often do these things with full *awareness* that we are doing so. In any case, these private behaviors also function as environmental surrogates when they are employed as explanatory devices.

Take feelings for example. We are sometimes told that "as a speaker receives instructions and gains experience the speaker *feels* more confident and *therefore* is able to give better speeches." But the evidence is simply that the instruction and practice produced the effective behavior! To be sure, instruction and practice can lead to better performance *and* feelings of confidence, but there is no reason to take the internal feelings as the cause of the improved behavior. Covert behaviors cannot explain overt ones. They are simply more behaviors in need of explanation.

Communication behaviors, both overt and covert, are functionally related to interpersonal conditions located outside us. For example, a compliment can make us both feel good about what we have done *and* increase the likelihood that we will do it again. In effect, our language community not only provides influence over what we do and say, but also over what we think, feel, imagine, and pay attention to. In turn, each of us has similar influences over other members of the language community.

Considerable confusion can result from taking covert behaviors as the causes of overt ones. For example, when feelings are taken as the cause of overt behaviors, we are often advised that something can be gained by "sorting them out." But what needs to be sorted out is our relationship to important things going on around us. A good listener is always appreciated and can provide the support and compassion that gets us through the day. But for talk about feelings to be more permanently beneficial it must eventually get around to the conditions in the environment that produce them, and, to the kinds of actions we might take to maintain, enhance, or change them. "Self" control is achievable only to the extent that we can discover how we are affected by conditions outside us and by learning to take effective action relative to those conditions.

It is easy to take covert behaviors as the causes of overt ones simply because they often occur just prior to what we do and say. However, if covert behaviors such as thoughts and feeling are employed to explain overt ones, how do we explain the thoughts and feelings? Inevitably we must return to the environment to explain both. Clearly, since covert behaviors sometimes precede and are correlated with overt ones, knowledge of them can sometimes lead to practical *predictions*. But *explanation* is another matter. To explain behavior we need to return to the external environment. For example, to explain why we sometimes say – or do not say – what we actually think and feel, we might point to the likely consequences of saying it.

A major problem with the method of introspection is that it only brings us into contact with certain classes of private behaviors that surface out of underlying neurological processes; it does not make contact with those processes. In contrast, we do make contact with events that occur in our external environment, and a good deal of useful knowledge can be generated by studying them. Eventually, neurologists will teach us much more about the role of the brain; but by that time we should already have a far more comprehensive view of the role of the environment. Also, what we eventually discover from the neurologists will necessarily be consistent with what we have come to understand by focusing on events and processes outside us.

Model building, of course, is an inherent part of generating knowledge about communication phenomena. But our models serve us well when they simply help to organize and make sense out of what it is that we are able to see. For the moment, most of what we are able to see consists of overt and covert communication behaviors and interpersonal events that are functionally related to their occurrence.

We do not get at a "deeper" or more profound level of analysis by converting interpersonal processes into corresponding surrogates which are then placed inside us. On the contrary, these hypothetical surrogates are typically couched in vague – if not mystical – terms that lose much of the detail and richness of our initial descriptions. At best, interpersonal surrogates can only duplicate what we come to understand by simply looking at what is currently available for us to see.

7

Teaching Interpersonally

Joseph A. DeVito

At Hunter College – in a seeming paradox being repeated throughout the country – we teach interpersonal communication in a large lecture format. Each section averages 300 students. But, the paradox thickens. Not only do we aim to teach the theories and skills of interpersonal communication through the usual pedagogical methods, but we also use these same theories and skills in our teaching. We attempt to approach the large lecture format interpersonally – something that all teachers faced with the large lecture class can effectively incorporate. Teaching interpersonally reverses the traditional one-to-many process and creates a one-to-one process repeated 300 times.

The tremendous ethnic diversity, as well as the huge age, economic, and intellectual differences that we confront daily at City University, present a strong case for at least exploring the possibilities for personalizing our teaching through an interpersonal orientation.

Depending on the reader's own teaching experiences and philosophies, this discussion may be thought of as (a) a reminder and explicit statement of principles followed normally, (b) an introduction to skills to be developed and refined, (c) an argument designed to convince the disbeliever, or (d) a statement of basically noble but impossible to achieve goals.

The validity and usefulness of this approach is seen most clearly – and may, therefore, be tested most directly – in the two central concepts of interpersonal communication: interpersonal relational development and interpersonal communication skills. I have elsewhere argued the first half of this approach, namely that teaching may be viewed as following the stages of normal relationship development and that relational skills significant to teaching are easily derived from this view.[1] Here I focus on the second half of this demonstration, namely that the skills of interpersonal communication are also the skills needed for effective teaching.

Teaching as Interpersonal Competence

A composite model of ten interpersonal communication skills, derived from both humanistic and pragmatic perspectives, is used to illustrate and argue the case for teaching interpersonally.[2] From the humanistic perspective – where principles are derived from an analysis of what humanists would claim should characterize meaningful interpersonal interaction – we get openness, empathy, supportiveness, positiveness, and equality. From the pragmatic perspective – where principles are derived from a scientific analysis of what works and what doesn't work – we get confidence, immediacy, expressiveness, other orientation, and interaction management.[3]

These qualities are not only used effectively or ineffectively by the teacher as a means of communicating. They are also the principles of interaction that the instructor teach by example and by virtue of his or her credibility and general status. This follows logically enough from the assumption that all behavior in an interactional situation communicates; we cannot not communicate.

The Skills of Interpersonal Competence

Here I identify on a macro level the general skill areas that these principles entail.[4] I conclude the discussion of each skill by noting one classroom experience I have used to illustrate how these skills are approached in one interpersonal communication course. The examples are intended to clarify further the skills rather than to suggest specific teaching experiences.

Openness entails the willingness to self-disclose as appropriate, to react openly and honestly to incoming stimuli (i.e., to give honest feedback), and to own our own statements (i.e., to use "I-messages," to accept personal responsibility for our thoughts and our feelings). Without self-disclosure there would be no humanness. Without open and honest responses and without owning our own thoughts and feelings we become passive conveyors, mere intermediaries in the learning process.

Openness requires the willingness to admit to uncertainty, to share relevant experiences (because ultimately education is a process of sharing experiences, whether those of Ivan Pavlov or Oscar Wilde), to reveal a personality that is vulnerable and strong, logical and emotional, virtuous and selfish.

One classroom experience I use that works well is to ask students to write anonymously a statement of an actively kept secret. The students are told that the statements will be collected and that some would be read aloud. When the students hear the statements that their peers have written, they can appreciate the feelings that accompany self-disclosure and some potential reactions to such disclosures. The benefits and dangers as well as suggested guidelines are then easily introduced.

Empathy, of course, is a feeling with the other person, feeling what and how the other person feels. But, empathy also entails the ability to communicate this feeling accurately to the other person. Without empathy teaching becomes a one-way process, much more efficiently handled by even the most elementary software. With empathy the teaching process becomes an exchange of experiences, an exchange that will produce cognitive as well as personal growth.

Empathy asks the teacher to possess both the ability and the willingness to feel (really feel) confusion, frustration, and test anxiety as does the student. Empathy asks us to feel failure and the accompanying feelings of lowered self-esteem, resentment, and depression.

Giving students a paper-and-pencil test of empathy quickly demonstrates the breadth and depth of empathic responses. Student and instructor examples of empathy – more often the failure to empathize – create a strong case for the need for empathic understanding. Techniques and principles follow.

Supportiveness refers to being descriptive rather than evaluative, spontaneous rather than strategic, and provisional rather than certain. Teachers especially need the skills of supportiveness because of our normal focus on evaluation (after all, it's our job), strategies (after all, that's what we do when we plan our classes), and certainty (after all, that's what I'm paid to be or someone else will be paid to be).

Supportiveness requires that the teacher recognize the value in being descriptive, spontaneous, and provisional. It requires a supportiveness for effort as well as for output, for conquering small hurdles as well as large ones, and for improvement as well as for success.

We practice providing active listening responses to specific cases. The inability of many to provide descriptive and nonevaluative responses demonstrates that supportiveness is extremely difficult but that it can be improved through the application of tested techniques and principles.

Positiveness includes stating positive attitudes and positively stroking another individual. What psychologists have long researched and discovered, namely that reinforcement works better than punishment and that positive reinforcement works best of all, good teachers know from experience. We also know that coercive power results in a decrease in both cognitive and affective learning. Yet, our tendencies to evaluate often lead us to forget such research findings. Positiveness asks that teachers communicate their enjoyment and enthusiasm in learning so that it becomes contagious.

To illustrate positiveness, we solicit positive responses to a student volunteer. We quickly learn that the difficulties involved in complimenting others are not insurmountable and that the compliment feels good whether you are sender or receiver.

Equality refers to the recognition of the equality of personalities. Equality means that both individuals are worthwhile and valuable people, and that each has something significant to contribute. Negative reactions to teachers are probably more often equality based than are any others. Talking down, interrupting, and disregarding different perceptions and perspectives seem among the most frequent criticisms of teachers, all clear violations of the equality principle. Equality requires that teachers honestly entertain objections to their academic conclusions and make the search for meaning a joint one.

We demonstrate equality by having students analyze their own interpersonal relationships, and perhaps those of significant others, in terms of equity – the fair distribution of rewards and costs. The experience vividly shows the role of equality in creating a satisfying interpersonal relationship.

Confidence means the absence of interpersonal anxiety, the control of communication apprehension, and the ability to communicate this sense of control. Negative reactions, ranging from personal dislikes to evaluations of ineffectiveness, follow invariably from verbal and nonverbal signs of anxiety.

The truly confident teacher is willing to admit mistakes, to alter preconceived plans on the basis of new evidence, and to encourage open and honest feedback on both the content and the structure and form of our teaching efforts.

A paper-and-pencil test of communication apprehension, designed to measure each person's reluctance to communicate in several different communication situations, demonstrates that we all experience apprehension and that our fears are relatively similar, yet manageable.

Immediacy refers to the ability to communicate a sense of contact, of liking, of togetherness. Without immediacy, teaching might well be conducted with a computer-generated image – not unlike Max Headroom. With immediacy, teaching creates union in the process of asking questions and searching for answers.

Immediacy suggests that we act on what we know to be true, namely that people respond more positively to those they like. Although never to suggest a personality contest, research does demonstrate that immediacy creates a climate better suited to achieving the goals of teaching and that nonimmediacy creates a detrimental climate.

Directing the class discussion to how you make a first date enables students to deduce many of the behaviors characteristic of immediacy. Generalizing them and identifying appropriate and inappropriate contexts are easy follow-ups.

Expressiveness includes the ability to communicate genuine involvement in the interpersonal interaction, encouraging expressiveness in others, and providing relevant and useful feedback.

In teaching, expressiveness involves nothing more than active involvement in the interpersonal interaction. It requires that the teacher possess the ability to command attention and interest through the presentation of subject matter and not through the threat of punishment.

Asking students – many of whom would at first argue that they have no difficulty with expressing their emotions – to formulate ways of communicating with a young woman [their own age, who has just ten days before her wedding heard that her fiance was killed in a car crash and you meet her as she is traveling alone to the morgue to identify the body] quickly illustrates some of the purposes, difficulties, and techniques of expressiveness.

Other-Orientation refers to focusing our communications on the other person, rather than ourselves, and communicating attentiveness and interest in the other person. Asking what the student knows (instead of what the student should know) and what the student needs to know (today and tomorrow and not ten or even two years ago) are inevitable questions in an other-oriented relationship. Focusing attention and interest on the other person (rather than, say, on an inert syllabus or textbook) likewise follow from other-orientation.

Other-orientation suggests that teachers direct their courses to the needs of the audience insofar as possible, to address (though not necessarily meet) the vocational orientation and expectations of the student, and to retain a flexibility that enables us to treat each individual individually.

We demonstrate other-orientation by focusing the course on the needs and interests of each student – aided no doubt by the obvious applications of interpersonal communication to all important parts of their lives – helps demonstrate my own other-orientation and the values of this approach.

Interaction Management is the ability to control the interpersonal interaction to the satisfaction and the achievement of the purposes desired by both parties. Like interpersonal communication, teaching is a transactional process. It is a process created out of the interaction of both parties who invariably direct the process to their desired purposes. The teaching interaction (or, more correctly, the learning that takes place) is actually a negotiated settlement arrived at through interaction between teacher and student. That the teacher often goes through an entire syllabus, while the students are still mentally on page one, is a frequent testimony to ineffective interaction management.

Interaction management in the classroom is seen in such daily activities as asking the right questions, presenting material in small and easily digestible pieces built on prior knowledge and information, and being challenging without intimidating.

Self tests for self-monitoring – the tendency to adjust the image of ourselves that we communicate to others on the basis of the outcome we desire – and Machiavellianism – the willingness to manipulate others for one's own end – show two nonobvious dimensions of interactional management. Here too are raised the ethical issues involved in this type and in all types of interpersonal interactions and that need to be covered in all such courses.

The large lecture format is surely here to stay; economic realities will see to that. It is a situation we can (a) tolerate and co-exist with, (b) fight to reverse the tide toward large classes, (c) take early retirement, or (d) manage the situation as effectively as possible, perhaps trying out the principles of teaching interpersonally as one management strategy.

Notes

[1]See my "Teaching as Relational Development," *Communicating in College Classrooms,* ed., Jean M. Civikly. *New Directions for Teaching and Learning,* No. 26 (San Francisco: Jossey-Bass, 1986), 55-59.

[2]This model, with the supporting research data, is most recently presented in my *Human Communication,* 4th ed. (New York: Harper & Row, 1988) and *Messages: Building Interpersonal Skills* (New York: Harper & Row, in Press for 1990 publication).

[3]These and related terms are defined in my *Communication Handbook: A Dictionary* (New York: Harper & Row, 1986).

[4]Numerous textbooks in interpersonal communication take a more micro approach and identify the specific verbal and nonverbal behaviors that these skills entail and will prove appropriate for the teacher who wishes to pursue this approach more fully. See, for example, my *Interpersonal Communication Book,* 4th ed. (New York: Harper & Row, 1986) and *The Nonverbal Communication Workbook* (Prospect Heights: Waveland Press, 1989.

Section Two

Values in Educational Communication

8

Formal Codes in Educational Communication

Richard A. Fiordo

Meaning, according to Klapp, does not grow from mere computerized data processing. Since the time of Socrates, we have used the slowness of conversation to ponder meaning in relation to another's words.[1] In education, underloading on meaning and overloading on data may produce conflict among our values, conduct, and relationships. What we value, how we conduct ourselves, and what type of relationships we pursue may have contradictory or complementary meaning to us. Peter Craigie warns of irreconcilable differences in our value systems – ethical, moral, religious, educational, and so on. The field of education prefers some values to others. Ethical school personnel are inarguably preferred. School personnel should communicate values of fairness and decency, for example, not bigotry and cruelty.[2]

If our values conflict or are misunderstood by our colleagues and students, communication may be abandoned or reduced to small talk. Although a necessary means to meaningful (and risky) communication, small talk stifles growth and signifies stagnation in interpersonal communication. When conversation fails to advance beyond the daily weather conditions, a communication caution light may be flashing. Through just and healthy relationships, values, and conduct, we may increase our competency in communication; that is, we learn when to enter, develop, and dissolve our human involvements. This chapter and the next two address our value orientations and human relations as professional educators.

From the curricula selected to the style of greeting bestowed upon a school bus driver, teachers make choices. The choices involve values. The values may be ethical. Ethics, being the study of good and bad or right and wrong, is embedded in teaching and educational communication generally. Teachers will fall toward one ethical pole or the other depending on the choices they make with respect to their students, colleagues, supervisors, parents, and others who serve in the schools.

Ethics is seen here as the study of right conduct and the good life. *Morality* is seen as the practice of what we believe is right and good. While ethics is theoretical, morality deals with what we do - that is, behavior and action. Applied ethics becomes morality. Theorized morality becomes ethics. Although ethics may pertain to personal morality, it may also refer to the study of the manner in which people ought to behave: that is, social ethics. An authority in ethics need not be moral; a moral person need not understand ethical theory.[3] For our purposes ethics will be used to cover morality and social ethics. Careful distinctions will yield to pragmatic usage.

We should also be able to distinguish the *teleological* doctrine of ethics (or values more broadly) from the *deontological* doctrine. Let us not be frightened by these profound concepts. In the applied context of this chapter, these gargantuan terms will have the following limited meaning. While teleological ethics holds that "rightness or wrongness of a specific action depends on the degree of goodness or badness of its consequences," deontological ethics maintains that the "rightness or wrongness of a specific action depends on whether or not the *kind* of action to which that specific action belongs is intrinsically right or wrong" – that is, a "particular action is right if and only if it can be called right under all circumstances, regardless of consequences."[4] The values discussed in this chapter and the next range from the teleological to the deontological. Please be alert to these crucial distinctions. Try, if you will, to determine which ethics (or values) lean toward the teleological and which lean toward the deontological.

Formal Codes

Richard Johannesen is a specialist in the field of ethics in human communication. He reports that formal codes of ethics in human communication have been proposed or adopted by various professional organizations.[5] The teaching profession constitutes one of these professional associations. Before discussing the Alberta Teachers' Association Code and Declaration, the powers and limits of professional formal codes will be, based on Johannesen's coverage, summarized. For an extensive treatment of communication ethics, see Richard L. Johannesen's *Ethics in Human Communication*.

In *The Empathic Communicator,* adapting his ideas to the field of teaching, Howell explains that "formal codes evolve from the experiences of many . . . people over considerable periods of time." The codes or prescribed standards are usually "uniform and stable" in their interpretation of problems when compared to "individual interpretations." Formal codes may be "consolidated in a list of 'should' and 'should not' statements that define approved ways of living for members" of that professional organization. The prescriptions protect the professional organization and allow members to work in relative harmony. The teacher who strays from the professional code, excessively at least, gets "punished for unethical conduct."[6]

Johannesen also tells us that Howell believes formal codes of ethics are fallacious because they pretend to erect universally accepted codes even though they do not.[7] Although each prescription of the code intends to offer good counsel, under some conditions the helpfulness of the code will prevail. It will not prevail under all conditions. To pretend it will apply in all cases when it only applies in some is false and frequently unintentionally unethical. Since professional codes presume universality, argues Howell, when applied to the letter, they often do more harm than good. For example, cultural differences "cannot be accommodated by a code of ethics."[8]

Endorsed by Johannesen as providing a "more balanced assessment,"[9] Hulteng maintains that when professional codes lack enforcement, these codes are "most influential with those who are *already* behaving responsibly and ethically." They tend to have "little effect on the ones who need the guidance most." Hulteng argues that danger awaits the naive who assume ethical matters have been settled because "a code has been drawn up." Doubtlessly, there is value in a professional code's establishment of what in principle will be generally accepted as right and wrong conduct. Broad and general or not, professional codes are beneficial. When we choose to respond to ethical violations, we have "at least some precepts by which to be guided."[10]

Johannessen notes that professional codes of ethics have worthy functions despite the deleterious results of codes lacking enforcement and codes worded so abstractly as to allow unethical practices to continue. Professional codes of ethics: (1) "can educate new persons in a profession by acquainting them with guidelines based on the experience of predecessors and by sensitizing them to ethical problems generic to their field,"(2) "can narrow the problematic areas with which a person has to struggle,"(3) "serve as a starting point to stimulate professional and public scrutiny of major ethical quandaries in the field," and (4) "may minimize the need for cumbersome and intrusive governmental regulations."[11]

For argumentative purposes to be served through formal codes of ethics, Johannesen endorses Crable for justifying the "useful argumentative function of codes." Crable, he affirms, holds that "formal ethical codes provide a visible and impersonal standard to which both critics and defenders can appeal in arguing the ethicality of practices."[12] Crable himself contends that formal codes serve to transform vague claims pertaining to unethical professional conduct into clear complaints.[13] Summarizing Crable's argumentative strategies for critics and defenders of formal professional codes of ethics, Johannessen suggests that to test the ethicality of a communicative act we must determine whether the act:

> (1) is ethically suspected even though it falls outside the boundaries of any established code; (2) is "clearly contrary to an established code; (3) is condemned, or justified, because one applicable code is superceded by another relevant code that takes precedence; (4) is ethically justifiable because "higher" purposes or values take precedence over the relevant code; (5) should be judged primarily by legal statutes rather than by an ethical code; (6) is unethical because, while the strict "letter" of the code was honored, the "spirit"

of the code was violated; and (7) is ethical because the code is irrelevant, improper, or too vague and ambiguous.[14]

An example of a formalized ethical code is the Code of Professional Conduct and the Declaration of Rights and Responsibilities, as stated by the Alberta Teachers' Association.

The ATA Code and Declaration

As professional guidelines in the general ethics of teaching, the Alberta Teachers' Association (ATA) distinguishes the Code of Professional Conduct from the Declaration of Rights and Responsibilities – from now on abbreviated as the Code and the Declaration. The Code and the Declaration are used here to illustrate formal codes in action. Counterparts to them can be found throughout North American teaching associations. The ATA Code and Declaration alert future and certified teachers to standards that have been codified and are utilized in the schools. Teachers and future teachers might also wish to investigate the Discipline Bylaws of the ATA *Members' Handbook*. The Bylaws outline behaviors, "other than the 'Code of Professional Conduct,' that may lead to charges of unprofessional conduct against teachers." Note well that the Code and Declaration do not constitute an ATA Code of Ethics. The Code and Declaration are "completely separate documents." Only the Code has the "force of legislation." The Declaration "does not have legislative authority." Adopted by the ATA in 1984, the Declaration constitutes "an attempt to define, in ideal terms the rights and corresponding responsibilities of teachers." While teachers who violate the Code are "subject to a charge of unprofessional conduct under the Discipline Bylaws of the Association," teachers who fail to exercise the responsibilities of the Declaration are "not necessarily subject to charges of unprofessional conduct."[15]

The Code and Declaration, revised, was enacted by Order in Council on 26 March 1986. Selections from these follow.

Code of Professional Conduct

The Code of Professional Conduct (with its twenty-two statements) stipulates minimum standards of professional conduct of teachers. It is not an exhaustive list of standards. Unless exempted by legislation, any member of The Alberta Teachers' Association who is alleged to have violated the standards of the profession, including the provisions of the Code, may be subject to a charge of unprofessional conduct under the Discipline Bylaws of the Association.

In relation to pupils

1. The teacher teaches in a manner that respects the dignity and rights of all persons without prejudice as to race, religious beliefs, color, sex, physical characteristics, age, ancestry or place of origin.

In relation to school authorities

8. The teacher protests the assignment of duties for which the teacher is not qualified or conditions which make it difficult to render professional service.

In relation to colleagues

13. The teacher criticizes the professional competence or professional reputation of another teacher only in confidence to proper officials and after the other teacher has been informed of the criticism.

In relation to the profession

20. The teacher submits to the Association disputes arising from professional relationships with other teachers which cannot be resolved by personal discussion.

The Declaration of Rights and Responsibilities for Teachers follows:

Declaration of Rights and Responsibilities for Teachers

The general purpose of education is the full development of the potential of each individual. Society, of which teachers are a part , establishes the goals of education and the organizational framework within which formal education occurs.

In its broadest sense, teaching is a process which facilitates learning. Formal teaching activities are based on the specialized application of the learning process adapted to meet the educational needs of the learner.

A teacher has professional knowledge and skill gained through formal preparation and experience. A teacher provides personal, caring service to pupils by diagnosing their needs and by planning, selecting and using methods and evaluation procedures designed to promote learning.

In Alberta, a teacher is a member of The Alberta Teachers' Association.

The Alberta Teachers' Association holds that teachers are entitled to the stated rights (10 statements are given) and must accept the corresponding responsibilities.

A selection of three of these rights are as follows:

1. Teachers have the right to base diagnosis, planning, methodology and evaluation on professional knowledge and skills, and have the responsibility to review constantly their own level of competence and effectiveness and to seek necessary improvements as part of a continuing process of professional development.

3. Teachers have the right to a voice in all decisions of a professional nature which affect them and have the responsibility to seek the most effective means of consultation and of collaboration with their professional colleagues.

7. Teachers have the right to fair and reasonable evaluation of professional performance and have the responsibility to give sincere consideration to any suggestions for improvement.

Code of Professional Conduct

The Code of Professional Conduct is prefaced by the statement that it "stipulates minimum standards of professional conduct" for teachers. Two terms in need of underscoring are *minimum* and *professional*. This code does not stipulate maximum standards nor general conduct. These minimum standards of professional conduct, however, seem challenging to fulfill for most teachers. In a self-report pilot study on teachers' adhering to this code, out of the eighty-two teachers polled, most declared some violation. Forty percent declared regular violation of this code. In relation to pupils, numbers one (prejudice), four (consideration), and five (confidentiality) suffered frequent violation. In relation to school authorities, number eight (protest) had been avoided. In relation to colleagues, numbers thirteen (criticism) and seventeen (suggestions) were abused. And, in relation to the profession, number twenty (dispute resolution) was violated.[16]

Any teacher or future teacher may violate one or more of the standards of the Code of Professional Conduct. To the extent that the violations occur, tolerance for the violations may become manifest in formal and informal complaints from pupils, authorities , and other colleagues. Depending on the school and its community, some rules of ethics may be more enforced than others. You will have to learn which breeches of ethics are tolerated in your school and community and which are not. The prudent approach would be to know what constitutes a violation and to avoid its violation. If you chose to violate an ethical standard, you would then be doing so deliberately and with knowledge that you may be chastized for doing so.

Which of the standards do you think you might violate? Write these out now. After student teaching, review your list and compare it with today's anticipations. After teaching for a year or more, compare what you may have violated with what you thought you would have violated.

Declaration of Rights and Responsibilities for Teachers

Knowing one's responsibilities can be unrewarding. With wisdom, the Declaration calls attention to both. We have rights in relation to responsibilities. Although teachers have rights, they "must accept the corresponding responsibilities." In appreciating our rights as teachers, we must confront our responsibilities. Linking rights to responsibilities becomes clear when we examine the ATA's Declaration. We will not analyze all ten items listed. Because of their communicative implications for teaching, several points will receive special attention.

Right number two pertains to pupil behavior that is "necessary for maintaining an optimal learning environment." The corresponding responsibility addresses the reasonable use of "methods to achieve such standards." If the necessary student conduct constitutes all students being seated, dressed in uniforms, hands folded, and looking straight ahead at the teacher, then reasonable methods must be employed to attain this standard. Threat of bodily harm, expulsion from school, removal from the hockey team and bribes would not constitute reasonable methods in Canadian schools. If the preferred pupil deportment involves students working in groups, dressed casually, and talking with one another about the task, reasonable methods must once again be utilized to attain this standard. Supportive words, kind glances, associated benefits, and rewards may constitute reasonable methods in Canadian schools. In short, teachers have the right to expect behavior suitable for learning in a classroom and the responsibility to elicit this behavior in a reasonable manner. Instead of complaining about a violated or unfulfilled right, a teacher must first analyze where responsibility for insuring the right has not been taken.

Right number four allows teachers "to criticize educational programs" as long as they "do so in a professional manner." Teachers may criticize within their rights if and only if they do so professionally. Interpreting this right and its concomitant responsibility involves judging what constitutes legitimate criticism and professional procedures. The criticism may attack the design of a needed program, the selection of relevant curricula in a program, inappropriate grading standards for the program, and numerous other educational problems tied to the program. The procedure might call professionally for the recognition of a problem and offer a solution to the problem. For example, a school district may have a speech therapy program that is obsolete. Teachers have the right to criticize its obsolesence and the responsibility to demonstrate with feasibility an improved version. To call attention to the problem entails more than a complaint. A way out of the problem is desirable as well. The way out would be professional – practicable and beneficial without assassinating the character or competence of teachers, administrators, or school boards related to the speech therapy program.

And, right number nine protects teachers against prejudicial discrimination based on race, religion, color, sex, physical characteristics, age, ancestry or place of origin. In return, teachers must "refrain from practising these forms of discrimination in their professional duties." Other responsibilities may conceivably be tied to this right. For ATA purposes, this suffices. To fulfill it is no small task. With communication as our concern, to avoid suffering from discrimination on these grounds and to avoid discriminating on these grounds constitutes a challenge to student teachers as well as veteran teachers. To suffer or inflict discrimination would involve the violation of a right and a responsibility. It would also involve unethical and unfair professional conduct. Since discrimination along these line occurs, the task of minimizing and eliminating prejudicial discrimination falls upon teachers. To make this ethic work, it must be practiced. Teachers should be protected from the tendencies of others to judge against them on racial, religious, sexist, and other grounds. When fairness is not shown, teachers may appeal to this right. When teachers discriminate on color, age, ancestry, and other grounds, those suffering may make their grievance known. The ATA Declaration states the responsibility applies to teachers' practising discrimination "in their professional duties." It may be preferable to avoid prejudicial discrimination altogether in a teachers' life and, perhaps, everyone's life. The humbler task is to avoid prejudicial discrimination professionally – in the professional duties of teaching.

To reject a person on grounds of race, religion, sex, or age insults this ethic. To accept such a person embraces this ethic. If a candidate for a teaching post or science project competition or school athletic team has several characteristics we do not prefer in terms of race, sex, or age, we must choose between insulting or supporting this ethic. When the candidate is superior, but of an undesirable color or age, we belittle the ethic by voting for the candidate who is inferior but of a desirable color or age. Relative to the professional duty, we rise or fall in our ethical choice. Based on what the job demands, we can be ethical by meeting the demands or unethical by surrendering to our prejudicial judgment. Whether the person victimized by prejudice is a WASP male or a metis female, the victimization is wrong and should be corrected. In its wisdom, the ATA recognizes this potential cruelty and provides protection against it in the schools in the performance of professional duties.

The right and responsibility does not require teachers to join interracial clubs or marry outside one's religion. It limits its ethical jurisdiction to the schools and the execution of professional duties. Teachers who abide by this right and responsibility have chosen to be ethical in their professional dealings. How teachers conduct their lives outside the jurisdiction of the ATA's Code and Declaration is subject to other standards.

Declaration and other formal codes for teachers limit themselves usually to transactions that occur at school or that pertain to school life. Codified teaching ethics tend to be practicable and endorsed through professional associations – the Alberta Teachers' Association, the Canadian Teachers' Association, and the like. The formal codes for teachers are usually accepted after a vote and endorsed in principle as workable and favorable. To the extent that the codified ethics are practiced, teachers work under conditions ranging from fortunate to hapless.

In the broader concern of communication ethics and teaching, the societal role of the teacher becomes a relevant consideration. The teacher as citizen, as churchgoer, as club member, as consumer, as neighbor, and so on can be important in the world outside the school and profession of teaching. Some activities outside the jurisdiction of the school may be seen as unethical even though a formal teaching code is not violated. The ATA Code and Declaration Ethics, once again, do not stipulate maximum standards of general conduct - just minimum standards of professional conduct. To get an idea of what maximum standards for general conduct are, we shall examine a selection of thinkers who have written on ethics in particular and values in general. of world religions.

Some student teachers do not see why their ethical lives outside the profession and school should be considered. Sometimes in some schools in some areas, teachers will take part in activities that are seen as improper, questionable, or even unethical in relation to teaching. The teaching role may conflict with some other role. Some examples include, depending on locale: being a barmaid, using illicit drugs, belonging to a gang, being a stripper (male or female), belonging to the KKK, managing an adult (pornographic) book store, promiscuous dating habits, being an alcoholic, and numerous others. If a teacher has a high profile in the area, the possibility of a conflict of interest may also be high. What constitutes a conflict of interest ethically to a teacher in a school at a Hutterite colony may differ significantly from a teacher in a school on a Native Reserve or another in a small town or large city. The lifestyles of teachers in diverse areas may be tolerated in varying ways at different levels. In order to understand the broader base for ethics, we will examine what humane thinkers have contributed. To see the microcosm of the school in its ethical relation to the macrocosm of society, we turn to authorities on humane transactions and communication ethics.

Notes for chapters eight, nine and ten are located at the end of chapter ten.

9

Humane Values in Educational Communication

Richard A. Fiordo

The thought of selected humane thinkers on right conduct and the good life has been condensed and applied to education. It would be worthwhile to listen to the echoes of their humane voices in the ATA Code and Declaration.

Starting with Aristotle, we find a value theory that has clearly been pleasing to educators for centuries with its stress on the benefits of contemplation and reason. With Aristotle as with the other humane thinkers covered, we can only highlight their value and ethical theories in this brief account. For a better grasp of the implications (that is, the limits and powers) of the contributions of the humane thought covered here, we recommend minimally, courses in value theory, ethics, psychotherapy, philosophical psychology, and rhetoric. To proceed with the limited information on values provided here alone may court disaster. The sketches here merely invite you to take a closer look. To acquire a respectable grasp of these humane principles requires an analysis of their presuppositions, paradigms, assumptions, premises, the conclusions implicit, and the conclusions actually deduced from the principles. Knowledge at this level requires far more effort. Please do not mistake the following summary for a treatise.

Aristotle

For Aristotle, the right act can be determined by the guide of the golden mean. "Moral virtue," says Aristotle, is a "mean between two vices, the one involving excess, the other deficiency." Clearly, locating the golden mean is not "a" simple task. Sometimes we must settle for silver or bronze. Aristotle warns us of the difficulty of finding the golden mean even if we have knowledge and wisdom. The vicious and ignorant easily confuse what is sufficient with what is deficient or excessive. For example, a brave person appears rash in relation to the coward and cowardly in relation to the rash person.[17] For Aristotle, "the right act is to do the right thing to the right person, to the right extent, at the right time, with the right motive, and in the right way." Merely to perform an "act in some cursory fashion does not render the act moral. It is also vital to consider "when, why, how, to whom, and how much." In other words, an ill-timed statement is equivalent to deception, and an "insufficient gift may prove harmful." Consistent with the higher goals of education, "ethical superiority and moral excellence necessitate innate discernment and learning of the highest magnitude."[18]

Epicurus

Although frequently confused with the hedonistic Aristippus and the Cyrenaics whose ethics entailed seeking and enjoying the "pleasures of the moment before the opportunity slipped by," Epicurus held that we may not die with the arrival of the next day. Instead, we may "live to suffer and regret the lasting baneful consequences of momentary pleasures." Subsequently, Epicurus argued "we do not choose every pleasure, but sometimes we pass over many pleasures, when greater discomfort accrues to us as the result of them." Not only might Epicurus think well of social exchange theory, but he might very likely enjoy a drink without drinking to excess. Reckless sex leading to the 1980s version of leprosy, AIDS, would not likely be his moral problem. Stressing the avoidance of pain and tolerating the enjoyment of pleasure (unless the pleasure is of the mind or soul), Epicurus declares the "pleasures of love" never profit us and we are lucky if these pleasures do not harm us. In short, legitimate pleasures include "all the pleasures of the mind, the avoidance of pain, mental tranquility, peace of soul."[19] As for orgiastic celebrations, see Aristippus and the Cyrenaics. Epicurian hedonism, unlike its popular misinterpretation, is comparatively conservatile – that is, more towards a cup of camomile tea than a carafe of wine.

Note that the *summum bonum* of Epicurus is prudence. All the other virtues spring from prudence. Prudence is bound to the pleasant life. He asserts that "it is not possible to live pleasantly without living prudently and honorably and justly, nor, again, to live a life of prudence, honor and justice without living pleasantly." Epicurus also accords friendship – a vital interpersonal quality – encomium: friendship is the greatest blessing for the "complete life" that wisdom allows us to acquire.

By nature we seek pleasure. To choose every pleasure indiscriminately is folly. All pleasures are good; all pains are evil. However, some pleasures should be shunned; some pains should not be avoided. Pleasures and pains should be weighed against one another: pleasures leading to discomforts should be resisted while pains leading to benefits should be endured. In the concise discourse of Epicurus, "the good on certain occasions we treat as bad, and conversely the bad as good." In conclusion, resembling Aristotle's stress on the rational, Epicurus maintains that it is "not continuous drinkings and revellings, not the satisfaction of lusts... and luxuries of the wealthy table, which produce a pleasant life, but sober reasonings."[20]

Epictetus

A stoical mode of ethical conduct is found in Epictetus. Indulgence in the pleasures of life decreases markedly from the hedonist to the stoic. Epictetus might be celebrated as a member of a task force yet scorned as a party animal and mourned as the life of a party. His ideas, though, have hueristic and liberating value, if not humor and vitality.

Epictetus urges us to be content with our circumstances. To complain about our conditions or plight is unwise, vexes the soul, and disturbs mental tranquility. We must exercise self-control to the level of self-mastery to attain peace of mind – that is, contentment. When we permit others to disturb our peace of mind, we allow ourselves to be reduced to slavery. We would not tolerate others abusing our bodies, yet we frequently permit others to abuse our mental tranquility by trusting our minds to disturbed and confounded people. We mindlessly permit such indignation shamelessly.

To gain peace of mind, we much accept and even welcome what cannot be altered. Otherwise, suicide is always an option. We can terminate our weary lives when we prefer. If we prefer to live despite our weariness, we may face the inevitable and unchangeable by either assuming an indifferent attitude towards it or accepting our plight willingly. Resignation removes the pain from our hapless circumstances. We must despise what we cannot improve: what is beyond our poor powers to add or remove. Contentment follows a life lived according to the natural laws governing us: mortality, survival, and the vicissitudes of life. By surrendering to all the demands of natural occurances, we resign ourselves to nature. A tranquil spirit follows.[21]

Sexually speaking, followers of Epictetus need not panic over AIDS, since sexual activity is seen as a "weakness, imprisonment, or slavery which ought to be avoided at all costs." Addiction to sexual activity is akin to the "cruel sufferings of slavery." If we fail to extinguish sexual habits, we "fall prey to its many pitfalls and consequential sufferings." Contentment correlates with sexual restraint. Incontinence spawns discontent.[22] The ethics of Epictetus, despite their sobriety, may be reborn in our sexually dangerous 1990s society.

St. Thomas Aquinas

Especially relevant to teachers working in the Roman Catholic separate systems in Canadian schools is the ethical system of St. Thomas Aquinas. Thomistic ethics would have value for public as well as separate school teachers, but his ethics would be of unequivocal value to separate school teachers.

St. Thomas urges us to realize both our human and divine nature. Ultimate happiness involves contemplating God and God's will. God's will is seen in natural law. While he encourages us to embody the virtues of temperance, fortitude, wisdom, justice, faith, hope, and charity (or love), he discourages us from committing mortal and venial sins. Both reason and revelation, he holds, lead us to truth.[23]

In discussing good and evil, St. Thomas tells us we act in our own best interest. We do not try intentionally to hurt ourselves even though we may hurt ourselves unintentionally. All of our actions strive toward "a good." Evil, however, is incidental and unintentional. Compared to good, evil occurs less frequently. Furthermore, evil does not exist on its own; "good itself is the primary cause of evil." Evil is a corruption of what is good. Anything that is evil exists in something that is good. Evil is "caused accidentally by good."

Since we all strive toward some good, the ultimate good we all strive toward is God. We tend as humans to imitate the divine nature of God. Our rational human nature leads us to understand God. As our penultimate goal, we lean toward being like God – that is, toward "a divine likeness." Our final objective is to discover what is good and true – that is, God. All of our deeds aim at knowing God.[24]

As for virtue, St. Thomas ranks charity (or love) highest in order of perfection over faith and hope. "Charity is the root of all virtues," explains St. Thomas. Being a theological virtue, charity (or love) need not depend on conformity to a mean – golden or otherwise. We can never "love God as much as He ought to be loved." Excess in love for God does not apply. Love "does not consist in a mean, but increases the more we approach to the summit." Charity (or love), in sum, indicates a "friendship with God as well as the love of him" – that is, "a mutual communion with a certain reciprocity of love."[25]

Sin is a sickness of the soul comparable to bodily disease. Mortal sins cause irreparable illness while venial sins do not. For example, sins that keep us from the love of God (e.g., blasphemy) or of our neighbor (e.g., murder) are mortal. Acts committed due to weakness or ignorance, for example, constitute venial sins. Venial sins are "not contrary to the love of God and one's neighbor." In sum, mortal sins cause irreparable harm to the Great Commandment of Jesus Christ – namely, love God entirely and love your neighbor as yourself – and venial sins do not.[26]

Communicating ethically in schools, separate or otherwise, would involve instructing some students who emerge from the tradition of St. Thomas Aquinas. Their worldview and values may resemble Thomistic ethics. Teachers unaware of Thomistic ethics would be wise to investigate them further since they will likely be judged by Thomistic students in light of Thomistic values.

James Martineau

As used in the universe of value discourse, intuitionism may refer to morality intuitively grasped. That is, intuitionism means that "moral value is inner, within the personality exclusively, *not* in overt actions" – overt action lacks the moral content of will, intent, motive and the like. Consequences are not of concern to the ethical intuitionist.[27] In the introspective light of intuitionism, James

Martineau's thought will be examined. As teachers, the decency of our intentions at times may be all we have remaining after colleagues and students criticize the outcomes of our policies and practices.

In Martineau's system of ethics, right and wrong acts are matters of motive or impulse. Even though the outcome of an act may be hurtful, if it stems from a good motive it is moral. Ethical deportment is judged by our "choice of the highest motive possible." When we are torn between a higher and a lower motive, we are moral when we choose the higher motive and immoral when we choose the lower motive. Morality is bound to duty. Without duty, morality would not be. Duty is a function of humans alone. However, duty should not be mistaken for wisdom. While duty implies our intentions, wisdom implies the sagacious way we handle circumstances we face. Wisdom helps us select ethical objectives, duty helps us fulfill them. When we may select the wrong objective, the act becomes foolish rather than sinful.[28] *Duty* consists in acting from the right affection," explains Martineau, while wisdom alone "consists in *pursuing the right end.*" Martineau's ethics of motive contrasts in this way with ethics of action or consequences: "Instead of meaning the worth of goodness by the scale of its external benefits, our rule requires that we attach no *moral value* to the benefits, except as signs and exponents of the goodness whence they spring; and graduate our approval by the purity of the source, not by the magnitude of the result."[29]

What is ethical can be located only in the "springs of action within us," not in the "effects of action upon us." The ethicality of our actions depends on the motives behind the actions. Morality, then, is internal and consists of "rightly *ordered* springs of action." "Rightly ordered" refers to a *"grade-scale of excellence* among our natural principles." What results is irrelevant to the standard of right action. Martineau offers a table for his thirteen springs of action. The lowest is vindictiveness; the highest is reverence with compassion just beneath it. The median motive of action includes antipathy, fear, resentment. Vindictiveness would typically be immoral and reverence moral. Resentment would lean in one direction or the other relative to circumstances.[30]

With respect to right action, once again, Martineau believes that "Every action is RIGHT, which, in presence of a lower principle, follows a higher: every action is WRONG, which, in presence of a higher principle, follows a lower." When confronting ethical problems, we have access to the Canon of Principles and the Canon of Consequences. The Canon of Principles allows us to evaluate duty and moral character. The Canon of Consequences allows us to evaluate wisdom and conduct.[31] Only the Canon of Principles is relevant to determining morality. The wisdom of our acts is gauged by the consequences. The morality of our acts are judged by our deliberate intentions.

As we see, Martineau does not ignore the external results of our actions; rather, he reclassifies the results of our actions as pertinent to our wisdom. Only our motives for our actions are relevant to right and wrong. Morality is restricted to intentions, prudent wisdom to effects. In the practice of teaching, as

Martineau orders human values, we are ethical to the degree that we chose the higher motive over the lower. If we act on the intention of sensual pleasure, when compassion is within our power, we act immorally. When our action springs from our love of liberty rather than our love of gain, we have acted morally.[32]

A teacher may give a low grade to his school's hockey star. The low grade may cause the hockey star to be ineligible for the team. The team's chances for a trophy will wane with the star player being academically ineligible. The consequences for the team may be painful. Yet, if the teacher sees it as his duty to put academic standards above athletic ones, his motive is right and so is his decision. Troublesome consequences do not affect the morality of his action. He has chosen the higher motive over the lower: that is, what is valid over what is easy. A principal of a school grants major benefits to the music teacher but minor benefits to the math teacher. She may have personal grounds for liking the music teacher and personal grounds for disliking the math teacher. The music teacher may be half the professional the math teacher is and contribute a third of what the math teacher does to the output of her school's program. The parents may even praise the principal's decision to support music over math and blame the opposite. Since the principal gives far more to the music teacher than she does to the math teacher, Martineau would consider her act wrong and immoral (despite even parental support) – or, at least leaning in this direction relative to her intent. Her act would be inarguably unethical if it sprang from vindictiveness. It would be relatively wrong if it came from gain or resentment. Once again, morality implies motives.

G. E. Moore

Those who believe consequences are germane to the ethicality of an act adhere to a school of ethical thought opposite to the intuitionist school. This school of ethical thought uses consequences as the guide to the rightness of an act. George E. Moore will be discussed as the representative ethicist of this school known sometimes as ideal utilitarianism or ethical realism. As the basis for an interpersonal ethic, Moore's ethical notions may be useful to some teachers in their school settings.

"Whether an action is right or wrong, Moore believed, "always depends upon its *total* consequences." He also argued that "if it is once right to prefer one set of *total* consequences A, to another set, B, it must always be right to prefer any set precisely similar to B." As for duty, Moore held that an "action is a *duty*, whenever and only when it produces the best possible consequences."[33] The right act "produces the best possible actual consequences" – not probable consequences or predictable consequences but actual results. Clearly, the right act does not depend on motive even though good and evil motives are taken into account.[34] A right or wrong act " *always* depends on its *actual consequences*,"[35] not on those we intend the act to produce. Since we never know the actual consequences of an act until later, we must act "in light of the best *foreseeable* consequences which may not be the best actual."[36]

Moore explains that " knowingly to do an action which would make the world, on the whole, really and truly *worse* than if we had acted differently, must always be wrong."[37] If a teacher steals a knife from a student who intends to injure another student with it, his stealing of the knife would be moral. A teacher who lies to a parent about a student's miserable performance in class would be moral if she knew the parent would abuse the child severely. Foreseeable disastrous results are consequences to be avoided. It is the teacher's duty only to act in such a way as to produce the best actual consequences under the circumstances. We must prefer the "best possible means to the best possible end."[38] However when we decide to do something that would lead to the best foreseeable consequences, we have to be able to do so accordingly. We may be willing but unable to do what is right. The ethical concern emerges from our choice among options when we can do what is right. If we are incapable of executing an action that is right, we cannot be held responsible. The act must be possible. As Moore maintained, a "voluntary action is right whenever and only when its total consequences are as good intrinsically, as any that would have followed from any action which [we] could *have* done instead."[39]

Moore accepts as inevitable the reference to consequences. Sometimes we choose the wrongful act and are praised because of its consequences. Sometimes we choose the rightful act and are blamed due to its consequences. Paradoxically, we sometimes "deserve the strongest moral condemnation for choosing an action, which *actually* is right." Paradoxically, we sometimes "deserve the strongest moral blame if [we do] not choose the course in question, even though it may be wrong."[40]

A teacher may violate the ATA Code or Declaration and try to get another fired on false grounds, yet this malicious prosecution may result in the prosecuted teacher being advanced professionally with subsequent funding coming to the school through the prosecuted teacher. The wrongful act becomes right due to the flow of consequences. The other side of this irony is the teacher who, forseeing a victory for the school team and the thrill of victory this swimmer will experience, recruits a student who is an outstanding synchronized swimmer. Instead, the synchronized swimmer fails her academic courses due to the pressures of training and competing for synchronized swimming. The swimmer must be suspended from the team which has come to depend on her high performance, and the team loses its chance at a team championship. The rightful act becomes wrong due to the flow of consequences.

As a critical reaction to Moore's values, Sahakian comments that we cannot do or even know when we act in line with the "best possible actual consequences." Probably, none of us has "even committed a single *objectively* right act" even though we may have been "successful in accomplishing many *subjectively* right ones."[41] In short, having your consequences be your exclusive rule for right and wrong has drawbacks. In the practice of hiring, for example, administrators may filter prospective teachers carefully using all the legal criteria for doing so. Yet, in spite of their noble efforts, teachers hired may – unforeseen by the administrator – molest students or teach doctrines of hate toward a minority. Do you think the administrator who hired the teachers who turned out to be a molester or hatemonger acted unethically in hiring these teachers who by their credentials and through their interview fulfilled all the current high standards for hiring teachers? Does your conclusion differ from the ethics of Moore or coincide with his ethics?

Josiah Royce

To the tune, lightheartedly speaking, of "Be true to your school," the value of loyalty addresses our fidelity and decisiveness. The developer of this ethic is Josiah Royce. Royce believed all ethical principles and all morality can be summarized by the supreme and intrinsic good of loyalty. Regardless of the worthiness of the cause, *loyalty* signifies the "willing and practical and thoroughgoing devotion of a person to a cause."[42] Two worthwhile causes may conflict. When this happens, we are obliged to be loyal to loyalty. Loyalty requires self-sacrifice, self-control, a personally valued cause, altruism, and others interested in the same cause. Loyalty has prerequisites: (1) one must have a cause, (2) one must choose the cause autonomously, (3) one must commit oneself willingly and thoroughly to a cause, and (4) one must have a sustained and practical dedication to a cause. Loyalty implies duty and obligation; it is the only justification for sacrifice.[43] The religious martyrs of Canada, the political martyrs of China's Pro-Democracy activists, the patriotic martyrs of Columbia's drug wars, teachers who risk jobs for educational reform, and the like exemplify Royce's loyalists. Loyalty is the standard for morality. Principles and actions that do not involve loyalty have no ethical value. Royce's ethic culminates in loyalty to loyalty.

Since Royce's value of loyalty can be attacked as justifying the conduct of pirates, Nero, Hitler, and Deng because their abuses can be seen as loyal, knowing what may be fitting and proper as a cause worthy of loyalty will help us temper the apparently extreme view of Royce. Royce maintained that autonomous and enlightened causes included friendship, the family, the state, humanity, and "all stable social relations capable of giving rise to causes that summon loyalty." Ultimately, conflicts in loyalty need not arise. If we are loyal to an evolving and developing system of universal human loyalty, we increase our human capacity for the advancement of humanity through the ethic of loyalty. Loyalties are contagious. As we evolve in our loyalties, we spread improved and preferred loyalties to others. Our loyalties, in other words, evolve from primitive to civilized. Loyalty transforms less enlightened values into more enlightened values – ethicality that did not address loyalty into ethicality that does.[44]

Royce judges a cause as good insofar as it is "essentially a *loyalty to loyalty,* that is, is an aid and a furtherance of loyalty in my fellows." He judges a cause as evil insofar as, despite the loyalty it arouses in us, it destroys "loyalty in the world of my fellows." An evil cause aims at "overthrowing the loyalties of others" and so promotes "disloyalty to the very cause of loyalty itself."[45] To "oppose another's spirit of loyalty," to render "loyalty impossible," to destroy loyalty, or to inhibit loyalty constitutes the "unpardonable sin of being *disloyal to loyalty.*" To be loyal to loyalty is the *summum bonum* involving deciviseness and fidelty. We must decide on a cause and be faithful to it. Indecision and infidelity with respect to a cause is lethal.[46] If someone remarks that you and I may be wrong, assuming a decent conscience as our guide, with Royce we may reply: "We are fallible, but we can be decisive and faithful; and this is loyalty."[47]

A teacher may decide on a cause and be faithful to it. She may choose to promote neurolinguistic programming as her cause. To the extent that she does what is within her power to implement this cause, she displays the ethic of loyalty. If she promotes neurolinguistic programming only when she finds support among her colleagues, she displays disloyalty to her cause. She is unfaithful. Her sin, according to Royce, is unpardonably disloyalty to loyalty.

As for students, loyalty to school and team and friends would not be uncommon. Of course, the loyalty may evolve in an upward and onward fashion. Yet, while your grade six students are in your class, their ultimate loyalty - if not obsession – may be to their local skateboard jungle. They will exercise self-control, make sacrifices, display personal devotion, demonstrate altruism, and promote the general welfare of skateboarding to other skateboarders as well as, perhaps, their posterity. As far as skateboarding is concerned, their Ecclesiastical dictum might be: "Loyalty, loyalty! All is loyalty!"

What do you think about being disloyal to loyalty? What if this teacher adhered prematurely to her cause of neurolinguistic programming? Perhaps, believe it or not, a preferred learning approach has become available. Would she be sinning against neurolinguistic programming through her infidelity to an alternative approach? Or, would she be loyal to the pursuit of the best learning theory available? Might her cause have been better defined for the value of loyalty in broader terms – for example, loyalty to the cause of learning theory or loyalty to the cause of advancing the study of learning?

Karen Horney

Thoughts on improving our conduct, values, and relationship were lucidly and profoundly set forth by the psychologist Karen Horney. Applying a selection of Horney's humane and healthy insights to the social psychology of education will constitute our limited effort. Horney's views on human psychodynamics prove useful. Horney saw aggression as a means we use to protect our security. Narcissism was seen as our "self-inflation and overevaluation owing to feelings of insecurity."[48] Basic anxiety, which is Horney's pivotal concept, refers to the "feeling a child has of being isolated and helpless in a potentially hostile environment."[49] Generally, whatever disturbs the security of children in relation to their parents produces basic anxiety. To cope with the basic anxiety, anxious children develop neurotic needs rather than rational solutions to their problems. If we were raised in a home where there was "security, trust, love, respect, tolerance, and warmth," unhealthy struggles within us would be avoidable and resolvable.[50]

When we are less fortunate in our childhood, we develop neurotic needs. The difference between our normal or healthy and neurotic needs is in degree. We all have inner conflicts. Due to childhood agonies from parental rejection, neglect, overprotection, and other forms of parental mistreatment, some of us have aggravated levels of inner conflicts. When our inner conflicts neurotically overwhelm us, we may avenge ourselves against those rejecting or mistreating us, be submissive to regain the love we think we have lost, wallow in self-pity to get sympathy, and so on. We may seek power over others if we cannot get love, become highly competitive where winning replaces achieving, or aim our hostility at ourselves as a means of berating ourselves. Instead of healthfully integrating needs of love, independence, and power, highly neurotic people may recognize only one of the needs while denying or repressing the others. The need for love, independence, and power correspond to Morris' orienting values of attachment, detachment, and dominance. Love means "moving toward people"; independence means "moving away from people"; and, power means "moving against people."[51]

As irrational solutions to problems (that is, "solutions" that do not work), we may develop perverse interpersonal strategies. Horney classifies ten neurotic strategies characterized by:

1. Indiscriminate wishes to please others and live up to their expectations – a neurotic need for affection and approval.
2. Fear of desertion and overvaluing love – a neurotic need for someone to take over in our life.
3. Over-restricting ourselves into unassertiveness – a neurotic need to live undemandingly within too narrow borders.
4. Glorification of power and contempt for weakness – the neurotic need for power.
5. Taking pride in our capacity to take unfair advantage of people – a neurotic need to exploit others.
6. Judging ourselves by fame – a neurotic need for prestige.
7. Vanity based on an inflated image of ourselves rather than fact – a neurotic need for personal admiration.
8. Driving ourselves, from basic insecurity, to be the best – a neurotic need for personal achievement.
9. Refusing to be committed to anyone or anything – a neurotic need for independence.
10. Striving to be impregnable, infallible, and unassailable – a neurotic need to be perfect.[52]

As educators, we may see these neurotic needs emerge in numerous ways.

We may not assert ourselves since we need neurotic approval from others who would reject us if we were assertive. We may surrender our rights to a team teacher who takes responsibility for us. We may belittle our contributions – actual and potential. We may show disrespect for any colleague who does not assume subordinate status. We may boast of our ability to use others at their expense. We may see ourselves as worthless unless our colleagues elect us to a prestigious position. We may fancy ourselves the fountain of all rationality in our school. We may wish to be legends in our schools and resent being legends only in our minds. We may avoid any interdependencies by involving ourselves as little as possible at work or afterwards. We may, lastly, adhere meticulously to trivial truisms to avoid reproach.

Do you see any of these unfortunate needs active in your life? Do you think some of them would plague you as a teacher? To which one do you seem most prone? What would you do to develop a real solution?

John Dewey

John Dewey's ethical pragmatism has extensively influenced ethics and educational communication. Dewey held that "every moral situation is a unique situation having its own irreplaceable good." Subsequently, fixed principles and rules do not apply to any particular case. Rather, we need to execute in a specific case "painstaking inquiry into facts and examination of principles."[53]

Unlike traditional ethicists, Dewey stressed that ethical theories dealing with values in general were not very useful.[54] Conduct is "always specific, concrete, individualized, unique." Judgments about which act should be "performed must be similarly specific."[55] We do not face ethical problems in general. We face specific ethical situations that may be problematic. We have to deal with a particular person or group that is uneducated, not humanity as a whole. We do not attain knowledge in the abstract; rather, we try to live knowledgeably in our daily lives. Instead of one goal in life (such as happiness, loyalty, survival, or God), Dewey contended that we have numerous goals. The person who pursues only one goal may be fanatical: that is, obsessive compulsive. For a time, we may pursue predominantly one goal, such as our health, due to circumstances. But, ordinarily, we pursue several other goals – for example, justice in our lives, our economic growth, our physical appearance, our family unity, spiritual development, or our social life.[56]

Dewey's ethics concerns itself with "what *ought* to be, not with what actually *is* the case." When we do not do as we should, according to Dewey, we have made a mistake. Mistakes are neither "unavoidable accidents to be mourned or moral sins to be expiated and forgiven." His view is positive. Mistakes serve as lessons learned from experience; they help improve our future actions. Error provides us with the obligation and opportunity to learn and develop. We grow ethically as we reconstruct and refine our standards and ideals continually. Taking responsibility for the improvement of our ethical flaws keeps us from ethical stagnation and empty ritualism. Ethically, we may continue to grow with vitality and flexibility. Our standards for judgment may advance as we mature.[57]

Sounding like a Zen master, Dewey urges us to be open to the uniqueness of each situation involving an ethical problem. Perhaps, this is easier said than done. However, assuming various acceptable values in Canadian society – the rights and freedoms in the new charter would suffice, when we analyze an ethical problem from the vantage point of one ethical value alone (bliss, survival, loyalty, etc.), we scan the situation through an abstract generality that biases and so blinds us to the facts of the situation before us. We may overlook evils, that is deficiencies or the problem of human ills. Whatever the greatest deficiency is the greatest good is found in its remedy. If two deficiencies are equivalent, their remedies constitute equivalent values: that is, they are equally good. When a student in your class suffers from malnutrition, the greatest good becomes nutrition. If another student in your class suffers from parental neglect, parental attention becomes the greatest good. In short, Dewey sees the good as the better. In other words, what is preferred or better among available remedies in any problematic ethical situation constitutes what is good.[58]

The attitude toward human ills that Dewey recommends is meliorism. Pessimism paralyzes our endeavors to improve ourselves and our world. Optimism overlooks, rather than corrects, our ills. Meliorism, the belief that the world gets better and we can aid in its betterment, is the most appropriate stance we can take on the problem of human ills. It helps us improve our circumstances despite the degree of deterioration that currently exists.[59] Furthermore, meliorism urges us to "study the positive means of goods and the obstructions to their realization, and to put forth endeavor for the improvement of conditions." Meliorism is felicific. Since happiness is found only in succeeding, when we progress or advance, we are succeeding: not a fixed and static level of success, but a continuing active process of moving onward in improving some situation. Dewey explains that perfection is not our final aim. Rather, the "ever-enduring process of perfecting, maturing, refining is the aim of living."[60] In brief, it is ethical to improve.

A teacher who is pessimistic may despair about a problematic ethical situation. She may allow an illness to become worse. An optimistic teacher may not acknowledge that an ethical problem exists. He too may allow the illness to become worse. A teacher who is a meliorist would assess the ethical problem and take positive steps to reconstruct it. For example, a teacher may have a colleague who criticizes her approach to classroom management in a manner that violates the ATA Code of Professional Conduct. The colleague gossips about her lack of classroom control and belittles her performance to other colleagues and students. Rather than despair at the malice of the human race or pretend the colleague means no harm after all, the teacher who is a meliorist might talk to the disgruntled colleague in order to remedy what is an irritable ethical situation. Treating the criticism from the colleague as a problem worthy of solution may improve the situation and remedy (or alleviate) the ethical malady.

Given the pluralism of Canadian society, Dewey's values prove useful indeed to teachers. With so many religious, racial, and ethnic groups in Canada, Dewey's view of morality being social allows for practical remedies to daily ailments. Morality involves conflicting values and their resolution through analysis and choice. Dewey defined moral conduct as "activity called forth and directed by ideas of value or worth, where the values concerned are so mutually incompatible as to require consideration and selection before an overt action is entered upon."[61] Canada's multiculturalism would serve as an appropriate setting for exercising Dewey's ethical method for confronting differences.

Dewey did not claim that morality should be social; he simply asserted that morality is in fact social: "Our conduct is socially conditioned whether we perceive the fact or not."[62] Self-interest as much as altruism is a function of social conditioning. Moral pressure comes from society and social interaction. Even our physical environment becomes socialized and humanized. What is right are the demands society and others pressure us to accept, if for no other reason, to live together in a suitable and progressive manner. Approval and condemnation are social responses to our conduct. We affect others, and others affect us. Our behavior and the behavior of others have consequences that reciprocally and interactively modify us and our ways. While we have rights, we also have obligations. Our freedoms go hand in hand with our responsibilities. When an ATA member exercises his right to complain about a colleague, he has the responsibility to do so in a manner considered professionally ethical – namely, he notifies the colleague of his complaint before presenting it to an ATA grievance board.

Dewey's focus on means to ends is frequently criticized as being overdone. His critics charge him with encouraging people to go somewhere, but fail to tell them where to go. As long as we are progressing, even if it is over Niagara Falls in a canoe, Dewey allegedly would endorse it according to the tenets of his instrumentalistic ethic.[63] Such a critique is sophomoric. Dewey critically and progressively accepted fundamental democratic rights and freedoms with their concomitant responsibilities.[64] Freedom of conscience would serve as a democratic end-in-view (or intended goal) and reflective thought as a means to transform the end-in-view to an accomplished end.[65] Ends without means do not exist. Ends cannot be judged without reference to means. We must deal with a relation of means-ends or means-consequences. The relation of means-ends or means-consequences must be "capable of being tested by observation of results actually attained as compared with those intended."[66] If we separate means from ends (or consequences), we eliminate an intelligent basis for adjudicating the ethical value of the ends.[67]

In his account of Dewey, Morris explains that as far as education is concerned, Dewey believed the goal of a democratic school is to "produce persons with an experimental habit of mind and with the moral character which can cooperate with other persons in associated action consonant with the democratic ideal." As the school produces such people, it becomes the "main agency for continually transforming an existing state of democracy in the direction of the ideal democracy."[68]

If the detractors of Dewey are right, the actions of the 27th Army of the People's Republic of China on 4 June 1989 in the incident at Tiananmen Square in Beijing would be ethically endosed since they were instrumentally superior to the means used by the former soldiers in bringing about the termination of the Pro-Democracy student demonstration. Do you believe Dewey's ethics would support the actions of the 27th Army? Do you believe the consequences the army sought to bring about – the termination of the student protests - justified, according to Dewey, the bloody means employed? Would Dewey's instrumental ethic endorse a teacher who skillfully uses the best means available to bring about a questionable consequence – for example, the expulsion, from school on marginal grounds, of a personally disliked student or the nomination of a personally liked student for student counsel despite the presence of other candidates with superior credentials? These questions are ultimately yours to ponder. How do you cast your vote?

Ethical responsibility is measured by our intelligence and education. We are ethically accountable "only to the extent of the light that is within" us. Two people are never the same, nor are their circumstances identical. Subsequently, each of us must be judged independently on matters of ethical duty, obligation, and responsibility. Smart and schooled people with material advantage will face greater ethical responsibility than dull and unschooled people lacking material advantage. Yet, we will not be weighed in terms of attaining or missing some fixed standard. Rather, we will be weighed by the direction in which we move. Our value scale is interval (or relative) instead of ratio (or absolute). We are bad when no matter how good we have been, we deteriorate: that is, we "grow less good." We are good when no matter how unethical we have been, we improve: that is, we "become better."[69]

Our ethical meterstick is, therefore, humanely elastic. As we grow, we move toward moral health; as we deteriorate, we move toward moral illness. Since different conditions prevail for judging individual worth, Dewey's relative notion of good and bad does not allow us to lord our moral achievement over another nor prostrate ourselves before the ethical splendor of another.[70] Morality with a fixed point fathers grounds for moral superiority and inferiority. While superior and inferior status may have an appointed place in bureaucratic hierarchies, they do not have an anointed place in Dewey's ethics. We become better or worse as teachers relative to our capacities and circumstances; we are perfecting or degenerating as teachers. If our progressing outweighs our regressing, we are good. Morality is, grammatically, adjudicated as the present progressive tense, and not the simple present tense – namely, "I'm getting better" or "I'm getting worse." As we examine ourselves, we can examine our students. Each becomes good or bad relative to individual capacities and circumstances. Thus, we declare at the end of a term: "You not only earned a grade of A, but you improved tremendously."

Simone de Beauvoir

"Existentialism," writes Kaplan, "is a philosophy which does not content itself with a mere description and evaluation." Returning to the classical philosophical tradition, existentialism insists that philosophy is fundamentally different from other intellectual pursuits. For existentialists, philosophy is not a body of propositions but a way of life." However, before assuming consensus on the part of existentialists, Kaplan notes that even an identification as "existentialists" is resisted. Is this vanity? What is the significance of such protectiveness? Existentialism explains "not just what propositions to accept, but what kind of life to live, and on what basis." Lessons learned at school fit in a textbook. We can look up answers in the back of the book. In contrast, existentialism deals with human life. No profound answers to the problems of life can be found in the back of a book. This one is no existential exception. If we can look up the answers in a book, we are not reading an existential book.[71]

Existentialism examines, then, the human condition. It looks at *possibilities* as well as constraints. *Choice* is crucial. For choice to remain meaningful, we must have alternatives. However, our alternatives give rise to *ambiguity*. No one choice permanently defines us. We choose continuously. With each choice, "some possibilities vanish forever while new ones emerge for the next choice." While we are always making something out of life, we never quite make it out because "life is inescapably ambiguous." While knowledge becomes interpretation, human conduct becomes a "struggle with the strands of ambiguity in which [our] existence is enmeshed."[72]

Recognizing the importance of ambiguity in human affairs, the existential philosopher and literary artist Simone de Beauvoir discussed the ethics of ambiguity. She held that "one of the concrete consequences of existentialist ethics is the rejection of all the previous justifications which might be drawn from the civilization, the age, and the culture." This constitutes the "rejection of every principle of authority." Treating a person as having freedom, an existential ethics risks in each case "inventing an original solution." Abstract ideas (such as nation, union, etc.) have no value in themselves. They have a value only in relation to living human individuals. If a nation or "union can be created only to the detriment of those it is trying to unite, the nation or union must be rejected. She repudiates idealisms and anything else that prefers abstractions to people. If an act distinguishes very little between us and others and if it allows us to fulfill ourselves in treating others as ends in themselves rather than as merely means to be manipulated toward ends, our conduct is likely to be ethical.[73]

De Beauvoir challenges every condemnation and justification of an act by its end alone or means alone before the unique and living facts of the case are taken into account. Since we conduct ourselves under limited real circumstances, we must concern ourselves with the uncertainties of ambiguous choices. We aspire to balance means against ends. We do not freeze; we continue to act in pursuit of ends. We define an end and realize it, knowing the "choice of the means employed affects both the definition and the fulfillment." For example, a political choice is an ethical choice. It is justified in concrete circumstances. We decide and gamble on that decision.[74] Respect for freedom has its difficulties. We must accept the ambiguities producing tensions in our struggle to perpetuate our continual liberation without ever seeking complacency.[75] Morality thus "resides in the painfulness of an indefinite questioning." Ethics furnishes no recipes: "there must be a trial and decision in each case." However, Simone de Beauvoir does not endorse trying to fulfill everyone's will. Since some people want to enslave others, such evil people must be fought.[76] Ethical conduct should not follow the line of least resistance. Ethical conduct must be consented to willingly regardless of the difficulties to follow. Freedom must triumph over tyranny. The triumph of freedom must be continual, progressive, and alive.[77] We must accept ambiguity in our daily lives to create and recreate our liberation.[78] Rather than flee from the present, we must use it as a time for choosing to liberate ourselves.[79] In education, if we choose a line of least resistence that opposes our sense of decency, we have made a choice against freedom. When we knowingly vote for a policy that restricts wholesome options, we have voted against liberations. Do you say things daily that deny your true feeling? Do you do things that restrict the options of others? Do you make choices that deliberately decrease your benefits and those of others? How existential a lifestyle do you think you live? Would Simone de Beauvoir agree?

The thinkers discussed represent a portion of the humane spectrum potentially useful to teachers. Students of education and teachers are encouraged to pursue ethical studies for purposes of educational communication. The list of worthy sources would fill a small phone book at least. As a suggestion of the ethical power that awaits the interested teacher, the following are proposed for continued study: Suzanne Langer, Martin Buber, Nikolai Berdyaev, Margaret Mead, Plotinus, Yu-Lan Fung, Maimonides, Socrates, Alfred North Whitehead, Ludwig Wittgenstein, Avicenna, Charles L. Stevenson, Rene Descartes, Mary Baker Eddy, George Santayana, Marie Hochmuth, Immanuel Kant, Bertrand Russell, St. Augustine, Henri Bergson, Jean-Paul Sartre, Daisetz Suzuki, Giordano Bruno, Mary Daly, Confucius, Stephen Toulmin, Philo Judaeus, Lao Tzu, Mary Whiton Calkins, Sri Ramakrishna, Nicola Abbagnano, Sri Shankaracharya, Averroes, Thomas Hobbes, Mencius, and numerous others.

Morris' Lifestyles

An approach to values that may benefit classroom teachers comes from the philosophy of Charles Morris. He proposes a total of thirteen patterns of value. Of the thirteen, seven are basic. He called them paths of life, ways to live, ways of life, and lifestyles. As a means for analyzing the lifestyles of your students, the seven patterns of value will be presented. Each was initially derived from a world religion.

Way 1 would be the Buddhist Path of Life, Way 2 the Dionysian Path of

Life, Way 3 the Promethian Path of Life, Way 4 the Apollonian Path of Life, Way 5 the Christian Path of Life, Way 6 the Mohammedan Path of Life, and Way 7 the Martreyan Path of Life.[80] Although the ways of life focus on healthy patterns of value and behavior (and we will focus on the healthy paths), Morris acknowledges that each healthy path may be hyperextended into a pathological one.

Ways of Life

Morris' ways of life offer criteria for us as teachers to order the complex preferences and relationships prevailing between us and our colleagues as well as between us and our students. The criteria consist of primary, secondary, and tertiary combinations of preferences for attachment, dominance, and detachment.

Morris sees these preferences as values. When organized systematically, the three preferred values of attachment, dominance and detachment become his seven major ways (or paths) of life – that is, patterns of value that direct our lives and integrate our "multifarious and competing interests." Each of the seven ways represents the "attainment of a dominant attitude (an apical interest) in terms of which all other interests are regulated." At least three factors influence us in selecting our way of life: our biological constitutions, our societal ideals, and our critical reflection. For example, each of us may be "inclined toward one or another of these paths of life, and in some cases ... may attain the congenial path without great difficulty." Yet, a congenial path may grace only some of us. Conflicts within us may lead us to be loyal to "a mode of life which promises release from conflict." Converting to a way of life that frees us from internal turmoil may "indicate a permanent reorientation of an entire life" or may be "merely a passing phase in the struggle of the individual for an as yet unattained (and perhaps never to be attained) integration." Morris warns that the "strenuous advocacy of a particular path of life is itself a sign" that we are "seeking this path of life and not merely following it." We must distinguish our ideal way of life from the life we are living.[81] seek its attainment."[81]

We may establish one way of life as our ideal, yet we may use another way of life – perhaps one that even violates our ideal – to mold ourselves and others into our ideal. In other words, the apical value for our ideal way of life may be detachment, yet we may pursue a detached way of life by temporarily (perhaps) incorporating a dominant way of life. We may change according to conditions and after reflection. Considering the "consequences of following any way of life" we decide to pursue, we "change to some degree" that way of life. There is no inevitability in selecting one necessary way of life as ideal for any one of us, for our community, or for humanity as a whole.[82]

While each path has conditions under which it would be appropriate, Morris intimates that the preferred path for the world as it is now may rest with the Path of Maitreya – a way of life that incorporates the benefits from each of the other ways but dispenses with their drawbacks. An account of the Maitreyan and the other six ways will follow. A diagram illustrating the components of the seven Ways of Life and their interrelationships is Figure 1.

Ways To Live

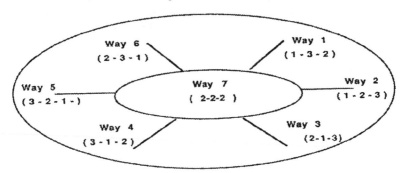

The orienting value (or interest) for Way 1 and Way 6 is dominance. The orienting value for Way 2 and Way 3 is detachment. The orienting value for Way 4 and Way 5 is attachment. Way 7 has no single value that consistently orients its follower. Rather, a dynamic balance of the three interests usually holds. Although slight fluctuations may occur circumstantially, the general norm is usually one of balance among the interests of attachment, dominance, and detachment.

In summary form, the seven ways are condensed for easy reference:

Way 1: preserve the best that humanity has attained

Way 2: cultivate independence of people and things

Way 3: show sympathetic concern for others

Way 4: experience festivity and solitude alternatively

Way 5: act and enjoy life through group participation

Way 6: constantly master changing conditions

Way 7: integrate action, enjoyment, and contemplation.[83]

For a thorough account, you are referred to Morris' *Paths of Life: Preface to a World Religion.* For our purposes, a middle range account will provide sufficient detail to grasp Morris' Ways to Live:

> WAY 1: In this "design for living" the individual actively participates in the social life of his community, not to change it primarily, but to understand, appreciate, and preserve the best attained. Excessive desires should be avoided and moderation sought. One wants the good things of life but in an orderly way. Life is to have clarity, balance, refinement, control. Vulgarity, great enthusiasm, irrational behavior, impatience, indulgence are to be avoided. Friendship is to be esteemed but not easy intimacy with many people. Life is to have discipline, intelligibility, good manners, predictability. Social changes are to be made slowly and carefully, so that what has been achieved in human culture is not lost. The individual should be active physically and socially, but not in a hectic or radical way. Restraint and intelligence should give order to an active life.

WAY 2: The individual should for the most part "go it alone," assuring herself of privacy in living quarters, having much time to herself, attempting to control her own life. One should stress self-sufficiency, reflection and mediation, knowledge of oneself. The direction of interest should be away from intimate associations with social groups, and away from the physical manipulation of objects or attempts at control of the physical environment. One should aim to simplify one's external life to moderate those desires whose satisfaction is dependent upon physical and social forces outside of oneself, and to concentrate attention upon the refinement, clarification, and self-direction of oneself. Not much can be done or is to be gained by "living outwardly." One must avoid dependence upon persons or things: the centre of life should be found within oneself.

WAY 3: This way of life makes central the sympathetic concern for other persons. Affection should be the main thing in life, affection that is free from all traces of the imposition of oneself upon others or of using others for one's own purposes. Greed in possessions, emphasis on sexual passion, the search for power over persons and things, excessive emphasis upon intellect, and undue concern for oneself are to be avoided. For these things hinder the sympathetic love among persons which alone gives significance to life. If we are aggressive we block our receptivity to the personal forces upon which we are dependent for genuine personal growth. One should accordingly purify oneself, restrain one's self-assertiveness, and become receptive, appreciative, and helpful with respect to other persons.

WAY 4: Life is something to be enjoyed – sensuously enjoyed, enjoyed with relish and abandonment. The aim in life should not be to control the course of the world or society or the lives of others, but to be open and receptive to things and persons, and to delight in them. Life is more a festival than a workshop or a school for moral discipline. To let oneself go, to let things and persons affect oneself, is more important than to do – or to do good. Such enjoyment, however requires that one be self-centred enough to be keenly aware of what is happening and free for new happenings. So one should avoid entanglements, should not be too dependent on particular people or things, should not be self-sacrificing; one should be alone a lot, should have time for meditation and awareness of oneself. Solitude and sociality together are both necessary in the good life.

WAY 5: A person should not hold on to herself, withdraw from people, keep aloof and self-centred. Rather a person should merge oneself with a social group, enjoy cooperation and companionship, join with others in resolute activity for the realization of common goals. Persons are social and persons are active; life should merge energetic group activity and cooperative group enjoyment. Meditation, restraint, concern for one's self-sufficiency, abstract intellectuality, solitude, stress on one's possessions all cut the roots which bind persons together. One should live outwardly with gusto, enjoying the good things of life, working with others to secure the things which make possible a pleasant and energetic social life. Those who oppose this ideal are not to be dealt with too tenderly. Life can't be too fastidious.

WAY 6: Life continuously tends to stagnate, to become "comfortable," to become sicklied o'er with the pale cast of thought. Against these tendencies, a person must stress the need of constant activity – physical action, adventure, the realistic solution of specific problems as they appear, the improvement of techniques for controlling the world and society. Our future depends primarily on what we do, not on what we feel or on our speculations. New problems constantly arise and always will arise. Improvements must always be made if we are to progress. We can't just follow the past or dream of what the future might be. We have to work resolutely and continually if control is to be gained over the forces which threaten us. We should rely on technical advances made possible by scientific knowledge. We should find our goal in the solution of our problems. The good is the enemy of the better.

WAY 7: We should at various times and in various ways accept something from all other paths of life, but give no one our exclusive allegiance. At one moment one of them is the more appropriate; at another moment another is the most appropriate. Life should contain enjoyment and action and contemplation in about equal amounts. When either is carried to extremes we lose something important for our life. So we must cultivate flexibility, admit diversity in ourselves, accept the tension which this diversity produces, find a place for detachment in the midst of enjoyment and activity. The goal of life is found in the dynamic integration of enjoyment, action, and contemplation, and so in the dynamic interaction of the various paths of life. One should use all of them in building a life, and no one alone.[84]

In terms of complementary and antagonistic values, Way 1 may complement Way 2. Way 3 may complement Way 4. And, Way 5 may complement Way 6. However, Way 1 may conflict with Way 4. Way 2 may conflict with Way 5. And, Way 3 may conflict with Way 6. The complementary Ways have one value of the same strength as the other member of the pair. The antagonistic Ways differ in the strength of two values. Only Way 7 serves as the harmonious hub. It alone draws from all, yet alienates none.

The seven Ways have complementary and oppositional relationships beneficial to us as teachers once we have learned to apply these categories with logical validity and empirical truth to ourselves and those with whom we work in our school settings. For example, once we establish that our principal follows Way 1, we know we will likely be in harmony with her if we follow Way 2; but, if we follow Way 4, we will likely be at loggerheads with her. If we follow Way 7, we will likely get along with her on most matters of import. If she follows Way 7, we would likely be graced by her integration of faculty, students, community, and board of education. We would, indeed, be blessed with a thoughtful doer who enjoys the people to whom she is responsible.

Additional comments on the benefits for all to be derived from Way 7 – namely, the Path of Maitreya – are in order. In our pluralistic, multidenominational, and multicultural Canadian milieu, people serving harmonizing purposes may be both preferred and beneficial to our general welfare. As teachers of students with diverse backgrounds, Way 7 may prove amenable to our educational aims. As counsellors and administrators, Way 7 once again may allow people from diverse origins from varied paths of life to work together in harmony and productively – or, at least with minimal quarrels and grievances. The cardinal virtue of Way 7 is "Maitreyan friendliness." This entails "abandon-ment and restraint, sympathy and severity, frankness and flexibility, challenge and considerateness, giving and withholding." In short, it requires a complex and vital friendship maintained through a dynamic balance of continual flexibil-ity.[85]

The Maitreyan ideal and Way of Life tempers the excessive tendencies of the other ideals and Ways without obliterating these variegated ideals and ways to live. As Maitreyan teachers and administrators, we would create the "most favorable environment for [our] development compatible with the development of other persons." With Way 7 as our ideal, we would "cherish diversity" in our schools (and lives) as well as foster an "attitude of detached-attachment" lead-ing us to relinquish our "possessive grip" on ourselves, others, and "on all things" in our lifetimes through our own efforts.[86] While being attached (that is, having desires) to objectives, we are not (as Maitreyans) addicted to or obsessed with the objectives. We can drop them when we wish or as cir-cumstances require. In other words, we can detach from our goals. Through detachment – objectivity if you like, we never allow our objectives to become cravings or obsessive compulsive neuroses. We pursue with indifference. We can end our pursuit of an objective without suffering the frustration of not hav-ing closure. In a sense, we are free. While we plan our school lessons, we may (but need not) complete every item that day. At a school meeting we may (but need not) go through the entire business agenda.

Morris cites Leonardo da Vinci as "a forerunner of the Martreyan ideal as operative in life." Over Leonardo's "long life of continual and restless activity," writes Morris, "is spread the mantle of a poignant detachment." In contrast, psychopathic behavior is "accompanied by an inability to incorporate the atti-tude of detachment into the adjustment to the particular problems set by the immediate environment."[87]

Way 7 has currency in the attitude of detached-attachment as far as other thinkers are concerned also. Ornstein explains that Zen masters "point out that 'worldly' activity can be a perfect vehicle for development, as long as one is free from attachment." As long as we are not in their service, "pleasures are leg-itimate." We must not cling to them. Quoting dervish wisdom applicable to detached-attachment, Ornstein emphasizes the point: When it is time for still-ness, stillness; in the time of companionship, companionship; at the place of effort, effort. In the time and place of anything, anything." [88] Insofar as we embody Way 7, we integrate attachment, dominance, and detachment.

With the exception of da Vinci, people who resemble the ideals of Way 7 have not been mentioned. Would you fill in the blanks on this item? Who do you know who embodies and practices the values of Way 7? Do you know any teachers, counsellors, or administrators who embody the Maitreyan Path, knowingly or not? Do you? If you lean in the direction of Way 7, to what extent do you embody and practice its ideals? Some students see Way 7 as little more than the Way of the Renaissance person. What do you think? Were you to follow Way 7 in teaching, do you believe you would enjoy what Morris says it promises? Do you identify with another way to live? Do you disagree with Morris on Way 7 as the preferred Way for our times? If you disagree, which of the Ways do you think is best? Do you think all of the Ways are ethical? Is Way 7 ethical as far as you are concerned? Which, if any of the Ways, do you see as unethical? If you try Way 7 or any other Way, please report your findings to your friendly local communication professor.

10

Truth and Honesty in Educational Communication

Richard A. Fiordo

In the television show "Baloney," an audience judges the veracity and falsity of several stories reported. One of the reporters is the soothsayer. The rest are pretenders. At the end of the round of stories, the pretenders are disclosed to the audience. Those audience members who voted for the soothsayer split prize money. What if this were done at the end of each class? Comical would be the situation and costly. Fear not. It will not happen on the budget assigned to education. The interest in finding truth in falsehood and honesty in deceit (or their opposites) in popular programming parallels the ancient esoteric concern with separating the false and the deceitful from the true and the honest in philosophy and science as well as mundane concerns at home, work, school, and anywhere else that we congregate. Our main concern is with separating truth and honesty from falsity and dishonesty in our classrooms and in our schools. What we do with the knowledge we gain from this critical separation is our ethical choice. Knowing the differences will be the first step.

Recognizing Truth and Falsity

Truth and falsity are awesome terms for what is so and what is not so. They may be interchanged with other concepts: education and miseducation, veracity and mendacity, information and misinformation, honesty and deception, as well as being correct and being mistaken. All have powers that stretch us beyond our reach.

At any specified moment, we know some things are true, some things are not true, and other things are undetermined. Ranked for our educational concerns, to know we do not possess the truth or falsity of something is good. To know we do not have the truth but we do know some of the false answers is better. To know what is true is best. Thus, "I know I do not know" is good; "I know what is false" is better; "I know what is true" is best. We move from what is less knowledgeable to what is more knowledgeable: from the indeterminate through the negative to the positive.

For example, we may know we lack information in degrees celcius about the boiling temperature of water, or we may know it does not boil at 20 degrees celcius nor at 50 degrees celcius. Or, we may know positively that water boils at 100 degrees celcius. The last condition exemplifies *positive* knowing or information. The second condition exemplifies *negative* knowing or information. The first condition exemplifies *undetermined* knowing or information. In everyday language, when we ask for "proof positive," we ask for positive information: what we know is the case rather than what we know is not the case.

To separate the true and honest from the false and deceptive, we may select falsity or select truth as our guide. Whether we prefer the positive orientation of searching for truth or the negative orientation of searching for falsehood, we have precious measures for our decisions. What is encouraged here, due to an educational bias toward positive information regardless of the intention of the source of a message, is to accept the responsibility of being accountable for the teachings we receive: that is, the positive information we inherit and assimilate. We must decide whether (or to what extent) the material taught us – the efforts of this text are of course included – is true positively. Positive information focuses us on the final possession – that is, what we positively have after we have considered misinterpretation, misunderstanding, misinformation, distortion, lies, omissions, misrepresentations, fabrications, concealments, imaginings, confusions, jokes, dishonesties, courtesies, amenities, self-deceptions, deceptions, illusions, and mistakes. Whether sources present us with falsehood deliberately or mistakenly, we inherit falsehood. The source – perhaps, an instructor - may have decent intentions in telling us to consume over a 100 grams of protein per day for our health; nonetheless, we must judge instruction. Teachers may honestly (although wrongly) instruct us that everyone is created equal in a physical sense. Hence, we obtain information; but, we must judge the correctness of this information. Although we pass a test, we may fail to acquire positive information. We are responsible, ultimately, for ourselves as far as our educations are concerned.

While we may know what is correct, we may also know what is incorrect. This is positive knowledge.[89] While we may not know what is correct, we may know what is incorrect. This is negative knowledge. With positive knowledge as the basis of our educational hunt for truth, we may tolerate those who with noble intentions mislead us. We may tolerate the pains and costs resulting from improper instruction emanating from those who honestly believe they held the correct answers to various questions but did not. We may overlook falsehood taught in honest ignorance of the facts, even though we may be intolerant of misinformation provided with malice. However, as far as positive information is concerned, whether we have been lied to or misguided, we function without a positive truth to guide us. We may be angry with those who lie and disappointed with those who misdirect, yet we are still ignorant. We are ignorant instead of enlightened. Pessimistically, we may have to count on ten percent of what we learn as constituting positive information. Operating on ten percent information efficiently can cost us dearly at the bank, at school, and in our daily relationships. We must filter the nonsense and falsehood from the truth. We must sift through the false professionals, false people, false organizations, and false information to acquire the truth – golden or otherwise. stories of Diogenes and Abraham in their searches for honest and true people repeat daily everywhere. Each of us must muffle the noise of ignorance and deceit and misrepresentation daily to locate positive knowledge.

We face an ongoing problem with establishing and maintaining knowledge: whether in the form of knowing we cannot recognize truth or falsity, of knowing we know what is wrong, or of knowing we know what is right. Our worldview is a mix of accuracy and inaccuracy. We should be continually updating and correcting misconceptions and falsehoods that erode even further if we do not correct them. We may, in our mix of beliefs and knowledge, have Mozambique confused with Mauritius, square root confused with exponents, Margaret Trudeau confused with Jackie Onassis, Sikhs confused with Muslims, and so on.

As we correct this misinformation, it may be replaced with other misinformation that we inherit daily: for example, that cactus plants grow all over the Jasper Park area of Alberta, that New Zealand hosted the 1988 Olympic Winter Games, that Alberta teachers will appreciate a 25% increase in salaries over the next two years, and so on. At any one time, we must face that we possess and teach faulty information. As ethical and intelligent teachers, we minimize the error by staying up-to-date with our field and correcting mistakes that creep in subtly. Whether we are misguided or not, we must operate in class on the basis of what we know at the time of the class. To establish what is true and what constitutes knowledge is beyond the humble powers of this discussion. A course in epistemology, logic, scientific methodology, and critical thinking is recommended to approach these lofty heights. Our aim here is to discuss honesty and deception with the focus on deception, while mentioning the ultimate concerns of truth and falsity.

While honesty refers here to telling the truth about what we believe to be so, deception refers to telling a lie about what we believe is so.[90] The options we have in this arena may include: (1) being honest while being true-to-fact, (2) being honest while being false-to-fact, (3) being deceptive while being true-to-fact (as in irony and fooling ourselves), and (4) being deceptive while being false-to-fact. Honesty does not guarantee being correct; dishonesty does not guarantee being wrong. Just as someone may honestly present us with obsolete information thinking the information is current, so someone may present us (accidentally perhaps) with valid information (thinking it is invalid and intending to deceive us). These four possibilities vary in amounts and frequency in our lives. A diagram will clarify the four:

	Honest	Deceptive
True-to-Fact	Honest I and True-to-fact	Deceptive III yet True-to-fact
False-to-Fact	Honest II yet False-to-fact	Deceptive IV and False-to-fact

With each of us, the four squares have different proportions. You may have a large Square I; I may have a large Square II; and so on:

You

Me

Given our educational interest in communication, we may also benefit from other categories: namely, what we know is so (true-to-fact) and what we know is not so (false-to-fact), regardless of honesty and deception. Tender loving honesty mixed with misinformation makes for an error that can be as difficult to correct as an error inherited with deception. A diagram will to explain what is chiefly relevant to our stockpile of positive information:

Knowing and Information

	True-to-Fact	False-to-Fact	Unknown
Know	I Positive Information	II Negative Information	III Undetermined Information
Do not know	IV No information (Ignorance)		

Positive information is more desirable than negative information, yet both are desirable modes of information. Ignorance is clearly undesirable. Honesty and deception considered and put aside, we ask: What do we know is true-to-fact? What do we know is false-to-fact? What do we know is undetermined? When we ask: What do we know is so? The answer constitutes positive information. When we ask: What do we know is not so? The answer constitutes negative information. When we ask: What do we know is unknown? The answer constitutes indeterminate information. We may know that putting an autistic student on a dunking stool will not improve or remedy the autism. However, we may not know what does. We lack positive knowledge. When a student passes out in a class due to walking pneumonia, a doctor knows penicillin (or a related drug) will likely remedy the pneumonia. Such information is positive. Negative and positive forms of knowledge both have utility. The biology teacher on a field trip instructs students what kind of berries must not be eaten (negative information) and what kind of berries may be eaten (positive information). When she encounters a berry she does not recognize, she faces knowing she cannot tell one way or the other.

Although our preferences may differ, with sound information as our educational goal the following objectives are suggested in this order of preference. Assuming we have knowledge of this information eventually, positive information we *know* is true-to-fact. Negative information we *know* is false-to-fact. Undetermined information we *know* indicates our ignorance of truth or falsity. Positive information may include honest and true information as well as deceptive but true. Negative information includes honest but false information as well as deceptive and false information. The perspective of positive knowledge allows us an overview of diverse types of information we might assimilate. Hence, we may gain positive knowledge from someone trying to deceive us.

The judgment on the ethicality of the deceiver who unintendedly gives us sound material should not be confused with the educational value of the truth presented. Poetic irony may suffice for deceivers with villainous intentions to get their proper due. Undetermined information tells us we fail to differentiate the true and honest from the false and deceptive or any combination of these. A diagram of the hierarchy follows:

Ranked Overview of Information

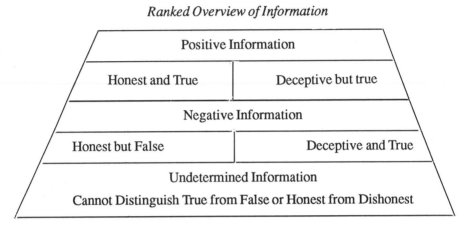

This model guides us toward a positive and negative educational base – that is, one that establishes what we know and do not know about content and the people who deliver it. In our context of educational communication, we rank the communication of positive information above negative information and negative information above undetermined information. Yet, we invite you to rank these as you like. Other perspectives may apply to schools as well. Choose, of course, as you see fit.

Honesty and Deception

If honesty is the best policy, then we should all adhere to truth and decency steadfastly in the face of danger. If honesty is the best policy, then by implication we would wish to implement the best policy. We would struggle to speak the truth and do what is right. Clearly, honesty may be the best policy – regardless of what we mean by best - under specifically defined circumstances. To say it is always the best policy has legitimate limitations. For example, we might consider it quite ethical to lie to a terminally ill student about a low grade or misdirect a violent student who asks us of the whereabout of another student desired as a victim.

Honesty and deception co-exist in any organization. "Boat rockers" and "whistle blowers" exist side-by-side with those committing or condoning deception or concealment. Sometimes, these opposing roles are exchanged. An educational organization is no exception. To shed light on crucial issues, its task is to keep the conversation going on communication ethics.[91] Since degrees of honesty and deception can be found in any classroom or school, when someone asserts there is no honesty or no deceit in a particular classroom or school, it would be proper to call an academic form of ghostbusters. – hallucination busters. Deception here refers to communicating what is intended to mislead others into believing what we do not believe.[92]

Even if teachers believe they should be totally honest regardless of painful consequences, as intelligent people, teachers must acknowledge the value of reaching a decision cognizant of the potential results rather than in ignorance of the possible results. In the Old Testament, Daniel was told he would be thrown to the lions if he prayed to anyone but Darius the King. Nonetheless, Daniel prayed to YHWH (Yahweh or Jehovah), his God, three times a day. Daniel was conscious of what would follow from his choice of action. Indeed, he was sentenced to the lions' den. His moral deed was enhanced through his knowledge of his future suffering. Had Daniel acted in ignorance of any consequential suffering, the nobility of his moral choice would suffer. Instead, many appreciate his dedication despite the punitive outcome he knew he had to face. To decide in the light of the outcomes of our decisions grants us an ethical standing we cannot have when we decide willfully to ignore the results of our choices. Truly, we may decide to act in a certain way without knowing what will follow and not being able to know what will follow. In such a case we know that we are gambling on consequences that may be abhorent. Once again, we dare to be decent.

In focusing on honesty and deception in school settings, we hope to call attention to the fact that schools constitute one more sector of employment that, despite efforts to the contrary, is not free of deception. In no way do these comments on the operation in education of honesty and deceit reflect circumstances that do *not* exist in the institutions of medicine, law, nursing, and social work. The functions of honesty and deception in corporations, business, marketing, sales, and journalism is not our concern and has been treated at length.[93] In short, honesty and deceit in varying proportions exist everywhere, including monasteries, seminaries, and retreats – the traditional moral pillars of society. For the cautiously minded, no insinuation is made here that honesty and deceit are distributed equally in all work settings. Some of us prefer to think there is more honesty than deceit in some fields than others and that some fields improve more than others. Clearly, the consequences of honesty and deceit vary tremendously: that is, either may produce far more distinguishable effects in one field than in another. For example, undercover police have to be (for the most part) deceptive in relation to their tasks in order to succeed, while teachers have to be (for the most part) honest in relation to their tasks in order to succeed. Honesty at an ill-timed moment may hurt undercover police just as deceit at an ill-timed moment may hurt teachers. in educational communication.

Burgoon, Buller, and Woodall summarize results of empirical research on deceit and honesty in human relations. Despite the humane presupposition in social communication that truthfulness is praiseworthy and deceit is reprehensible, lying remains a common communication strategy. Furthermore, deception is necessary for "controlling information, maximizing rewards, and minimizing costs." Deception is a "highly adaptive and competent communication strategy essential for survival." In short, we find in "everyday interactions that honesty is not always the best policy." As a method of controlling information, deception serves as a communication strategy (educational or otherwise). As a communication strategy, deception may be judged morally in terms of the "motives of the deceiver." Sometimes the selfish motives hurt others, and sometimes the unselfish motives benefit others.[94]

While lies are told, deceivers usually lie to avoid hurting another, to avoid damaging the relationship, and to protect the deceiver – especially from the opinion of the person deceived. We also deceive "in the interest of tact or politeness," of convincingness to others, and of gaining a "margin of success when in a low power position." Gender differences are present as well. Recent studies suggest men think deception is "more permissible than women do." Women lie, however, for reasons of affiliation – especially when trying to avoid relationships."[95] Both genders also deceive through misinformation and untruths: exaggeration, tall tales, evasion, lies, misrepresentation, and fantasy.[96] We generally will also use the following reasons to support their deception: (1) to avoid hurting others or ourselves, (2) to benefit others, (3) to promote fairplay, (4) to protect what is true with a lie, (5) to advance separate truth, and (6) to retain the confidence others have in our truthfulness.[97] The honest and responsible person may be hard to find.

Research focuses on a receiver's skill at recognizing deception rather than on a source's skill at deceiving. As assessed by Burgoo, Buller, and Woodall, sometimes we separate the deception from the truth uttered by a stranger. However, we are accurate "only slightly above chance." We would be "almost as accurate" if we "relied entirely on guessing." Should we become suspicious, then, to defend ourselves from deception, especially the malicious brand? Becoming suspicious or raising our suspiciousness need not increase our ability to separate honesty from deception. Rather, we should improve our notions about how to detect deception. With young children, the ability to detect deception progresses as they age and develop. In a range of ages from grades six to twelve, younger children decipher with less accuracy than older ones.[98] In short your young students will not detect deception as often as your mature students.

In covering this subject matter, the stress has been on the teacher distinguishing truth and honesty from falsehood and deceit coming from students and others in the context of the school. Since deception and falsehood have a place in human communication, when to extinguish them becomes our moral choice. After separating veracity from mendacity and openness from concealment, when would you condemn veracity and openness? When would you condemn mendacity and concealment? How close is this thought to your beliefs about the true and straightforward reigning over the untrue and devious? Would you judge this idea as viable, naive, or suicidal with respect to your career as a teacher? Would you explain your judgment?

Account-Dependent and Account-Free Communication in Education

Scientific explanations, moral inference, and legal justification would rank as sophisticated human endeavors. When we provide sound and legitimate accounts, we attain a professional standard few attain. To account for events or actions with intelligence constitutes a worthwhile challenge. However, for brief moments we may wish to dispense with accounting for actions and events. Whether we dispense with learned explanations and justifications or any other manifestation of giving accounts (such as, attribution, fabrication, inference, rationalization, and reasoning. We dispense with the pervasive communicative act of accounting – of answering to the word *why* (and sometimes the word *how*). In short, when we answer to *why* or *how,* we render an account.

An account includes any of the preceeding terms designating responses to *why* or *how* (attribution, fabrication, etc.). When we reply regularly to the explicit or implicit interrogative of *why* and *how,* we become *account-dependent.* When we do not reply to *why* or *how,* we become *account-free.* For the most part, we continually draw inferences, mythicize, offer paradigms, presuppose, offer reasons, rationalize, justify accusations, attribute causes, explain, infer motives, and the like in our attempts to account for *why* we do as we do or something acts as it does as well as *how* someone or something acts as it does. We reason on grounds ranging from the sublime to the ridiculous, the wise to the foolish, and the sane to the insane. We may explain away our kindness or our cruelty, our attractiveness or unattractiveness, and our wealth or poverty. We justify for better or for worse, yet we justify. Our world requires it and we provide it – perhaps, volunteer it. We explain and rationalize "by means of purely intellectual processes, but we understand by means of the cooperation of all the powers of the mind in comprehension."[99] Communication generally, social intercourse, and educational discourse might suffer impoverishment without it. So, we account or become "no-accounts."

In the style of the general semantics notion of E-Prime (E') language (or English devoid of any form of "to be")[100] and the Pollyanna Hypothesis (that we use positively evaluative (E+) words more often in more places and more easily than negatively evaluative (E-) words),[101] we suggest another notation to distinguish communicative discourse that accounts for as much as possible from communicative discourse that accounts for as little as possible. Just as we may communicate (or teach) in E' with E+ words, so we may communicate (or teach) in an account-dependent manner (symbolized as A) or in an account-free manner (symbolized as -A). The account-dependent and account-free notions emerge in part from attribution theory.[102] Account-free communication is phenomenological in the practical sense defined by Walsh and Vaughan – namely, descriptive of "phenomena without interpretation, explanation, and evaluation."[103] We attribute (or account for) causes and motives to behavior frequently. Until, however, we move from amateur psychologists to professionals or from amateur reasoners to logicians, we risk more than psychologists and logicians do as far as faulty attribution and inference is concerned. Our accounts may resemble stories or myths more than value inferences. By imposing an account-free norm of communication on ourselves periodically, we discover what communication without rationalization might be. The rhetorical scholar Marie Nichols and the semanticist Richard Dettering would encourage, in Wittgenstein fashion, students to remain silent and say nothing about causes or motives when rationalizing became suspect. Both encouraged their students to be occasionally account-free. When in doubt, we should not give worthless accounts unless we want communicative filler.

Thus, we render accounts for legal, ethical, political, scientific, commercial, and even comical purposes. In order to produce desired outcomes and needed results, we offer accounts of phenomena, ourselves, and others with or without wisdom. Account-free discourse purges our communication of rationalization. Accounting for events and actions is simply prohibited. Whether the account is sober and intelligent, legal or scientific, fabricated or bizarre, the account is out of place in account-free discourse.

To speak account-free presents us with a challenge. We may describe and predict phenomena. We may not explain them whether or not the grounds are considered germane and valid in our realm of interest – for instance, science, art, religion, philosophy, commerce, law, or even the occult. In Pap's definitions of *explicandum* and *explanans,* while the *explicandum* constitutes a "fact to be explained," the *explanans* constitutes the "assumptions in terms of which a fact is explained."[104] In Canadian society, we may explain facts through science and its assumptions. However, we might also explain facts through religion and its assumptions. The school issue pertaining to instruction on creation versus evolution exemplifies two diverse explanations of the facts. In account-dependent discourse, we would remain in the universe of scientific discourse for the explanation of evolution and within the universe of religious discourse for the explanation of creation. After several courses in scientific method, legal method, philosophical method, and so on, we might have an improved chance to assert with learned confidence that an explanation is sound with respect to the assumptions being made in various disciplines. If a hierarchical bias exists in Canadian society, it would likely be towards science. For our purposes, science need not (nor should not) be seen as the final arbiter in our explanations since metaphysical explanations are other than and outside the reach of science.

In much of our daily educational discourse, we may amuse (yet fail to enlighten) ourselves on true and valid explanations of facts. Account-free discourse may relieve us of nonsense from others as well as ourselves. When we impose the restrictions of being account-free on our communication, we avoid uttering and attending to explanations – whether they are true or false, enlightening or confusing, lucid or garbled. We block and inhibit our tendencies and the tendencies of others to provide accounts. As Jack Webb of the old TV series *Dragnet* was famous for requesting, "the facts, please, just the facts": facts here referring to what presents itself to us – to our senses - without an account of why.

Account-free teachers would ask students for lucid and detailed descriptions of the facts – that which was observed or witnessed. The unseen and unseeable, the laws of nature, the ways of God, the operation of spirits, the laws of society, kismit, or any other intangibles will not be permitted in the account from the students – only the facts may count. Teachers cannot ask *why* about the facts; they can only ask *what*.[105] When a student fight occurs in a hall, teachers communicating account-free would ask the students what happened. As the students explained why it happened, the teachers would return to what was observed.

A description based on account-free communication might sound like this: the girl with the short hair collided in front of the water fountain with the girl with the long hair. The short-haired girl then slapped with an open hand the upper back of the long-haired girl. The long-haired girl then punched with a tightened fist the short-haired girl in the solar plexus region. The principal then placed himself between the two girls. The slapping and punching stopped as soon as the principal stood between them.

While account-dependent communication might satisfy our dramatic bloodlust, it may be little more than a fictional or imaginary fabrication. Account-dependent communication might sound like this: That long-haired (Sally) troublemaker got what she deserved today. She has a grudge against the short-haired girl (Molly) because Molly stole her boyfriend. Besides, Sally has a chip on her shoulder anyway because her parents are mean to her, and she has a temper that flares up like crazy. She is a hot-tempered red-head. Molly has been patient with her for months now. She knows she can whip her because she takes tae-kwan-do. She has avoided a fight with Sally because her parents would ground her, and her tae-kwan-do instructor would suspend her from practice. Fate was in charge, though, at the water fountain. They were destined to collide. In fact, I think they crashed into each other accidentally on purpose. The principal hates Sally and likes Molly. So when he saw Molly get hit, he just wanted to punch Sally out himself, but did not because he knows Sally's father is a lawyer and will sue him for everything he is worth. And, he does not want to lose his big house and his new Volvo. Besides, when he broke them up, he threw Sally against the lockers to make Molly look good and to punish Sally for picking the fight with her.

How exciting the rationalized event is compared to the described event! Yet, with the joys of fabrication and fiction aside, what in fact has been accomplished?

If we turn to other accounts that occur in Canadian society, we encounter alternatives to this school account. If we observe that a teenage couple engages for five minutes daily in hugging and kissing for six months or more, we might account for this sustained affection on several grounds. Science might explain their conduct as a function of high homophily with low heterophily linked with a history of random intermitant reinforcement. The Ancient Greeks might have explained them as being shot through with Cupid's arrow – a mere metaphor in our time. Astrology might explain them as a Scorpio and a Virgo: that is, a Water sign and an Earth sign – "Water seeks a home which it finds within the Earth." A humorous version of this astrological explanation is a comical line by Rodney Dangerfield: "My former wife is an Earth sign and I am a Water sign – together we made mud!" As one astrological guide says: "These two elements were designed each to need the other. But too much water can turn Earth into mud or quicksand."[106] Rodney eventually faced the quicksand. The affectionate couple may as well some day. A final explanation of this affectionate couple comes from the occult explanation of reincarnation. Clearly, the verification of reincarnation lies beyond the powers of contemporary science. An occult explanation of our affectionate couple might be that their relationship is not the "result of chance." Their relationship is "an episode in a serial story begun long before." In some way, this couple has been "related to each other in other lives." In one life, the couple met in Persia and in another life in Egypt. These former relationships account for "their strong mutual attraction."[107]

Again, conversion may become quite thrilling when the account-dependent mode of educational communication is utilized. How comparatively worldless the conversation would have been had the account-free mode of educational communication been practiced! What have we as teachers gained with the one mode and lost with the other? A cynic might order: "Don't poison my mind with your accounts. Leave me to witness life." What do you think? Which mode of accounting do you prefer? And, ironically, *why*?

Attribution Theory

Attribution theory itself deserves special attention. In conversation, we may hear causes attributed to anything from S-R (stimulus-response) grounds to metaphysical grounds. When we ask why or how, we start attributing one or more causes to some behavior, attitude, or belief. Whether rational or foolish, the attributor offers reasons. The scientist on matters of science, and the judge on matters of law would likely offer reasons that are predominantly valid although bias would likely seep even into explanations from these learned minds: contraries would comingle. Zen practitioners and gestalt therapists discourage us from asking why. This assists us in minimizing our attributional accounts. Observing may increase and rationalizing may decrease. Since much communication and rhetoric function through rationalization rather than ratiocination, attribution plays an important social role even if it serves to contaminate our soundwaves with gibberish. Without attribution (since conversation without attribution would be cut drastically), we restrict ourselves to the logical role of the fictional Mr. Spock of Star Trek where we either know, as Wittgenstein admonishes, or we remain silent. Our social life would be much quieter – perhaps, for the better. However, this world is not likely to become as rational as Mr. Spock's this week. So, we must deal with it in its current form of saturated accounts: rationalization, attribution, and inferences. Like it or not, as teachers we should be able to distinguish foolish (or at least socially unacceptable) accounts (reasons, attributions) from wise (or at least socially acceptable) accounts (reasons, attributes).

To illustrate the variety of human attribution, several perspectives will be taken on explaining a result or condition. Burke discusses the downward way of explanation – for example, science's reductionist accounts of phenomena to their simplest material level – and the upward way of explanation – for example, religion's elevating accounts of phenomena to their loftiest (or most celestial) intangible level.[108]

If we attribute causes to a successful effort at team teaching, we will assign divergent causes and reasons to the success of the team teaching as we assume diverse perspectives from science, religion, and astrology. Socrates was known for his dialectic in which he chose every possible perspective from which to examine something as his method of establishing truth.[109] Although less skilled and ambitious than Socrates in this case, the perspective of science and astrology will be used as grounds for attribution. No effort will be made to reflect the specialist – namely, the scientist or the astrologer. The unprofessional who dabbles in science or in astrology will serve as our ground for attribution. Hence, for better or for worse, the viewpoints of the scientific and the astrological will be reflected.

We ask: Why was that team teaching effort at Northwest High School, then, so successful? The scientific viewpoint might attribute the success of the team teaching to group synergy, the proper balancing of a member with skills in accomplishing tasks with a member skilled in human relations, and supportive administrative practices. The astrological viewpoint might attribute the success of the team teaching to one member of the team being born in the year of the Dragon and the other in the year of the Monkey. The sincerity and sensitivity of the Dragon member compliments the business skills of the Monkey member. Furthermore, none of their students were born in the year of the Dog or the Tiger. Dog and Tiger children would not harmonize with the Dragon teacher or Monkey teacher.[110] These diverse and asymetrical, if not contrary, attributions pertaining to the success of the team teachers inspire little confidence that corroborative evidence has been presented. If both are faulty accounts, which faulty account would you prefer? Which shows your bias?

In our educational context of communication, "attribution theory deals with the ways people infer the causes of behavior."[111] It is concerned with "how an observer assigns causation to the actions of another"[112] and attempts to "define more exactly [the] process by which people make judgments about other people's behavior."[113] As classroom teachers, we have to explain course content as well as conduct; attribution theory will at least improve our understanding of how we explain conduct.

Attribution theory suggests how we come to understand our behavior and that of others. While scientific psychology tries to "ascertain the actual causes of behavior," attribution theory or "naive psychology centres on [our] perceived cause of behavior in ongoing interaction."[114] According to the attribution theorists, we are amateur psychologists when we infer the mainsprings of human action.[115] Attribution theory holds that: (1) we try to "determine the causes of behavior" – that is, answer the question, why are you doing that? (2) we "assign causes systematically," and (3) the cause we explain or the "attributed cause has an impact on [our] own feelings and behavior."[116]

The attribution theories of Heider and Kelley lead eventually to distinguishing situational from dispositional attributions. Situational attributions rationalize our actions through external causes outside our power. Dispositional attributions rationalize our actions through internal reasons or predispositions to respond, such as, beliefs, attitudes, or motives.[117]

In the classroom, we serve as amateur psychologists. We will tend to think the cause of proper conduct or of misconduct stems from the situation in which we act or from dispositions within us. The preference we have for attributing causation to one or the other constitutes our attributional style. Because we are not being objective or scientific in our analysis, we are subject to misinterpretation rather than accurate perception and interpretation of the causes.[118] However, while everyone is subject to distort the causes of behavior, as amateur psychologists, we are more likely to than scientific psychologists. In short, our "own self-interest often guides what may appear on the surface as 'objective' attribution." For instance, a persistent error in attribution involves attributing the cause of conduct too often to human disposition rather than to the situation in which people operate. We attribute, furthermore, the cause of other peoples' conduct too often to disposition and the cause of our own conduct too often to situation. This means we judge others by their dispositions and ourselves by circumstances.[119] Their locus of control is internal while ours is external.[120] Others sin. We are forced by circumstances into error: a comfortable account (or story) for us.

When accounting for our own actions, the self-serving bias takes hold. This bias results in us taking credit for the positive consequences flowing from our actions but denying any responsibility for the negative consequences flowing from our actions. Subsequently, in accounting for actions of ours that have had costly outcomes, we attribute their cause to environmental conditions. In accounting for actions of ours that have had profitable outcomes, we attribute their cause to internal dispositions. Generally, we attribute our negative behavior to circumstances beyond our control that victimize us and our positive behaviors to our fine moral character.[121]

In a school, we may attribute malice to others for deeds we would forgive ourselves for due to circumstances that imposed themselves on us. We may attribute noble effort and ethical intelligence to our successful handling of a classroom problem while believing another teacher has succeeded through friends in the administration and parents at the Board of Education. Simons uses Bandura to support a position that offers a direction to pursue (if not a solution to) the problem of attribution: we are neither "driven by inner forces nor buffeted helplessly by environmental influences." Since we "can forsee the probable consequences of different actions and alter our behavior accordingly," we "can reward ourselves or withhold rewards from ourselves, depending upon whether we have reached our goals."[122]

To pronounce on the causes of a student's behavior on a report card epitomizes such blind and biased attribution. For example, on a report card, a student's evaluation may be sufficient with a description or evaluation alone. However, the common practice of attribution may show its confused head through the comments of this teacher who was also an amateur (that is, naive) psychologist: "Samantha has difficulty sharing her ideas in social studies class due to her feelings of inadequacy and low self-esteem. These uneasy feelings seem to be tied to the culture shock she is experiencing."

Both classical and Skinnerian (that is, S-R) conditioning theories "make as few inferences as possible about what goes on inside" us when we encounter a stimulus.[123] While S-R theories of behavior may be criticized as simplistic and unsatisfactory accounts of the whole person, to lean cautiously toward the descriptive base of scientific S-R psychologists might benefit us as teachers. Instead of pronouncing on matters we know not, such as the internal mediating states of motivation within us and others, we will pronounce firmly on what we have witnessed through careful observation – not on what we have inferred naively from our sweepingly biased scanning of our students and colleagues. We should challenge ourselves to be periodically account-free. Our culture urges us to be account-dependent. Do you deserve a break today from being account-dependent? What might happen if you try?

Notes

[1]Orrin E. Klapp, "Meaning Lag in the Information Society," *Journal of $unication, 32*:2 (Spring 1982), 56-60. See also, Marilyn Ferguson, *The Aquarian Conspiracy: Personal and Social Transformations in the 1980s* (Los Angeles: J. P. Tarcher, 1980), especially Chapter 6 on "Liberating Knowledge," 145-187.

[2]Interview with Dr. Peter Craigie on "Irreconcilable Differences in Religion," Calgary, Alberta, 15 January 1981. See also, Richard Fiordo, "The Keegstra Case: The Anti-Semitic Argument in Modern Day Alberta Schools," in Frans H. van Eemeren, Rob Grootendorst, J. Anthony Blair, and Charles A Willard, eds., *Argumentation: Analysis and Practices, Pragmatics and Discourse Analysis* (Dordrecht-Holland: Foris, 1987), 278- 288.

[3]William S. Sahakian, *Systems of Ethics and Value Theory* (New York: Philosophical Library, 1963), 2-3; P. H. Nowell-Smith, *Ethics* (Baltimore: Penguin Books, 1969), 11-35; *The Journal of Educational Thought: Moral Education Special Issue, 15*:1 (April 1981); G. Debrock, "Ethics, Order, and Grace," *Man and World: An International Philosophical Review, 18*:3 (1985), 295-315; and A. D. Hunt and R. B. Crotty, *Ethics of World Religions* (Minneapolis: Greenhaven Press, 1978).

[4]G. Debrock, "Ethics, Order, and Grace," *Man and His World: An International* Philosophical Review, *18*:3 (1985), 295.

[5]Richard L. Johannesen, *Ethics in Human Communication*, 2nd ed. (Prospect Heights: Waveland Press, 1983), 143.

[6]William S. Howell, *The Empathic Communicator* (Belmont: Wadsworth, 1982), 187-188.

[7]Johannesen, 144.

[8]Howell, 197.

[9]Johannesen, 144.

[10]John L. Hulteng, *The Messenger's Motives: Ethical Problems of the News Media* (Englewood Cliffs: Prentice-Hall, 1976), 225-233.

[11]Johannesen, 145.

[12]Ibid.

[13]Richard E. Crable, "Ethical Codes, Accountability, and Argumentation," *Quarterly Journal of Speech, 64*:1 (February 1978), 23-32.

[14]Johannesen, 146.

[15]*The Alberta Teachers' Association Members' Handbook* (Edmonton: The Alberta Teachers' Association, 1988).

[16]A pilot study conducted from 1988 to 1989 by this author among teachers and graduate students with teaching experience.

[17]Aristotle, *Nicomachean Ethics*, translated by W. D. Ross (Oxford: University Press, 1915), 1109a 20-21 and 1108b 19-20.

[18]Sahakian, *Ethics and Value Theory*, 13. William Sahakian was used as the interpretive philosopher. His explanations were clear and appropriate for general educational purposes. His accounts of selected philosophers were applicable, relevant, and useful to teachers and future teachers as well as counselors and administrators in the field of education. I hope the readers find these selections beneficial to their ethical inquiries in educational communication. My brief handling of the selected philosophers can do little more than introduce students to the complex and challenging world of communication ethics.

[19]Ibid., 138-139.

[20]Ibid., 140-141.

[21]Thomas Gould, ed., "Introduction" in *The Moral Discourses of Epictetus* (New York: Washington Square Press, 1964), XVI-XVII.

[22]Sahakian, 147 and 154-155.

[23]Ibid., 220-221. See also, F. C. Copleston, *Aquinas* (Baltimore: Penguin Books, 1967), 200-201.

[24]St. Thomas Aquinas, *The Summa contra Gentiles*, in the *Basic Writings of Saint Thomas Aquinas*, translated by Laurence Shapcote, edited by Anton C. Pegis (New York: Random House, 1945), Bk. III: Ch. 3, 10, and 25 ; Margaret Gorman, *General Semantics and Contemporary Thomism* (Lincoln: University of Nebraska Press, 1962), 103-105; and Copleston, *Aquinas*, 210-211, 217-218, and 228-229.

[25]Sahakian, 231-232.

[26]Ibid., 234. See also, Copleston, 206-208.

[27]bid., 44.

[28]Ibid., 88-90.

[29]James Martineau, 3rd ed. *Types of Ethical Theory* (Oxford: Clarendon Press, 1898), 72 and 26.

[30]Ibid., 70, 49, and 266.

[31]Ibid., 270-276.

³²Ibid., 266.

³³George E. Moore, *Ethics* (London: Oxford University Press, 1912), 106-107.

³⁴Sahakian, 342-343.

³⁵Moore, 121.

³⁶Sahakian, 343.

³⁷Moore, 112.

³⁸Sahakian, 343.

³⁹Moore, 140.

⁴⁰Ibid., 121.

⁴¹Sahakian, 350.

⁴²Josiah Royce, *The Philosophy of Loyalty* (New York: Macmillan, 1908), 16.

⁴³Sahakian, 352-354.

⁴⁴Ibid., 357-358.

⁴⁵Royce, 119.

⁴⁶Sahakian, 355 and 359.

⁴⁷Royce, 195-196. See also, George H. Mead, "The Philosophies of Royce, James, and Dewey, in Their American Settings," *International Journal of Ethics*, 40 (1930), 211-231.

⁴⁸Calvin S. Hall and Gardner Lindzey, *Theories of Personality*, 2d ed. (Toronto: John Wiley and Sons, 1970), 135.

⁴⁹Karen Horney, *Our Inner Conflicts* (New York: W. W. Norton, 1945), 41. See also, Karen Horney, "The Flight from Womanhood," in Jean Baker Miller, ed., *Psychoanalysis and Women* (Baltimore: Penguin Books, 1973), 5-20.

⁵⁰Hall and Lindzey, 135 and 137.

⁵¹Ibid.

⁵²Karen Horney, *Self-Analysis* (New York: W. W. Norton, 1942), 54-63. See also, William S. Sahakian, ed., *Psychology of Personality: Readings in Theory* (Chicago: Rand McNally, 1965), 134-149.

⁵³John Dewey, *Reconstruction in Philosophy* (New York: Henry Holt, 1920), Ch. 7. See also, John Dewey, *The Quest for Certainty* (New York: G. P. Putnam's Sons, 1957), 223-228.

⁵⁴Sahakian, *Ethics and Value Theory*, 319. See also, Jonas F. Soltis, "Dewey and Thorndike: The Persistence of Paradigms in Educational Scholarship," *Canadian Journal of Education*, 13:1 (Winter 1988), 39-51.

⁵⁵Dewey, Ch. 7.

⁵⁶Sahakian, 319-320.

⁵⁷Dewey, Ch. 7. See also, Dewey, *The Quest*, 254-286.

⁵⁸Sahakian, *Ethics and Value Theory*, 320-322 and 332. See also, Abraham Kaplan, *The New World of Philosophy* (New York: Vintage Books, 1963), 44-45.

⁵⁹Sahakian, 322-323.

⁶⁰Dewey, Ch. 7. See also, G. J. Emerson and Maryann Ayim, "Dewey and Peirce on Curriculum and the Three R's," *The Journal of Educational Thought*, 14:1 (April 1980), 24-25.

⁶¹John Dewey and James H. Tufts, *Ethics* (New York: Henry Holt, 1908), 209.

⁶²John Dewey, *Human Nature and Conduct* (New York: Henry Holt, 1922), 316.

[63]Sahakian, 337.

[64]Charles Morris, *The Pragmatic Movement in American Philosophy* (New York: George Braziller, 1970), 157-167. See also, Emerson and Ayim, "Dewey and Peirce," 28-31, for additional critical commentary on Dewey. See especially, John Dewey, *Freedom and Culture* (New York: G. P. Putnam's Sons, 1939), 103-130.

[65]Sahakian, 329-331 and 336.

[66]John Dewey, "Theory of Valuation," *International Encyclopedia of Unified Science*, Vol. II, No. 4 (Chicago: University of Chicago Press, 1939), 24-25.

[67]Sahakian, 329. See also, M. R. Konvitz and Gail Kennedy, eds., *The American Pragmatists: Selected Writings* (New York: World, 1965), 174.

[68]Morris, 162. See also, Dewey, *Freedom and Culture*, 124-126 and 155-176.

[69]Dewey, Reconstruction, Ch.7. See also, Kaplan's *Philosophy*, 19, for an account of pragmatism's contextualism.

[70]Sahakian, 324. See Kaplan, 40 and 41, for an explanation of pragmatism's objective relativism and liberalism.

[71]Kaplan, *Philosophy*, 99-100.

[72]Ibid., 117. See also, William Barrett, *Irrational Man: A Study in Existential Philosophy* (New York: Doubleday, 1962), 246-247. For additional commentary, see: Nicola Abbagnano, *Critical Existentialism* (New York: Doubleday, 1969), 224.

[73]Simone de Beauvoir, *The Ethics of Ambiguity* (New York: Citadel Press, 1967), 142-145.

[74]Ibid., 145-149.

[75]Ibid., 96.

[76]Ibid., 133-136.

[77]Ibid., 155.

[78]Ibid., 9 and 10.

[79]Ibid., 76-78. See also, Barrett, *Irrational Man*, 247 and 263.

[80]Richard A. Fiordo, *Charles Morris and the Criticism of Discourse* (Bloomington: Indiana University Press and Lisse: Peter de Ridder Press, 1977), 153-155.

[81]Charles Morris, *Paths of Life: Preface to a World Religion* (Chicago: University of Chicago Press, 1970), 183-184 and 209.

[82]Ibid., 184 and 210.

[83]Charles Morris, *Varieties of Human Value* (Chicago: University of Chicago Press, 1932), 1-2.

[84]Ibid., 15-18. For a reproduction, see Fiordo's *Charles Morris*, 185-187.

[85]Morris, *Paths of Life*, 170-171. See also, Fiordo's *Charles Morris*, 154-156.

[86]Morris, *Paths of Life*, 172 and 210-213.

[87]Ibid., 163-164.

[88]Robert E. Ornstein, *The Psychology of Consciousness* (San Francisco: W. H. Freeman, 1972), 159-160.

[89]Lilly-Marlene Russow and M. Curd, *Principles of Reasoning* (New York: St. Martin's Press, 1989). See especially the sections on "Truth, Relativism, and Skepticism" on pages 34-37 and on "Causal Reasoning on pages 270-298. The present discussion on what constitutes positive information derives in part from these sections. Thanks must also be expressed to Stephen Toulmin, Richard Rieke, and Allan Janik's

chapter on "Grounds" in *An Introduction to Reasoning*, 2d ed. (New York: Macmillan, 1984), 37-44.

[90]Paul Watzlawick, *How Real Is Real? Confusion, Disinformation*, Communication (New York: Vintage Books, 1977). See especially the chapter on "The Benefits of Confusion" on pages 27-42 and the chapter on "Deception in Intelligence Work" on pages 118-139. For another view, see R. D. Laing, *Self and Others*, rev. ed. (London: Tavistock, 1961), p. 110: "In our daily discourse, we employ, among others, two notions of 'truth.' One is the 'truth value of a proposition,' the relation of words to things. If A says 'p is the case,' what is usually termed the 'truth value' of the proposition 'p is the case' has nothing to do with A's relationship to this proposition. However, in daily discourse it is frequently more important for us to gauge A's relation to the proposition: whether A is telling the truth, whether he is lying, or whether he is deceiving himself, and so on."

[91]M. David Ermann and R. L. Lundman, *Corporate Deviance* (Toronto: Holt, Rinehart and Winston, 1982), especially pages 37-101. See also, R. Arnett, "Keep the Conversation Going," *Ethica*, 5:1 (September 1989), 1-2.

[92]Richard L. Johannesen, *Ethics in Human Communication*, 2d ed. (Prospect Heights: Waveland, 1983), 104. See also, A. Isenberg, *Aesthetics and the Theory* of Criticism (Chicago: University of Chicago Press, 1988), especially pages 245-264 on "Deontology and the Ethics of Lying."

[93]For example, see: Clifford G. Christians, Kim B. Rotzoll, and Mark Fackler, *Media Ethics: Cases and Moral Reasoning* (New York: Longman, 1983); Ermann and Lundman, *Corporate Deviance*.

[94]Judee K. Burgoon, David B. Buller, and W. Gill Woodall, *Nonverbal Communication*: The Unspoken Dialogue (New York: Harper and Row, 1989), 263.

[95]Ibid., 266.

[96]William W. Wilmot, *Dyadic Communication*, 3rd ed. (New York: Random House, 1987), 239.

[97]Sissela Bok, *Lying: Moral Choice in Public and Private Life* (New York: Vintage Books, 1979), Chapters 2 and 6. See also, Leo F. Buscaglia, *Loving Each Other: The Challenge of Human Relationships* (New York: Fawcett Columbine, 1984), especially Chapter 2 entitled "Loving Each Other Through Communication," 75-87.

[98]Burgoon, Buller, and Woodall, especially 275, 280, and 287. Dilthey quoted in, R. D. Laing, *The Divided Self* (Baltimore: Penguin, 1970), 32.

[99]Stephen W. Littlejohn, *Theories of Human Communication*, 2d ed. (Belmont: Wadsworth, 1983), 185.

[100]D. David Bourland, "A Linguistic Note: Writing in E-Prime," *General* Semantics Bulletin, 32 & 33 (1965-66), 113. See also, J. Samuel Bois, *The Art* of Awareness, 3rd ed. (Dubuque: Wm. C. Brown, 1978), 359-360.

[101]Jerry Boucher and Charles E. Osgood, "The Pollyanna Hypothesis," Journal of Verbal Learning and Verbal Behavior, 8 (1969), 1-8.

[102]See Edward E. Jones et al. *Attribution: Perceiving the Causes of Behavior* (Morristown: General Learning Press, 1972).

[103]Roger N. Walsh and Francis Vaughan, eds., *Beyond Ego: Transpersonal* Dimensions in Psychology (Los Angeles: J. P. Tarcher, 1980), 263.

[104]Arthur Pap, *An Introduction to the Philosophy of Science* (New York: Free Press of Glencoe, 1962), 181 and 423.

[105]In its extreme manifestation, account-free communication would resemble the Zen masters' choice to "act rather than explain, to demonstrate rather than expound": Garma C. C. Chang, *The Practice of Zen* (New York: Perennial Library, 1970), 171. Furthermore, one of Zen's tasks is to "shift one's attention from the abstract to the concrete": Alan W. Watts, *The Way of Zen* (Toronto: Vintage Books, 1957), 126-127. Also, Western philosophical explanations do "not greatly intertest the Zennist" since "most of the questions asked by Western thinkers are either frivolous or, worse, impertinent": Lucien Stryk and Takashi Ikemoto, eds., *Zen: Poems, Prayers, Sermons, Anecdotes, Interviews*(New York: Anchor Books, 1965), iii. Finally, Zen has the "tendency to resort to concrete objects and happenings": D. T. Suzuki, "An Interpretation of Zen Experience," in Charles A. Moore, ed., *The Japanese Mind: Essentials of Japanese Philosophy and Culture* (Honolulu: University of Hawaii Press, 1971), 133.

[106]Linda Goodman, *Love Signs: A New Approach to the Human Heart* (New York: Harper & Row, 1978), 1151 and 1153.

[107]Gina Cerminara, *Many Mansions* (New York: Signet Books, 1967), 123-128.

[108]Kenneth Burke, *The Philosophy of Literary Form: Studies in Symbolic Action*, rev. ed. (New York: Vintage Books, 1957), 17-18 and 107-112.

[109]William S. Sahakian, *Systems of Ethics and Value Theory* (New York: Philosophical Library, 1963), 159.

[110]From a bulletin available through a lecture on the Chinese zodiac, Calgary, June, 1989.

[111]Littlejohn, 185.

[112]Herbert W. Simons, *Persuasion: Understanding, Practice, and Analysis*, 2d ed. (New York: Random House, 1986), 52-53.

[113]C. G. Morris, *Psychology: An Introduction* (Englewood Cliffs: Prentice-Hall, 1979), 561.

[114]Littlejohn, 185-186.

[115]Simons, 53.

[116]Littlejohn, 185.

[117]Stephen W. Littlejohn and D. M. Jabusch, *Persuasive Transactions* (Glenview: Scott, Foresman, 1987), 112 and 94.

[118]Littlejohn, 186.

[119]Littlejohn and Jabusch, 66.

[120]Bonnie R. Strickland, "Internal-External Control Expectancies: From Contingency to Creativity," *American Psychologist, 44*:1 (January 1989), 1-12.

[121]Joseph A. DeVito, *Human Communication: The Basic Course*, 4th ed. (New York: Harper & Row, 1988), 57-58. See Strickland's "Internal-External" on pages 1 and 12 for a description of explanatory styles. See also, C. Peterson and L. C. Barrett, "Explanatory Style and Academic Performance Among University Freshman," *Journal of Personality and Social Psychology*, 53 (1987), 603-607.

[122]Simons, 52.

[123]Ibid., 51.

11

Evidence and Advocacy for Educators

Kathleen Mahoney

Introduction

A convincing argument (whether it be in social conversation, school debate, or before the Courts) usually requires more than the speaker's opinion in order to persuade a listener or judge. The response to arguments based solely on opinion usually is, "where is your evidence?" Without supporting evidence, a case or a claim is nothing more than an assertion which cannot satisfy a burden of proof in either debating or legal contexts of argumentation.

In this chapter, evidence and its interrelationship with education and communication, are discussed. Techniques to evaluate and classify evidence are provided. The two most important evidentiary considerations, relevance and admissibility, are identified and explained by reference to legal principles and rules. Related to these considerations are the sources of evidence, counter balancing factors to admissibility, the probative force evidence may have and the burden of proof and presumptions applicable to argumentation. These elements are discussed generally and then applied by using a hypothetical example of sexual assault by a school principal of a student, where both civil and criminal actions are taken.

Relevancy

Debate, whether it is legal or extra-legal shares many common traits. Disputed issues are always involved and advocates are required to develop arguments in favor of one position while attacking the other. By this process of adversarial comparison each side tries to show its position is superior to the other. At the end of the process, an objective third party decides the winner and loser.

The main differences between the two forms of debate are their rules and procedures. Obviously legal cases have more at stake than debating competitions and as a result, the procedural and substantive rules, especially those pertaining to evidence, are far more complex and rigorous in their application than the rules of debate or argumentation in general. But as debate rules are modelled on legal evidentiary rules, an understanding of basic legal elements of the law of evidence are nevertheless essential for those interested in debating skills or in argumentation generally.

One of the most fundamental principles of the law of evidence is that "proof must be relevant to a disputed issue."[1] This proposition requires an understanding of the concept "relevance" as well as what a "disputed issue" means. Relevancy includes the relationship between the propositions for which the evidence is offered and the issues in the case.[2] In other words, if evidence is adduced which goes toward proving a proposition which is not an issue or related to the matter in issue, then it can be said to be irrelevant. For example, if a person is charged with murder as a result of being found holding a smoking gun standing over the corpse of the victim of a gunshot wound, evidence of his driving record, if an attempt was made to enter it into the record, would be found irrelevant. This is because the accused is not before the Court on a driving charge nor does a motor vehicle enter into the facts of the case. On the other hand, results of a paraffin test performed on the accused showing he had fired a gun would be relevant because the evidence is directly related to an issue before the Court and within the range of allowable controversy in the lawsuit.

The relevance test is also applicable to smaller propositions within the larger framework of the controversy. In our example of the murder charge, if certain witnesses had heard the accused threaten the victim, such testimony would be relevant in order to establish the required mental element for the crime.

The rule then is, evidence is relevant if it tends to prove the existence versus the non-existence of a fact in issue; evidence is irrelevant if it does not tend to prove the existence or non-existence of the alleged fact to which it is directed or if the existence of that fact is not provable in the case.[3]

The scope of the relevance rule in debate is limited to the resolution put before the debaters. In civil law, the scope of the rule would be defined by the record put before the judge. The record generally includes the plaintiff's statement of claim, the defendant's statement of defence and the plaintiff's reply. These documents set out a statement of facts upon which the parties will rely in their argument. Evidence at the trial must relate only to the facts alleged in the record.

In criminal matters, the rule applies to the information or indictment the Crown has placed before the Judge.[4] The indictment documents the circumstances of the alleged offence, and is normally a short concise statement such as "John James Doe, on or about the 9th day of June, 1989, at the Township of Tinkersmith in the County of Athabasca, did unlawfully murder Julie Mayscroft contrary to the Criminal Code of Canada."

Unlike civil proceedings, the information or indictment in a criminal proceeding defines the factual issues in a much broader way, giving the Crown and the defence more latitude to enter evidence.[5] Nevertheless, in all legal proceedings and in debate the scope of admissible evidence is determined by the description of the "disputed issue" in the pleadings or the resolution as accepted by the parties.

Admissibility

In the search for truth, it is a fundamental principle that logically relevant evidence should be received. However, there is another precept which says that a rational system of evidence has many exceptions. Consequently, tests of admissibility other than relevancy and logical connection exist and must be considered.[6]

One of the most common exceptions to the relevancy test is the hearsay rule. Certain evidence may be clearly relevant to an issue yet be ruled inadmissible because it is "hearsay."[7] For example, using the hypothetical murder described above, if the Crown prosecutor attempted to use the evidence of a witness who testified he knew the accused intended to shoot the victim because a third party in whom the accused confided told him so, the evidence, although relevant to establishing intent to kill, would be ruled inadmissible because of the hearsay rule. The rationale underlying the rule is its inherent unfairness. The accused cannot cross-examine the maker of the damaging statement and the third party was not under oath to tell the truth at the time the statement was made. These deficiencies are contrary to the format and purpose of witness examination in the modern Anglo-American trial process and undermine the accuracy of fact determination. As a result, hearsay evidence is always questionable and often inadmissible.[8]

Evidence can also be inadmissible on other grounds. For example, s.24(2) of the Canadian Charter of Rights and Freedoms dictates that evidence which tends to bring the administration of justice into disrepute is inadmissible. An example of this kind of tainted evidence would be a confession obtained by the police from the accused murderer who was not informed of his right to counsel at the time of arrest. The confession, although highly relevant would be inadmissible as a breach of s.24(2).

Another rule of admissibility requires that all forms of direct evidence be authenticated. Authenticity requires the proponent of the evidence establish that the evidence is genuine. If a document is used as evidence for example, care must be taken to determine who prepared it and under what circumstances. Normally this requires the testimony of the author of the document or someone who saw the author create or sign the document, such as the attesting witness to a will. Where a physical object, such as an alleged murder weapon is being tendered as evidence, it must be established that it is the same weapon which was taken from the accused at the scene of the crime which then went to the testing laboratories and later to the courtroom. If the judge decides the item is genuine and relevant it will be assessed as part of the total evidence. If authenticity is not established, the judge is bound to ignore the evidence.

Sources of Evidence

The uses and limitations of evidence often depend upon its source. Evidence can take many forms: judicial notice, public records, writings, photographs, expert reports, testimony of witnesses and personal inspection. Some of the more common sources are discussed below.

Judicial Notice

Normally when a judge makes a decision on disputed facts, she only considers the evidence that is put before her. However, there are situations where judges are required to determine questions without the benefit of evidence. One of the most important of these is judicial notice. Judicial notice is based on the assumption that the judge or trier of facts has a fund of generalized knowledge and a knowledge of specific facts which she can relate to the proceeding. The test for the application of the judicial notice principle may be expressed by saying that the court, including the judge and jury must take judicial notice of generally accepted information that is beyond dispute amongst reasonable people. Put another way, a court must take judicial notice of what everyone knows and uses in the ordinary process of reasoning about everyday affairs.

The concept of judicial notice is essential to a rational system of justice. Without it, courts would be forced to hear arguments on propositions no reasonable person would consider arguable. For example, arguments disputing the inherent dangers of handling a loaded gun would be contrary to widely held accepted knowledge and would likely not be admissible because judicial notice would be taken of the obvious.

There is a danger of misuse of judicial notice however, that must be considered. A judge may erroneously regard a source of information as of indisputable accuracy when it is not, or he may accept socially defined stereotypes as being indisputably correct. For example, some judges in custody disputes have taken judicial notice of the "fact" that stay-at-home mothers are the best kind of mothers. On the basis of this assumption they decide to give custody of the children to the father whose new wife stays at home in preference to the biological mother who works outside the home. While this view may have been accepted as the common understanding in the past, more recent evidence convincingly shows the assumption to be a gender biased, unfair stereotype of women, limiting their freedom and potential. To protect against these and other kinds of misuse, an opponent is permitted to dispute judicial notice by submitting evidence to the contrary.

The way judicial notice is invoked is as follows: the party seeking judicial notice of certain evidence must ask that the assertion be accepted as established fact not requiring proof. If the opposition believes the evidence is refutable, she must raise an objection. Once an objection is raised, the party seeking to establish the assertion must tender evidence in support of it unless the judge denies the objection.

In summary, the party seeking judicial notice has the burden of (1) convincing the judge that the matter is not disputable amongst reasonable people and (2) readily accessible sources of indisputable accuracy demonstrate that fact. If the judge decides the matter does not fall within the domain of judicial notice, the ordinary rules of evidence apply.

Public Documents and Records

Public records are often the strongest and most important evidence an advocate can use in argument. Public documents include any documents issued by or with the approval of a government agency. They could include Parliamentary debates or hearings reported in Hansard, legislation, position papers, birth and death certificates, deeds, court decisions and transcripts of trials.

Even though evidence that forms part of the public record is highly regarded because of its official nature, it is never unassailable. Public records can be examined for their quality and objectivity, validity, authenticity and accuracy.

For example, a report of a government expert committee may state that economic sanctions applied to South Africa are ineffective in the fight against apartheid yet a deeper examination of the report may reveal that the witnesses upon who the committee relied to form its opinion were unreliable or they were lobbyists hired by the South African government.

Public and Private Writings

Writings, both public and private are often used sources of evidence. Public writings consist of published material other than public records including academic journals, textbooks, maps as well as tabloid newspapers, novels and magazines. The weight and acceptance of this kind of evidence largely depends on the reputation or prestige of the publication. Those writings which command greater respect in the public eye will be assigned the greater weight and will be the most readily accepted by judges. For example, an item about the financial position of IBM reported in the *Financial Post* will carry more weight than a similar item in the *National Enquirer* or the *Calgary Sun*.

Private writings on the other hand, are writings meant only for private use. Diaries, letters, documents of private companies, wills and contracts are some examples. Where private writings are inadmissible because of hearsay or authenticity problems,[9] they are often useful for providing leads to sources of admissible evidence. For example, sales records of a store may indicate that a gun identical to the one used in a murder was purchased on a certain day. Even though this evidence would be hearsay and difficult to authenticate on its own, it could be used to find out whether any salesperson recognized the accused as a purchaser of the gun on the day in question and lead to obtaining admissible testimony which could authenticate the sales slip and be of great weight in linking the accused to the murder weapon.

Testimony of Witnesses

The most common and probably the least reliable source of evidence is the testimony of witnesses. It is unreliable for the reasons discussed below, yet within its context there is a whole spectrum of reliability. For example, testimonial evidence given before a Court or government body is considered to be of greater weight than that obtained outside the courtroom. Evidence given under oath carries legal sanctions for perjury and contempt and is more reliable and more likely to be true than casual conversation or statements made in an informal setting outside the courtroom. Like written evidence, the source of the testimonial evidence is important for purposes of the weight and credibility the judge will give it. When a professor testifies about a particular area of expertise and is backed up by numerous publications in prestigious academic journals, the evidence should carry great weight. On the other hand, when a person with a long criminal record who is testifying to avoid prosecution as an accomplice gives evidence, the evidence should be received with some degree of skepticism.

Other problems inherent in testimonial evidence[10] which should be noted arise from the fact that different persons perceive events differently. The keenness of the senses, the length of time the senses were exposed to the event and the level of attention the witness directed to the event all contribute toward how the event is perceived. Memory also plays a key role in testimonial evidence. The accuracy and reliability of the evidence may vary depending upon the time lapse between the occurrence of the event and the witness's recollection of it. A deposition recorded at the scene will usually carry more weight than the testimony of a witness describing what he saw months or years before. Psychologists say the amount of detail remembered drops off sharply in the first few hours and days after the event.[11] Furthermore, studies indicate that the more unpleasant the facts, the more detail the witness is likely to forget.[12] In addition to the problems relating to truthful witnesses outlined above, some witnesses deliberately lie about what they know. Often the most accomplished liars portray a very convincing demeanor while truthful witnesses may appear nervous, confused and contradict their former testimony.[13] The credibility of witnesses is a matter for judicial determination, but there are no fail-safe methods to determine conclusively the truthfulness of a witness. Thus, testimonial evidence in many cases is inherently unreliable.

Probative Value of Evidence

Counterbalancing Factors

All relevant evidence by definition has probative value, but as was seen in the earlier discussion, relevance is not always enough. Sometimes relevant evidence is ruled inadmissible because its probative value is outweighed by other counterbalancing factors. Four factors which may result in relevant evidence being excluded are, first, the danger that the facts offered may unduly arouse the trier's emotions of prejudice, hostility or sympathy; second, the probability that the proof and the answering evidence that it provokes may create a side-issue that will unduly distract the trier from the main issues; third, the likelihood that the evidence offered and the counter-proof will consume an undue amount of time; fourth, the danger of unfair surprise to the opponent when, having no reasonable ground to anticipate this development of the proof, he would be unprepared to meet it.[14] When these evidentiary issues arise, a judge is required to balance two intangibles – probative values and probative dangers. In order to avoid having evidence ruled inadmissible on these grounds, the advocate must discover evidence which has more than a bare minimum of probative worth so that distraction, time-consumption or prejudice and surprise are outweighed.

Partial Proof

Evidence which supplies only partial proof in a series of facts is of little probative value in itself. What the advocate must often do to meet the required burden of proof is bring several pieces of partial evidence together to create a strong combined effect. For example, in our hypothetical murder the prosecution would be required to prove "mens rea" or an "evil intent" on the part of the accused beyond a reasonable doubt. However, evidence used to prove the intent element of the offence would constitute only a small part in the series of facts that would be required to prove the charge of murder.

Corroborative Proof

Corroborative proof means cumulative or additional proof. It's function is to strengthen or confirm other evidence. Corroborative evidence may come from a different source than the evidence it supports. For example, if the accused murderer in our hypothetical case testified that the Crown charged the wrong person, claiming he was out of town on the day of the murder, an airplane ticket in the accused's name showing him elsewhere on the critical date would corroborate his alibi. If the accused could produce several witnesses to testify he was in another city at the time in question, the corroborative proof of his defence would be even stronger.

Presumption and Burden of Proof

Presumption

A presumption is a legally recognized connection between two situations each consisting of a fact or group of facts.[15] In legal argument and in debate, a presumption may assist a party in meeting the burden of proof required to win their case. One of the most common presumptions is in favor of the *status quo*.

The concept of presumption assumes that the status quo will continue or that the value accepted at the present time will remain the same. It is in this way presumption favors the status quo until a good reason has been presented which justifies change.

To demonstrate the evidentiary effect of a presumption, one can consider the abortion issue as an example. Prior to January, 1988, to have an abortion outside of an accredited hospital was a crime. The criminalization of abortion was the *status quo*. Subsequently, the Supreme Court ruled that the existing abortion law was unconstitutional and struck it down.[16] The *status quo* then became one of no laws limiting abortion. Partisans on both sides of the abortion debate are actively trying to change the status quo. Pro-choice activists would like to see legislation which would guarantee access to abortion services to all women on an equal basis whereas pro-life groups would like to see new criminal legislation curtailing a woman's right to choose and giving the fetus a constitutional right to life. The pro-choice side has the advantage of a presumption against the criminalization of abortion. Their burden is limited to showing good and sufficient reason for legislation which would go the next step and affirmatively guarantee access to abortion. The pro-life partisans, on the other hand, start with the burden that the *status quo* value is wrong. On top of that, they must make a convincing case for re-criminalization as well as the creation of new rights for the fetus at the expense of women's rights. Clearly the pro-life activists have a much heavier burden of proof to meet.

Burden of Proof

Burden of proof is connected to the notion of presumption because it is assigned to the advocate who wishes to challenge the status quo. A good and sufficient reason for adopting a proposition must be provided and must convince the judge deciding the argument. Unless the burden of proof is met, the advocate fails to win the decision and the opponent need not argue anything other than support of the status quo. In law, there are two main standards of proof underlying the burden of proof. They are the civil standard, which is proof on the balance of probabilities, and the criminal standard which is proof beyond a reasonable doubt.

An example of how these concepts operate is provided in the following example.

Let us assume we have a situation wherein an elementary school principal has been charged with sexually assaulting children under his care. The Crown has brought charges under the Criminal Code and the parents of the affected children have brought a civil suit against the school principal for the harm done to their children.

Establishing the Elements of the Criminal charge.

With respect to the criminal charges, it is necessary to look at the Criminal Code[17] to see what the school principal would be charged with. Section 271 provides that any person charged with, and convicted of, sexual assault can be imprisoned for a maximum of 10 years. Section 265 defines sexual assault and assault as occurring when a person:

a) without the consent of another person, he applies force intentionally to that other person, directly or indirectly;

b) he attempts or threatens, by an act or a gesture, to apply force to another person, if he has, or causes that other person to believe upon reasonable grounds that he has, present ability to effect his purpose; or

c) while openly wearing or carrying a weapon or an imitation thereof, he accosts or impedes another person.

This section applies to all forms of assault, including sexual assault, sexual assault with a weapon, threats to a third party or causing bodily harm and aggravated sexual assault. The section goes on to address consent. It says "for the purposes of this section, no consent is obtained where the complainant submits or does not resist by reason of:

a) the application of force to the complainant or to a person other than the complainant;

b) threats or fear of the application of force to the complainant or to a person other than the complainant;

c) the exercise of authority."

Within this framework, then, sexual assault occurs when "force" is applied to another without that person's consent. The assault does not have to conform to a stereotypical image wherein the victim is bruised or has broken bones. Any form of touching without the consent of the other party can fit within this section of the Code.

Sections 139 and 153 of the Criminal Code also apply to our hypothetical case. Section 139 expressly provides that consent is no defence if the victim is under 14 years of age. Given that the accused in our example is an elementary school principal it is almost certain that his victims were not 14 years of age. As a result, even if the children in question "agreed" to his sexual advances such agreement will not be a defence for our accused.

Section 153 is also applicable. Under this section any individual who is in a position of trust or authority vis-a-vis a young person and who touches, either directly or indirectly, that young person, is guilty of an indictable offence.

The first thing that the Crown must show is that the elements of the offences are present. The elements specified under s.153 would seem to exist in our hypothetical case. The accused, as a principal of an elementary school, certainly exercises authority over his pupils. Moreover, a person occupying such an administrative post is clearly in a position of trust. One of his chief responsibilities is to ensure that students under the school's care are properly supervised and educated. These elements could be established by evidence in the public records of the school and School Board or by testimonial evidence of some official possessed of this information.

With respect to the sexual assault charge, the Crown must establish an application of force without consent. Section 139 clearly establishes that consent is no defense in cases where a child has been sexually touched. The element of force can be established by adducing proof that a school principal holds power over school children and here used his authority to achieve his end of sexually touching the children.

To establish the fact of touching, physical evidence or testimonial evidence of victims or witnesses will be required. Bruises, scratches, semen, torn undergarments and the like may provide physical evidence of a sexual touching. If the victims were attended by doctors, their reports may provide relevant documentary and testimonial evidence of the assault.

Finally, as is unlikely that there will be any eye witnesses to the crime, the primary witnesses will be the victims themselves.

Under s.16 of the Canada *Evidence Act,* the child victim will be allowed to testify in these proceedings so long as he or she is able to communicate the evidence and understands either the nature of a solemn oath or the importance of telling the truth. It is important to note, however, that the Courts are likely to accord greater weight to testimony to evidence given by a child who understands the nature of a solemn oath. In such a circumstance the child "shall" give testimony. In circumstances where the child does not understand the nature of an oath, but appreciates the importance of telling the truth, the court has discretion in calling the witness, as is suggested by the wording "may" testify.

Burden of Proof

In a criminal trial, the Crown has the burden of proving its case. There is a presumption of innocence in favor of the accused which must be displaced by a standard of proof beyond a reasonable doubt. This means the accused has no affirmative burden to prove his innocence. Merely raising a doubt about the prosecution's case will be enough to secure an acquittal.[18] Furthermore, an accused is under no obligation to testify or even call evidence. The accused can hear the case presented by the Crown and through his right of cross-examination and rebuttal, demonstrate the weaknesses in the Crown's case to the point where a reasonable doubt is raised.

None of this should be taken to suggest that if an accused has a defence that he need not call evidence to support it. Anything that can be done to increase the possibility that either a judge or a jury will have a reasonable doubt about the prosecution's case must be brought forward by the defence.

Reasonable Doubt

A "reasonable" doubt is not a simple misgiving that one might have about a particular facet of the Crown's case. The law recognizes that nothing is certain in life and it is only rarely that an accused is found smoking gun in hand and the Crown is able to call unshakable eye witnesses all of whom perfectly corroborate each other. In almost any criminal litigation that results in a conviction there will be some inconsistencies and uncertainties in the Crown's case.

A reasonable doubt does not, however, amount to vague uncertainties that one might entertain about the prosecution's case. A reasonable doubt is:

... that state of the case which, after the entire comparison and consideration of all the evidence, leaves the mind of the jurors in that condition they cannot say they feel an abiding conviction to a moral certainty of the truth of the charge ... The evidence must establish the truth of the fact to a reasonable and most certainty; a certainty that convinces and directs the understanding, and satisfies the reason and judgment of those who are bound to act conscientiously upon it.[19]

If on the basis of all testimony received, as well as any other evidence that might tend to corroborate the Crown's case, a verdict of guilty is returned, the criminal would be sentenced by the judge.

The purpose of a sentence in a criminal action is punishment and deterrance. Evidence from both sides is tendered about the accused's character, criminal record or other matters relevant to sentencing. It can come from public records, testimony, professional assessments or other sources as long as it is relevant and meets the normal admissibility requirements.

After the sentencing is concluded, the next step would be to institute a civil action. Normally, the civil action would not be allowed to proceed until such time as the criminal action had been dealt with by the Courts.

Establishing the Civil Action

The civil action against the school principal would be taken by the parents of the children. The suit would probably rest upon three independent civil causes of action: (1) battery – unwanted touching perpetrated against the children; (2) mental distress caused to the children and (3) mental distress caused to the parents. In addition, the parents might also take an action against the School Board for negligence on the basis of its failure to adequately protect the children from the principal.

The purpose of these actions would be for the plaintiffs to gain compensation from the defendants for damage suffered. Unlike a criminal action, the purpose of a civil action is not to punish or deter but rather to provide compensation.

In a civil action, the burden of proof is much lower than in criminal cases. In a civil action, the winning party must be able to show that on a balance of probabilities its view of what took place is the more likely version of events. This is much less onerous to prove than the beyond a reasonable doubt standard of proof. The balance of probability standard is described as follows:

... [The] party must prove his proposition by a reasonable preponderance of evidence. Their term, "preponderance of evidence," means such evidence as, when weighed with that opposed to it, has more convincing force, and from which it results that the greater probability of truth lies therein. It does not mean that a party must demonstrate his case, exclude all possibility of error or produce in your mind, absolute certainty. In civil matters courts act on the balance of probabilities.[20]

In order to win in a civil action against the school principal the following would be required. First, evidence of the criminal conviction would probably suffice to establish the occurrence of the battery: this would be a matter of public record and would be adduced as such. Secondly to prove mental distress, psychiatric evidence would be required. An expert in the area of psychiatric medicine or psychology would be called to testify. Thirdly, a causal link would have to be established between the actions of the defendant and the symptoms of mental distress and in all likelihood, some physical symptoms of distress would probably have to be demonstrated to corroborate the testimony of the psychiatrist. This evidence could come from experts in psychology or psychiatry backed up by testimony of those who may have observed changes in behavior patterns. These could include teachers, friends, social workers, parents and the victims themselves.

Once the plaintiff established the injuries, the court would then calculate the amount of damages the defendant will have to pay. The amount will be based on the severity of the injuries. In the give and take of the action, opposing counsel would try respectively to maximize and minimize through evidence, the injuries that flowed from the tortious act, on the balance of probabilities standard.

Presumptions in Civil Actions

It is unlikely that any presumptions would lie in this hypothetical case, but they do occur in civil actions. A civil presumption describes a relationship between a basic or known fact and the existence of a presumed fact. For example, if a barrel rolls out of the second story window of a warehouse and falls on someone it will be presumed that the barrel was negligently handled in the warehouse and that such negligence caused the injury to the person who had the barrel fall on him. The presumption favors the injured plaintiff and casts the burden of displacement of the presumption on the defendant. The plaintiff need only prove the circumstances of the event. Unless the defendant adduces evidence of some other plausible cause which would place fault elsewhere, the plaintiff wins.

Conclusion

As has been raised many times in this discussion, legal evidence is a great deal more complex and rigorous than is the evidence that is required in daily communication or school debate. What is crucial to both, however, is the principle that claims must be supported by evidence for argument to take place. This chapter considers sources and types of evidence, weight and credibility it may be given and general principles regarding admissibility, relevance and burden of proof. These legal concepts should assist educators in planning and researching their arguments.

Notes

[1]Hart and McNaughton, Evidence and Inference in the Law, Evidence and Inference 48, 48-59 (D. Lerner ed. 1958)

[2]In law, this aspect of relevance is often called "materiality," but for our purposes, will be included in the larger concept of relevancy.

[3]Schiff,Evidence in the Litigation Process, 2nd ed. Carswells, 1983, p. 15.

[4]C.C. sections 493, 496, 504-07, 720, 736.

[5]Substantive legal doctrine plays an important role in relevancy issues, beyond fact allegations in pleadings, information, indictment of written particulars, but no further discussion is offered because substantive law is beyond the scope of this more general discussion.

[6]J. Thayer, A Preliminary Treatise on Evidence at the Common Law 264-66.

[7]For example see *Bond et al. v. Martinos* [1970] 2 O.R. 319, 10 D.L.R. (3l.) 536 (Ont. C.A.); *Peake's Ltd. v. Higgins,* (1930) 2 M.P.R. 80 (Sup. Ct. N.B.A.D.)

[8]For a detailed discussion on exceptions to the hearsay rule, see Schiff, supra note 3 p. 295-450.

[9]See p. 5-7, supra.

[10]There are many sources of information about the difficulties inherent in testimonial evidence. See for example, Wigmore, The Science of Judicial Proof, 396 et seg. (1937); Wellman, The Art of Cross-Examination, 142 et seg. (1936); Nahstoll, Observation and Memory of Witnesses, 48 A.B.A.J. 68(1962); Marshall, Evidence, Psychology, and the Trial: Some Challenges to Law, 63 Colum. L. Rev. 197(1963).

[11]Brown, Legal Psychology 88-89 (1926).

[12]Coburn & Fahr, Amnesia and the Law, 41 Iowa L. Rev. 369, 370-75(1956); Siegal, Inability to Remember – Its Analysis in Medicolegal Orientation, 45 J. Crim. L. 151, 152, 156(1954).

[13]Healy & Healy, Pathological Lying, Accusation and Swindling 265-66(1915). Credibility of Certain Lay Witnesses: The Psychopathic Liar on the Witness Stand, 1 Current Med. for Attorneys, No. 5, p. 21(1954) as cited in Schiff, infra, note 3. Schiff, supra note 3.

[14]Schiff, supra note 3 p. 73-74.

[15]Supra note 3, p. 1142.

[16]*R. v. Morgentaler,* [1988] 1 S.C.R. 30.

[17]R.S.C., 1985.

[18]*Woolmington v. The Director of Public Prosecutions,* House of Lords (England), 1935 [1935] A.C. 462, 104 L.J.K.B. 433, in Schiff, supra pg. 1103.

[19]*Commonwealth v. Webster* (1850), 5 Cash, (59 Mass.) 295, 320 in Schiff, supra, at pg. 1121.

[20]Haines, "Criminal & Civil Jury Charges" (1968), 46 Can Bar Rev. 48, 86, in Schiff, supra, at pp. 1135-36.R.S.C., 1985.R.S.A., (1980), s.20(1).

12

Social and Communication Issues in Testing

Claudio Violato

Testing – both psychological and educational – is a form of communication. The test is a measurement instrument which can be used by the tester (teacher or psychologist) to assess some very specific characteristic of the testee (pupil or client) and communicate information about the testee's standing on that dimension. Classroom tests, for example, can give feedback both to the pupil and the teacher about the pupil's achievement, the teacher's effectiveness and the appropriateness of the instructional material. Similarly, psychological testing may reveal changes in personality which in turn communicate information about the effectiveness of the therapy that has been employed. Testing, in short, constitutes an evaluative form of communication. Teachers are linked with pupils and clients with therapists through testing and the information it yields about the various people and processes involved. As measurement instruments which provide precise and rigorous information, tests constitute formal communication processes.

Whether it be in schooling and education, in industry, in government or in medicine and psychology, virtually everyone has a stake in testing. Testing has become a matter of social and political as well ad educational concern. Today, as it frequently has been in the last 70 or so years, testing is much in the news and is once again under public scrutiny and, sometimes, attack. It is our purpose in this chapter to examine some of the most contentious issues and major concerns that have arisen over testing. Particularly, we shall examine the following topics related to standardized testing: (1) A Brief History of Testing; (2) The Nature-Nurture Controversy; (3) Testing and the Mass Media; (4) The Invasion of Privacy Issue; and (5) Limits of Testing.

147

A Brief History of Testing

The origins of testing are lost in antiquity. In China for example, several centuries before Christ there was an elaborate system of civil service examinations. Testing was also a normal part of the education of the ancient Greeks. Both Plato and Socrates used expert oral questioning of their students as they saw teaching and testing as inextricably intertwined.[8] Some of the earliest records of testing, however, can be found in the Bible. There is a story in the Bible of an oral test that was used to distinguish between men of Gilead from members of the tribe of Ephraim. The latter pronounced "Shibboleth" without the "h" following the "S":

> Then they said unto him, Say now Shibboleth; and he said Sibboleth: for he could not frame to pronounce it right. Then they took him, and slew him at the passages of Jordan (Judges; 12: 5-6, King James Version).

This is a *final* exam and negative feedback indeed. Failure on this short test produced rather drastic consequences. Fortunately, failure on modern-day tests rarely produces such extreme outcomes.

The origins of standardized testing date back to the 1890's with Joseph Rice's spelling surveys.[15] Rice was attempting to develop norms of spelling ability for different aged children. The next major event in standardized testing was the translation and revision of the Binet scales of mental age by Lewis Terman of Stanford University in 1916. It was not until after the widespread application of standardized testing in World War I for military personnel selection, however, that testing received broad popular attention. As the United States entered into the war in 1917, the American Psychological Association (the official body that represents psychologists in the U.S.) offered its services to the U.S. Army. Psychologists were called upon to develop tests and screening devices for the new recruits. This resulted in the now famous Army Alpha Verbal Test for literates and the Army Beta Nonverbal Test for illiterates. In a very short period, these tests were administered to millions of recruits.

After the end of the first World War, psychologists turned their attention to civilian testing. A variety of achievement, abilities, interest and aptitude tests were developed and standardized. The 1920's saw an unprecedented, and as yet still to be matched, activity in intelligence testing. Educational testing (e.g. standardized achievement tests), in somewhat delayed fashion, experienced its peak development and use between 1930 and 1950.[5]

Both educational and intelligence testing had been on the decline since the 1950's. Now, however, there has been an increase in educational testing in the last eight or nine years owing to provincial legislation (Alberta and B.C. for example) of mandatory testing at various grade levels in the school system.

The latest public controversy over testing has occurred in the early 1970's and then again in the late 1980's. These were the acrimonious debates that were triggered by Arthur Jensen and then resuscitated by Phillipe Rushton on the question of the heritability of IQ. To students of psychology this is known as the nature-nurture or environment-heredity controversy. We shall examine this issue in the next section because of its importance and because of so much confusion surrounding it.

The Nature-Nurture Controversy

Probably the most controversial and emotionally charged issue related to testing is the nature-nurture controversy. While this controversy has been prevalent in psychology and education as a whole, nowhere has it been more hotly debated than with reference to IQ and intelligence. Indeed, with the possible exception of the theory of evolution, no scientific topic has been as filled with a confused mixture of passion, science, politics, and philosophy.

In its simplest form, this issue centers around the extent to which IQ and intelligence are genetically determined. On the one side, the environmentalists such as American psychologist Leon Kamin and anthropologist Jay Gould claim that IQ and intelligence are environmentally determined. On the other side, Berkley psychologist Arthur Jensen and Canadian psychologists Phillip Vernon and Phillipe Rushton assert that the evidence suggests a genetic interpretation. In actuality, Kamin, Gould, Jensen, Vernon and Rushton are all interactionists agreeing that both genes and environment play a role: the debate centers around the relative importance of each. Virtually all psychologists – and just about everybody else for that matter – hold very strong and emotionally laden views about this environment-genetic controversy. The friction and heat that is generated by this issue, frequently creates more confusion than clarity and leaves the antagonists even more fixed in their original views regardless of the direction that the evidence points. It is very important, therefore, that we examine the scientific evidence bearing on this matter as objectively and dispassionately as possible.

The modern day debate was initiated by Arthur Jensen when he published his 1969 article in the *Harvard Educational Review*. In this article by the title "How much Can We Boost IQ and Scholastic Achievement?" Jensen challenged the orthodox environmental doctrine which holds that IQ is almost completely environmentally determined. Jensen suggested that the well-known differences in performance on IQ tests by Blacks and Whites (approximately 15 points on the average) might in fact be due to genetic differences between these groups. Among other possibilities, Jensen suggested that: "A not unreasonable hypothesis [is] that genetic factors are strongly implicated in the average Negro-White intelligence differences."[11]

This was soon picked up by mass media and distorted – Jensen was denounced and branded as a racist. The repercussions were not limited to the world of social sciences but soon spread throughout society as a whole. Soon discussions of "Jensenism" were appearing in psychology textbooks and in the popular press such as *Time, Newsweek* and *Psychology Today*. Even television became embroiled in the fracas when, in mid-1975, CBS produced and aired a documentary, *The IQ Myth,* which strongly denounced "Jensenism." The vehemence of reaction grew so great that Jensen frequently had to be protected by body guards when giving public appearances. The debate has continued to the present, with Rushton's recent articles and television appearances. Geraldo Rivera devoted an entire episode of *Geraldo* to Rushton's work and his views have been debated by David Suzuki on national television. National newspapers such as the *Globe and Mail* have given extensive coverage to the issue. *Time* devoted an entire page to Jensen's 1980 book, *Bias in Mental Testing,* which was advertised as a definitive study on the question of environment and genes. This unprecedented attention given to an academic debate by the popular press and television, attests to its compelling and gripping nature. Unfortunately, several misunderstandings and misinterpretations have confused the issue. These include: (1) a tendency to equate IQ and intelligence; (2) a tendency to equate IQ and achievement; and (3) a failure to acknowledge the voluminous research data – particularly studies of twins – on this point.

The IQ and Intelligence

Many people equate IQ and intelligence. In fact, IQ and intelligence may be only marginally related. Much of the controversy about the heritability of IQ arises from the misconception which equates IQ and intelligence.

The IQ is a relatively recent concept that began with the work of Alfred Binet in France at the turn of this century. Intelligence, on the other hand, has its roots in antiquity. The early Greek philosophers such as Plato and Aristotle speculated about and debated the nature of intelligence. Charles Darwin offered an analysis of intelligence in his book *The Descent of Man* (1871) as did his cousin, Sir Francis Galton, in his book, Hereditary Genius (1869). Despite at least two thousand years of discussion and debate, however, there is yet no suitable definition of intelligence. Even among psychologists, there is very little agreement on the nature of intelligence.[1,22,6] Jean Piaget could do little better than define intelligence as the process of adapting to the environment through assimilation and accommodation.[14] Still other psychologists, such as Howard Gardner, wish to define intelligence within the framework of an information processing model which includes creativity, social behaviour, motor abilities, and athletic ability among others.[3] It is obvious that hardly anyone can agree on a suitable definition of intelligence. Indeed, there are nearly as many definitions of intelligence as there are people defining it.

The IQ on the other hand, is narrowly and precisely defined. The Intelligence Quotient has its origins in the work of Alfred Binet at the beginning of this century. In 1904 Binet was appointed by the French government to a committee to investigate the causes of retardation among public-school pupils. As a consequence of this work, Binet saw the need to develop a screening device which could identify children who might encounter probable difficulties in their later schooling. Binet reasoned that language and numerical skills are important for success in school. Children who are underdeveloped in these skills, are likely to face difficulty. Thus, Binet constructed a test which measured verbal and numerical reasoning. By giving the test to large numbers of different age children, Binet was able to develop norms of "mental age." That is, the mean score for eight year olds on the test was said to represent a mental age of 8, while the mean score for 9-year-olds represents a mental age of 9, and so forth. Thus, a child who takes the test and receives a score that is the same as the mean score for 6-year-olds was said to have a mental age of 6. It was then possible for Binet to determine whether a child had a retarded, normal or advanced mental age. Children with retarded mental ages (that is, less than their chronological age) could receive special attention from teachers (and others) so as to anticipate possible learning difficulties which may otherwise arise. This, of course, was the beginning of formal remedial education. The German psychologist, William Stern, took the next logical step when he divided mental age (as determined by the test) by chronological age and multiplied this quotient by 100 to produce the familiar IQ:

MA (Mental Age) x 100 = IQ (Intelligence Quotient)
CA (Chronological Age)

Thus, we have the well known IQ with a mean of 100.

Binet, in his later work, was joined by Theodore Simon, a French psychiatrist, so that the later tests came to be called the Binet-Simon Intelligence Tests. This test was a valuable beginning as it provided a way to identify slow learners. In 1916, the Stanford University psychologist Lewis Terman, using the Binet-Simon test as a model, produced a test for use in the United States. This is now known as the Stanford-Binet Test of Intelligence. Since that time, many other tests have been developed for use in North America including the Wechsler tests (Wechsler Intelligence Scale for Children-Revised [WISC-R]; Wechsler Adult Intelligence Scale-Revised [WAIS-R]) and the Lorge-Thorndike test.

IQ is based on a very well-defined set of tasks which are calibrated on a norm-referenced basis. A great part of the controversy over IQ testing arises for most people because they equate IQ and intelligence, however intelligence may be defined. For most people the concept of intelligence has philosophical and metaphysical dimensions. Implicit in this is that persons of higher intelligence have more human value than those with "less" or lower intelligence. The very attempt to quantify what for some is sublime (i.e., human intelligence) is an outrage; to then attach more or less worth to some persons over others (an IQ score) is a further outrage. However, IQ is none of these things. Objections to IQ about its inability to predict a person's eventual happiness, their success at marriage or earning power are also frequently raised and, after all, shouldn't "intelligence" be related to these things. Perhaps "intelligence" should be, but we would be surprised if the IQ is since it was never intended to predict or be related to these things. IQ, as an index of measured intelligence, reflects a narrow range of skills which cannot but poorly predict global issues such as success in life.

Perhaps the most unfortunate development was the transformation of mental age into the IQ because the very term invites misunderstanding and the equating with intelligence. If the same ratio were known, as say, the performance quotient (PQ), much of the acrimony and heated debate surrounding IQ testing might fade away. Unfortunately, a further complication arises because many people tend to equate IQ with actual achievement.

IQ and Achievement

A few years ago, a *New York Times* reviewer in discussing the IQ controversy, called the claim that IQ cannot be raised a "counsel of despair.[7] This probably is the major source of bias against testing: this belief threatens people's hopes and expectations for themselves, their children and others they care about. They think that if IQ is genetically fixed then people are entrenched in their "stations" in life with little or no hope for betterment or improvement. This, of course, is not true and reflects a popular misunderstanding.

What people actually do – the grades they achieve, the jobs they get, the professions they enter – is achievement or the outcome of their total efforts plus circumstances and opportunities. This includes how hard they work, their interests, motivation, family environment, the schools attended, and so forth. A high IQ by no means guarantees success in life nor does a modest IQ guarantee failure or inability to better one's condition. Many psychological studies bear this out.

In 1921 Lewis B. Terman – the Stanford University psychologist who developed the Stanford-Binet intelligence tests – undertook a study of high IQ children. He selected 1,528 young people between ages 3 and 19 who had IQ's 135 or above. This group has been studied intensively in the last 60 years. The majority of men and women in this study have done well in their careers, "but there's nobody in the group who is a real genius – no Einsteins reports psychologist Robert Sears who is now in charge of the study."[4] Many of these people distinguished themselves in careers in science, law, medicine, education and literature. Two-thirds of the whole sample have gone to college and a few are millionaires. At the same time, many in the sample never rose above menial work such as janitors, hot dog vendors at baseball games, waitresses and clerical workers. Moreover, while many of the most successful people reported a high satisfaction with their career and life in general, many reported high dissatisfaction as well. Clearly high IQ is no guarantee of success or happiness.

Since the 1920s there now have been studies numbering in the thousands which have investigated the relationship between IQ and achievement. A summary of these studies indicates that, generally, IQ and achievement are correlated. Approximately 25 percent of the variance in achievement is accounted for by IQ. Conversely, 75 percent of the variance is due to other factors (effort, work, interests, motivation, family life, etc). This clearly suggests that achievement itself is almost wide open and certainly not determined solely, or even largely, by IQ. What we make of ourselves depends largely on their efforts and not IQ. Can this be called "a counsel of despair?"

Unfortunately, many people (such as journalists and others) confound IQ and achievement and interpret the scientific finding that IQ cannot be changed to mean that people who are not successful are destined to pass this on to their children. This of course, is simply a misunderstanding and reflects an extremely superficial knowledge. We must always clearly draw the distinction between IQ and achievement.

The Twin Studies

The least convincing but most controversial data on the question of the heredity of IQ is the data on group performance differences. These data show that typically, caucasians outscore blacks on IQ measures while orientals outscore both groups.[16,17,20,21] In his highly controversial 1969 article, Jensen reviewed some of these data and suggested genetic differences as a possible explanation. Such inferences cannot be made on the basis of these data, however, because ethnicity of these groups is hopelessly confounded with socioeconomic status (SES). And it is well known that socioeconomic status is correlated with both achievement and IQ with higher SES people typically scoring higher on both measures than lower SES people.[9,23] The average differences between blacks and whites on IQ tests, therefore, may simply reflect socioeconomic differences among these groups rather than genetic differences.

There is, however, compelling evidence from other sources which clearly point to a significant hereditary component of IQ. These are the so-called "twin studies" or more correctly, the studies of familial relationships. These studies involve determining the correlations between IQ's of people with varying degrees of genetic relationships with a particular focus on twins.

Several testable hypotheses can be generated from the identical twin situation. First, if the "nature" view of IQ is correct, then we would expect the IQ's of identical twins to be essentially identical (within the limits of measurement error) since they do not differ genetically. Second, if the "nurture" view is correct, then we would expect the IQ's of identical twins to be no more similar than that of fraternal twins. Moreover, the situation exists where identical twins have been reared together (same environment) or have been reared apart (different environment). The latter situation may occur when the infants are given up to adoption to different families. This situation provides a naturally occurring "manipulation" of the environment: that is, an "experiment."

A study by two University of Minnesota psychologists, T.J. Bouchard and Matthew McGue, summarizes 111 studies of the world literature on familial resemblances in measured intelligence (IQ).[2] Bouchard and McGue included only studies which met strict standards of research and publication; the 111 studies represent the best and most rigorous which have been done by dozens of scientists involving more than one-quarter of a million cases. This may be the largest sample ever assembled bearing on the heritability of a human trait, physical or psychological. The data point to a substantial heritability of IQ. Similarly, in an authoritative review of evidence bearing on the nature-nurture controversy, psychologists Sandra Scarr and Louise Carter-Saltzman, have drawn the following conclusions:

> The gains made by adopted children reared in improved environments are not dramatic . . . and differences between separated [identical] (MZ) twins are not large . . . Heredity does play a substantial role in determining individual differences in intelligence.[18]

Since most experts in this area estimate that approximately 50-80 percent of the variation in IQ is due to genetic differences.[7] Quite clearly, heredity is important.

Testing and the Mass Media

Testing can be and is a highly controversial topic. It is also a very popular topic for mass media. Newspaper and magazine articles, popular books and television programs dealing with testing and IQ are common place. Indeed, much of the controversy surrounding testing and IQ is probably the result of mass media treatment.

The Harvard psychologist J.R. Hernstein has observed that, particularly with reference to the heritability of IQ, the controversy is an ersatz one created by the national press. As we have seen, there is strong evidence about the extent to which IQ is heritable. As Hernstein has noted, however, in public discussions and mass media treatments, the idea that genes account for a large portion of the variation among IQ's seems controversial and associated with a few men of allegedly questionable character. He has identified at least four important factors which transform a scientific consensus into something that appears controversial:

1. The national press favors "sociological" explanations of society, perhaps because when most editors and senior reporters went to school, optimism about the potentialities for social reform was high.

2. A few professors are available to provide the anti-genetic arguments. They rarely publish their arguments in the technical literature; when they do, the arguments usually fare poorly. They gather little or no data of their own, but instead tend toward *ad hominem* charges against the scholarly consensus . . . Mostly, they are not psychologists; few of them have genuine psychometric expertise. The more extreme attacks on the heritability of IQ tend to be political, not scientific.

3. The professors just characterized could not so influence the national press without the tacit cooperation of many scholars who study, and the merchants who sell, tests. An unspoken agreement grants peace and prosperity, respectively, to scholars and publishers who stay out of the public debate.

4. Egalitarians share the bias against testing with social scientists who do not like psychology. Some sociologists, economists, and political theorists share a strain of anti-psychologism based on the premise that, in the study of society, the important direction of causality is from group to individual, rather

than vice versa. Individual psychological variables, such as IQ scores, are a mote in the eye of social theorists whose vision takes in the human landscape as a whole.[7]

The lay public which, in this case, includes many social scientists, educators, teachers, physicians, politicians and other groups, professional and nonprofessional alike, generally come to believe the mass media "environmental" view of IQ. The public, moreover, is led to believe that psychologists themselves are divided on this point and that the hereditary view is promulgated by a few "shady" researchers of questionable character and sinister motives.

Both Arthur Jensen and Cyril Burt have been vilified and attacked in a vitriolic manner by the mass media and members of the academic community. This is, of course, quite understandable since the weight of the scientific evidence favors the "genetic" interpretation – the media are then left to *ad hominem* arguments. One of the tactics of the anti-hereditarians is to claim that because Cyril Burt's data may be invalid (see Table 1), the whole of the genetic stance must collapse. The impression is created that the whole of the argument rests on the work of Cyril Burt. Whether or not Burt's data is fraudulent, however, is irrelevant since hundreds of other studies have been conducted since that time and they point to a genetic view of IQ. Another tactic is to attempt to discredit the researcher by imputing dark, racist and sinister motives to his work. Arthur Jensen has been attacked in the mass media in this way as has Phillipe Rushton.

The Case of Sir Cyril Burt

Sir Cyril Burt, the only psychologist ever to be knighted, was born in England in 1883 and died in 1971 at the age of 88. Burt was regarded as one of the world's great psychologists as reflected in *Time* magazine's eulogy that he was the most "powerful and influential psychologist since William James." His greatest contributions were in the areas of quantitative methods and psychological testing. Burt is generally thought to have played a decisive role in the British Education Act of 1944 which legislated the use of psychological tests for assigning students into various educational streams.

The hereditary view of intelligence, while not new with Burt, found in him one of its most prominent promulgators. He had, for decades, generally been regarded as the most authoritative psychologist on the matter. On October 24, 1976, Oliver Gillie in an article in the *The Times,* launched a direct attack on Burt claiming that he had published fraudulent data to support his view that intelligence is largely inherited. Gillie summarized four main charges:

1. That Burt had guessed at the intelligence of parents he interviewed but later treated these guesses as hard scientific data.

2. That Burt invented two "collaborators" who wrote papers supportive of his position and criticizing those of opposing views.

3. That Burt reported correlations exact to the third decimal place which is a virtual statistical impossibility. In three studies of the correlations of IQ scores

of identical twins reared apart, the coefficients reported were exactly 0.771; for identical twins reared together the correlations reported were 0.944.

4. That Burt concocted data to fit the predictions of his favorite genetic theories.

Since these allegations were made, it seems very likely that Burt is guilty on all four charges.[10] His two "collaborators," Margaret Howard and J. Conway, have never been found nor is there any documentation to establish their association with Burt. Much of Burt's data seems too improbable to accept as real; few psychologists accept Burt's data as valid.[11,13] Indeed, these data are rarely, if ever, included in reviews of the heritability of IQ.[2] While it is certain that Burt's reputation as a scientist has been damaged, his idea that IQ has a large genetic component is supported by the scientific evidence.[18] Carter-Saltzman, 1982). Burt, the man, may have lost credibility, but his theories continue to remain credible.

A third common tactic of the mass media is to ignore evidence or events which undermine the environmental position. Such a tactic is exemplified in the case of Richard Heber who was once the director of the Milwaukee Project. This project was an interventionist program that attempted to raise the IQ's of preschool ghetto children. Throughout the 1970s, Heber and his spokesmen claimed dramatic results for their interventionist program. They claimed that they could raise the underprivileged children's IQ by 33 points to a mean IQ of over 125. These indeed were startling and dramatic results and were widely reported in the popular press like the *Washington Post, The New York Times,* and *Time.* Unfortunately, as it turns out, these claims were undoubtedly false and fraudulent. In 1981, Richard Heber and an associate were sentenced to seven years in prison (see Table 2) for diverting institutional funds to their own personal use such as raising horses. Nonetheless, the popular consciousness has absorbed and retained the unsubstantiated claims that IQ is very malleable.

The Case of Richard Heber and the Milwaukee Project

On July 30, 1981, Richard Heber and an associate were convicted of numerous counts of diverting institutional funds and were sentenced to three years in prison. Several months later, Heber was sentenced to an additional four years. He began serving his sentence in 1981 in a federal prison in Bastrop, Texas.

Richard Heber was probably best known as the director of the Milwaukee Project which was an interventionist program that attempted to boost the IQ's of preschool ghetto children. Heber, however, had also been director of the Center on Mental Retardation and Human Development at the University of Wisconsin; he had also chaired President Kennedy's panel on mental retardation in the early 1960's. Heber was well known to psychologists for his work in the field of intellectual development and compensatory education.

In the early 1970s the Milwaukee Project and Heber broke into the national news when it was claimed that the IQ's of ghetto children were raised by 24-35

IQ points by the interventionist program. *Time, The Washington Post,* and *The New York Times,* to name just a few, publicized these results widely asserting that the environment is primarily, perhaps solely, responsible for the lower IQ's of economically deprived groups.

Conversely, the hereditarian stance was denied and ridiculed. The Milwaukee Project was held out as a beacon of hope for dramatic and lasting changes to IQ by interventionist programs.

Unfortunately, all of these claims are undoubtedly false as no other psychologist has yet been able to replicate them or even come close. Heber and his associates probably made these claims so as to continue to receive large federal grants. Patrick Fanigan and Heber diverted at least $165,000 of the center's money to their personal bank accounts. With it and other money, they bought hundreds of acres of land in Wisconsin, Iowa, Florida and Colorado. They also set up a horse training business which involved considerable time, travel and capital.[7]

All of this is incomparably more important than the allegations made towards Sir Cyril Burt. Yet the national press which gave so much publicity to the fraudulent claims in the 1970s, remains remarkably silent on this case. The claims by Heber of raising IQs dramatically have permeated the public consciousness and many continue to believe these claims. Apparently, the popular press is unwilling to publish anything which could correct these unsubstantiated claims. Just as in the Burt case, however, the lack of credibility of a supporter of a theoretical position does not necessarily invalidate the theory. The extent to which IQ can be raised by compensatory education is still a matter for research to settle.

Right from the start the scientific community has been eager to scrutinize Heber's work. The data, however, were never published in any substantial way in technical reports. All that is really available are the claims of Heber and his spokesmen. The truth is that nobody can really evaluate what was done to the children in the Milwaukee Project or what the results were. It is unlikely, however, that Heber's claims are substantiated since no one has been able to replicate his alleged results. The best that has been achieved are modest and transitory increases in IQ. The extent to which IQ can be raised by some sort of educational or psychological intervention is still a matter of controversy and can only be settled by further research. This similar silent treatment has been given to the Bouchard and McGue study which supports the hereditary stance of IQ.[2] While this should have been big news for the nature-nurture controversy, virtually no mention of it was made in the press. The press, apparently, selectively reports the position of the environmentalists.

In summary, then, the press tends toward a systematic anti-testing position and frequently creates a "controversy" where none exists. This has been the case with the nature-nurture debate. Serious students of testing and other people, however, should view media treatment of these subjects with extreme skepticism.

The Invasion of Privacy Issue

With the proliferation of personal data banks maintained by credit bureaus, and the advent of computers that can easily access such information, the public has become more and more concerned with maintaining individual privacy. In testing, this has become a major issue as well. This is especially true of personality testing where very intimate and personal questions about sexual behaviour and fantasies are sometimes asked. Such questions ask persons to make public some covert and personal aspects of the respondent's inner life. When can we justify the use of such revelations? When is the social need to know greater than an individual's right to keep his own secrets? Thorndike and Hagen have proposed that seven major questions need to be addressed in determining whether or not the social need for disclosure overrides the right to privacy:[19]

1. For whose benefit will the information be used?
2. How relevant is the information to the decisions that must be made?
3. If the information is to be gathered for a social good, how crucial is that good?
4. How "personal" is the information that is sought?
5. Has there been provision for "informed consent"?
6. To what extent may consent be assumed?
7. Is the individual's anonymity protected?

When the social or personal benefits are regarded to be high, invasion of privacy is accepted. This is very common practice in medicine for example. Countless thousands of women daily submit to gynecological examination which certainly must be regarded as an "invasion of privacy." Similarly, countless thousands of people daily undergo surgery which also is "invasion of privacy." Nevertheless, people readily and voluntarily undergo these procedures largely because of the real or perceived benefit that accrues to them. Society as a whole benefits as well when invasive medical intervention can control or eradicate contagious diseases. A similar principle could govern testing in education and psychology: if the benefits outweigh the right to privacy, testing is acceptable. Even so, however, testing does have limits.

Limits of Testing

One sector of society which includes students, lay people, teachers and even some psychologists, denounces tests as completely useless at best and even sinister and wicked at worst. At a recent symposium on tests and testing at the University of Calgary, in Canada, for example, one professor of psychology proclaimed objective tests as the "devil's invention." At the other extreme, another sector of society uncritically accepts test scores as having absolute meaning and precision. For this latter group, test scores are cloaked in inherent value and meaning. Still others herald tests as the keepers of standards in education. Without a rigid and imposed testing program it is asserted, education would collapse into hopeless chaos. Finally, a last group of people see tests as perpetrating and even causing racial discrimination, sexism, the denial of certain human rights, the subversion of democratic principles and so forth.

None of these extreme views, of course, are correct. Tests by themselves are neither the keeper of educational standards nor are they the perpetrators of injustice and evil. *Tests are measuring instruments which can provide reliable and valid information with which to improve the quality of decisions.* The decisions, however, are always made by a person (teacher, psychologist, counsellor and so forth) and this responsibility cannot be turned over to a test. The decision to launch or not to launch the space shuttle on a particular day is made by people; but it is based, in part, on as much reliable and valid information as possible. Even so, the decision can be flawed. Similarly, the quality of decisions by teachers and psychologists can be very much improved by reliable and valid test data, but these decisions are not flawless. Ultimately, decision makers cannot abdicate their responsibility to tests.

It is also important to remember that test scores always include measurement error. Therefore, a test score must be seen and interpreted in this light. If the measurement error is large, the test score is virtually meaningless. Even if the measurement error is small, we must not forget that tests generally measure a very narrow and specific characteristic. Few if any psychologists, for example, would assert that an IQ score neatly and definitively sums up a person's "intelligence" and life chances. Nor would many math teachers assert that a score on an algebra test is a definitive measure of the student's math ability. In the hands of the wise and competent user, tests can be powerful tools in the service of benefitting humanity. Applied by the incompetent, tests can be instruments of evil and injustice serving those who wish to discriminate against others.

Noted References

[1]Boring, E.G. (1923). Intelligence as the tests test it. *New Republic, 5*, 35-27.

[2]Bouchard, J.T., & McGue, M. (1981). Familial studies of intelligence: A review. *Science, 212* 1055-1059.

[3]Gardner, H. (1984) Frames of mind. New York: Wiley & Sons.

[4]Goleman, D. (1980). 1,528 Little geniuses and how they grew. *Psychology Today, 13*, 28-43.

[5]Haney, W. (1981). A short history of social concerns over standardized testing. *American Psychologist, 36*, 1021-1034.

[6]Hebb, D.O. (1966). *A textbook of psychology* (2nd ed.). Philadelphia: W.B. Saunders.

[7]Hernstein, R.J. (1982). IQ testing and the media. *The Atlantic Monthly,* August, 68-74.

[8]Hopkins, K.D., & Stanley, J.C. (1981). *Educational and psychological measurement and evaluation.* (6th edition). Toronto: Prentice-Hall.

[9]Jencks, C., et al (1972). *Inequality: A reassessment of the effect of family and schooling in America.* New York: Basic Books.

[10]Jensen, A.R. (1980). *Bias in mental testing.* New York: The Free Press.

[11]Jensen, A.R. (1974). Kinship correlations reported by Sir Cyril Burt. *Behavior Genetics,* 4, 1-28.

[12]Jensen, A.R. (1969). How much can we boost IQ and scholastic achievement? *Harvard Educational Review,* 39, 1-123.

[13]Kamin, L.J. (1974). *The science and politics of IQ.* Potomac, Md.: Erlbaum.

[14]Piaget, J. (1952). *The origins of intelligence in children.* New York: International University Press.

[15]Resnick, D. (1980). Minimum testing historically considered. *Review of Research in Education,* 8, 3-29.

[16]Rushton, P. (1988). The reality of racial differences: A rejoinder with new evidence. *Personality and Individual Differences,* 9, 1035-1040.

[17]Rushton, P. (1988). Race differences in behaviour: A review and evolutionary analysis. *Personality and Individual Differences,* 9, 1009-1024.

[18]Scarr, S., & Carter-Saltzman, L. (1982). Genetics and intelligence. In R.J. Sternberg, *Handbook of Human Intelligence,* Cambridge: Cambridge University Press, 792-896.

[19]Thorndike, R.L. & Hagen, E. (1977). *Measurement and evaluation in psychology and education* (4th ed.). Toronto: Wiley, 611-615.

[20]Vernon, P.E. (1978) *Intelligence: Heredity and environment.* San Francisco: W.H. Freeman.

[21]Vernon, P.E. (1982). *The abilities and achievement of Orientals in North America.* Toronto: Academic Press.

[22]Wechsler, D. (1958). *The measurement and appraisal of adult intelligence* (4th ed.). Baltimore: Williams and Wilkins.

[23]White, K. (1982). The relation between socio-economic status and academic achievement. *Psychological Bulletin,* 92, 463-481.

Section Three

Gender and Culture in Educational Communication

13

The Teacher's Role in Gender Balancing

Suzanne McCorkle

As future teachers, you face an important decision – will you help to sustain gender and ethnic stereotypes or will you be a force for positive change? There is no neutral ground on this issue, for those who ignore the problems of ethnic and gender imbalance are doomed, consciously or unconsciously, to perpetuate the communicative patterns which sustain bias. This chapter examines how racial and gender bias are embedded in our current educational system and what you as teachers can do to help students break the bonds of traditional gender and ethnic stereotyping.

Gender Bias: Myth and Reality

"Gender" is the key term which recognizes that communication and role differences between men and women are not biologically ordained, but are a learned, cultural pattern. *Removing Bias: Guidelines for Student-Faculty Communication,* a Speech Communication Association publication, states: "Currently sociologists and psychologists generally agree that the term 'sex' refers to biological components (hormones and chromosomes) while 'gender' is used for the learned and cultural behaviors loosely associated with biological sex".[1]

It is important to use the term "gender" rather than "sex" when discussing behaviors. Behaviors caused by hormones or genetics are relatively unchangeable. When we talk about "sex stereotyping" the perception is that these differences are biologically ordained and, hence, unchangeable. The label "gender stereotyping" can be perceived as a cultural manifestation, and, therefore, changeable.

Surprisingly, some experts argue gender bias is not "real" or not important. Four attacks on the need to confront gender and ethnic stereotyping in education merit discussion.

Myth 1: Excellence and equity are in competition. Some argue we cannot have overall excellence if gender equity is a priority. *Phi Delta Kappan* guest editor Charol Shakeshaft explains the logic and effects of this myth.

> Since the call for excellence was first sounded in 1983 in *A Nation at Risk,* a lot of loose talk has blamed the so-called lack of excellence in the schools on the pursuit of equity. . . .
>
> President Reagan, for instance, claimed that one reason that the schools were failing was the attention that had been focused on female, minority, and handicapped students. He asserted that, if the federal government and educators had not been so preoccupied with the needs of these special groups of students, education in the U.S. might not have succumbed to the "rising tide of mediocrity." What the President failed to note is that, if these three groups of students are eliminated, only about 15% of the school population remains. . . . The logic behind the attack on equity goes something like this: excellence and equity are different; equity threatens to take resources away from excellence; therefore, let's abandon equity as a national concern so as to pursue excellence exclusively.[2]

Sadker, Sadker, and Klein point out the central ethical flaw in the argument that equity and excellence are incompatible:

> How can education be excellent if it is not fair? A Teacher may be effective in educating white males, but if female and minority students are not achieving, can this be called educational excellence? . . . If excellence is only for some, democracy cannot survive.[3]

1. True False	Boys talk more than girls in elementary, secondary and postsecondary classrooms.
2. True False	There is widespread sex segregation in classrooms at all educational levels.
3. True False	Teachers are more likely to punish girls than boys for calling out answers during classroom discussions.
4. True False	Boys receive more praise from teachers than girls.
5. True False	Teachers give boys more academic help than they give girls.

Adapted from "Sexism in the Classroom," by M. Sadker and D. Sadker, 1985, *Vocational Education Journal* 60: 30.

Myth 2: The Culture of Schools is Feminine. So Girls Have the Advantage. A quiz provided by Sadker and Sadker demonstrates the fallacy in the logic that because there are more female teachers, girls have an advantage in the educational environment.[4] If you answered false to any of the questions in above, you subscribe to Myth 2. The section of this chapter on "How Sexism is Built into the Educational System" will illustrate how girls are disadvantaged in the current system.

Myth 3: Existing Laws are Sufficient to Solve the Problem. Ayim points out that laws only achieve *formal* equality of opportunity, meaning there are no "legal or quasi-legal impediments" to equality. However, on a *substantive* level of equality, where the disadvantaged group actually receives equal treatment in proportion to their numbers, women and girls remain either invisible or unrewarded. As long as the problem remains embedded in cultural attitudes, legal action alone cannot remedy it.[5]

Myth 4: We Have Enough Equity Now. While some social change may be occuring, statistical data show that women have not achieved equity.

> Women are nowhere near possessing substantive equality of opportunity . . . The areas in the paid work force where women are concentrated, clerical work and the service industries, are frequently referred to as female ghetto areas because they have become identified with low salaries and stunted opportunities for advancement. And, even in these traditional female areas, women earn much less than male co-workers. In all employment areas, including the professions, women workers are concentrated in the lower echelons, and their earnings are a fraction of the earnings of male workers in the same field. . . . Women, especially old women, are much more likely to live beneath the poverty line than men, and female-headed single-parent families are much more likely to be poor than male-headed single-parent families. . . . Canadian women do not enjoy substantive equality of opportunity with men. . . .[6]

Sadker, Sadker, and Klein remind us that equity requires active work and won't simply "go away": "the idea that sexism will disappear naturally, becoming extinct as time and environment change, does not reflect reality "[7]. Specific examples of how sexism and racism persist will be presented in the section "How Sexism is Built Into the Educational System."

While most educators committed to equity in education are of one mind about the above myths, experts differ widely on how gender bias should be conceptualized and confronted.[8] One trend in the literature of educational discrimination takes the *compensatory approach*. The compensatory view suggests that women and ethnic groups have been systematically discriminated against and need extra help to balance past inequity. This view assumes that women and minorities should strive to succeed within the existing cultural system, i.e., to compete within the system which works well for white males and to become more like white males.[9]

In contrast to the compensatory approach is a *gender-balanced* approach.[10] Gender-balance advocates see bias as a function of the social and economic factors which denote power and status, rather than as functions of gender or ethnic traits; i.e., gender bias is built into the Western world's white, patriarchal power structure and is not exclusive to women, but is aimed at any non-white, non-establishment group.

Looking at bias as a function of power makes its manifestations more subtle and pervasive. For example, women have been allowed into college buildings and classrooms for several decades, yet what is taught has not changed and remains from a white-male research base, about white-male history and philosophy, geared to entry into white-male culture, and implicitly – if not overtly – functions to maintain the perception that women and ethnic groups are inferior.[11]

Researchers and theorists from the gender-balancing perspective see a need for more deeply rooted cultural changes to a more pluralistic society. Rather than helping women and minorities to compete for power within the existing structure, gender-balance advocates argue the social structure itself has characteristics which are detrimental for both men and women and which should be changed. Sadker, Sadker, and Klein delineate how gender stereotyping damages boys *and* girls:

> Although sexism is frequently associated only with females, in reality sex bias is a two-edged sword; males are also victims. . . . research indicates boys are stereotyped earlier and more harshly than girls. Boys who are quiet, passive, or unathletic find themselves at a disadvantage and may even suffer social and psychological consequences for their inability to conform to the male sex-role stereotype. "Real" men are supposed to be athletic, competitive, and aggressive. Boys who do not fit this mold have their own special set of problems, both within and beyond school walls.[12]

A gender-balancing approach demands dramatic and systematic changes within the entire school system and would result only from determined political action. Whether you choose to become involved in the larger political issues or not, there are many actions you may take in your own classroom to confront gender bias.

How Sexism is Built Into the Educational System

A substantial body of research documents the presence of sexism and racism in the educational system and in teacher classroom behaviors. The following briefly summarizes some of the ways the educational system and individual teachers discriminate against women and minorities.

First, the historic purpose of education was (and is) to train white males to succeed in a white-male world.[13] Beyond the obvious former prejudices that persons of color could not learn and that learning was physically damaging to the "delicacy" of females, the patriarchal value system created the goals of education which remain in use today. For example, the decisions on when to teach specific instructional concepts generally are set at the level of male maturation.

> Although females mature earlier, are ready for verbal and math skills at a younger age, and have control of small-motor skills sooner than males, the curriculum has been constructed to mirror the development of males. Decisions about the grade in which students should learn long division, read *Huckleberry Finn*, or begin to write essays are based on the developmental patterns of boys (and primarily white boys), not on the development patterns of girls (or of minority students). The result is that girls are often ahead of the game in

some areas and never in the game in others. Some grow bored, others give up, but most learn to hold back, be quiet, and smile.[14]

Further, traditional teaching techniques mirror the aggressive and competitive characteristics of dominant (white male) Western culture. Shakeshaft argues that this may not be the best learning environment for girls (or boys) who do not necessarily subscribe to the win/lose philosophy of life.

An examination of the use of competition as a learning style provides an illustration of the ways in which male development guides instructional style. From the bluebirds against the cardinals in a spelling bees to the boys against the girls in a game of math facts, pitting student against student in a win/lose contest is a common and accepted means of instruction in U.S. schools. Students learn not only how to compete but that competition is a worthy endeavor.[15]

Second, research on white boys often is generalized to represent all students.[16] This bias follows as an effect of white-males' definition of themselves as the only valuable people (historically men defined themselves as the only "human" group). Philosopher Mary Daly argues that describing the world only through the eyes of white males, necessarily created an unrealistic understanding of the "human" condition:

Men have provided us with a false picture of the world . . . not just because their view is so limited, but because they have insisted that their *limited* view is the *total* view. They have insisted that their *male* experience of the world is the *human* experience, and this has necessitated denying the experience of women where it is different from the experience of men.[17]

Consequently, research either excluded women completely or discarded the results about women and girls when they differed from the results about boys and men.[18] The logic for discarding data on women was that it "skewed" the results because it was "different" from the male data. Much of the research base in education, consequently, was flawed and is being redone. Research on what is best for different groups of students also must be conducted and the basic assumptions of curricular and instructional technique reassessed.

Third, teachers interact more with males than with females. Contrary to the public image of chattering girls, boys talk more to teachers and receive both more quality and quantity of feedback from teachers.[19] This is partly an effect of cultural stereotypes of boisterousness, energy, aggressiveness, and challenge as positive masculine behaviors and of protest, challenge, and assertiveness as negative feminine behaviors.[20] Recent studies found boys continue to be more verbally aggressive than girls and the difference increases with age. The educational effect is that boys demand attention and are rewarded; girls demand attention and are rebuked for being unladylike.[21]

Studies on teacher-student interactions indicate that within coeducational classrooms, teachers, regardless of sex, interact more with boys, give boys more attention (both positive and negative), and that this pattern intensifies at the secondary and college levels. Girls get less teacher attention and wait longer for it. When they do get attention, it is more likely that the teacher will respond to them neutrally or negatively . . . The reinforcement girls do get is likely to be for passivity and neatness, not for getting the right answer.[22]

One study found teachers present 56 percent of their time with males and 44 percent with females. At this rate, a female would receive 1 800 fewer hours of teacher attention over the span of her education.[23] Teachers often did not know girls' names or learned them later, could report fewer details about girls as students, and often lumped all female students together as "the girls" when discussing classroom behaviors.[24] Compounding these facts is an often held teacher perception that they treat boys and girls exactly the same.[25] The belief that "If I think I treat boys and girls equally, I do treat them equally" is not valid. Unconscious cultural assumptions about gender lead the most well intended teachers into gender biased behaviors.

Fourth, curriculum remains male-based. This bias has two phases. In the first phase textbooks, movies, and other instructional materials, directly stereotype women (doctors are male; nurses are female). In the second phase, an occasional mention of women or minority contributions may be made in classes, but women and minorities generally remain invisible. When mention of women is made, it focuses on women who have "made it" in the white male value system and have become astronauts or scientists. Shakeshaft explains how an occasional unit on women's studies is an inadequate response to gender bias.

> Although a unit on women's history in a social studies class may deliver the message that women have a place in history too, it also announces that there are two kinds of history: American history, which is important and about men, and women's history, which is peripheral. Certainly teaching a section on women's history is better than not teaching anything about women at all. However, the failure to integrate female experiences into the general curriculum drives home the message that girls and their experiences are somehow "other," that they are not part of general literature and history.[26]

Fifth, females are excluded in the gender biased language of textbooks and teachers. Research shows the "generic he" is perceived by students to mean male, not male or female.[27] Use of the "generic he" does limit perceptions of what career and life options are appropriate for females. Shakeshaft elaborates:

> . . . in one study in which young children were asked to draw a picture of a caveman, they drew pictures of a man. When they were asked to draw cave people, they included women and children. Male-exclusive language in the classroom relentlessly chips away at female self-esteem. If a girl always hears the "he" means everyone, while "she" means females only, that girl is learning that females are less important than males. Those who argue that gender-exclusive language is unimportant should change all their "he's" to "she's" and see how important it really is. If the issue of language were truly irrelevant, there would be little resistance to changing it.[28]

Texts in the speech communication field follow the same historic pattern of gender biased language. Randall's survey found 84 percent of college speech communication textbooks failed to consider sexist language.[29]

Sixth, some teachers permit the verbal victimization of women in their classrooms.[30] When racist or sexist terms, jokes, or pictures are permitted in the educational environment, the message is communicated that women and minorities are not whole people and are appropriate targets for victimage. Teachers have become more adept at disciplining racist comments, but remain insensitive to the prevalence and effects of verbal victimage of women and girls.

Seventh, females learn gender-linked, low-power speech patterns. As discussed above, men and boys talk more than girls and women, yet popular mythology believes exactly the reverse. This belief/reality gap creates a teacher perception that however little girls talk, they talk too much. In addition, boys learn an assertive way of talking; girls learn to use qualifiers and nonverbal behaviors which are perceived as less intelligent. Other learned low power behaviors include: males select most topics of discussion, males interrupt females, comments made by females often later are attributed to males.[31] These behavioral patterns encourage teachers to perceive girls as less intelligent and to reduce the opportunities available to girls in the classroom (if one believes females are less intelligent, less capable at math, or unable to be leaders, the teacher is less likely to call on females for those classroom activities). Houston explains how the norm that women use low-power communicative behaviors is enforced in the classroom:

> If teachers fail to notice the gender of the student who is talking, if they pay no attention to who is interrupting whom, whose points are acknowledged and taken up, who is determining the topic of discussion, then they will by default perpetuate patterns that discourage women's participation in the educational process.
>
> The *teacher* may well try to ignore gender, but the point is that the *students* are not ignoring it in their sense of how the interactions should go and who is entitled to speak in the educational area. Gender may be excluded as an *official* criterion, but it continues to function as an *unofficial* factor.[32]

Eight, teachers differ in how they give instructions to boys and girls. Teachers tend to instruct males and then let them perform the task or manipulate the equipment; teachers tend to do the task *for* females.[33] While the impact of these findings is greatest on math and science laboratory classrooms, teachers in all disciplines should be aware of this unconscious pattern of gender bias. It is difficult for learning to occur when half the students are not given a chance to experiment.

Finally, the degree to which gender bias is embedded in the system is apparent in its lack of a place on the social or educational agenda. A 1981 survey of educational texts showed no texts included curricular resources on sexism, one-third of the texts did not mention sexism at all, five times as much space was allocated to males than females in foundations of education texts, and stereotyping continued in many texts.[34] While the text you are reading now deserves praise for including gender bias, the discussion of bias is partitioned into the "women's chapter" – one might ask why gender bias and its remedies are not an agenda throughout the text?

The sum effect the gender imbalance built into the educational system and teacher behaviors is the perpetuation of a "socially created" reality which produces damaged people.[35] It is important to remember that the current social structure is a reality created by society's values and customs, not an unchangeable or immutable "truth." The current educational system is rigged. It is rigged to help white males at the expense of women and minorities. To date, teachers have unwittingly been the primary tools in perpetuating bias in the classroom.

The Teacher's Role in Gender Balancing

Ideally, your educational theory and speech-communication methods courses already have discussed gender and ethnic balancing, and you will receive more specific training upon arrival at your first teaching assignment. Unfortunately, many teachers will not be offered these opportunities. What, then, can you do as an individual teacher to balance gender in your classroom?

Two levels of activity can help to gender-balance any classroom: (1) teaching a specific content unit confronting the assumptions and communicative behaviors of sexism and racism, and (2) gender-balancing communication as an everyday classroom activity.

A Teaching Unit on Gender-Balancing

A unit on historic social values and how they promote gender and racial bias can set an agenda in the classroom which communicates the message that sexist and racist behaviors are undesirable and will not be tolerated. It is necessary to examine the social attitudes which encourage sexism and racism, rather than just to "say" we should not be sexist or racist. Sexist attitudes and behaviors are so embedded in our lives that most teachers and students are unaware of the subtle, yet pervasive, effect of sexism and the extent to which our own behaviors perpetuate sexism. In *Removing Bias: Guidelines for Student-Faculty Communication,* Jenkins explains why teachers must change their basic perceptions before progress can be made in gender-balancing:

> We are often unaware of the social and cultural differences among people, because of gender, race, ethnicity, and/or age, that affect our everyday communication. It is precisely those elements of life which are most natural, most unconscious, and most automatic which we need to examine in order to promote bias-free learning opportunities in the classroom.[36]

A classroom unit has the further advantage of getting students to understand the negative effects of sexism (and racism) on men and women and to create new norms to replace old sexist and racist habits. While the teacher may unilaterally attempt to gender-balance, if the agenda is not clear on *why* balance is important, the students will enforce the existing social norms.[37] One adaptable approach to a gender sensitive unit in the speech communication classroom is adapted from a widely used values clarification exercise on the characteristics of a competent, mature adult (Fill in the blank: "A competent and mature adult is . . ."). Have students list characteristics of mature adults and then discuss why these characteristics are important to happiness at home and success at work. Then have students list characteristics of men and women (Fill in the blank: "Men are . . ." and "Women are . . ."). Discuss: Which characteristics listed for men and women are different from those listed for mature adults? Why are the lists different in terms of social stereotyping? Which elements on the "men" and "women" lists are counterproductive to competence in the workplace or happiness in family life? What are the effects of the negative behaviors and stereotyping on men and women?

Presentation of a gender-balancing perspective will be similar to a unit on interpersonal communication in that individuals are valued rather than put-down. For example, women can simultaneously be encouraged to unlearn submissive behaviors and be valued for their role as primary childrearers. "Woman stop serving as looking-glasses reflecting men at twice their natural size, we can cease to project images of ourselves as less capable [by playing 'stupid'] and we can start asserting the validity of our own meanings and experiences".[38] Concurrently, students need to recognize the difficulty and importance of childrearing in a culture which gives lipservice to the value of motherhood, but no economic support. Girls and young women would benefit from "reality training" to combat the romanticized cultural myth that all one's problems are solved once one becomes a wife and mother. They need to realize that single-parent families led by women comprise most of those living in poverty and that our legal system has a dismal record of collecting child support payments. Young adults need dramatic and visceral exposure to the economic facts of life which result from choices to drop out of school, become pregnant, or avoid acquiring skills because "someone else will be around to take care of them." Corporations like U.S. West sponsor helpful programs centred around the choices made while in school that affect one's later earning power.

A gender sensitive unit offers further opportunities to discuss women's culture. Tetreault calls for textbooks to include the everyday contributions of women's work within the home – "childbearing, childrearing, and housework. Textbooks must document women's efforts to break out of their traditional sphere of the home in a way that uses women's activities, not men's, as the measure of historical significance".[39] Women's strengths must be recognized and valued (patriarchal value systems de-value women's contributions under the logic that women are only valued as counterpoints and support systems for men, so if a woman does something, it inherently can't be valuable). Acker illustrates how women's strengths are devalued in education: ". . . women interested in teaching are criticized for bringing 'such damning characteristics as altruistic motivations, desires for pleasant social relationships with colleagues, and preferences to work with people rather than things' to professional life".[40]

The gender sensitive unit may be expanded by converting any of the issues in the next section into mini-lessons. A unit which carries gender-balancing as a primary objective *is* an interpersonal communication unit and well-suited for the speech-communication curriculum. Interpersonal communication is a prime area for junior high and high school students, as many of their other developmental difficulties stem from lack of interpersonal communication competence.[41]

Sample exercises and gender sensitive instructional units can be found in numerous sources. Some are listed at the end of this chapter.

Gender-Balancing as an Everyday Activity

In addition to a specific unit which teaches gender-balancing, the teacher must alter his or her own gender biased communication patterns.

First, become aware of your own patterns of behavior. Studies show teachers perceive they give equal time to boys and girls when they actually give boys more time. Videotape your own classroom and count the number of interactions with boys and girls to check for balance of time given to each gender. Further, check the tape for the types of feedback given to see if the gender biased responses, discussed elsewhere in this chapter, are present. *The Sex Equity Handbook for Schools* gives some examples of how you can code for discrimination while watching classroom videotapes.[42]

Research indicates that teachers can change their communicative behaviors when sensitized to gender imbalances.[43] However, change is difficult and requires disciplined procedures, like learning to balance time spent with each group by alternately calling on boys and girls. Spender notes that even after training, when she *felt* as if she were calling on and responding to boys and girls equally, or perhaps even overcompensating and calling on girls more, the maximum time she ever spent with girls was "42% and on average 38%, and the minimum time with boys 58%. It is nothing short of a substantial shock to appreciate the discrepancy between what I *thought* I was doing and what I actually *was* doing.[44] Teachers also respond to girls' questions with terse answers, while the same question asked later in the same period by a boy will receive serious and lengthy consideration.[45] Teachers must unlearn these habits.

As you work towards balancing time spent with boys and girls, you should expect protest from the boys and be prepared to lead discussions on why these feelings occur and why gender-balancing is important. Spender explains that just as teachers unconsciously "feel" that two-thirds of the time should be spent with boys, so do students.

> It should not be surprising that the students should share a similar notion of fairness with their teachers, for we are all members of the same society which accords more significance to males. In the classroom where teachers were trying to allocate their time equally, their efforts did not go unnoticed by the

students, and despite the fact that the teachers were unsuccessful, and were able to spend only slightly more than one third of their time with the girls, many of the boys protested that slightly more than one third was unfair, and that they were missing out on their *rightful* share of teacher attention.[46]

Our patterns of male favoritism are so ingrained that balancing teacher-student interaction is more complicated than having good intentions – it requires training, planning, and periodic behavior checks. If your microteaching has not focused on gender-bias, you should request this training from your education department and methods teachers.

Second, gender-balance the examples used in your instructional units. Examine your textbooks and unit lesson plans. Are all the examples male-oriented? Are women invisible? Spender provides an analysis of the pervasiveness of women's "invisibility" as a function of male control of language, as well as a function of the focus in textbooks on male history:

> Men, for example, have defined what they do as work, and where women do not do the same things as men, they are classified as *not* working, regardless of the number of hours they spend engaged in physical chores. A woman who may spend more than twelve to fifteen hours per day (seven days a week) in cleaning, cooking and caring for children, who may have interrupted nights and demanding days in which there are no rest periods, can find herself saying "Oh, I don't work. I'm only a housewife." This demonstrates the male monopoly on meaning, for in the face of overwhelming evidence to the contrary, such women have learned to deny the realities of their own life (in which they work harder and longer than men in general, according to the UN statistics) and to take on the male definitions of the world in which the only *real* work that is performed is undertaken by men.[47]

Spender further notes that U.N. economic statistics only report for-hire "male" work, although women *do* the work which produces 60-80 percent of the world's food.

When preparing lessons, remember that women can be valued both for their success within the world of business and industry and within the larger social structure. Examples are not hard to create – we often hear about the "men" who pioneered the West; women also were there driving the wagons, plowing the fields, and dying. One can simply ask: What were the lives of these women like? In public speaking units, examples can be drawn from women speakers like Barbara Jordan, Sojourner Truth, or local political figures. In interpersonal or listening units, you can gender balance classroom examples by showing both men and women in a variety of roles and occupations. A doctor or scientist should be named "Jane" as well as "John"; a nurse can be named "Bill" rather than always "Betsy."

In general, oppose the assumption that "women's work" is unimportant simple because it is done by women. If you, as the teacher, do not gender-balance, you are helping to deny women their own experience, "to accept men's definitions of them as inferior, to believe that they are less valuable, and to collaborate in the business of keeping women off the record. And the dependence of one sex, emotionally and financially, on the other, gets constructed."[48]

Third, gender balance language usage and terms. "Man" and "mankind" can be replaced with "people" or humanity." A "gentleman's agreement" becomes a "mutual understanding." Instead of calling the class "you guys," refer to them as "students" or "people." De-genderize masculine and feminine terminologies by not giving gender to cars, boats, or animals. Hence, "she is a beautiful boat" becomes "the boat is beautiful"; "the horse ate his oats" becomes the "the stallion ate his meal" or "the horse ate its oats." Use parallel terminology. If you would not refer to men as "boys" do not refer to women as "girls" (suggesting females never become mature adults). If you would not refer to a doctor as male, do not preface a female's occupation with "woman" ("woman dentist" suggests it is remarkable that a woman could become a dentist).[49]

Fourth, avoid implicit as well as overt gender or racial put-downs. It is bad instructional technique to avoid recognizing the attempts of any group to ask questions, to look surprised when a minority student gets a right answer, or to give feedback to women based primarily on appearance or neatness. We must become more sensitive to overt gender stereotyping. A friend recently heard a high school principal respond to her daughter's interest in occupations that involved travel by suggesting she become an airline stewardess. The administrator only recognized that her comments underrated the student's potential when the parent listed off pilot, military officer, business executive, translator, and several other, higher status, occupations that require travel.

It is also bad instructional technique to allow males to abuse females verbally. Some may excuse systemic vilification of girls as a normal phase that boys go through of hating girls.[50] Clearly, verbal abuse is "normal" only if one is learning white-male superiority.[51] And the "phase" boys go through may be solidifying the attitudes which permit later spousal abuse at home and sexual harassment in the workplace. Permitting these behaviors implicitly condones them. Teachers must develop the same sensitivity, recognition, and responses to sexual harassment that we have developed to racial slurs.

Fifth, do not allow sexist or racist humor. Jokes which are at the expense of women, men, or ethnic groups must be negatively reinforced. It will be necessary to take time in class to discuss how racist and sexist humor victimizes particular groups of people. Jenkins elaborates on more subtle forms of gender-biased humor. An example of sexist humor is the male instructor who smiles and says he "didn't hear a question because he was distracted," as he drools at an attractive student (suggesting the student's primary role in life is sex-object) or makes a joke with the rest of the class about topics like rape, affirmative action, girls' sports, etc. This "humor" demeans all women and suggests serious topics are trivial and funny. Jenkins suggests the teacher use student laughter at serious topics as a springboard for discussion, by saying something like:

"I noticed that some of you laughed when I brought up the topic of sexual harassment. Why do you think such laughter occurs?" or "I'm noticing a lot of you laughing, even though this topic is very serious and/or tragic for a number of people. It is a little uncomfortable talking about things we don't usually discuss, isn't it?"[52]

Sixth, set and enforce rules about interruptions of other speakers. A no-interruption rule creates a new norm and helps males unlearn the gender biased habit that males may freely interrupt females (suggesting anything a female says is not important). An interruption rule can be introduced as an integral part of a "Listening" or "Interpersonal Communication" unit, or be introduced as a general rule of communicative competence.

Seventh, ensure that girls get as much time with equipment as boys and that you do not fall into the pattern of "doing tasks for" girls and letting boys experiment for themselves.[53]

Eight, structure a unit in public speaking classes on powerless speech. Women and other historically powerless individuals use more of what has become labeled "powerless speech."[54] These credibility robbing speech patterns include: hedges/qualifiers ("Kinda" or "I guess"), hesitation forms ("uh," "um" "you know"), tag questions (ending a sentence with "isn't it" or other tagged-on questions to seek confirmation),[55] and disclaimers ("I don't know much about this but . . .") Johnson suggests showing students a demonstration tape which presents a message in powerless speech and then repeats the message without the powerless verbal behaviors.[56] Discussion can follow on what makes speech more or less credible, what contexts we are more likely to use powerless speech in, and how we can make our speeches more credible by eliminating low power behaviors.

Ninth, develop a support group of teachers and/or parents. Because gender-balancing alters the power structure perpetuated through gender stereotyping, some hostile response is inevitable.[57]. While negative responses may be mitigated by showing how gender stereotyping hurts males,[58] protests will abound. Help yourself in meeting the challenges of gender-balancing by establishing a group of like-minded teachers and parents who can support each other, provide an environment for practicing new skills, and develop strategies to cope with adversity.

Conclusion

Gender-balancing is more than a women's issue. Putting gender inequity on the social agenda and then doing something about it cuts to the core of the historic social patterns which advantaged some groups and disadvantaged others – assigning women and minorities to positions of low or no pay, low status, and low self-esteem. In a real sense, training for gender balance is "prosocial" training which builds more fully functioning adults.[59] Ayim asserts that gender-balancing is beneficial for society:

Neither logic nor the concept of a cohesive society are jarred by the possibility that everyone be adventurous, like math and science very much, not be excitable in a minor crisis, be skilled in business, be very direct, and be capable of making decisions easily. For one set of people to like math and science very much does not presuppose that another group dislike these disciplines, . . . For one set of people to be very gentle, very aware of the feelings of others, not to use harsh language, to express tender feelings with ease, and to enjoy art and literature does not demand another set of people defined by the opposite poles of these features. Furthermore, the greater the number of people in any society who possess these features, the happier and healthier such a society would be.[60]

The financial structure of modern society virtually requires women to work regardless of family structure. To survive in the modern workplace women and men must learn to work together. Teachers who do not actively work to counteract gender-bias in their classroom implicitly are supporting the existing discriminatory practices. In the case of gender bias, ignoring the problem perpetuates it – and does nothing to prepare students to be mature, competent adults. In the words of Rita Bornstein:

> As educators, your role is to ensure that your students break out of group stereotypes to explore and pursue a wide variety of school and life options. You will be strengthening individual students to resist the continuous bombardment of messages they receive regarding sex-, race-, and class-appropriate roles, jobs, and behavior.
>
> You have the opportunity to break the vicious circle that may otherwise imprison your students for the rest of their lives.[61]

Instructional Resources for Lesson Plans and Classroom Exercises

Chapman, A., ed. 1986. *Feminist Resources for Schools and Colleges: A Guide to Curricular Materials.* 3d ed. N.Y.: The Feminist Press.

Bate, B. 1988. *Communication and the Sexes.* N.Y.: Harper and Row, Publishers.

Berryman, C.L. 1979. Instructional Materials for Teaching a Course in "Women and Communication." *Communication Education* 28: 217-24.

Foster, J. 1983. *A Packet of Secondary Classroom Activities to Teach Students about Sex Role Stereotyping.* ERIC document ED 289 757. Available from Michigan Department of Education, Office for Sex Equity, P.O. Box 30008, Lansing, MI 48909.

Jenkins, M.M. 1983. *Removing Bias: Guidelines for Student-Faculty Communication.* Available from: Speech Communication Association, 5101 Blacklick Road, #E, Annandale, VA 22003.

Kaser, J.S., M.P. Sadker, and D.M. Sadker. 1982. *Guide for Sex Equity Trainers.* New York: Longman.

Parker, B. 1984. *Nonsexist Curriculum Development: Theory into Practice. The Handbook of the Curriculum Design Project at the University of Colorado. Boulder.* ERIC document ED 286 773. Available from Women Studies Program, University of Colorado, Boulder, CO 80309.

Sadker, M.P., and D.M. Sadker. 1982. *Sex Equity Handbook for Schools.* New York: Longman.

Smith, M.A., and S.K. Edson. 1980. Exercises: Experiential Learning About Sex Roles. In *Sex Equity in Education,* J. Stockard, et al, eds., 195-222. N.Y.: Academic Press.

Weiner, E.H., ed. 1980. *Sex Role Stereotyping in the Schools.* Washington, D.C.: National Education Association.

14

Multiculturalism and Educational Communication

John W. Friesen

"You've come a long way, baby," boasts the commercial message of its product, and to some extent this can also be said of multicultural education and communication. The development of the field has been gradual and not always in a productive fashion. At the present time there are a number of related challenges to be worked out which will decide the future direction to be taken. In fact, much of what passes for sound educational communication procedure in the field often lacks a solid theoretical base. Before these kinds of issues can be identified and discussed, however, it will be useful to show the relationship of multicultural education and communication to the "parental" concept of multiculturalism generally. This is perhaps best accomplished through a brief historical analysis.

Origins of the Concept

In Canada a formal policy on multiculturalism was formulated and inaugurated on October 8, 1971, but this action was not without significant political background. In fact, its origins may be traced as far back as the birthdate of the nation because the country's population has always been ethnically heterogeneous. Cultural clashes between societies began as early as the sixteenth and seventeenth centuries when the French entered. Those who remained in the Maritimes then differentiated themselves as Acadians and gradually developed a lifestyle all their own. In the West, the Metis nation emerged, preceded by the influx of the British and followed by the immigrants who made their way to the West.[3]

Finally, in the late nineteen sixties, after a lengthy and thorough time of study, the Federal Government's Royal Commission on Bilingualism and Biculturalism announced that Canada had *two* official languages and *two* official cultures. If the statement was intended to settle anything, its originators

177

were wrong. In fact, it *began* the process of analysis insofar as the identity of the nation was concerned, with many ethnocultural groups demanding "equal time." In 1972 the government established an office of Minister of State for Multiculturalism and the following year set up the Canadian Consultative Council on Multiculturalism.

Some writers have pointed out that the original policy on multiculturalism has built-in defects and unresolved difficulties.[3,16] In the first place, it is hardly possible to identify a nation through a series of cultural identities. Also, to foster such an arrangement hardly augers for national unity. Each ethnocultural community or subculture will have its own goals and value system and these are bound to clash at some point in time. The fact that the rights pertaining to cultural identity are enshrined in law makes little difference in reality because equality is difficult to guarantee in a scheme built of variations and even contradictions. Illustrations for this point are numerous. Consider the following: (1) the Aboriginal concept of land ownership versus the European notion of land title; (2) the Anabaptist (Mennonite, Amish, Quaker, etc) belief in pacifism versus public opinion in times of war; or (3) Hutterite communalism versus the Canadian farmer when it comes to land purchases. The fact is that most of these differences can be accommodated through negotiation and toleration but even that process is usually undertaken through institutional practices that are distinctly cultural in both origin and practice. Most Canadian institutions, particularly government and education are British in origin with some American influence, though they also reflect French impact further east. Inevitably conflicts are resolved on the basis of political power, and familiarity with established traditions within the power basis is certainly an advantage.[4]

Current federal programs in multiculturalism are ample in both scope and purpose, affecting five major programs: Cultural Development Program, Ethnic Histories, Canadian Ethnic Studies, Teaching of Official Languages, and Programs of the Federal Cultural Agencies.[8,21] The latter include activities and programs of such agencies as the National Film Board, the National Library, the Canadian Radio-Television Commission, the Canadian Broadcasting Corporation, the Canada Council, etc. Some of the activities funded through the Secretary of State are educational in nature and depend largely on the objectives and imagination of the body applying for funding.

Multicultural policies on the provincial level vary a great deal in nature and intensity. Some provincial governments have enacted legislation while others have stuck to the practice of sponsoring related events. The Province of Manitoba was first on the scene, establishing a multicultural policy in 1972; Saskatchewan followed two years later, and Alberta passed the Alberta Cultural Heritage Act in 1984. Ontario, meanwhile, established the Ontario Advisory Council on Multiculturalism in 1973 affecting such departments as Citizenship and Culture, Attorney-General, Community and Social Services, and Correctional Services etc.[29]

The Province of Quebec has refused to acknowledge the validity of the concept of multiculturalism, opting instead for interculturalism, as an appropriate reality for a nation with two official languages and two cultures. The policy's originators see Quebec as a distinct society within the nation and as a threatened minority which is not ready to give in to the surrounding assimilative forces. The New Brunswick policy is similar in orientation (reflecting the only truly bicultural area within the nation), and opting for the guarantee of equality, appreciation and preservation for all of its citizens.[5] At the far end of the scale is a reluctant Prince Edward Island, featuring a unicultural Anglo composition, and Newfoundland, which recognizes the validity of promoting multiculturalism through heritage language instruction, ethnic cooking and fiddle music.

It is difficult to underestimate the importance of establishing policy insofar as social justice is concerned, and this is particularly true of multiculturalism. The variations of cultural motif are immense, but the underlying rights and needs required by all Canadians are fairly consistent. When a close investigation of cultural expression is undertaken it will be discovered that there are greater commonalities among people, regardless of ethnic affiliation, than there are differences. The penchant of the media to sensationalize apparent human differences constitutes an unfortunate camouflage for the important fact that all people are very much part of the same human family.[27]

Governments are not always very quick in formalizing policy, and this has particularly been true with regard to multiculturalism. Sometimes this is because of the lack of speed in legislative "due process." Even then, there has been ample legislation in Canada to assure human rights in the various domains, including multiculturalism. The Federal Bill of Rights and the Canadian Charter of Rights and Freedoms are just two examples. The Canadian Multiculturalism Act of 1988 is more specific and promotes the principle that multiculturalism is a basic element of the Canadian heritage and identity. It also promotes the preservation and enhancement of heritage cultures and actively assists racial minority communities in overcoming discriminatory barriers. The latter function is particularly important because prejudicial treatment and discrimination are harder to handle without specific legislation to lean on in seeking to rectify injustices. Without the enshrinement of specific and comprehensive human rights in legislation, there is little certainty that equity will be achieved in this sector.

Improving Policy Implementation

Despite the virtues of pursuing equity in the multicultural sector, the endeavor has drawn more than its share of critics. One of the first was the late John Porter, one of Canada's leading sociologists. Porter saw multiculturalism as a fraud perpetuated by the British in order to maintain the present social order which he referred to as a "vertical mosaic." He therefore argued that recognition should not be given to cultural differences. Porter was joined by other scholars who described the multicultural policy as a hoax designed by the federal government to camouflage the fact that power is vested in the hands of the dominant Anglo culture, thus forcing other ethnic groups to continue their struggle for a recognition of their rights.[2] 1981).

Academics are not alone in raising questions about the formulation of multicultural policy. The media have also raised a number of emotionally-charged issues, e.g. that the promotion of multiculturalism amounts to offering only some citizens money for having an ethnic background. They have also contended that multiculturalism may contribute to ghetto-building and promote ethnocentrism if ethnocultural communities are encouraged to continue to practice their separate lifestyles apart from other citizens. Such separateness can also reduce the hope of Canada ever developing anything remotely approaching a nation. In fact, the country may eventually become so fragmented that it will be at best an agglomeration of ethnic principalities. It may be argued that a measure of criticism can be very healthy for an emerging field, helping its promulgators to clarify which ends to pursue and thus avoid duplication, contradiction or contrary purposes. However, those "contradictions" may be central to the functioning of a pluralist society because the needs of its component sectors will vary. The definition of pluralism implies divergency in either or both of structure and function. That which works in one arena may not auger well in another.

In applying the principle of pluralism to the Canadian scene it becomes evident that the nation is composed of a number of quite divergent communities, i.e. Aboriginal peoples, Charter nations (French and English), immigrant groups and newcomers. Each community cluster has special arrangements pertaining to their history and place in the nation. The Aboriginal peoples have the right of first occupancy and special legislation to protect their interests: granted that these interests have not been honored in the past, i.e. treaty rights and land claims. The Charter nations have set the format and procedures for most national institutions and still have control over them. The immigrant groups of the 1890-1914 period particularly were largely agricultural peoples (at least in the West), and although many of them have migrated to urban areas, their heritage identities are still evident in rural ghetto-like settlements across the prairies. People who have migrated to Canada in the last two decades (newcomers) have pretty much had to take what they could get in terms of any institutional adjustment to their needs, and only a minor ripple of flexibility has been evident in that sector. Possibly the most significant change has been with regard to schooling through the development of the English-as-a-second-language field. Other adjustments, while at first appearing to be of significant value to educational communication, may, on closer examination, reveal portentous challenge.

The Subsector of Multicultural Education

Definitions of multicultural education abound, but what they have in common is the observation that schooling is the institution best suited to undertake the fulfillment of the underlying mandate. Essentially, the mandate of multicultural education is twofold: to assist in the perpetuation of pluralism, (1) as a social goal; and, (2) as an individual right. This means that the school has the responsibility to teach about heritage cultures as a rightful component of Canadian society, and to make proper note of the contributions which the various heritages have made to the national culture. Students are to be taught to appreciate the cultural and ethnic diversity of the nation, and to learn that cultural diversity and individual choice are vital aspects of the western value system.[26]

The second part of the mandate has to do with the individual. For the past decade or so educators argued persuasively that if individuals are to develop to their full potential, they have a right in any learning setting to experience acceptance of themselves with all their strengths and weaknesses. Simultaneously they must also learn to see their peers as individuals having equal worth and dignity, regardless of *their* backgrounds.[26] 1986, 3-4). These objectives are to be reflected in the curriculum as well as with teaching strategies. Instructional materials are to be free of bias and stereotyping and must include information about the various heritages existent in the region and/or national makeup. Teaching methodologies should aim at promoting an enhanced self-concept on the part of the student, and seek to relate to human needs and feelings and attempt to maximize the creative powers of the student. When these objectives are fully operationalized, an enhanced student motivation will result. In this sense multicultural education becomes the teacher's special talisman – a boon to improved learning. By the way, the needs of teachers should also be taken into account in this kind of reform. Their situation is unfortunately too often neglected when innovations in educational communication are envisaged, and this is unfortunate. The teacher is still the key to effective education.[7]

When the multicultural phenomenon in educational communication first gained momentum in North America, the initial activities were of the "fun-food-festival-and-finery" variety. Today there is *still* too much of this kind of enterprise in the sense that it purports to promote the development of tolerance and understanding. As exercises for entertainment or interest, the sponsorship of ethnic potluck dinners, songs and dances has certain value; however, eating together or participating in a sing-song will do little to create an attitude of empathy or understanding. When these events come to a conclusion, most people will still be oblivious to the meaning of cultural diversity. In the earlier stages of the development of multicultural education it seemed to be a good idea to sponsor these activities as a form of communication and awareness-building, but it is now time to get down to serious business.[7]

One of the more established practices in multicultural education has been the identification of curriculum themes and teaching procedures appropriate to multicultural concerns in the classroom.[22,14,28,12,15] While the resultant research has unearthed very insightful endeavors in educational communication, there is still too much emphasis on practical concerns to the exclusion of philosophical deliberations. It is one thing to employ good teaching techniques, but it is quite another to be able to rationalize the underlying assumptions pertaining to their selection and employment. By taking the time to indulge in a little of the too much neglected process of "philosophizing," educators may not only have the benefit of being good practitioners, they may also be able to articulate the justification of those practices. This process has more than a singular advantage and this chapter is not intended to launch a campaign to make teachers become philosophers. More importantly, a rigorous analysis of any envisaged educational adjustment should provide awareness of the complexity of its underlying premises. In light of the frequent changes constantly being proposed for education generally (an enterprise which is always justified as an attempt to meet contemporary needs), a fairly lengthy agenda should soon emerge.

In the interests of limited space, and because of the urgency of the need for their proper implementation, two specific frontiers will be discussed on which teachers must forge a meaningful multicultural path. These have to do with (1) operationalizing cultural diversity in the classroom; and, (2) enhancing the concept of individuality in that context. In each instance it may be helpful first to consider each objective in the context of multiculturalism generally and then bring the discussion specifically to the realm of multicultural education and communication.

(1) *The Conundrum of Cultural Diversity*

Like the nature of a pluralist society itself, the idea of providing equality and fair treatment for all citizenry is a many-faceted and complicated objective. That subject is currently also the target of philosophical analysis. This is as it should be. In the first instance, government policy-makers and politicians who seek to implement those policies, are often accused of passing out political plums to specific ethnocultural groups who apply for and who manage successfully to obtain funding for their projects. To be quite blunt, when this happens it is probably not too much out of sync with the way politicians normally function. After all, the job of a politician is to play to the constituency; the squeaky wheel gets the grease. Of course, If such funding is merely for political purposes, i.e. to assure re-election, (and if such can be proven), there is little need for further discussion. If, however, the funding is allocated on "valid" grounds, its practice may be deserving of examination. For example, were the funds applied for through approved channels? Were they allocated on an equalitarian basis? Were they expeditiously expended? Essentially this line of scrutiny also probes the feasibility of seeking *seriously* to promote cultural patterns in Canada which may differ significantly from that of the mainstream. It is also necessary to raise the caution that to fail to support the practice of diversity (including financially), is to fall prey to, or at least be accused of promoting cultural assimilation.

The lending of strong support for culturally diverse practices logically raises the question of the degree to which such should be fostered. At what point should support be softened or withdrawn altogether? Should ethnocultural groups be hindered if their cultural practices are contrary to populist social and moral practices? Is the criterion of possible damage to the "national interest" the ultimate criterion? Is it the *only* criterion? On what grounds can the national interest be identified or measured?

There is a psychological question aspect to this deliberation. For example, people who emigrate to Canada are sometimes led to believe that they will be free to practice their way of life in an uninhibited fashion after establishing themselves in this country. They are expected to believe such a policy because it is promulgated by spokespersons sometimes just a little too anxious for a population increase even if it is attained on dubious grounds? A look at the Canadian scene shows that the extent to which immigrating cultural practices can be maintained is considerable. (Note at least the seeming tolerance toward the isolationist practices of Hutterites, Amish, the Old Believers, Chinatown, the Sikh community, etc.). There are even some cultural groups in Canada who maintain an active "homeland concern" after taking up residence in Canada. This finds expression in group activities which support a variety of programs in their country of origin. In some instances monies are raised and sent back to the homeland to "support the revolution," or help with other such causes.[9] If the dedication to other nations' causes is tolerated by Canadian citizens, it would appear that very few limits are placed on the function of cultural diversity within our national parameters. Undoubtedly there are also many Canadians who have serious misgivings about the liberality of our cultural pluralism.

Critics sometimes caution that a policy of unrestricted pluralism encourages the development of cultural ghettos. This, theoretically, allows the formation of exclusive communities that function without particular regard for the national interest. Hutterite colonies are frequently targeted in this kind of discussion, and evidence shows that their preference for isolation may, in fact, not be tolerated. Legal undertakings against them in Alberta, for example, have been extensive. Legislation against their land purchases in the past were no doubt propelled by citizens who either misunderstand or were intimidated by their communal lifestyle. A host of related suspicions have also been popularized, most of them entirely unfounded. The myths about Hutterites include that they do not pay income taxes, they enjoy the luxury of publically-supported private schools, and they do no business in nearby small towns, thereby forcing the towns to an early death, etc. All of these myths are entirely without foundation.[24]

Several decades ago, when the population of their colonies was rising rapidly (assisted by the Hutterites' disdain for birth control), there was fear in the agricultural community that the Hutterites would eventually take over that industry. After all, agriculture is the one industry in which they prefer to engage. In 1947, in response to public concern, the Social Credit Government of Alberta passed a law that restricted Hutterites from buying additional farmland. The law stipulated that the Hutterian Brethren were permitted to buy a maximum of 6,400 acres for each new colony only if the site was at least forty miles from an existing colony. The law was amended in 1960 to omit the forty mile clause but allowing no sales to Hutterites without a hearing before a community property control board *and* approval by the Legislative Cabinet.[10] The law has since been appealed because the Human Rights Act, subsequently passed by a Conservative provincial government, rendered the Communal Properties Act obsolete.[8] At the same time a watch-dog committee was established to determine how much land the Hutterites would buy when they were again allowed to do so. The Brethren *did* buy a higher proportion of land in the next five years than they did in the years preceding the Act passed, but nothing further was done to hinder their expansion. In the final analysis, the Bill of Rights prevailed. In retrospect, it seems somewhat ironic that during this time of restriction, people who were Canadian citizens were actually immobilized in seeking to expand their farms while foreign companies were unrestricted in purchasing any amounts of farmland in the province. This is an illustration of how quickly political restrictions can be formulated when independence and/or eccentricity is/are seen to violate the principle of the nation's (province's), best interest. In other words, under specific cirumstances, even an innocuous act like buying land can be interpreted as threatening to "the national interest."

A second example of the same restrictive attitude has been put forth by Chief John Snow of the Goodstoney Band of the Stoney Indian tribe near Calgary. Snow has argued that the desire to provide land in Alberta for incoming settlers at the turn of this century motivated the government to "dream up reasons" to limit the lifestyle of the Indian people. The government accused the Indians of killing too much game and of not making use of their lands for agricultural purposes. This justified taking away their land. Snow pointed out that a people who lived in harmony with nature for many thousands of years were not about to change their philosophy so radically that they would suddenly abuse the balance of nature by killing off wildlife in excessive amounts. In relation to land use, the Stoney people were hunters and fishermen. Naturally they did not *farm* the land.[25] Again it becomes evident that the justifications manufactured for the purpose of limiting minority lifestyle can be "creative," but unkind.

The Classroom Context

The context of the classroom constitutes a more confined arena in which to test the viability and communicability of multicultural principles, particularly the concept of "encouragement of diversity." Translated into the learning situation, this objective juxtaposes the two intents of: 1) helping students to become aware of their individual origins and those of others; and learning to accept themselves (and others), with all their strengths and weaknesses; and, 2) teaching students to understand the heterogeneous peoples of the country, who share universal concerns, yet add the unique spice of diversity to our common culture.[26] A brief amplification of the two corollaries may serve to elucidate this point.

The extent to which diversity can be communicated in the classroom has logistic limits. These pertain to both student behavior and teacher expectations.

For example, it is easy to make the claim that current teacher training programs provide teachers with a flexible philosophy of education, and that such an approach takes individuality into account. If this is believed, experience will show that even such an orientation is insufficient to anticipating the circumstances which teachers can experience in relation to variations in student behavior brought about by their cultural origins and allegiances.

There are many instances of unique or "unorthodox" student behavior which a teacher may misunderstand and think to be inappropriate, and act accordingly. This means that the teacher may discipline the student, ignore the behavior in question, or even pass judgment on the student. The resultant communication between teacher and student may actually hinder the learning process or even do damage to a student's self-esteem. Untrained in the nuances of a specific culture, a teacher may misinterpret the actions of a student and deem them to be disrespectful, rude or even belligerent, when in effect the student may only be acting out culturally-learned behavior cues.[15] For example, a teacher in a Native community may find older students helping younger classmates with their answers and decide that such behavior comprises or borders on cheating. In the context of an Indian community, however, it is quite natural for this kind of thing to happen; in fact, it is *expected* that older brothers and sisters will help out.

A primary difficulty in seeking to accommodate individual pupil needs, derived from a cultural context, emanates from the educator's lack of preparation in knowing how to communicate interculturally and provide effective intercultural teaching. Too many teachers still do not comprehend how important personal background is in explaining why individuals behave the way they do. Without knowing how to go about the process of understanding a particular cultural context, teachers are at least partially handicapped in trying to assist the student in the process of self-discovery and enhancing self-image. By the way, this is true whether or not the "off-norm" behavior of the student is culturally-motivated or otherwise motivated.

The bulk of a teacher's time is taken up with the responsibilities of the teaching mandate, i.e. teaching the three "R's" and providing information about citizen rights and responsibilities, etc. This fact does not have a direct bearing on the question of teacher facility in handling culturally-related student behaviors, but it *is* a fact of the profession. After all, each pupil has to be taught that all citizens must obey the law, pay taxes of various kinds, respect individual property, and, if they want to be employed, speak at least one of the two official languages.[18] Charged with this agenda, there is very little time left over for the teacher to decipher much information about individual students. This does not excuse the teacher, of course, but it does comprise somewhat of an explanation. Even the talisman promise of multicultural education may be too much for the weary teacher to appreciate at times; in other words, "what's the use" of such information if there is insufficient time to operationalize it?

The extent to which cultural diversity may function as a significant educational communication factor in the classroom has realistic limitations. Aside from drawing attention to selected ethnocultural holidays, costumes, foods, etc., or implementing a field trip to a local Indian reserve, a Hutterite colony or Chinatown, multiculturalism is still a limited curricular theme. Students who have learning problems related to their cultural background, e.g. recently arrived immigrants, are often assigned to E.S.L. classes, away from the regular classroom. Teaching the regular curriculum and promoting national values simply take up too much time to care for the "irregular" student. In addition, as schooling continues to take up additional family and social responsibilities, e.g. family life and sex education, consumer education and health education (including AIDS) etc., "cultural" elements become a lower-end-of-the-scale priority. Perhaps this deficiency could be reduced somewhat if the realization that multiculturalism very fundamentally relates to basic human rights were comprehended. A few explanatory comments may serve to elucidate this observation.

(2) *Promoting Human Rights and Equality*

The quest for equality and the guarantee of human rights is a longstanding venture in Canada. The lateness with which the vote was extended to females and Aboriginal peoples is a good case in point. To some eyes, the newly adopted Canadian Charter of Rights and Freedoms is supposed to change all that. True, it also has implications for the multicultural scene since it affects virtually every sector of Canadian life. In the final application of the Charter, however, it may be the courts which dictate the meaning of the inherent principles.[17] The fact that education is a provincial matter may muddy the process of applying the Charter somewhat even though some will argue that certain rights are universal. These include the right to learn, the right of access to state institutions that promote learning, and the right to pursue learning commensurate with one's abilities and personal needs.[23]

A backward look usually furnishes ample fuel to depict the shortcomings of a people, and the case of the banishment of the Japanese Canadians during World War II is useful here. Berger argues that even the entrenchment of the Canadian Charter of Rights and Freedoms is no absolute guarantee that such an act might not be repeated. Berger points out the *non obstante* clause of the Charter and warns that in the final analysis, . . . it is difficult to say how often legislators may exercise their power to override the Charter provisions."[1] As comforting as the existence of the Charter may be to members of particular cultural backgrounds, there is no statute that can be drafted that will guarantee the complete protection of minorities. In a real sense, every individual is "at the mercy of his/her peers."

Probably the most comprehensive work on multicultural rights to date is by Evelyn Kallen, and covers the gamut in terms of legal, biological, political, etc. aspects.[1] Kallen addresses the question of group versus individual rights in Canada, clarifying that the Charter has its greatest impact with reference to individual rights; at the group level, Canada's ethnic "enclaves" cannot lay claim to the same kinds of collective rights. The three groups she makes reference to include the Charter nations of French and English, the Aboriginal peoples, and the immigrants. Each group stakes its claims on a different kind of national transformation, and to some degree, the three sets of claims are in conflict.[13]

A common concern on the part of Canadians who seek justice through the guarantees of the Charter of Rights and Freedoms usually do so on the grounds of having been the object of discrimination. Often the process is so subtle that overt action is required to stop the flow. Traditionally, institutions have adopted three approaches: (1) ignore racial or ethnic cleavages and enforce universal and individual merit; (2) seek to "restore" balance by instituting quotas and affirmative action type programs; or (3) steer a midway course between the first two alternatives. While the latter approach generally avoids the exacerbation of interethnic differences or the stigmatizing of certain groups, it does further the reality of group inequities and perpetuates the problem of ethnic and racial particularism.[19]

In a real sense the Canadian Charter of Rights and Freedoms does not guarantee multicultural rights. The Charter has no specific powers in that regard. The central difficulty is that laws that violate human rights cannot be overridden. Only rarely, therefore, was the 1960 Federal Bill of Rights employed as an effective ruling.[23] 1985, 10). In addition, even an entrenched Charter can prove to be ineffective when the spirit and enthusiasm are not there to sustain it. As it stands, elements of the Charter are "interpretive." They do not confer rights, but rather allow a behavior translation which, in the case of multiculturalism, would be consistent with the preservation and enhancement of the multicultural heritage of Canada.

The Educational Context

A more limited spatial and philosophical arena in which to wrestle with the challenge of communicating equality is the classroom. Most multicultural programs in this context barely scratch the surface of the underlying principle – to promote respect for individuality and basic human rights. Related school programs still feature foods, festivals and finery as fundamental components. Often school staffs will devote an evening, a school day or even a week to sponsor special celebrations. Potluck dinners sporting ethnic dishes, dress-up parties and traditional dances of various kinds prevail across the country. The result of having participated in such activities is probably a full stomach, the enjoyment of a bit of entertainment or even a temporary feeling of goodwill, but any lasting value is dubious. Basically these programs draw attention to the "surface" differences among ethnocultural communities but little more than that.

Attempts to give multicultural education a more meaningful thrust in terms of honoring human rights has emanated from several sectors. In the first instance, information about the various cultural communities is readily accessible today. Multicultural clubs and centres abound, many of them financially supported by the various levels of government. These institutions try to provide information about cultural uniquenesses and specialties, and attempt to promote intercultural understanding through contact. Of course, many of their activities are of a lighter nature in terms of promoting tolerance and understanding, but efforts are underway to develop more depth. Leaders in these communities have also made themselves available as public relations personnel and as guest speakers for a variety of forums. They have lobbied governments for more significant programs. Consciousness-raising has become a high priority item on the agenda, and the nature of resultant programs has been restricted only by the imagination. Still, a dilemma remains. How can multicultural programs in educational communication be designed that more nearly fulfill the mandate of assuring equity for groups and individuals?

Attention is again focussed on the school. Here multicultural programs in educational communication are being designed that seek to cultivate attitudes of understanding and respect for the person. The emphasis in this process is on "cultural background" but that is only one means by which to operationalize the desired goal. It is only one avenue. Educators must never lose sight of the truth that every person is unique and this reality will be manifested in many different ways. The objective of illustrating and trying to teach respect for human individuality, then, can also be achieved through other kinds of emphases as well, e.g. noting physical differences (height, weight, shape, hair color – or lack of it, etc.), differences in perception and taste (or even minor eccentricities) and differences in communication habits and styles. What needs to be recognized is not so much the fact of individuality, but the implications thereof. We need to concentrate on outlining the parameters which we will heed when we acknowledge differences and try to accommodate them. Accommodation in this case implies the recognition and granting of full human rights to every individual. In a multicultural context of educational communication this may even imply furnishing instruction (even counselling), in a student's native language. A glossing over of the truth that everyone is entitled to basic human rights (in this context, the right to sound learning opportunities), by any approach will jeopardize the whole enterprise. When multicultural educators push out of proportion the celebration of differences via fun-foods-festivals-and-finery, or practice those exclusively, they do the whole business of education a major disservice.

School programs which underscore basic human rights involve such concepts as communication and caring and even confrontation. To use just one example, in some educational circles the phenomenon of the field trip has been extolled as an excellent vehicle for teaching/learning about other cultures. Kehoe cautions that intercultural contact per se can be quite damaging. People who hold antagonistic attitudes toward a certain ethnic group hold reduced negative stereotypes if they have less communication with the group in question.[14] Ijaz and Ijaz postulate that when intergroup contact is undertaken, a specific set of criteria need to be met if enhanced understanding is to be realized. These include:

1. communicators must see each other as having equal status;
2. communicators should jointly engage in activities that involve superordinate goals and necessitate cooperation;
3. there should be a general pleasantness about the situation;
4. there should be institutional support for the venture; and,
5. the "visiting group" should communicate with high-status members of the group or community being visited.[11] Ijaz, 1981).

In a further consideration of the required criteria for successful intercultural communication, Mountjoy has drawn attention to the necessity of extensive pre-and post-contact discussion and counselling. These sessions allow the participants to integrate the experiences into a positive and developmental model rather than reinforcing negative stereotypes or creating new ones.[20]

Based on the foregoing, it would seem that the efficacy of potluck dinners and festivities will not substitute as legitimate options in multicultural education. They comprise an inadequate route for promoting intercultural understanding and cannot substitute for procedures that foster equality in human rights. Even tried-and-true techniques, such as field trips, are subject to specific conditions. Two things may therefore be concluded: (1) multicultural education should function within, or at least keep in view, the parameters of a "greater" pedagogical truth, namely the responsibility of respecting basic human rights; and, (2) when multicultural activities and programs *are* initiated, care should be taken to ensure that they accomplish the goals of the enterprise. When these principles are put into practice, multicultural educators will reap the full benefit of the "talisman effect" of multicultural education. Having experienced an acceptance of themselves as unique human beings, both students and teachers will communicate new dimensions of human potentiality within themselves.

That, after all, is what education is supposed to be about.

Noted References

[1]Berger, Thomas R. (1987). "The banished Japanese Canadians," in *Ethnic Canada: Identities and Inequities,* Edited by Leo Driedger, Toronto: Copp Clark, 374-394.

[2]Burnet, Jean. (1981). "Multiculturalism: ten years later," *The History and Social Science Teacher,* Vol. 17, No. 1, Fall, 1-6.

[3]Burnet, Jean. (1984). "Myths and Multiculturalism," in Ronald J. Samuda, et. al. (eds). *Multiculturalism in Canada: Social and Educational Perspectives,* Toronto: Allyn and Bacon, 18-29.

[4]Dahlie, Jorgen and Tissa Fernando. (1981). *Ethnicity, Power and Politics in Canada,* Toronto: Methuen.

[5]Driedger, Leo. (1978). *The Canadian Ethnic Mosaic,* Toronto: McClelland and Stewart.

[6]Friesen, John W. (1977). People, Culture and Learning, Calgary: Detselig Enterprises. Friesen, John *When Cultures Clash: Case Studies in Multiculturalism,* Calgary: Detselig Enterprises.

[7]Friesen, John W., Karen B. de Vries and Esha R. Chaudhuri. (1986). *Multicultural Education Journal,* handbook no. 2, Vol. 4, No. 1, Edmonton: Alberta Teachers' Association.

[8]Friesen, John W. (1987). *Reforming the Schools – for Teachers,* Lanham, Md.: University Press of America.

[9]Glazer, Nathan. (1980). "Toward a sociology of small ethnic groups: a discourse and discussion," *Canadian Ethnic Studies,* Vol. XII, No. 2, 1-16.

[10]Hostetler, John A. and Gertrude Enders Huntingdon. (1967). *The Hutterites in North America,* New York: Holt, Rinehart and Winston.

[11]Ijaz, M. Ahmed and Helene Ijaz. (1981). A cultural program for changing racial attitudes," *The History and Social Science Teacher,* Vol. 17, No. 1, Fall, 17-20.

[12]Ijaz, M. Ahmed and Helene Ijaz. (1982). "We can change our children's racial attitudes," *Multiculturalism,* Vol. V, No. 2, 11-17.

[13]Kallen, Evelyn. (1982) *Ethnicity and Human Rights in Canada,* Toronto: Gage.

[14]Kehoe, John. (1981). "Effective Tools for Combatting Racism in the School," *Multiculturalism,* Vol. 4, No. 3, 3-39.

[15]Kehoe, John. (1984). *Multicultural Canada: Considerations for Schools, Teachers, and Curriculum,* Vancouver: Faculty of Education, University of British Columbia.

[16]Lupul, Manoly R. (1982). "The Political implementation of multiculturalism," *Journal of Canadian Studies,* Vol. 17, No. 1, 93-102.

[17]McLeod, Keith A. (1985). "Editorial," *Multiculturalism,* Vol. IX, No. 1, 2.

[18]McLeod, Keith A. (1989). (Ed.). *Canada and Citizenship Education,* Toronto: Canadian Education Association.

[19]Moodley, Kogila A. (1987). "The predicament of racial affirmative action," in *Ethnic Canada: Identities and Inequities,* edited by Leo Driedger, Toronto: Copp Clark, 395-407.

[20]Mountjoy, Terry. (1987). "The contact hypothesis," *Saskatchewan Multicultural Magazine,* Vol. 6, No. 3, Fall, 4.

[21](n.a.). (1976). "Federal departments and agencies responsible for implementing the multicultural policy," *Canadian Library Journal,* Vol. 33, 227-30.

[22]Pasternak, Michael G. (1979). *Helping Kids Learn Multi-cultural Concepts,* Champaign, Ill.: Research Press.

[23]Ray, Douglas. (1985). "Human Rights in Education," *Multiculturalism,* Vol. VI, No. 1, 10-12.

[24]*Report on Communal Property.* (1972). Edmonton: Alberta Select Committee of the Assembly (Communal Property), Government of Alberta.

[25]Snow, John. (1967). *These Mountains are Our Sacred Places,* Toronto: Samuel Stevens.

[26]Tiedt, Pamela L. and Iris M. Tiedt. (1986). *Multicultural Teaching: a Handbook of Activities, Information, and Resources,* Boston: Allyn and Bacon.

[27]Van den Berghe, Pierre. (1981). *The Ethnic Phenomenon,* New York: Elsevier.

[28]Wagner, Hilmar. (1981). "Working With the Culturally Different Student," *Education,* Vol. 101, No. 4, Summer, 252-58.

[29]Welch, Robert. (1981). "Ontario Multicultural Policy," *Multiculturalism,* Vol. IV, No. 3, 23-24.

Section Three

Organizational Communication in Education

15

Organizational Communication: Implications for the Educator

Frank D. Oliva

Introduction

Achieving Objectives Through Communication

Human beings organize to achieve their goals and objectives. This includes defining and arranging positions, roles and functions in complex relationships. Organizations consist of people engaged in concerted action of elaborate and complex human activity who strive to accomplish some particular human endeavor. The basis for this coordinated human endeavor is communication. As Daniel Katz and Robert Kahn, two prominent organizational psychologists, observed, "Communication . . . is the very essence of a social system or organization".[31] Probably the most graphic illustration of this, in a negative sense, is the complete disruption in Genesis of the building of the Tower of Babel through the imposition and rapid development of unique language patterns on those engaged in the construction.

The Effectiveness of Communication in Organizations.

Today corporate leaders frequently call for improved communication within their organizations hoping, as a result, for an increase in productivity. One of the most recent proclamations of this nature was made in 1986 by Roger Smith, Chairman of the Board of General Motors Corporation. In an address to a group of Columbus businesspeople in Ohio he attested that "good communication is the key to organizational effectiveness; if people in organizations communicate better their organizations will work better."[9] However, not all scholars of communication agree with this position. Thomas Martin Jr, President of the Illinois Institute of Technology claims that the inevitable result of improved and enlarged communication between different levels in the hierarchy is a vastly increased area of misunderstanding." A European scholar, Ormo Wiio, as reported in Daniels and Spiker,[9] states: "The more communication there is, the more difficult it is for communication to succeed."

Organizational Communication

Historical Overview

The study of organizations and the role of communication within them has been ongoing for most of this century. Consequently, when communication scholars began to turn their attention to the study of organizations they initially borrowed heavily from the concepts developed by such fields of study as organizational psychology, organizational sociology and organizational behavior. Thus, in a real sense the study of organizational communication began as an interdisciplinary field of study. Researchers in communication have, in recent years, endeavored to focus on human communication.[9] In opposition to this focus, management theorists Hersey and Blanchard in their book *Management of Organizational Behaviour: Utilizing Human Resources* have maintained that the means to motivating employees to higher production levels is based on motivation theories in which the behavior of individuals is explained through the satisfaction of physical, psychological or social needs.[22]

The role of communication, they believe, is a means of motivating organizational members or that it is merely one of several peripheral contributing types of motivated behavior in an organization leading to organizational effectiveness.

The Role and Definition of Organizational Communication.

How important a role does organizational communication play in the effective operation of an organization? Goldhaber reported that "organizational communication has been called the life-blood of the organization; the glue that binds the organization; the oil that smooths the organization's functions; the thread that ties the system together; the force that pervades the organization and the binding agent that cements all relationships." Further he has detected three common strands from the many approaches to, and definition and perceptions of, organizational communication:

1. Organizational communication occurs within a complex open system which is influenced by and influences its environment,

2. Organizational communication involves messages and their flow, purpose, direction, and media and,

3. Organizational communication involves people and their attitudes, feelings, relationships, and skills" Consequently he defines organizational communication as follows: "Organizational communication is the process of creating and exchanging messages within a network of interdependent relationships to cope with environmental uncertainty."[16]

Skills needed in Communicating within Organizations

The development of perceptions relating to organizational communication studies which led to this definition are included in: the flow of information within an organization[32]; the "skills" of communicating in business and the professions (eg. speech making, listening, interviewing, counselling, selling, persuading); the flow of data that serve the organization's communication and intercommunication in some manner[42]; "speech communication," as opposed to written communication, within a system of overlapping and interdependent groups[7]; and communication skills such as listening, speaking, writing, interviewing and discussing within the fields of organizational structure and motivation.[21] More recently the field of organizational communication has been perceived to include not only the formal but the informal communication within the organization.[18,47,20] Finally, the perception of the scope and extent of organizational communication has developed to include interaction between management and the organization's employees and external-publics.[3]

Recent Theoretical Developments

Researchers in recent years have become concerned that the field of organizational communication has become fragmented and disorganized.[9] Arising out of a sociological model of organizations developed by Burnell and Morgan, Putnam classified various approaches to the study of organizational communication. Burnell and Morgen's model, which follows, divides organizations into four perspectives. The horizontal continuum represents views of reality ranging from objective to subjective. The vertical continuum of order ranges from regulation to radical change. The four quadrants then represent four basic perspectives of organizations: functionalism, interpretivism, radical structuralism and radical humanism.[40]

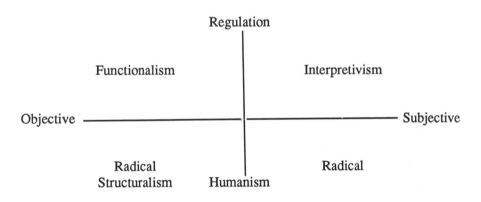

Figure 1. View of Organizational Reality and Order in Four Perspectives on Organizational Communication

Functionalists and radical structuralists, although differing in their views of order, take an objective view of reality. Interpretivists and radical humanists take a subjective view of reality. Radical structuralists and radical humanists endorse fundamental change in the existing order of organizations while functionalists and interpretivists prefer a regulative view of order.

Functionalism

Functionalism continues to be the dominant perspective in organizational communication studies but it has developed from a traditional form into a very different contemporary form. Traditional functionalists regarded organizations as machines and communication in those organizations was perceived in a formal and machine-like process. Communication effectiveness, in this view, involved two conditions:

1. the process of message sending and receiving are both reliable and accurate and,

2. the message receiver understands and responds to the message in the way the sender intended.

Contemporary functionalists have changed their view of reality to a more subjective stance in that not only are the concrete aspects of the organization important but so are the ways the organizational members perceive and subjectively experience organizational communication (Falcrone and Werner, 1978). However, the functionalist researcher usually wishes to understand the organization members' perceptions of reality in terms that the researcher defines. The contemporary functionalists view of order allows for change in the organization either for the improvement of organizational effectiveness or to reduce power inequalities.[39]

Interpretivism

The interpretivist regards organizations as cultures which are subjective rather than objective, emerging from the shared experiences of the people who comprise it.[38] Organizational reality is socially constructed through communication.[40] The interpretivist researcher endeavors to measure this reality not in the terms he defines but from the frame of reference of the organizational members. In addition the interpretivist scholar is interested in the symbols and meanings involved in the organizational behavior leading to socially constructed realities. Proceeding from illustrations and stories of organizational members' experiences, the interpretivist researcher analyzes and describes the themes which reveal, for example, the relationship between management's communication style and employee communication. The interpretivist's goal is to reveal those communicative activities that occur in a variety of settings to produce the unique character of the organization. 1987). The functionalist's approach, on the other hand, would be to measure these two conditions and statistically analyze those measurements.

Radical humanists and radical structuralists differ significantly on their views of reality but both begin with the assumption that at least some of the features in most organizations are inherently undesirable, oppressive and harmful. Therefore, fundamental changes are necessary.

Radical Humanism

Radical humanists locate the source of this oppression in systems of language and meaning. An example of this is that sexual discrimination of women in organizational circles results from a language which demeans and debases women. Common ways of talking about women influences ways of thinking about, and ultimately acting towards, women.

Radical Structuralism

Radical structuralists attribute oppression, on the other hand, to power differences and inequalities that exist in the design of the organizational structure. They would argue that discrimination against women is a result of, not only language problems, but also physical segregation and isolation from sources of power. However, both radical humanism and radical structuralism are relatively uninfluencial currents of thought in organizational communication. This does not mean that their viewpoints should be ignored for they offer many valuable insights about the process of communication in organizations.

Although interpretivism is also a minority view of organizational communication it has gained adherents rapidly because of the following two major sources of dissatisfaction with functionalist views:

1. the disorganized and fragmented state of the field during the 1960's and 1970's and,
2. the managerial bias of the functionalist's views.

Interpretivism is seen to present a serious alternative to the traditional concepts and methods of functionalist social science. The question is not which of these perspectives is best but rather which will serve the situation under scrutiny more effectively. Functionalism is best suited for describing and relating variables in organizational communication processes. Interpretivism, on the other hand, is more appropriate for questions about the role of communication in members' experiences of organizational life.[9] In some circumstances rather than an "either – or" approach to these two perspectives a "both – and" strategy may prove the most effective.

Patterns of Organizational Communication

It is appropriate at this stage to examine the patterns of organizational communication, which from the traditional functionalist view divides the topic into function and structure. Although these concepts will be treated separately here for simplicity they are in fact closely related. As Farace et al indicated "Both function and structure are intimately linked together, and major breakdowns in either can render the communication system of an organization inoperative."[14]

Communication Functions

Traditionally the functions of organizational communication in open systems are grouped into three processes:[9]

1. transformation of energy and materials via input, throughput and output,
2. regulation of system processes and
3. system growth or adaptation.

Farace et al describe three communication functions associated with these processes under the headings of production, maintenance and innovation. The production function encompasses all forms of communication within the organization which are related to the coordination and control of all production aspects of the organization. The maintenance function relates to all communication which endeavors to ensure that the organization continues to function at a steady state of operation. Organizational policies, procedures, rules and negative feedback (which is designed to prevent the organization from deviating from its goals and objectives) are included in the maintenance function. Farace et al suggests that the maintenance function extends further.

> "Maintenance communication is that which (a) affects the member's feelings of personal worth and significance (b) changes the value placed on interaction with co-workers, supervisors, and subordinates, and (c) alters the perceived importance of continuing to meet the organization's production and innovation needs."[14]

This view has led theorists like Goldhaber to create a fourth functional category called the human function.[17]

The innovation function covers communication which relates to any form of change in the organization. This would include the development and implementation of new ideas and strategies and could extend to changes in organizational philosophy, values, structure, functions and even behavior. The general purpose of the various functions of organizational communication is to reduce the level of uncertainty within the organization and is therefore generally inversely proportional to the size of the organization.

Communication Structure

Communication structure has long been defined by the traditional functionalists in terms of concrete messages flowing along lines of communication. Many researchers today, however, particularly the interpretivists favor the view that communication structure involves the patterns of interaction between and among people within the organization. This view is consistent with that of the functionalist because these patterns of interaction can be observed. However, interpretivists believe that structure is not, in itself, an objective property of communication but an idea shared by the members of the organization.[41] Owens is of the opinion that structure is both an objective property and a subjective idea because not only can it be observed but it is understood in terms of our ideas about structure.[37] It follows then that communication structure can be viewed in two different ways. Structuralists have generally described organizational communication in formal and informal systems. To encompass the subjective discussion researchers have begun to view communications structure as a network.

Formal communications are generally associated with the hierarchically structured official channels within an organization. These channels are directionally oriented such that organizational communication is seen as flowing downward, upward and horizontally in line with the organizational authority structure. Informal communication systems have been defined "as not rationally specified" in the sense that the formal lines of communication are not followed.[43] Information is passed quickly, more often accurately than not, via the "grapevine" in cluster transmission patterns. Although the concepts of formal and informal communication are often referred to there appears little or no agreement among researchers on how to distinguish between the two systems. Should the patterns of interaction among members of an organization be emphasized it is usual to do so by means of network relationships. These patterns are best studied by means of a technique known as network analysis which reveals linkages between and among individuals and group structures as well as other network roles.

The Organizational Environment

In developing his definition, Goldhaber decided to include the environmental dimension.[16] This was an important and significant conceptual step in the understanding not only of organizational communication but also of the influence the organization has on the environment and vice versa. The implications of this to the educator are important in that the school system interacts significantly with the community at a number of levels.

Goldhaber viewed organizational communication as a process of ongoing, continuous and changing organizational communication in a dynamic open system which creates and exchanges messages among its members and between its members and the environment. This is illustrated in Figure 2.

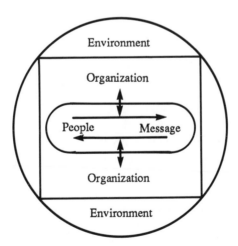

Figure 2. Paradigm of Organizational Communication

The Environmental Dimension

Early research focussed on the directionality of message flow, communication channels and networks and it was believed that organizational communication was determined almost exclusively by the structure of the organization.[27]

As the focus of research moved to systems theory increasingly more emphasis was placed on organizational behavior with particular reference to the relationship between the organization and its environments. Generally in organizational theory the environment refers to those activities outside the boundaries of the organization whether they are objective or subjective in nature. However, recent studies have revealed the need to include internal aspects of the organization when considering the organizational environment.

Two such aspects of the environment which provide valuable insight to the study of organizational theory in general and organizational communication in particular are those which concern themselves with the organizational culture and organizational climate. Organizational culture, centres on the internal context of the organization but views the organization from the point of view of what it "is" rather than what it "has." Organizational climate on the other hand also deals with the internal organizational environment but pays attention to the internal atmosphere or set of characteristics which constitute the organization's practices and procedures. As Jelnick, Smircich, and Hirsch state, culture is the emerging "explanation of choice" for organizational researchers, and climate has been historically the "explanation of choice."[29]

Organizational Culture

Organizational culture as defined by Owens is "the body of solutions to external and internal problems that has worked consistently for a group and that is therefore taught to new members as the correct way to perceive, think about, and feel in relation to those problems." The culture of an organization develops over time and in doing so it acquires the status of assumptions regarding the nature of reality, truth, time, space, human nature and human relationships. Eventually it becomes taken for granted, and finally reaches the stage of shared philosophies, ideologies, values, assumptions, beliefs, and attitudes that knit a community together.[37] If the community is an educational institution and all the participants – teachers and administrators - agree implicitly or explicitly with the interrelated psychological qualities inherent in the culture of the organization, then all members of the organization can approach problems and decisions with unity because "this is the way things are done around here."[33]

Organizational culture is "a learned pattern of unconscious or semiconscious thought, reflected and reinforced by behavior, that silently and powerfully shapes the experience of a people" the purpose of which is to "provide stability, foster certainty, solidify order and predictability, and create meaning."[10] Generally in the past research into organizational culture has concentrated on evidence derived from the observation of organizational behavior. However, more recently, it has been seen necessary to study the impact of the elements of the environments within which the organization finds itself. One of these elements involves the symbolism incorporated into the organizational culture in the form of rituals, myths, traditions, and language through which the attitudes and values of the organizational members are transmitted from one generation to another. In schools symbolism of this nature would include the daily schedule of classes particularly with respect to the bell, the attitude to teacher authority, the seating arrangement of the classroom and the means by which information is disseminated to the students.

The study of organizational culture has also revealed the existence of multiple cultures in the sub-units which make up the total organization. In the educational setting differing cultures will be found among the student population, the teachers in a given school and the administrators in the central School Board Office. In addition to this it is possible that the cultures of each individual school may differ within a particular school district and that the cultures of each department within a particular school may differ. Recognition of the existence, nature and function of organizational culture is not only important to management style but also to the structure and foundation of organizational communication.

Socialization

The mechanism through which an organization exercises maintenance and control of the organizational culture is socialization. Through this process the participant identifies personally with the accepted values, attitudes and expectations of the organization or departs from it. Socialization has been defined as "that part of the learning process which deals with the acquisition of requisite orientations for satisfactory functioning in a role."[25,1]

It is a continuous process beginning in early childhood and continuing throughout life. Most primary socialization is complete by adulthood but the learning of new role orientations accompanies each change of status. This is commonly observed in modern society, where occupational roles are embedded in an organizational setting, and in the socialization required after a change in an occupational role. Organizational socialization is concerned with the processes by which requisite role orientation of offices, statuses and positions are acquired by the members of the organization for the purpose of formative influence of the values, norms, expectations and sanctions of the organization. By this process, role ideology and role performance of personnel are carefully molded.

Within the school organization three types of peer groups can be seen to exist namely consensual, diffuse and job specific.[46] This typology of peer group is based on the respective distribution of the elements of the primary group, namely face-to-face contact, diffuse interaction, group solidarity and membership stability.[8] Within these three peer group types there exists four effective means of group control.[46] Briefly, these are firstly, selective recruitment which ensures that new members will enter the peer group with similar values, attitudes and work habits; secondly, socialization which defines the role of the individual work settings as they reshape the attitudes and values of the members; thirdly, selective expulsion which facilitates the departure of deviants or the expression of unresolved pressures of adjustment to the work setting; and lastly isolation or ostracism by peers for a long-term group member who resists group pressures.

The neophyte teacher is subjected to a double socialization process. Initially, socialization to professional norms and values occurs during teacher education where a more theoretical focus is provided. The second phase of socialization begins when, as new teachers to a school, they are confronted with the norms, values, attitudes and expectations of their more experienced colleagues. In this situation the neophyte teacher is particularly vulnerable to formal and informal socialization pressures. Waller describes the situation thus:

> The significant people for a school teacher are other teachers, and by comparison with good standing in that fraternity, the good opinion of students is a small thing of little price. A land mark in one's assimilation to the profession is that moment when he decides that only teachers are important.[45]

Organizational Climate

Organizational climate is a term which has enjoyed wide usage in the past. It can be defined as "the study of perceptions that individuals have of various aspects of the environment in the organization." During the 1960s Halpin and Croft developed the Organizational Climate Description Questionnaire based on their studies of the "attributes of leadership and group behavior" existing in selected elementary schools.[19] The studies which followed tended to focus on the data gathered from adults, almost invariably teachers and occasionally administrators. In recent years pupils and students have been included in the process of data gathering. It is important to point out that studies in organizational climate depend heavily on the perceptions of the participants usually elicited by the use of questionnaires.

Organizational climate is related to organizational culture in so far as it is subsumed by it and reflects the individual perceptions of the organizational members of the values and belief systems contained in the environment in which the organization operates.[37,13]

However, it is the culture of an organization which influences the development of the organizational climate because the organizational culture determines the inherent values and belief systems of the individual organizational members which in turn influence their perceptions of the organizational climate particularly with respect to organizational performance. Research completed by Kante in which highly successful American Corporations were compared to less successful corporations drew the conclusion that high performing corporations had a culture of pride and a climate of success.[30]

The External Environment

The internal organizational environment to a large degree influences the performance of its members and ultimately the success of the organization in achieving its goals. However, no matter how much pride is manifested through the organizational culture nor how much success is developed through the organizational climate, the organization must come to terms with its external environment. The management of the external environment – the relevant publics including clients, voters, communities, regulators and legislators – is achieved through public relations image building and public affairs and issues management.[9] Public relations and image building, the "identity an organization wants perceived by its relevant publics,"[17] is a process by which specific organizational characteristics and behaviors are developed through various means of communications. Educational organizations, particularly school systems strive to assure their stakeholders that the teachers in their schools are providing the optimum opportunities for their students. While corporations employ professional public relations experts to perform this task, school systems rarely go to such lengths.

Public affairs and issues management differ somewhat from the more traditional activities of image building. Issues management involves the identification and tracking of public issues that may affect an organization. In some cases it is necessary for the organization to make changes to respond to the publics from whom these issues arise. The organizational change must also be communicated to the publics involved. In other cases, organizations combine issues management with issues advocacy. This essentially is a process by which the organization strategically attempts to shape public opinion on certain issues before political action regarding such issues results in legislation or regulation which the organization believes will adversely affect its operation.

The external environment of all levels of educational systems is generally known as the community. The community can be considered to include those stakeholders in education extending from the local to the provincial even to the national and international arenas.[15] Community involvement in education facilitates the dual role of education in society – namely directing the path of society as well as reflecting the cultural values of society to the young. Because of its precious role in society, education needs community involvement from all levels. In this way the external environment is of the utmost importance to the educational organization and effective communications between it and the environment ensure that the organization not only functions effectively but becomes an integrated part of the environment.

The School System

Systems theory is generally credited to a biologist, Ludwig von Bertalanfy, who, in 1950, outlined a notion which has been developed to describe, explain and predict organizational behavior. He wrote, with the science of biology in mind:

> An organism is an integrated system of interdependent structures and functions. An organism is constituted of cells and a cell consists of molecules which must work in harmony. Each molecule must know what the others are doing. Each one must be capable of receiving messages and must be

sufficiently disciplined to obey. You are familiar with the laws that control regulation. You know how our ideas have developed and how the most harmonious and sound of them have been fused into a conceptual whole which is the very foundation of biology and confers on it its unity.[36]

Social scientists substituted the work organization for organism, group for cell, and person for molecule in the biological statement above to capture the basic concepts involved in analyzing complex situations in organizations. School systems have been described as organizations in that they are "an integrated system of interdependent structures and functions." An organization is constituted of groups and a group consists of persons who must work in harmony. Each person must know what the others are doing. Each one must be capable of receiving messages and must be sufficiently disciplined to obey . . ."[4] Systems theory contains two central important concepts which enable the social scientist to examine organizations in their entirety. These are:

1. the concept of subsystems and,
2. the concept of multiple causation

Systems can be divided into two main classifications – "open" and "closed." Social systems theory generally deals with "open" systems because it is difficult to envisage organizations such as schools or school systems which do not interact with the environment in which they exist. Interestingly enough, Halpin and Croft in their influential studies on organizational climate of elementary schools "concentrated on internal organizational characteristics as though they function independently from external influences" and further used the terms "open" and "closed" to describe the profiles of schools that represented selected characteristics of organizational climate.[37]

Sociologists have long considered the school as a social institution. Durkheim considered the school as an institution wherein society recreated itself in its young.[11] Weber as quoted by Boocock believed that the school was a place where individuals acquire the experiences and credentials which define their subsequent position in society. His analysis emphasizes the structure of the school organization and the role it plays in the control of students through the functional division of labour and the hierarchy of offices which provide a structure of authority on legally defined power.[6]

Published in 1932, Willard Waller's *Sociology of Teaching* was one of the first full-length sociological analyses of the school. It follows the traditions set down by Durkheim and although it lacks the quantitative analysis, its discussion of the school as a social organization provides a persuasive explanation of low levels of student motivation and performance. The school's institutionalized dominance and subordination which characterized the teacher-pupil relationship produces the view of a fortress of despotism in which the school is in constant danger of being beseiged from within. The teacher represents and maintains the social order in the school, whereas the students have only a negative interest in the feudal superstructure providing the material in which teachers are expected to produce results. Similar criticism of schools based on this theme have come from writers such as Kohl[34], Kozol[35], Holt[23,24], and Silberman.[41] Another sociological explanation study which attempts to explain the antagonism between teacher and student revolves around the fact that schools are susceptible to the problems peculiar to service institutions where one or more groups or categories of roles perform a service or function for another group or category of roles. Schools, as in other involuntary institutions such as prisons and mental hospitals and other organizations which serve involuntary clientele, focus on the maintenance of order and control to such a degree that it becomes an integrative theme.

Philip Jackson's *Life in Classrooms* is a combination of the author's own observations of several elementary classes over a long period of time. In his view the classroom, in many respects is analogous to a crowd, for only in schools do large groups of people spend several hours each day literally side by side. It follows, he asserts, that a major function of the school is crowd maintenance or the control of mass behavior. To accomplish this, a clear hierarchy of authority is needed as well as an institutionalized sequence of events which ritually defines and organizes the school day. The only useful quality developed in the child is the patience to endure the delays, distractions and interruptions which characterize the classroom.[28] In other words, ritualism replaces relevance in that the school curriculum is fixed in advance, the subjects are introduced in the same way, teachers press home the same concepts and test in the same manner. What the student has learned is how to endure. to endure.

During the 1960s educational anthropologists began to study seriously school problems in the United States as a result of the social and political crisis of that time. Until this time conventional researchers had assumed that schools were primarily agencies for formal education and because of this were not usually studied in relation to their linkages to other institutions.[26] In the field of sociology the interpretive school of thought has encouraged researchers to investigate the processes by which those involved in education construct, define, and manage their everyday world. The central focus of sociology has become the need to reveal "what constitutes reality for the participants in a given situation, to explain how these participants came to view reality in this way and to determine what are the social consequences of their interactions."[2]

Interactionist Peter Wood in his book *Sociology and the School: An Interactionist Point of View* asserts that interactionism has much to offer the practicing teacher. Contributions, through interactionist studies, have been made, he argues, in the areas of better teaching through a more relevant and realistic curriculum; less conflict in schools through a more accurate diagnosis of the problems; better understanding, possibly leading to the enhancement of one's own teaching career as well as that of others and a better understanding of how both school and society are inexplicably riddled with inequalities, and how they are reproduced. Further, it may be possible to gain a greater appreciation of how the constraints governing the teacher's task are partially created in the school and acted out such that a sounder base for institutional and curriculum reform may result.[48]

The interactionists would argue that the problems in educational institutions today are due to the functionalist view that the school exists in society to recreate society's values and/or provide a mechanism "to meet the manpower needs appropriate to an expanding economy."[2]

Because of recent criticisms of education, as outlined earlier, the functionalist stance has fallen into dispute. It has been criticized for under estimating the importance of conflict and ideology and for exaggerating the role of technology. Further, it has been criticized for neglecting to examine the content of education. However, had it not been for functionalism the sociological study of education, particularly in the post-war years would not have advanced because sociologists of the functionalist school illustrated clearly the connection between education and the other important social institutions such as economics and politics. Because in the realm of organizational behavior no concept relies so heavily on social systems concepts as organizational culture, it follows that the notion of person-environment interaction and the underlying shared cultural values, philosophies, beliefs, expectations, attitudes and norms are important in the shaping and eliciting of human behavior. Goldhaber's definition of organizational communication, then, as "a process of creating and exchanging messages within a network of interdependent relationships to cope with environmental uncertainty,[16]" needs to be modified to emphasize the interaction not only across interpersonal sub-units but also across organizational environments many of whom have developed their own cultural values, philosophies, attitudes and norms.[12] Not only are the formal lines of communication based on levels of authority (an important consideration in the effective administration of educational systems) but the patterns of interaction revealed in the informal communications networks are also important to consider because they reflect and are themselves reflected by the cultural philosophies, attitudes and expectations both of the organization and the members of it. The words of F. Kenneth Berrien[4] are applicable here. "Modern society is a network of social systems growing increasingly complex, overlapping, competitive, sometimes cooperative, in which as individuals we find ourselves enmeshed." One such social system is the educational system. To understand it and maximize its performance within society it is necessary to understand the theory and processes of organizational communication which enables it to function.

References

[1]Barnell, G. and Morgan, G. (1979). *Sociological Paradigms and Organizational Analysis.* London: Heinemann Press.

[2]Barton, L. and Walker, S. (1978). "Sociology of Education at the Crossroads." *Education Review:* Vol. 30, 269-283.

[3]Bernstein, B. (1976). "Organizational Communication Theories: Issues Analysis" Paper presented to the International Communication Association, Portland, Oregon.

[4]Berrien, F.K. (1976). "A General Systems Approach to Organizations" in *Handbook of Industrial and Organizational Psychology.* Chicago, Ill: Dannette, M.D., Rand McNally and Company.

[5]Berrien, Kenneth F. (1976) A General Systems Approach to Organizations in Marvin D. Dunnette (Ed.). *Handbook of Industrial and Organizational Psychology.* Chicago: Rand McNally and Co., 42.

[6]Boocock, S. (1973). "The School as a Social Environment for Learning Social Organization and Micro Social Process in Education." *Sociology of Education,* Winter 1973, Vol. 46, No. 1.

[7]Bormann, E. and Howell, W. Nichols, R. and Shapireo, G. (1969). *Interpersonal Communications in the Modern Organization.* Englewood Cliffs, N.J.: Prentice-Hall.

[8]Cooley, C., Angel, R.C. and Carr, L.J. (1933). *Introductory Sociology.* New York: Scribners, 208-215.

[9]Daniels, T.D. and Spiker, B.K. (1987). *Perspectives on Organizational Communication.* Dubuque, Iowa: Wm. C. Brown.

[10]Deal, T. (1985). "Cultural Change: Opportunity, Silent-Killer, or Metamorphoris?" in Kelman R. Et. A. (Eds.) *Gaining Control of the Corporate Culture.* San Francisco: Jossey-Bass, 301.

[11]Durkheim, E. (1956). *Education and Society.* Translated by Fox, S.D. Glencoe, Ill: Free Press.

[12]Euske, N.A. and Roberts, K.H. (Eds.) (1987). Evolving Perspectives in Organizational Theory: Communication Implications, in Jablin, F.M., Putnam, L.L., Roberts, K.H., and Porter, L.W. *Handbook of Organizational Communication: An Interdisciplinary Perspective.* Newbury, P.K.: Sage Publication, 42.

[13]Falcione, R. and Warner, E. (1978). "Organizational Climate and Communication Climate: a State of the Art," Paper presented at the International Communication Association, Chicago, Ill.

[14]Farace, R.V., Monge, P.R. and Russell, H.M. (1977). *Communicating and Organizing.* Reading, MA: Addison-Wesley.

[15]Giles, T.E. (1978). *Educational Administration in Canada.* Calgary: Detselig Enterprises, 99-102.

[16]Goldhaber, G.M. (1983). *Organizational Communication.* Dubuque, Iowa: Wm. C. Brown, 3rd Ed.

[17]Goldhaber, G.M. (1986). *Organizational Communication.* Dubuque, Iowa: Wm. C. Brown, 4th Ed., 336.

[18]Greenbaum, H. (1971). "Organizational Communication Systems: Identification and Appraisal." Phoenix, Az: Paper presented at meeting of the International Communications Association.

[19]Halpin, A.W. and Croft, D.B. (1962) *The Organizational Climate of Schools.* Chicago Midwest Administration Centre, The University of Chicago.

[20]Haney, W. (1973). *Communication and Organizational Behaviour.* Homewood, Ill: R.D. Irwin.

[21]Haseman, R. Logue, C. and Freshley, D. (1969). *Readings in Interpersonal and Organizational Communication.* Boston: Holbrook Press.

[22]Hersey, P. and Blanchard, K. (1982). *Management of Organizational Behavior: Utilizing Human Resources.* New York: Wiley and Sons, 2nd Ed.

[23]Holt, J. (1964). *How Children Fail.* New York: Delta.

[24]Holt, J. (1967). *How Children Learn.* New York: Pitman.

[25]Hoy, W.K. (1969). "Pupil Control Ideology and Organizational Socialization: A Further Examination of the Influence of Experience on the Beginning Teacher." *The*

School Review. September-December 1969, Vol. 77, 3-4, 258.

[26]Husen, T. and Postlethewaite, T.N. (Eds. 1985). *The International Encyclopaedia of Education, Research and Studies.* Oxford: Vol. 8. Pergamon Press.

[27]Jablin, F. Putnam, L. Roberts, K. and Porter, L. (1987). *Handbook of Organizational Communication: An Interdisciplinary Perspective.* Beverly Hills, California: Sage Publications.

[28]Jackson, P. (1968). *Life in Classrooms.* New York: Holt, Rinehart and Winston.

[29]Jelnick, M., Smirich, L. and Hirsch, P. (1983). "Introduction: A Code of Many Colours." *Administrative Science Quarterly,* 28, 331-338.

[30]Kanten, R.M. (1983). *The Change Martyrs: Innovation and Entreprenership in the American Corporation.* New York: Simon and Schuster Inc., 49.

[31]Katz, D. and Kahn, R.L. (1978). *The Social Psychology of Organization.* New York: Wiley and Sons, 2nd Ed.

[32]Katz, D. and Kahn, R.L. (1966). *The Social Psychology of Organization.* New York: Wiley and Sons.

[33]Kelman, R., Saxton, M., Serpa, R. and Associates. (1985). *Gaining Control of the Corporate Culture.* San Francisco: Jossey-Bass, 19-20.

[34]Kohl, H. (1976). *36 Children.* New York: Signet Books.

[35]Kozol, J. (1970). *Death at an Early Age.* New York: Bantam Books.

[36]Lwoff, A. (1966). "Interaction among Virus, Cell and Organization." *Science.* 152, 1216.

[37]Owens, R.G. (1987). *Organizational Behaviour in Education.* Englewood Cliffs, New Jersey: Prentice Hall, Inc., 3rd Ed. 166.

[38]Pacanowsky, M. and O'Donnell-Trijillo, N. (1984). Organizational Communication's Cultural Performance. *Communication Monographs,* 50, 192-206.

[39]Pace, R. (1983). *Organizational Communication: Foundations for Human Resource Development.* Englewood Cliffs, N.J.: Prentice-Hall.

[40]Putnam, L. (1982). "Paradigms for Organizational Communication Research: An Overview and Sysnthesis" *Western Journal of Speech Communication,* 46, 192-206.

[41]*Silberman, C.E. (1970). Crisis in the Classroom.* New York: Vintage Books.

[42]Thayer, L. (1968). *Communication and Communication systems.* Homewood, Ill: R.D. Irwin.

[43]Tompkins, P.H. (1967). "Organizational Communication: A State of the Art Review" in G. Richetto (Ed.) *Conference on Organizational Communication.* Huntsville, AL: NASA, George C. Marshall, Space Flight Center.

[44]Trijillo, N. (1985). "Organizational Communication as Cultural Performance: Some Managerial Considerations." *Southern Journal of Speech Communication,* 50, 201-204.

[45]Waller, W. (1961). *Sociology of Teaching.* New York: Russel and Russell.

[46]Warren, D.I. (1970). *Sociology of Education.* "Variations on the theme of Primary Groups: forms of Social Control within School Staffs." Vol. 43, 3, 290.

[47]Witkin, B. and Stephens, K. (1972). "A Fault Free Approach to Analysis of Organizational Communication Systems." Paper presented to Western Speech Communication Association, Honolulu.

[48]Wood, P. (1983). *Sociology and the School: An Interactionist Viewpoint.* London: Routledge, Kegan, Paul.

16

Selection of Educational Personnel and Organizational Communication

Neal Muhtadi

Excellent leaders surround themselves with excellent talent.[4,14] They recognize the impact of people and their attitude on the success or failure of the organization.[11] Consequently, they pay close attention to the selection and hiring of future employees and the role they may play in the organization in relation to communication with others.

The main purpose of this chapter is to explain the grounds of management and communication that guide the selection of educational personnel. This will be accomplished by outlining steps involved in the hiring process. Ideas presented are practical and should prove useful in helping teaching and administrative candidates.

Among the tasks of leadership that superintendents of schools perform are: planning for the selection of the best possible staff for the district; developing and implementing an effective staff development program for members of the administrative, teaching and non-teaching team in order to ensure ongoing renewal; and implementing a supervisory system that promotes quality instruction for the learner. Planning for the selection of quality staff for the district is an arduous and time-consuming task. People, not things, drive the educational enterprise; efforts expended in selecting staff are certainly merited.

Generally, the superintendent or members of his/her team follow these steps in the selection process:

1. Identifying position vacancies.
2. Developing a job description for each position.
3. Preparing advertisements for vacancies.
4. Arranging for receipt of applications.

5. Coding applications by subject and position.
6. Screening applications and checking on required data.
7. Confirming receipt of applications and communicating to the applicant additional requirements if necessary.
8. Rating each application based on the strength of the resumé – excellent/outstanding or preferred, average or good potential, poor or disregard. (Figure 1).
9. Checking references and affirming or altering ratings of applications. (Figure 2).
10. Shortlisting candidates.
11. Interviewing candidates.
12. Developing a profile for each candidate based on the interview responses and comments.
13. Deciding and offering selected candidates the various jobs.

Once acceptance is received, board approval and written confirmation follows. In most cases a job offer from a management team member, albeit verbally, is considered legally binding. Paperwork that follows is generally a formality.

The Advertisement

Applicants are advised to give careful attention to job-postings and advertisements where desired skills, qualifications and deadlines for position vacancies are described. For an application to receive serious consideration it must satisfy the stated criteria. Timeliness, completeness, brevity and presentation are major characteristics of excellent applications. They are some of the quality indicators of excellence and caring.

Depending on the desirability and location of the district, personnel managers receive many applications for a single advertisement. This may change with the projected teacher shortage. In the Fraser Valley, British Columbia, Canada, it is not infrequent that an advertisement will generate eight or nine hundred responses. For an application to stand out among so many it must be complete, informative, attractive and on time. As an assistant superintendent of secondary schools I received an average of twenty applications a day. Some applications were poorly prepared and lacked the necessary information and desired attractiveness. Due to time factors, I paid less attention to these applications as one may expect.

Desirable Attributes of an Excellent Application

Generally, a complete application includes the following:

1. Application: The main intent of a letter of application is to convince the reader that the writer is fully qualified and is worthy of an interview. Therefore, every effort must be made to outline carefully and succinctly areas of strengths,

attributes and accomplishments that put the candidate in excellent stead for the position.

2. *Statement of Philosophy:* Research supports the idea that values and beliefs motivate people.[12] Oliver North's beliefs underscore his decision to commit an illegal act in the Iran scandal. In his decision to prohibit the colonel from holding public office, Judge Gesell was undoubtedly convinced that North's values may be inconsistent with public expectations and trust. Education law is rich with examples that illustrate public expectations of teachers and others who hold positions of public trust. This is evident in board actions to suspend or terminate teachers who behaved, although consistent with personal beliefs, inappropriately. A teacher may believe that public knowledge or awareness of his/ her sexual habits, anti-semetic beliefs, racial and religious prejudices is impertinent to teaching; yet, in reality, values are pertinent. Students come from varied backgrounds and beliefs. They are a captive audience and an impressionable group. Teachers' actions, explicit or implicit, must be perceived as righteous and moral by all stakeholders. The statement of philosophy must consider the implications of teaching and modeling ethical behavior.

In reviewing a statement of philosophy, a personnel manager must be convinced that this candidate believes in helping students succeed and commit to lifelong learning. Children are our future; educating every student to the fullest extent of his or her capacity is the responsibility of every educator. A philosophy that is inconsistent with this belief renders necessary re-examination of one's vocational goals.

3. *Academic preparation and experience:* Organizing a resumé requires careful planning. Candidates must outline clearly and succinctly academic qualifications, as well as the sequence and nature of their experience. Knowledge and experience in technology is a desirable skill that merits mentioning We live in the Information Age; teaching through technology, with technology and about technology are important areas that deserve educators' attention.

Copies of transcripts of marks, letters of praise, awards and scholarships are essential data that should be appended to the resumé. References must be clearly identified and contacted prior to inclusion in the curriculum vitae. This is necessary in order to maintain currency of information and use of proper etiquette.

4. *Certification status:* Copies of teaching credentials and certification status are important data that should be included in the resumé. If a candidate is a student teacher who is nearing graduation, it is advisable to write a letter to the certifying agency, e.g. the College of Teachers or teacher licensing department, requesting a written response for qualification requirements. The response should indicate certification status upon graduation. A copy of this letter is a useful piece of information. Uncertified teachers are not permitted to teach in British Columbia public and publicly-supported private schools. Teaching certificates are required in most jurisdictions in Canada and the

United States.

5. *Evidence of caring.* Related data indicating commitment, involvement, caring and affection for children give the resumé added strength. Education is a people business; caring and involvement reflect ones concern for people and desire to help them succeed.

Creativity and imagination in the preparation of the resumé enhances the candidate's chances for being shortlisted. Examples of creativity may be:

1. Using color schemes for the various components of the resumé.
2. Highlighting important information by using bold letters or graphic features.
3. Indenting pages to highlight major parts of the curriculum vitae as appears as follows:

The Resumé

Jane M. Black

Address   4356 North Hampton Avenue
Vancouver, British Columbia Y7S 6M3

Education

1987-89   **University of London. Master of Arts** – Science

1982-86   **University of Alberta. Bachelor of Arts** – Music.

1978-81   **Biola College.** Seminars on religious education and music.

1961-72   **Redwater School. Grade 12 Diploma.**

Experience

1988-89   **School District No. 7 (Thorhild, Alberta)**
Volunteer tutor, grades 2 and 3.

1986-88   **Alberta Heart Foundation.** Office Manager.

1973-76   **Edmonton   Recreation   Department.**   Swimming
instructor, levels 1-4 life-saving.

1971-73   **Woodlands School.** Volunteer tutor and softball
coach for handicapped children.

Areas of Related Experience

Redwater Recreation Department. Squirts basketball coach.

Edmonton Theatre Guild. Director, *Oliver.*

Armenian Relief Agency. Volunteer, medical supplies.

Redwater School. Chairman, "dry-grad" committee.

St. Ann's Church. Instructor, grade 7 confirmation.

Edmonton School district. Member, Community-
school relations committee.

Leadership Roles

1987-88   **President – Thorhild County No. 7 Chamber of**

Commerce.

1984-85 **General Secretary – Edmonton General Hospital Board.**

1975-77 **Candy Striper – Edmonton General Hospital.**

1971-72 **President – Redwater School Students' Council.**

References

Miss Helen Sabo
Principal, Redwater School
2354 Provincial Road
Redwater, Alberta, V3M 3N1
(403) 496-3211 (school)
(403) 496-3785 (residence)

Dr. Douglas Major
Administrator – Edmonton General Hospital
1850 - 82nd Avenue
Edmonton, Alberta V2E 1G1
(403) 432-3114 (office)

Reverend Al Tinka
Mayor – Redwater Municipality
1211 Lacombe Street
Redwater, Alberta V3M 2N1

Several days after mailing the resumé, as a sound communication strategy, it is advisable to check on the receipt of the application. If possible, contact should be made with the person responsible for coding, rating and shortlisting. Contact with the superintendent, if it is a small school district, is recommended. Accessing district staff by telephone may prove very challenging; creativity, tact and tenacity however, may pay dividends in the long run. Personal communication and contacts, when done well, are very useful.

The Interview

In order to maximize a candidate's potential for employment, proper preparation for the interview is not only desirable, but essential. This preparation may involve several tasks including the following:

1. Knowledge of the area – It takes little effort to research an area. Some of this information is readily available at the nearest Chamber of Commerce, Canadian Automobile Association, or provincial and state information offices. Understanding the community, its economy, values and politics is not an arduous task. Similarly, understanding the school district, its mission, values, beliefs, aspirations and general characteristics helps the candidate to plan for the interview and to formulate future career goals.

2. Knowledge of the school system – Is the school district large? How many teachers does it employ? Is it committed to staff development and

professional renewal for its staff? Is the school district known for its quality schools? What is the average age of school teachers? How involved are parents in the education system? Do they view education as a shared responsibility where parents and teachers work cooperatively in the development of student intellectual, social and vocational goals, or are these duties relinquished to teachers and administrators?[13] H.J.,1984). These are important questions that deserve serious consideration.

3. Knowledge of the selection process is beneficial. Hiring practices differ from one school district to another. Some involve all stakeholders in the educational enterprise – principals, teachers, parents, trustees and student leaders. Others limit the process to the principal and district staff. If a district is a proponent of shared leadership,[14] (Gardner, 1986), it is likely to use the former approach. Knowing the audience and the school community helps the candidate to prepare for the interview.

4. Displaying Thinking and Assertiveness Qualities – It is not unusual for the interviewer to conclude the interview by inviting questions from the candidate. There is always the temptation of inundating the interviewer with a flood of questions. This is not advisable. Rather, the candidate should prepare three or four thoughtful and searching questions for the interview. In addition to displaying assertiveness qualities, the interviewee must demonstrate his/her capacity and disposition to engage in quality thinking. Effective teachers consistently promote in their classroom higher order thinking.[14]

5. Knowing and anticipating the interviewer's questions must receive careful consideration. This requires rehearsing and researching questions that are generally asked during interviews. Employers design questions that elicit specific answers to help them in the development of an idiographic profile for each candidate (Figure 1). This exercise seeks information relating to specific themes such as personal values, mission,beliefs, interpersonal relations skills, organizational and motivational attributes and the candidate's commitment to ongoing renewal.

Examples of questioning strategies of communication used during interviews follows: asked during interviews.

Mission and Belief Questions

– Why did you choose teaching over other professions?

– Why this school district?

– If you were to select the ideal profession what would it be and why?

– What is the goal of every teacher?

– Comment on the following statement: " I love teaching Geography; it is the only reason why I am a teacher."

– Comment on the following statement: " Medicine and law are excellent professions. They pay well in comparison to teaching; I will encourage my kids to become doctors and lawyers."

– Do you believe a teacher makes a difference? If yes, why?

All of the above questions are designed to elicit answers that demonstrate the candidate's values and beliefs in teaching as being an honorable profession. Again, one must remember that values and perceptions drive everything.[12]. A strong belief based on love and caring for every child; an unwavering determination to inspire students to learn and a sincere effort to improve public perception of education and educators are decided assets.

An interviewer looks for answers that clearly reflect the candidate's desire to help people grow and attain self-actualization. All answers must focus on the student and his/her growth and success.

Interpersonal Relationship Skills Questions

– Describe an excellent teacher to me. What makes one teacher better than another?

– Perceptions are reality. How do you want to be perceived by your students?

– What do students mean when they say: "We want our teacher to be fair"?.

– Explain to me what is empathy?

– What would you do if a student is tardy?

– How would you react to students who miss deadlines?

– Do you want your students to like you?

– Should teachers strive to build rapport with their students ? If yes, why?

– Comment on the following statement: "Student / teacher relationships must be based on mutual respect."

– What actions would you take if a student tells you in confidence :"I hate my parents."

– Describe a good listener to me.

– What do you do if you have a very talkative student who tends to dominate class discussions?

– What would you do if you suspect a student is cheating on examinations?

– How do you feel when you fail?

How do you feel when students fail?

– A student informs you that her best friend is going to run away from home, what would you do?

Answers to these questions are communication strategies designed to help the interviewer or interviewing team to determine how caring, emphatic and objective the candidate is. Teachers must be good listeners, rapport builders, positive, empathic and objective. These attributes aid understanding, positive relations and interaction with pupils. They also support student individual safety, belonging, self-esteem and self-actualization needs.[8] 1959).

Creativity and Resourcefulness Questions

– How do students learn?

– What is meant by the statement: "I want to be a guide by the students' side, not a sage on a stage"?

– Comment on the following: "When I lecture to students I learn a lot. I think lecturing is the best way for students to learn."

– Describe an excellent lesson to me.

– How do you inspire students to learn?

– Can teachers learn from students? Tell me more.

– What periodicals and books have you read recently?

– What magazines do you subscribe to?

– Where do your ideas come from?

– What is a creative person?

– Describe a resourceful teacher to me.

– Comment on the following: "Students do not learn if they do not experience success."

– Comment on the following: "My teacher is very inspiring. She varies lesson activities and plans exciting field trips."

– What is meant by the terms: positive reinforcement, feedback and recognition?

– If students fail a test what do you do?

– Is it possible to force students to learn?

– The verb educate comes from the Greek word "educare," or drawing out, what does this mean to you?

– How important is enjoyment to learning? How do you plan enjoyable lessons?

– Describe an educated person to me.

– What is meant by continuous progress and individualized instruction?

The questions are communication strategies designed to unveil candidates as innovators, change-agents and effective lesson planners. They intentionally vary lesson activities and make them relevant, interesting and enjoyable. In their view, the subject is not as important as the individual.[5,6] They believe the student is a thinking and curious individual, who is capable of being self-reliant and making decisions based on careful analysis, sound judgment and values. Candidates view teachers as feeling fulfilled when the learner is successful. They believe students learn best when they are actively involved in the lesson.[2]

Work Orientation, Productivity and Gestalt Questions

– How important are deadlines in your view?

– What do you do if a student hands in late assignments?

– Do you expect complete work from students?

– How do you feel when a job is half done?

– How do you usually spend your summer holidays?

– Comment on the following statement: "I do not need to write down lesson plans. They are all in my head."

– What is meant by the statement: "My lesson plans are based on student ability levels, not grade levels."

– Do you expect as much of yourself as you do of your students?

– Should students receive from instructors written course outlines and expectations? Tell me more.

– Do you set personal and professional goals for yourself? How important is goal-setting to success?

In this communication strategy, the questions are designed by the interviewer to discover answers relating to the candidate's ability to organize and structure lessons, to help the learner meet deadlines and establish meaningful goals. Candidates' answers must clearly reflect a positive attitude toward the learner as a unique individual. Lesson planning is individualized.[5] it is not subject or grade oriented. For a candidate to receive maximum points on this section of the interview, he or she must be perceived as highly committed to hard work and accountability for student success.[7]

Self-analysis questions:

– What are your views on students marking their own homework?

– Should students be allowed to assign themselves marks for tests?

– How important is self-assessment to learning?

– What are the main components of an excellent project?

– Tell me three strengths that your have.

– Tell me three weaknesses that you have.

– What would your best reference tell me about you as a teacher? in 0

Answers to these questions reveal the candidate's views on self-assessment and evaluation as a learning tool. Students can learn from this formative method of evaluation. It also determines if a person views the role of a teacher as a judge, or as an enhancer, supporter and guide of student success and learning. The latter is a sign of an effective teacher, the former is indicative of a role that is inconsistent with existing effective school research and practice.[10,3]

Subject-oriented Questions:

In the past most questions during interviews were subject related. The interviewer's communication strategy aimed at testing the candidate's subject knowledge base. Today, subject questions are less frequent for the following reasons:

1. The screening process addresses subject qualification through the examination of university transcripts that accompany the application. Major and minor subject concentrations are clearly stated on credentials from accredited Canadian and American educational institutions, rendering unnecessary subject in-depth questions. However, in cases where candidates are not recent graduates, subject questions become necessary.

2. The reference checking process is very revealing. It tends to provide candid verbal comments on an applicant that are seldom available in written form. Admittedly, this seems odd and unfair, but it is reality.

Questions relating to knowledge of the subject may be asked where a district subscribes to a specific philosophy or teaching approach. Reading instruction is an excellent example in this regard. If a district believes that the best way to teach reading is by the phonics method.[1] the interview questions would emphasize this approach.

Increasingly, educators are becoming aware of the need to individualize learning by focusing attention on curriculum. It is not unusual for a teacher to disregard provincial and state curriculum guides. Consequently, questions on curriculum sources and implementation are becoming an integral part of the interview process. Selecting excellent employees and seeking employment opportunities in education require careful planning and preparation. Efforts expended in this regard pay handsome dividends to employers and employees.

Noted References

[1]Chall, J.S. (1983). *Learning To Read: The Great Debate* (2nd ed.). New York: McGraw Hill.

[2]Champagne, A. *The Cognitive Psychology Perspective.* ERIC Document No. ED 247148.

[3]Etzioni, A. (1984). *Self-discipline, Schools, and the Business Community.* Final Report to the U.S. Chamber of Commerce, Washington,D.C. ERIC Document No. ED 249-335.

[4]Gardner, J.,W. (1986-87). *Leadership Papers.* Vol.1-11. Leadership Studies Program, Independent Sector, Washington,D.C.

[5]Goodlad, J.I. (1984). *A Place Called School.* (New York: McGraw Hill.)

[6]Goodlad, J.I. and Anderson,R.H. (1959). *The Nongraded Elementary School.* (New York: Harcourt, Brace and World.)

[7]Ginsburg, A. and Hanson, S. (1985). Values and High School Success. Final Report To the U.S. Department of Education, Washignton, D.C.

[8]Maslow, A.H. (1959). Cognition of Being in the Peak of Experiences. *Journal of Genetic Psychology 94:43* (March, 1959.)

[9]Merman, S. & McLaughlin, J. (1983). *OUt-Interviewing the Interviewer.* (Englewood Cliffs, N.J.: Prentice Hall.)

[10]Morris, V.C. et al. (1984). *Principals in Action: The Reality of Managing Schools.* (Columbus, Ohio: Charles E. Merrill Publishing.)

[11]Peters, Thomas J. &. Waterman, Robert H.(1982). *In Search of Excellence.* (New York:Warner Books.)

[12]Shute, W., Webb, C., Thomas, G. (1989). Preparing School Administrators for the 21st Century: Completing Conceptual Frameworks. A research paper presented at the AASA conference, San Francisco, 1989.

[13]Walberg, H.J. (1984). Families As Partners In Educational Productivity." *Phi Delta Kappan,* Vol. 65, No.6, pp. 397-400.

[14]Resnick, L. & Klopfer, L. (1989). *Toward the Thinking Curriculum: Current Cognitive Research* (Toronto: ASCD).

Suitability for the Position

	Disregard [ ]	Good [ ] Preferred [ ]
Mission and beliefs Values and the profession		
Interpersonal relations Skills: caring, listening, empathy		
Organizational Skills: Ability to plan well, inspire, motivate, set and attain goals.		
Productivity: Modeling high expectations, diligence, gestalt.		
Self-Analysis skills: Objectivity, fairness, self-assessment and improvement.		
Subject-related skills: Knowledge base, cultural literacy, curriculum development and implementation.		
	Poor	Average Outstanding Potential

Figure 1

Instructions for the Referee

All applicants for substitute and regular teaching positions to our district are required to have at least two confidential reference reports completed by a Supervisor (Principal or Superintendent), Sponsor Teacher or University Faculty Sponsor or Professor. The candidate identified below has named you as a referee with whom we can make further contact. Please answer the questions below and the ratings on the reverse side. Once completed, the form should be returned in a confidential sealed envelope to this office.

Applicant Information

_____

Last Name of Applicant   First   Middle

General Information

Between what dates have you known the work of this applicant?

From_____ to _____

What was your relationship to the applicant?

_____

Why did the applicant leave the position?

_____

_____

Have you written a formal student teacher or teacher evaluation report for this candidate?

No _____ Yes _____ If yes, what year? _____

Referee Information

_____   _____

Name of Referee (PRINT)   Title

_____   _____

Institution

                                 _____

                                          Address

_____   _____   _____

Signature of Referee   Phone No.   Date

Figure 2

Reference Criteria

Instructions – Indicate in the appropriate column your rating by a check mark.

Criteria	Weak	Fair	Satis-factory	Good	Except. Strength
Belief in the role of the teacher as a developer of children					
Positive rapport with children					
Positive rapport with adults					
Empathy					
Ability to resolve interpersonal conflicts					
Work ethic, enthusiasm, energy					
Classroom management skills					
Plans for individual student success					
Organizational and planning skills					
Knowledge of effective teaching strategies					
Ability to apply knowledge of effective teaching strategies					
Knowledge of subject area(s)					
Professional attitude/ethics					
Verbal and non-verbal communication skills					
Willingly assumes additional responsibility					
Leadership qualities					
Maturity judgment					
Models learning/ongoing professional development					

Additional General Comments:

_____

_____

_____

Would you recommend employing this candidate to work with children? Yes [ ] No [ ]

If you could, would you employ (or re-employ) this candidate? Yes [ ] No [ ]

Figure 3

17

Communication in Educational Organizations

Paul S. Licker

"The goals of education in our District are to develop students to the best of their abilities in the formal curriculum and to instill appropriate values for them to be active and contributing citizens in our society."

> – The first fifteen seconds of the welcoming address of an elementary school principal to the first meeting of the Parent Advisory Group of her school

"The School Board has examined its policies and has discovered that its Excellent Student Program (ESP) is overspending its budget by 10%. Hence we will be instituting an Excellence Fee next year in the amount of $120 per student in the ESP. We are sorry to have to do this, but every program should be self-supporting."

– Note found in lunch kit

"Oh, yes, Mrs. McCallum, I think Johnny is doing quite well. . . . Well relative to what you ask? We think well relative to his own abilities. Can he spell, read, write, add, or think? I don't know, Mrs. McCallum, we'll review that at the next Parent Open House."

> – Phone call at 4:00 p.m. near the end of term

"Use of this room by unauthorized personnel is strictly forbidden. Authorization can be obtained in writing from the school Secretary. Only school employees and recognized students may request authorization."

> – Memo posted on conference room bulletin board

"School policies are entirely in the hands of the school Principal, in consultation with the Vice-Principal and teachers. Parents' advice is also to be taken into account, along with the wishes of students and recognized parent groups. No decision affecting hours, locale and labor relations may be taken without prior consultation with the Assistant District Supervisor."

> – Page 132 of the Manual for Schools

Organizational Principles

These quotations illustrate five important ways organizations work in schools (Figure 1). Every organization, and a school is certainly a common organization, follows these principles. When schools are functioning well, when students are learning, parents satisfied, and teachers feeling fulfilled, these principles manifest themselves to everyone's advantage. But when schools appear confusing, obstreperous, even mean, to parents, students, and teachers, these same principles are operating in a negative fashion. This chapter explores these five principles, with reference to the school situation and particularly with reference to communication. For communication is the means through which these principles act, the vehicle for the human interaction that makes schools living organizations.

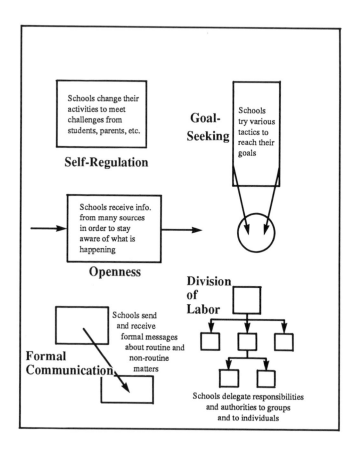

Figure 1. Organizational Principles

Goal-Seeking

A school is an organization of a specific type we call a "social system." By this we mean it is a set of components that interact to meet a goal held by people together (i.e., by a "society"). The goals are "social" in nature because they affect society at large and are in turn affected by society. The education of children, raising literacy among the populace, and providing life-skills training are three social goals.

A "system" is really a set of things that interact. The terms "system" and "systematic" are so widely used (and mis-used) that it's difficult to give an example of a non-system. Surely a school, a class, a project group, a discussion group, and a radiator are systems. But so are testing keys, grade books, pedagogies, class rosters and lesson plans. The key thing here is that in each of these systems, the components work together (or are forced to work together) to meet a goal.

Most social systems based on communication among individuals seek several goals, either sequentially or simultaneously. In fact, goal-seeking may be considered the primary activity of social systems. These goals embody the purposes for which the systems are formed, the criteria by which their performance and value to members is measured, and the activities which consume the greatest proportion of the system's resources.

These three concepts (purposes, criteria, and resources) need to be explored independently, especially with respect to the role of communication. Although a system may have a goal, it is arguable whether or not the components of the system share that goal. In fact, it is possible for the components to have entirely different and even conflicting goals and yet the system can be said to be seeking its own goal. Consider the goal(s) set up in the quotation above:

> The goals of education in our District are to develop students to the best of their abilities in the formal curriculum and to instill appropriate values for them to be active and contributing citizens in our society.

It is doubtful whether at any given moment all or even most of the components (i.e., students, teachers, administrators) are seeking this particular goal. Many will, if pressed, admit that their "short-term" goals (social contact, meeting friends, getting through homework, controlling a class, preparing schedules) contribute to the long-term goals in some vague way. In many cases students may not even know the published goals of an educational system. Nonetheless, the organization (i.e., the way individual components are related into groups, units, classes, schools), fed and maintained by communication among the components (groups, units, etc.), contributes to the ability of the system as a whole to seek and attain its goals.

Next, a system is judged in terms of its effectiveness (that is, how well or frequently or reliably it meets its goal(s)) and its efficiency (that is, how carefully it expends its resources in meeting those goals). It is a truism that almost anything can be bought, it's only a matter of knowing the price. Most social systems however are not willing to pay extremely high prices to meet goals and this shows up in goal statements that tend to be conservative, because those who frame these statements often have good knowledge of the costs involved. Most teachers, for example, are willing to invest only so much effort in motivating students to learn.

This invokes the concepts of accountability and performance measurement: we can't know how well we're doing if we cannot obtain relevant and adequate measures of performance. Key in this is communication of both goals and results and properly informing everyone of the criteria by which judgments will be made. Generally those who frame goals without also carefully spelling out how performance relative to those goals is to be judged are courting disaster. The teacher who is either unaware or chooses to ignore performance judgments is going to have a short career. If no one is aware of the standards and measures then the entire schooling system breaks down. While it is possible to have destructive arguments over these measures (consider many strikes by teachers' unions over class size, for example), the arguments will be over something else – after the fact – without this prior knowledge.

Finally, goal-seeking is a major user of a system's resources. For what other reason would a system consume these resources, anyway? These non-goal-oriented activities are often termed "overhead" and consist of two major categories: maintenance and defence. Maintenance activities keep a system functioning at current or proper levels (these may not be the same, of course) by rebuilding, retraining, or replacement. Maintenance activities do not contribute directly to goal attainment, but without them goals are difficult to meet. Defence activities try to keep other systems from intruding. Parents often are upset at school systems that seem to spend a lot of their taxes on building barriers that prevent them from accessing teachers and administrators. At least they may appear to be barriers. Open communication channels between teachers and administrators on the one hand and students and parents on the other can go a long way toward relabeling these activities – unless they really are defensive maneuvers!

Goal-seeking is closely related to another principle of organization, that of self-regulation. It is because some systems are self-regulated, meaning they can keep themselves on target, that they reach goals other than by chance. We turn now to that principle.

Self-Regulation and Feedback

Organizations operate on the principle of self-regulation. By this we mean that organizations like schools continually scan the environment they are in, locating situations that are considered in need of improvement and then taking action to improve the situation. Figure 2 illustrates this principle in action. Let's consider how a school board might operate consistent with this principle.

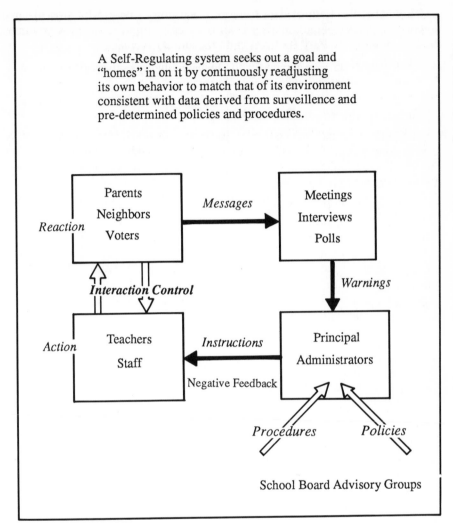

A Self-Regulating system seeks out a goal and "homes" in on it by continuously readjusting its own behavior to match that of its environment consistent with data derived from surveillence and pre-determined policies and procedures.

Figure 2. A Self-Regulating System

First, the School Board has normal operating procedures. Consider the Excellent Student Program. It's a relatively expensive trial program for outstanding students integrated with regular students in the classroom. During the first three years of its life, the ESP program has functioned well and everyone is satisfied. But it's been noticed that ESP has costs and the overrun, approximately 10% of the ESP budget, represents real taxpayer dollars that have to be made up. This is noticed in data gathered in the Board Controller's office by examining regular accounting statements and reports. This surveillance function is one of many such activities school boards regularly carry out. Others include sessions with parents and teachers, union meetings, maintenance reports and so forth.

This particular item of data triggers a warning to Board decision makers downtown. They operate on a series of policies and procedures. For example these come from the P&P (Policies and Procedures) manual:

5.4.1 School Board programs for non-impaired students will operate at a break even point after the first three years of operation.

7.2.1 It is established procedure to levy fees on parents of students in special programs which do not meet budget targets.

Note that the established policy is that programs break even and that there is a procedure (parent levies) that is relevant to this policy whenever a situation might arise that requires decision. There may be many possible procedures – we've indicated only one here.

Based on these policies and procedures – themselves alterable by School Board committees, public referenda, or executive decisions taken by appointed officials – the School Board has decided to levy a $100 fee on parents of ESP children. This decision and the corresponding procedures for putting it into effect are sent to school principals for action. They will have to collect the fees and forward them to the Board Controller's office. This is an example of feedback which tends to correct a situation considered harmful. In effect the feedback reduces the a difference between desired and actual situations.

When the principals put this decision into effect, money is collected and, in principle, the balance sheet of the ESP program is brought into closer balance. Of course, parents may pull their children out of the ESP program to save money (reaction) instead of paying fees (action) and thereby signal a significant loss of income (data) to a program that has a fixed cost, resulting in an indication (warning) that more needs to be done. It may happen that the Board will take a closer look at its policies and/or procedures in this case rather than institute another action in line with existing P&P. This results in a kind of spiral cycle of communication (Action, Data, Warnings, Command, etc.).

This basic principle of self-organization is the means by which organizations like School Boards, schools, parent groups, even individuals, cope with uncertainty in their environments. The effectiveness of self-organization depends, however, on the value (validity and appropriateness) of the policies and procedures as well as the effectiveness of the communication links obvious in Figure 2. For example, if the Controller's office failed to issue reports regularly, decision-makers in the downtown Board offices would not know anything was wrong. If principals failed to put decisions into effect, failed, in other words, to carry out the actions they were "commanded" to do, nothing would happen. This does not mean that things would get worse. It is possible for the environment (i.e., students, children, parents) to change to make the program less expensive without Board actions.

Openness

As a general principle, organizations that seek goals have to be open to inputs from their environments. Otherwise, as is clear from Figure 2, they are "blind" and can only reach goals by chance. What is less obvious is that open-ness has other virtues, not directly related to goal-seeking, such as obtaining resources, discovering threats, doing long-range planning, and changing poli-cies based on the performance of existing ones. However, we cannot discuss openness without considering what is "open."

In everyday speech, we consider ourselves "open to suggestion" if we are willing to consider, at least, the ideas of others. "Open-mindedness" means that we do not prejudge situations based on prior, perhaps unrelated, experience and do not generally let first impressions dictate how we treat others and their ideas. And an "open-door policy" means that workers can come to their supervisors and parents to a school principle to discuss ideas and concerns without having to leap through hoops unnecessarily. One principal once told his staff that he had an open door policy, only to have one teacher quip "Yeah, but you're never there!"

All these uses of "open" tell us that openness is a complex attribute. It means allowing access, allowing free flow of information and emotion, and not prejudging a situation. In an organization, openness also means having well-defined procedures for obtaining and sharing information and letting others know when their attempts at communicating have been successful. One manager in a research organization routinely threw his mail into a trashcan without opening it. He explained his actions thus: if it's so unimportant that you have time to write it down and send it to me, then I don't want to see it. Need-less to say, most people never found out that their comments weren't being read. Fortunately most of us don't have this kind of attitude.

Let's examine these four components of openness: *access, free flow, lack of prejudgment, feedback.* An organization needs to have well-defined access paths. There are four sorts of paths necessary: upwards, downwards, incoming and outgoing. As will be discussed later, upwards and downwards channels of communication are necessary because organizations of any complexity or size will divide work, responsibility and authority into small, coordinated chunks. Incoming channels (parents wishing to speak with principals, interest groups wanting to address parent groups) should be simple, easy to use and reliable. No one wants to have to fill out forms to talk to the principal, no one likes play-ing telephone tag just to get an appointment to see a teacher and students become disillusioned with adult society when told "you should have seen me first" after they get into trouble or when their idea has become stale. And remember the open door policy: open doors, like answering machines, are fine, but no one likes addressing empty space.

Outgoing channels are often formal in nature (memos, for example) and will be discussed in some detail in the next section. Many well-intentioned and finely-performing schools seem to fail or have political troubles not because they aren't doing their jobs well but because they don't manage their public images well. Sending important messages home in Johnny's lunch kit may suffice at the output side ("Well, Mrs. Jones, we DID send a message home with the kids"), but using such unreliable channels to distribute timely and controversial messages is not being "open" in the true sense.

An open organization permits free flow of information, ideas, emotions, impressions, and so forth. Of course, "free" may mean many things and too much information may be worse than too little.

Free flow is enhanced through frequent scheduled contacts, multiple channels of communication, advance communication about how communication is to take place (what theorists call "metacommunication"), agreement on what things mean (parents often are confused by education jargon even so simple a term as "report card" means different things to professional educators and parents), and lack of filters on topics. This latter is important. Sometimes we will agree that certain things will not or need not be discussed. This metacommunication is a filter to improve efficiency. At other times, however, this sort of agreement may not exist and attempts by one communicator to limit another's words or ideas this way are clearly seen as hypocrisy in the presence of "openness." While it is necessary sometimes to filter our interactions to avoid "information overload," it is easy to err by restricting communication too much. Most principals and teachers are inundated with information and often decide in advance to limit mail, phone calls or interviews in what might seem an arbitrary fashion to parents and students. Certainly the *policy* at least has to be explained. A better strategy is to inform parents and students of how to communicate more efficiently.

Prejudgment is obviously a sort of filter on open communication. Organizations prejudge messages in a variety of ways, decreasing their openness to their environment. Prejudgment of the source, the content, and the importance of a message may limit the value of the message and harm the communication relationship.

Before expanding on this, however, we should consider why people prejudge and what value this is. For an organization, there are always many sources of information some of which are better than others. That is, information may be more reliable, more understandable, more compact and usable from some sources than others. Every attempt to acquire information, too, is targeted on specific content. And finally, every organization places a value on information and will, as already pointed out, expend only so many resources to get it. These are all prejudgments and they are often functional. The difficulty arises when individuals in organizations make prejudgments based on stereotypes, time pressure, superficial similarities to unhappy past situations, and so forth; these prejudgments stand little chance of being functional except by chance.

Teachers and school administrators have to make special efforts not to prejudge students, parents, and interest groups falsely and unwisely. Often prejudgment is the result of habit acquired through functional behavior as mentioned above. But more likely is the inadvertent filtering of important information based on stereotypes. Then prejudgment starts to look like prejudice; the first may have some value; the latter is distinctly unfair.

Feedback is the final component of organizational openness. It is critical that openness also appears to be open. Parents often have the feeling that their concerns are being ignored simply because school administrators fail to tell them that their concerns have been noted and what will become of these notes. As feedback is critical for all communication and as school organizations cannot reach their goals without being open to communication from their social environments, feedback plays a double role of insuring that channels established at high cost to schools, parents, and students are maintained in an "open" state.

Formal Communication

A brief review to this point is in order. Organizations seek goals; social organizations, like schools and classes seek social goals such as instruction. These goals are attainable because these organizations are self-regulating: they home onto a goal and alter their behavior in order to reach their goal. In order to do this, they have to be open to information from their environment. Since the environment is a social system, this information may come in a traditional information format such as forms and reports, or it may appear as emotional messages and opinions of students, teachers, parents or other school systems.

Our attention now turns to the formats themselves. Much of the communication that goes on in social systems is "formal." That is, it is stylized in format, limited in terms of subject matter, and regulated in terms of timing, source and destination. Consider a registration form, requisition forms or bills. These are messages, but severely limited ones, on a specific medium (paper), with specific information restricted to specific parts of the page and specific vocabulary required in each of these parts. Not all so-called formal communication is as rigid as these paper forms, but one factor – regulation of format and content – is paramount.

In organizations, formal communication is favored because it fits in neatly with the need organizations have to regulate their own behavior quickly. If messages are scheduled, easy to receive and hard to misinterpret, little time and energy is lost and matters that need attending to can be focussed on rather than on what a message means. Formal communication – "paperwork" to many – is also a burden because it is so limited. The normal range of human thought and emotion is enormous and most forms work to restrict this range to an infinitesimal fraction. Thus, when a memo from the principal asks for teachers to list their major curriculum-related equipment needs for the coming year in a checkoff fashion, it's not surprising that Mr. A, who wants the latest in microcomputers to demonstrate a particular kind of graphic processing to his art class, and Ms. B, who isn't really sure if she needs an electronic timer for her chemistry lab but would like to try out a number of them to see if they're any good, are confused and frustrated. Formal communication is not necessarily the best means of expressing things – it's just rapid and clear to the person who created the form.

Formal communication is also functional because it relates specifically to an organization's needs to meet its goals. So long as goals are really attainable, clear, and understood by everyone, formal communication can do the job. Unfortunately, these three characteristics are rarely found together and, in view of the fact that most complex social organizations also divide labor (see the next section), most people do not have only the simple messages that formal communication allows.

That's why informal communication is another characteristic of social organizations especially schools, where so much formal communication is already present. Now you may be confused: why are both kinds of communication characteristic of social organizations? Isn't this just a way of saying, after all, that there is a lot of variety in how people communicate in organizations? Yes, at one level what is being said here is that the formal/informal distinction is not the most important one. But, critically, there is a role for each type of communication. Although they coexist within the organization, they serve different functions in different ways. Informal communication serves to keep social functions going: the chit-chat in the coffee room lets the teachers know what everyone is doing, parents drop by a classroom and volunteer their time to find out what's happening there, students share their thoughts on the latest music fad with teachers, the principal and assistant principal discuss school board politics. None of this really "runs" the schools, but without it people wouldn't understand each other and would have difficulty forming relationships built on trust.

Another role for informal communication is to get information where formal channels do not work well. For example, the principal may have a teacher in for a work-related interview, say about curriculum. It's likely that an insecure teacher may not wish to expose problems, particularly to a principal who may look stern and unforgiving or merely be out of sorts today. The formal communication (interview) is not going to get information shared. Then, after the interview over coffee, when the teacher and the principal are discussing the local university, many exchanges may actually focus on curriculum matters, disguised as a critique of the undergraduate education program. Teachers will chat up the school secretary to get information that would be far more difficult to obtain in a limited form or may seem far more threatening in a memo. In other words, informal communication may apparently serve one of the functions of formal communication, but in a different way and at a different time.

Formal communication patterns tend to follow specific lines and these lines are engendered by the way work is divided in organizations. In fact, commonly when people refer to "the organization," they are actually talking about the way formal communication flows within the organization. This is the topic to which we'll turn our attention now.

Division of Labor

The final principle of organization is division of labor. This literally means that tasks are divided into chunks and made the responsibility of subsystems in the organization. We are all familiar with this principle from our earliest days in school working in groups or on teams. However, this seemingly simple principle really implies a number of fairly subtle things.

For instance, dividing labor is useless unless the goals, too, are divided and unless those subsystems' work is coordinated. This means that (1) a great deal of communication is necessary to inform people about goals, criteria, and methods for meeting those goals, (2) there has to be a coordinator, and (3) there has to be some systematic way for the subsystems to report on their activities to the coordinator.

To many minds, this implies a bureaucracy and, in fact, a bureaucracy is based strictly on these ideas. Bad bureaucracies focus exclusively on the mechanisms – how activities are coordinated – and ignore the content – the goals and the people working to meet them. Good bureaucracies temper, through communication, the need for coordination with the needs of those coordinated.

One important "formula" for making division of labor both effective and efficient is

RESPONSIBILITY = AUTHORITY

By this is meant that responsibility for getting some piece of a job done (some part of a goal) should have a corresponding authority over use of resources to get the job done. Too much responsibility creates unnecessary tension and anxiety; too little may result in inefficient use or wastage of resources.

Viewing division of labor as going from top (overall goals) down to smaller goals, reporting on performance (i.e., meeting responsibilities) is met through communicating in an upward fashion; coordination (i.e., exercising authority) is accomplished through sending messages in a downward fashion. When authority and responsibility are roughly equal, the two vectors are in a state of balanced tension. Student groups may, for example, be given some responsibilities for fund-raising for the school but no authority to say how they go about doing the fund-raising. In many cases there are few problems. But if the instructions are out of synch with the real world of student canvassing, then those directing the efforts (student-run organizations) may feel the imbalance as students report failure.

This balancing act is necessary in healthy organizations; an imbalance in either responsibility or authority can have dramatic and bad effects on performance. In some cases, people with small responsibilities for staff functions can make others' lives miserable by trying to exercise too much authority. Consider the "petty bureaucrat" who controls the conference room. Too much swaggering authority can make it difficult, if not impossible, for staff to meet and discuss problems and plan for solutions. The opposite problem can occur when school administrators heap too much responsibility on teachers who haven't the time an resources to meet them. Consider a teacher who has to handle 30 students, meet parents, serve on committees and work with student clubs and is then asked to coordinate an end-of-year planning session without any time off (time is a resource) or funds to do it.

An Example for Analysis

> Student lunch hours are too long. We think that we have a way to shorten the school day and help teachers find the time they need to meet and plan together. Our Parent Advisory Group has endorsed this concept. We will shorten lunch hour by 12 minutes daily and dismiss students at 1:30 every third Thursday. Please indicate below whether or not you support this idea by checking either the APPROVE or REJECT box below. Please return this form to the school by Thursday. To simplify things, if you support the idea, you don't have to return this form.
>
> – Note found in lunch kit on Monday afternoon

Let's look at this brief example in light of the five principles of organization we've examined.

1. Goals: what goals are being pursued, what criteria are being used to measure goal attainment, what resources are being directed toward goal attainment?

2. Self-Regulation: What is the self-regulation mechanism here, what critical events in the environment are being watched, what is the program or policy?

3. Openness: How open is the organization to input from its environment in terms of access, free flow, prejudgment, and feedback?

4. Formal Communication: What is the format of communication here, how is formal communication determining organization, and how functional is the formal communication?

5. Division of Labor: What do we know about how "labor" is being divided here, what kinds of coordination are necessary, and how effective is that coordination in terms of reporting, authority and responsibility?

Goals

We speak now only of goals that the intended changes seem aimed at. There seem to be two goals here: cutting down on wasted time in lunch periods and providing teachers with time to meet to do planning. These goals seem consonant in this example (i.e., time being wasted now on overly-long lunch periods will go toward increasing teachers' time for planning). The goals are clearly stated in the message.

Goal attainment measures seem obvious, although there may be other goals (for example, working parents may not be home to receive their children), so it is not clear that all the stakeholders in children's education share the goal-attainment measures. Finally, apparently the only resources expended at the moment are those necessary to reproduce the message and hand the copies out to students. The cost of the scheme, however, may be found by subtracting the benefits that teachers gain from the costs involved in changing bussing contracts and the time working parents may have to take off every third Thursday afternoon.

Self-Regulation

This message is being sent home with the students in order to determine what parents think of this idea (one already endorsed by the parent group). It seems obvious that parent opinion is an important concern for the principal and that the responses to the survey will be used to gauge parent opinion so that appropriate actions can be taken later either to institute or cancel the proposed changes in school schedule. However, there is no indication of what the policy is, what proportion of parents need to approve or reject the change, for example.

Openness

Access seems good on first glance, but note that Johnny's lunch kit is not a very reliable means of communication. Many parents will not receive the notice and the principal has stated that "No response" will be treated as approval (a disastrous assumption, as any public relations expert will tell you). Free flow is inhibited to an extent by the limitations of the form; parents aren't asked for suggestions, only to approve or reject one idea. The door doesn't appear "open." It's also apparent that the principal has prejudged the situation by providing only a single suggestion and by indicating the ambiguous fact of a prejudgment by the parent advisory group (which concept have they endorsed and what do they think the implications are?). Finally, the principal has not indicated how feedback will be used to inform parents that their responses have been taken into account.

Formal Communication

The format is obviously formal in the extreme. The message itself is limited in content to the issue at hand and the return message is merely going to be an X in a box. The directive tone of the message seems to indicate that while the principal is asking parents for the authority to change the school schedule (something one might assume in any case), in fact, the principal is communicating that the change is preferred regardless of whether or not parents respond. In other words, the parents are responsible to the principal, not the other way around! This sort of formal communication, especially couched in the terms it appears in, is hardly functional and the probability of a great deal of informal communication is almost total.

Division of Labor

There seems to be a split in responsibility for school scheduling, although the principal has ultimate responsibility. Decisions about the schedule are made by the principal, with the advice of the parent advisory group. The principal coordinates these efforts. Less obvious is the indication that parents are given great responsibilities with little authority other than that implied weakly in the notice to submit a vote. While the notice doesn't say a great deal about division of labor, the fact that principals are often given this kind of discretion points to that very division. How principals and other school administrators actually carry out their responsibilities is another question. Messages such as these make it difficult.

Section Five

Verbal and Nonverbal Communication

18

Communication Style in Education

Lynne Hughes

This chapter will examine some of the most essential elements of style, which very generally refers to the kind of language the writer or speaker chooses, and the way he or she arranges this language. The discussion of style will therefore deal mainly with diction and sentence construction; appropriate and inappropriate word choice and effective and ineffective sentences will be presented. The relationship among the writer or speaker, the writing or speaking situation, and the reader or audience will also be addressed. The information in these areas is by no means exhaustive; however, the reader should come away with a relatively sound perspective on what constitutes effective style.

Most of the material in this chapter is equally applicable to writing and speaking, except where noted. There are, nevertheless, some differences between the two forms of communication that should be kept in mind. Speaking to a group has the advantage that speakers can rely upon voice to add emphasis; writers have only the written words to convey their message. Determining audience response can occur more quickly in speaking, as there is immediate feedback, even while the presentation or speech is taking place. Thus speakers are able to adjust their work to meet audiences' requirements.

The tasks of writers are easier than speakers in other ways. Nervousness or stage fright is obviously not a problem, and writers are able to submit polished final versions, whereas speakers' final efforts may not be as effective as they would like them to be. Writers can present more information or examples than speakers, as a reading audience is able to take in more than a listening one. This advantage is particularly useful in a paper which seeks to persuade or influence – often a large number of reasons help sway opinion.

Despite the differences between oral and written discourse, the primary goal of both writers and speakers is to communicate their ideas clearly and fully to the readers or audience. Whether the goal is to inform a group about an issue, to persuade a group to act or think in a certain way, or simply to entertain an audience, writers and speakers will not be well-received if their essays or presentations are confusing and tedious. Thus style, when successful, helps a speech or paper become interesting and easily understood. These qualities are highly desirable in both written and oral work, and the ways of attaining them are similar in both endeavors.

Diction or word use is a major component of style, and can play a large role in the success or failure of communication. Writers and speakers can be perceived as educated, intelligent, thoughtful, and imaginative if their word choice suits the occasion. Inappropriate language often appears when writers and speakers have failed to take into account their subject and audience. The following kinds of language are usually best avoided:

1. *Slang.* Slag words have their place in particular types of discourse; however, they are inappropriate in most discussions because of their lack of precision, their tendency to become outdated, and the fact that they are not always easily understood by everyone. Examples include: *out to lunch, ticked off, screwed up, stuff.* Words that generally sound immature or juvenile should also be avoided: "That attitude drives me crazy"; "The movie was just wonderful, and I liked it a lot."[1]

2. *Cliches.* Trite expressions ought to be left out of most writing and speaking. Like slang, they tend to be over-used and lead to stale rather than vibrant communication. Although cliches are permissible in some informal presentations, they should be used carefully, and expressions like the following would be better replaced with less worn, more imaginative phrases:

a whole new ball game	down the road
hard as nails	sadder but wiser
the bottom line	history tells us
caring and sharing	the patience of Job
state of the art	the key factor
it is interesting to note	at this point in time

3. *Jargon.* Jargon refers to technical or special language of a profession or trade. It is legitimate when writers and speakers are addressing members of a particular profession, as they would be familiar with the terms. When an audience is general, consisting of different kinds of people with various backgrounds, however, jargon should be replaced with translations into everyday language. A linguist, for example, would stay away from terms such as free variation, and aspiration, and distinctive feature if he or she were writing or speaking to a general audience.

4. *"Big Words."* It is best to avoid pretentious diction or words that are too complex or formal for the context. Although some writers and speakers feel that this kind of diction makes them appear learned, frequently it confuses and annoys audiences rather than impresses them. It is preferable to trust your own voice and vocabulary; wherever possible, choose the smaller, simpler word. For example, "After receiving an answer in the

affirmative, the employee commenced his study" needs simplification: "After getting permission, the employee began his study." "Not a year passes without some evidence of the fundamental truth of the statement that the procedures and techniques of education are more complicated and complex than they were two decades ago" is better expressed as "Each year shows that methods of education are more complex than they were twenty years ago."[2] This revision not only makes the statement more easily understood, but it also substantially reduces the number of words.

5. *Concrete vs. abstract words.* Writers should try to use as many concrete nouns as possible. Concrete nouns are those which readers can easily visualize – *buildings, dogs, people,* etc. Abstract nouns or those words that refer to concepts or ideas, while definitely required at times, should be kept to a minimum, for example: *freedom, courage, discussion, behavior.* Remember that the most memorable communication creates definite images in audiences' minds.

6. *Omnibus words.* Words like *aspect, factor, thing, concept, situation* should be used carefully. They are appropriate in particular contexts, but they are too often used as all-purpose words and contribute little to the sentence in which they appear. For example, "The educational aspect of the workshop should be examined" might be better stated as "We should determine how educational the workshop will be."

Unnecessary or redundant words appear in almost everyone's writing and speaking from time to time. In his famous essay on language, "Language, Politics and the English Language," George Orwell explains why so much modern writing includes a great deal of padding:

> The attraction of this way of writing is that it is easy. It is easier – even quicker, once you have the habit - to say "In my opinion it is not an unjustifiable assumption that" than to say "I think." If you use ready-made phrases, you not only don't have to hunt about for words; you also don't have to bother with the rhythms of your sentences, since these are generally so arranged as to be more or less euphonious. When you are composing in a hurry – when you are dictating to a stenographer, for instance, or making a public speech – it is natural to fall into a pretentious, Latinized style. Tags like "a consideration which we should do well to bear in mind" or "a conclusion to which all of us would readily assent" will save many a sentence from coming down with a bump.[3]

Anyone who has tried to create rhythmic sentences without these crutches can agree with Orwell about the difficulty of eliminating redundant words and phrases. Nonetheless, those who are successful will find their writing and speaking much more concise and pleasurable to read or to listen to. The following words and phrases on the left can be replaced by the ones on the right:

at this point in time	now
in this day and age	now; today
prove conclusively	prove
alternative choices	choices

basic fundamentals	basics; fundamentals
completely eliminate	eliminate
because of the fact that	because
owing to the fact that	because
in view of the fact that	because
make a purchase	purchase; buy
prepare an analysis of	analyze
take action	act
make contact with	contact
each and every	each; every
one hundred in number	one hundred
blue in color	blue

These phrases can be totally eliminated:

it is obvious that
it is clear that
it is essential that
there are
there is
it was felt that
as it were
so to speak

Nominalization – the conversion of a verb into a noun – also occurs when writers want to sound more impressive, but this often creates stilted and wordy sentences. For example, "Examination of the data took place," "Discussion of costs occurred," and "Preparation of the lessons was done" can be rewritten as "The data was examined," "The costs were discussed," and "The lessons were prepared."[4] In the revisions, the main point of the sentence is made directly, and the nominalized verbs – "examination," "discussion," and "preparation" – became the main verbs.

The active voice is preferable to *the passive voice* in most cases. In the former, the subject of the sentence performs the action (I reviewed the book); in the latter, the subject receives the action or is acted upon (The book was reviewed by me). The active voice provides for more direct communication and fewer unnecessary words.

One of the easiest ways of arranging language into effective *sentences* is through choosing grammatical types of sentences. Used well, these types can add color, emphasis, and clarity to essays and presentations. There are four basic kinds of sentences:

1. *Simple* (one independent or main clause): The teacher started the class.
   The sentence remains simple even if the subject and/or the verb are compounded: The teacher and his aid started the class.
2. *Compound* (two independent or main clauses, joined by a coordinating conjunction or a colon or semicolon):
   The teacher started the class, and he walked to the blackboard.

The scholar was very productive: she wrote six articles and reviewed several books last year.
The principal met with the teachers; together, they constructed their policy.

3. *Complex* (one independent or main clause and at least one dependent or subordinate clause):
Although the principal met with the teachers, they were unable to construct their policy.
When the polling booths closed, the telecast began.
The salesperson returned our deposit although she was not obliged to do so.

4. Compound-complex (at least two independent or main clauses and at least one dependent or subordinate clause):
Because the game was nearly over, we left our seats and we headed for the parking lot.
Until the decision is made, the committee cannot proceed and the work that was to be done must wait.

All of these kinds of sentences can achieve particular effects. The simple sentence, for example, usually works best when it serves to announce a topic that will be discussed, when it emphasizes an idea immediately following, or when it deals with a very simple concept. The compound sentence often states issues of equivalent value or presents balanced ideas or contrasts, while the complex sentence illustrates more complicated thought, as it subordinates and reveals relationships between ideas. The compound-complex sentence usually deals with the most complex ideas of all, and is often found in formal, technical, or highly specialized papers or presentations.

Consider this paragraph from Vincent Massey's speech, "Uncertain Sounds":

Why do I call language such as I have cited, bad? For several very simple reasons. First, it is verbose. It says in three pages what could be said in one. Secondly, it is ugly. It has neither shape nor form, harmony nor rhythm. Thirdly, it is obscure. The writer, having to say what might easily be clear after one reading, seems to take pleasure in compelling us to a second or even a third. After sorting out all the clauses and phrases and connecting words, we are still left wondering exactly what the writer means. And this is not surprising, for the sins of this form of writing are not confined to their effects on the reader.[5]

Here Massey wants to accomplish two tasks: to emphasize how ineffective much modern language is, and to illustrate the relationship between the writer and the reader. He succeeds in his former task by citing his reasons in short, simple sentences. These reasons stand out much more clearly in their isolation than they would have in longer, more complicated sentence types. (Note also the emphatic second sentence fragment, which calls attention to the word "simple.") Massey next communicates a more complicated concept – what happens between the writer and the reader – by using the complex and compound-complex construction in the last two sentences.

The following paragraph appears in Martin Luther King, Jr.'s essay, "The Answer to a Perplexing Question":

> We must pray earnestly for peace, but we must also work vigorously for disarmament and the suspension of weapon testing. We must use our minds as rigorously to plan for peace as we have used them to plan for war. We must pray with unceasing passion for racial justice, but we must also use our minds to develop a program, organize ourselves into mass nonviolent action, and employ every resource of our bodies and souls to bring into being those social changes that make for a better distribution of wealth within our nation and in the underdeveloped countries of the world.[6]

Here King first uses a compound sentence to emphasize the equal importance of praying for and working towards peace. The last sentence is compound-complex, which again reveals the equivalent values of passive and active efforts and also conveys the complexity involved in the struggle for a better world. The relative length of this last sentence reflects the enormity of the task as well.

Sentences can lose their effectiveness if there are basic errors in them. The following faults most frequently occur:

1. *Sentence fragments.* The fragment or incomplete sentence (a word, phrase or dependent clause which does not contain a subject and a finite verb) should be avoided in most writing. For example, "The discussion lasted four hours. A long, tedious, and basically unproductive event" would be better put as "The discussion, lasting four hours, was long, tedious, and basically unproductive." In speaking, of course, when grammatical rules do not have to be followed so closely, fragments used for emphasis are acceptable. These ought not to be used too often, though, as they can lead to an overly dramatic effect.

2. *The comma splice.* One of the most common writing errors, the comma splice consists of two main or independent clauses joined together by only a comma: for example, "Many issues were dealt with at the school board meeting, only a few problems were solved." The comma splice can be corrected in the following ways:

   1) Replace the comma with a period: "Many issues were dealt with at the school board meeting. Only a few problems were solved."
   2) Replace the comma with the semi-colon: "Many issues were dealt with at the school board meeting; only a few problems were solved."
   3) Join the two clauses by a coordinating conjunction: "Many issues were dealt with at the school board meeting, but only a few problems were solved."
   4) Make one of the clauses into a dependent clause: "Although many issues were dealt with at the school board meeting, only a few problems were solved."

3. *Mixed construction.* This kind of fault involves shifting from one sentence pattern to another in the middle of a sentence. A frequent error of this kind occurs in the "this-is-when" construction: "A good book is when you can't put it down." Remember that when "is" functions as a linking verb, it must join two nouns and not a noun and a "when" clause. The correction would read: "A good book is one that you can't put down."
Another mixed construction appears in the "reason is because" sentence; for example, "The reason he is returning to school is because he wants to get his doctorate." The sentence is not grammatical because "is" is a verb of definition and nouns have to be defined in terms of other nouns. The word *reason* must be defined by a word or words that function as a noun. Therefore, the sentence can be written correctly in two ways: "He is returning to school because he wants to get his doctorate"; or "The reason he is returning to school is that he wants to get his doctorate."

4. *Lack of parallelism.* Words, phrases, or clauses that form a series and serve the same function should be expressed in the same grammatical form – in parallel form. Sentences which lack parallelism often seem clumsy and can be confusing. For example, "Her duties included recording minutes, supervision of staff, training new employees, and maintenance of office supplies" would be better written as "Her duties included recording minutes, supervising staff, training new employees and maintaining office supplies."

5. *Dangling modifier.* Modifying words must modify a word that is directly stated in the sentence, not merely implied. For example, "Having studied the report, the decision was made" makes little sense. "Having studied the report, the committee made its decision" clarifies the sentence.

6. *Shifts.* Writers and speakers should be as consistent as possible in the use of number and person. Unless the context requires it, shifts from the singular to the plural should be avoided. For example, "teacher" should be either singular or plural in the following sentences: "The teacher initially needs detailed lesson plans. As they gain experience, however, teachers spend less time laboriously planning their classes."
Shifts between first person (I, we), second person (you), and third person (one, he/she, they) also generally should be absent in writing and speaking. "If one has to deal with a very emotional subject, you need to stay as calm as you can" ought to read, "If you have to deal with a very emotional subject, you need to stay as calm as you can." Throughout an essay or presentation, the use of person, like the use of number, should be as consistent as possible, given the context.

7. *Incomplete comparisons.* All comparisons should be complete to avoid confusion. Sentences such as "Our course selection is wider" need to be expanded to "Our course selection is wider than that of the college in British Columbia." Illogical comparisons need to be re-worked also: "The library here is larger than the University of Lethbridge" makes more sense as "The library here is larger than the library at the University of

Lethbridge."

As mentioned, the audience whom the writer or speaker is addressing must be taken into account when choosing style. Frank A. Brown, Jr. has written the following three paragraphs which can help illustrate the importance of audience. They all deal with the same subject, but his audiences are very different in each and thus he must alter his style accordingly.

> 1. "Recent studies have provided reasons to postulate that the primary timer for long-cycle biological rhythms that are closely similar in period to the natural geophysical ones and that persist in so-called constant conditions is, in fact, one of organismic response to subtle geophysical fluctuations which pervade ordinary constant conditions in the laboratory (Brown, 1959, 1960). In such constant laboratory conditions a wide variety of organisms have been demonstrated to display, nearly equally conspicuously, metabolic periodicities of both solar-day and lunar-day frequencies, with their interference derivative, the 29.5 day synodic month, and in some instances even the year. These metabolic cycles exhibit day-by-day irregularities and distortions which have been established to be highly significantly correlated with aperiodic meteorological and other geophysical changes. These correlations provide strong evidence for the exogenous origin of these biological periodisms themselves, since cycles exist in these meteorological and geophysical factors."[7]

The article from which this paragraph was taken appears in *Physiological Zoology*. Obviously the audience is a specialized group who would be familiar with the scientific jargon; only a scholarly audience would not need definition of "long-cycle biological rhythms," "metabolic periodicities," and "interference derivative." Because the concepts are rather involved, complex and compound-complex sentences can be used.

> 2. "Familiar to all are the rhythmic changes in innumerable processes of animals and plants in nature. Examples of phenomena geared to the 24-hour solar day produced by rotation of the earth relative to the sun are sleep movements of plant leaves and petals, spontaneous activity in numerous animals, emergence of flies from their pupal cases, color changes of the skin in crabs, and wakefulness in man. Sample patterns of daily fluctuations, each interpretable as adaptive for the species, are illustrated in Fig. 1. Rhythmic phenomena linked to the 24-hour and 50-minute lunar-day period of rotation of the earth relative to the moon are most conspicuous among intertidal organisms whose lives are dominated by the ebb and flow of the ocean tides. Fiddler crabs forage on the beaches exposed at low tide; oysters feed when covered by water. "Noons" of sun- and moon-related days come into synchrony with an average interval of 29+ days, the synodic month; quite precisely of this average interval are such diverse phenomena as the menstrual cycle of the human being and the breeding rhythms of numerous marine organisms, the latter timed to specific phases of the moon and critical for assuring union of reproductive elements. Examples of annual biological rhythms, whose 365 day periods are produced by the orbiting about the sun of the earth with its tilted axis, are so well known as scarcely to require mention."[8]

This paragraph appears in a science journal, and its audience seems to be scientifically knowledgeable as well, but not as specialized as the previous one. The language is relatively formal, the sentences are fairly lengthy, and there are few simple sentences.

> 3. "One of the greatest riddles of the universe is the uncanny ability of living things to carry out their normal activities with clocklike precision at a particular time of the day, month and year. Why do oysters plucked from a Connecticut bay and shipped to a Midwest laboratory continue to time their lives to ocean tides 800 miles away? How do potatoes in hermetically sealed containers predict atmospheric pressure trends two days in advance? What effects do the lunar and solar rhythms have on the life habits of man? Living things clearly possess powerful adaptive capacities – but the explanation of whatever strange and permeative forces are concerned continues to challenge science. Let us consider the phenomena more closely."⁹

This excerpt, the least complex and most informal of the three, originates in *Saturday Evening Post*. Its audience would consist of intelligent readers with diverse backgrounds, who most likely have an interest in general science that explains fascinating phenomena. The diction, while not simplistic, consists of words that most would understand. The sentences contain fewer words than the two previous paragraphs; the sentences are mostly simple or compound.

Ultimately, style involves consideration of all the elements in the rhetorical situation – the speaker or writer, the subject, and the nature of the audience. Speakers and writers need to ensure that their sentences and diction particularly suit the occasion and the group addressed. When style is appropriate, it helps provide clarity, interest, and enjoyment in a presentation or paper, which are key qualities in effective communication.

Notes

[1]Many of the word use and sentence errors appear in the *Detailed Marking Code*, The Effective Writing Service, The University of Calgary, 1984.

[2]Glenn Leggett, C. David Mead, and William Charvat, eds. *Prentice-Hall Handbook for Writers*, 7 ed. (Englewood Cliffs, New Jersey: Prentice-Hall, Inc., 1978), 315.

[3]George Orwell, "Politics and the English Language," *The Essayist*, 4 ed., ed. Sheridan Baker (New York: Harper and Row, 1981), 275-276.

[4]For an even more direct revision, the sentence can be written in the active rather than the passive voice: "We examined the data"; "The group discussed the costs"; "The teacher prepared the lesson."

[5]Vincent Massey, "Uncertain *Sounds*," *Speaking of Canada* (Toronto: MacMillan Co., 1959), 189.

[6]Martin Luther King, "The Answer to a Perplexing Question," *The Essayist, 5 ed., ed. Sheridan Baker and C. Jeriel Howard (New York: Harper and Row, 1985), 68.*

[7]Frank A. Brown, Jr. and Emma K. Terracini, "Periodisms in Mouse 'Spontaneous' Activity Synchronized with Major Geophysical Cycles," *Physiological Zoology 35* (January 1962): 27.

[8]Frank A. Brown, Jr., "Living Clocks," *Science* 130 (4 December 1959): 1534.

[9]Frank A. Brown, Jr., "Life's Mysterious Clocks," *Saturday Evening Post* 233 (24 December 1954): 18.

19

Oral Interpretation in Education

Madeline Keaveney

Literature is a social institution; it is one of the ways that we talk to one another. Through literature we experience a sense of the other by contacting other individuals, other places, other times.[1] Far from being peripheral to our lives, literature continues to be central to our human experience. Although literature is not identical to our daily realities, it touches upon reality and gives us a rich framework from which to judge our experiences.[2]

Oral interpretation helps us to share our experience of literature with others. It is a highly communal process whereby we communicate to an audience the intellectual, emotional, and aesthetic facets of a literary work. We embody the text, giving it social, oral, and visual substance; by using our voices, bodies, faces, and gestures we flesh out the textual clues available to the silent reader.[3]

Oral interpretation is both an art and a skill. It is a means of elucidating, clarifying, explaining. It is a disciplined sharing of meaning through verbal and non-verbal language. Historically, literature was first an oral art, practiced by diverse cultures as a means of preserving cultural identity, teaching cultural values, and entertaining. Literature is first accessible to a child orally. Through the skilled use of oral interpretation, we can make these first literary experiences enlightening and memorable and can encourage the reading and sharing of good literature.[4]

In this chapter we will examine how an understanding of point of view, narrators, and characterization can enrich oral interpretation performances. Then we will discuss general criteria for selecting literature for oral performance. Finally, we will look at how storytelling, the oral performance of folktales and poetry, and the use of group performance can be integrated into an oral performance program.

249

Point of View

Point of view is a concept central to the understanding of oral interpretation. Technically speaking, it is the perspective (angle) from which the narrator (storyteller) descries (describes, sees, illuminates) persons, places, and events (the world of the story).[5] It is the physical and psychological position that the narrator takes in revealing plot (the sequence of changes in human relations) and character.[6] If you asked each person in your class to attend a baseball game and to come back to class to tell you what each saw, certain features of each story would be the same – the score of the game, the time of day the game was played, etc. But the stories would have many differences that can be accounted for by remembering the concept of point of view. The physical position of the storyteller – whether he was seated in a box seat or the bleachers – will, in part, determine what he is able to see and report. The amount of knowledge of the game that the storyteller brings to this particular game will, in part, determine how much the storyteller is able to understand of what he sees. The ability of the storyteller to explain and describe will affect the story told. The degree of objectivity and interest of the storyteller will affect the story told; if the storyteller knows a player on one of the teams, he will tend to pay more attention to the feats of that player than he will to what the entire team is doing.

This example may seem to have little to do with oral interpretation or literature, but it illustrates how our perspective changes our view and helps to determine what we see, how we interpret what we see, and how we are able to describe what we see. The point of view of a particular literary selection determines how we come to see the fictional world. Understanding the point of view utilized in each literary piece we choose for performance will enable us to present orally the vision and experience of life embodied in that particular literary text.

Narrators

The narrator or storyteller is the person in the piece of literature in whom the point of view is lodged. Generally speaking, narrators are either first-person narrators or third-person narrators, i.e., they either tell stories about themselves or tell stories about others.

First-person storytellers are generally participants in the action of the story they tell. Because this storyteller is saying "I am going to tell you a story about something that happened to me," the storyteller is subjective, i.e., because she is a character in the story recognized by other characters, the story she tells is distorted by her own prejudices, biases, ignorance, etc. As readers or listeners we only know what the narrator chooses to tell us about herself or others; we receive the narrator's interpretation of reality rather than any objective documentation. Thus, the first-person narrator's interpretation of self and others in the story should be suspect. On the other hand, this narrator is credible; she was there as an eye-witness to events. She can tell us her thoughts and feelings at the time of the events of the story as well as now. However, because she is involved in the story, she may have a limited ability to evaluate accurately her own actions and feelings, let alone those of other characters in the story. It is this tension between subjectivity and credibility that is the hallmark of the first-person narrator.

These characteristics of first-person storytellers should not be surprising. Many of us tell stories about significant events in our lives. In so doing we may exaggerate how eloquent we were, how unfairly we were treated, etc. Our listeners will seldom know the reality of the situation we describe but will be limited to the details we choose to give. A character in our story that we have presented negatively may, in reality, be an extremely reasonable person. Our listeners have only our character portrayal from which to judge. So, too, in the literary stories we encounter, we must depend on the narrator for the details of the story we are told.

In contrast to the first-person narrator, the third-person narrator tells us a story about others. He may tell us the thoughts and feelings of one or more characters (thus exercising the literary option of omniscience) or he may tell his story based on what he has observed and surmised. He is, therefore, more objective because he is not centrally involved in the story, but less credible than the first-person narrator. However, even though he is less subjective than the first-person narrator, he is not entirely objective. If he has access to the mind of a character, he will tend to identify with and sympathize with that character, while, at the same time, being able to shape our responses. He may be limited to his own thoughts, feelings, and conjectures about others, but he is still a human being with human prejudices and the human capacity for ignorance and misinterpretations.[7]

Take, for example, the story of "The Three Little Bears." This story is told by a third-person storyteller who gives us details about Goldilocks and each of the three bears. In most versions of the story, Goldilocks is portrayed as a careless, rude girl who enters a private home uninvited and steals and destroys private property. We can only imagine what the story would have been like if Goldilocks had been the narrator and we had seen the story from her point of view.

Although an understanding of narrators may not necessarily lead to better oral performances of literature, such an understanding should help to make us more sensitive to the narrative character and his/her effect on the story being told.

Characterization

In choosing to present orally a selection of literature, we are faced with problems that the silent reader does not encounter. We must use both verbal and nonverbal means to fully communicate the literary piece. This means suggesting, as appropriate, the age, sex, nationality, and cultural background of the narrator or characters, as well as a character's personality and how that character differs from others.

The voice is the major tool at our disposal. Through pitch, pace, and volume we can, for example, communicate the sex of the narrator or character, as well as differences in relative social position, age, and emotional health. Through changes in pronunciation and articulation we can help the audience to understand the cultural backgrounds of different characters. The strategic use of pauses can increase emotional intensity and also differentiate characters. Additionally, we can use facial expressions, gestures, and body stance to suggest sex, age, relative sizes of characters, and a character's emotional makeup. All of these nonverbal tools add a dimension of intellectual and emotional depth to the literary selection and bring out qualities inherent in the literature but ones that may be missed by the inexperienced reader. An oral performance of a good piece of literature is memorable, a feast for the eyes and the ears.

Selecting Literature for Performance

Before examining specific types of literature to perform, we need to look at criteria for selecting literature that will lend itself to oral performance. The first, and most important, guideline is to choose something that is of interest to both the performer and the audience. Literature that is orally performed should not be perceived by the audience as just another way to get course content across, even though a well performed literary selection can enhance the curriculum. The literature and the performance of the literature should add something to the lives of the listeners. Secondly, the literature chosen should be at least partially accessible to the audience from a single oral presentation. There is a difference between what a child can read herself and what she can understand from a dynamic performance. A successful oral performance can address an audience's interest, and, at the same time, make accessible literature that is too difficult or confusing for silent reading. At the same time, there is literature that is too difficult for oral performance, with confusing characters, a wandering plot line, or vocabulary too conceptually advanced for the audience. The wise performer will perform such literature only when he is fully able to explain potentially confusing parts to the audience.

Thirdly, the literature selected should be worthy of the performance effort, presenting unique characters who have universal human appeal. Simplistic literature isn't worth the time of the performer or the audience. The theme or message of the literature should stretch the thinking of the audience. In addition, the literature should be well written, with memorable style and language usage.

Finally, attention should be paid to the emotional coloration of the performed selection. Many examples of literature that are part of our heritage present different racial or ethnic groups pejoratively or depict women in a demeaning manner. These literary pieces should be used cautiously. Children imitate the models we present to them in literature and absorb literary values.

Presenting a variety of literary models that introduce children to differing value systems and world views will help them to live in and make judgments about our increasingly multicultural world.

Storytelling

Storytelling is an ancient art. From time immemorial human beings have told stories to satisfy their curiosity, provide models of competence, entertain, and share a sense of belonging and the wonder of the world around them. Because storytelling is often a child's first contact with literature and literary education, it is especially important that serious attention be given to how storytelling can affect children.

Storytelling has many values. It can be a shared activity between adult and child. Children are natural storytellers who delight in having an adult make the effort to enter their world. The conversational stance of storytelling is closer to the child's world than the more distance and formal world of silent reading. It is also an activity that brings the imagination into play and encourages fantasizing by offering a direct avenue to knowledge and a means for children to understand and express thoughts and feelings, while, at the same time, allowing children to savor life in worlds different from their own. Storytelling allows us to see and hear imaginary worlds unfolding in front of us, worlds that may represent a welcome respite from the struggle of silent reading. It is an activity that provides an excellent opportunity to exercise listening skills that are important for success in school and life. And, finally, storytelling often allows us to deal indirectly with issues that the child may need to address. A child may be unable or unwilling to talk about a sensitive topic, such as, divorce; a well told story dealing with the issue may help the child understand what is happening to him through the thoughts and feelings of the characters in the story.

Before picking a story for oral performance, some attention should be given to age-appropriate interests and abilities. Young children, in the three to six year old range, love repetition, as evidenced by the delight that children have in repeating new words and sounds. Because children of this age have limited literary experience and limited attention spans, stories with simple talking animals, concrete familiar objects, and repetitious plots work well. Stories focussing on the senses are particularly effective, as are stories about characters and activities that are part of the young child's world. Children in the six to nine year old age group are more sophisticated consumers of stories. They are learning to read and are being exposed to a wide variety of stimuli. Tales of travel, primitive times, folktales, and simple history stories are effective. Children in the nine to twelve year old age group are looking for role models; stories of danger, action, and mystery, as well as stories about favorite sports and animals, are particular favorites.[8]

Once the performer has thought about the age group to whom the story will be presented, the next step is to prepare the story for performance. Whether the story chosen is one the performer has created or is a prose narrative familiar to the audience., the performer should thoroughly read or think through the story, perhaps making sketchy notes, so that key story episodes and their relationship to one another can be identified. At times, if the story is a child's favorite, the performer may even choose to tell the story word for word, but this first step in preparing a story will still be important. After key episodes have been identified, the performer needs to think through the structure of the story, identifying major plot lines and any subsidiary plots. Knowledge of the plot, coupled with knowledge of the key episodes, will help the performer to move smoothly from one section of the story to the next, using interesting and refreshing word choice aimed at audience understanding and enjoyment. Next, the performer should think about the characters in the story and how he can make those characters memorable. Attention paid to physical and psychological details will pay off in increased interest and pleasure on the part of the audience. Finally, transitions should be considered so that the story segments flow smoothly, capturing and retaining audience attention.

The next decision that needs to be made is whether any visual aids will be used with the stories. Because visual aids add interest to any presentation, it is always tempting to use them to augment performance interest. Pictures, appropriate costumes, objects, puppets, and flannel boards are favorites of almost all audiences. However, the wise performer will vary her performance style, sometimes telling stories with visual aids and sometimes opting to use only her voice, body, and the power of the story to enrich the experience of the audience. Next, the performer will probably want to consider the environment in which the story is going to be told. A warm, comfortable atmosphere is desirable, with clear sight lines for all of the audience. An uncluttered area is also best, since the storyteller will want to be able to help the audience focus on the story being told. And, the area chosen should be one where everyone in the audience will be able to hear comfortably. In short, the ideal storytelling area is one wherein the audience can be comfortable but one wherein focused listening and viewing are possible.

Once all of these steps have been addressed by the storyteller, he should think about how he wants to begin the storytelling. For a young, rowdy audience, a simple finger play or quiet song can be used to set the mood and to get the audience focused on the storytelling activity. For all audiences, the introduction should be long enough to give any necessary information, set the mood, and motivate the audience to listen. The introduction is an opportunity for the audience to settle down while the storyteller creates a bond between himself and the audience.

The final step in the storytelling preparation process is practice. Special attention should be given to character names and words that are difficult to pronounce. The performer should work for characters who are vocally and physically differentiated from one another. Clear diction, with appropriate volume and pace, as well as interesting vocabulary, will insure that the story will be accessible and enjoyable to the audience. Facial expressions and gestures should be rehearsed that add to the power of the story. And the performer should continue to practice until she knows the story well, to insure quality eye contact with the audience. If these simple guidelines are followed, the storytelling experience will be exciting for both the performer and the audience.

Folktales

Folktales are another almost universal literary form that have been traditionally used in most cultures both to entertain and to teach, thereby perpetuating standards and binding societies together.

Basic folktales are stories regarded as fiction, although many contain a lesson or moral. Tales of talking beasts and fairy tales (with magic objects and enchanted people) would fall into this category. Often the function of these tales is to pass on a culture's rules or values. Because they are often short, with a relatively simple plot and vocabulary, basic folktales are a natural choice to perform for children.

Myths, another kind of folk literature, are stories that are often considered true stories of what happened in the past and are usually told to keep an ethic in tact. These stories often explain the origin of facets of a culture or illuminate the ways of gods with humans. An understanding of myths, particularly those from Greece and Rome, is an indispensable part of any child's education in literary and cultural allusions. However, because myths are often part of the religious life of a particular culture, some knowledge of the original cultural setting and any performance taboos is desirable, so that the integrity of the myth can be maintained. Finally, legends are also popular choices for oral performance, particularly for older children who see role models in the stories of Betsy Ross or St. Francis of Assisi. Older children also react positively to fables, because the brief narratives often focus on notions of good and evil, appropriate and inappropriate behavior. Although fables may be selectively shared with younger children, the often high level of abstraction in fables makes them more appropriate for an older audience.

In sharing any kind of folk literature with an audience, we are often introducing the audience to a culture different from their own. In addition to the pleasure we derive from such tales, we reinforce and share the standards that bind societies together and bridge the generations.

Poetry

Poetry is mysterious, wonderful, evocative. It alters our view of the world, because it concerns itself with human doubts, frailties, triumphs, and disappointments.

Children's poetry is often didactic, meant to teach a lesson. It tells a story, with a plot and interesting characters. Poetry that is dramatic, much like a mini-play, is also appealing to children. And poetry that is expressive, reflecting observations, emotions, and impressions of the world and the creatures in it will capture a child's imagination.

Performing poetry orally for an audience has many values. A skilled performer can instill in the audience a love for and an appreciation of the power of language. Because poetic language is compacted, each word carries a great deal of weight; oral performance can lighten the burden of understanding. The oral performance of poetry brings out the musicality and rhythm in poems and emphasizes these elements particularly attractive to children. Additionally, the oral performance of poetry can help an audience grapple with the often strongly emotional but evasive meaning in a poem. Images that might be confusing in a silent reading are embodied and clarified in oral performance, helping the audience to experience the poem's sensations. Because poetry is pleasing to the ear, an oral performance can be both more enjoyable and more understandable than a silent reading. In addition to the selection criteria noted earlier in this chapter, oral performers should be alert for poems that combine the child's love of language sounds and music with the child's love for story and action. For beginning poetry listeners, short poems that deal with experiences and emotions in the child's world will help the child begin to experience poetry positively. Poems with sensory appeals, nonsense, and humor are also appropriate, as are poems that feature melody and rhythm.

When first seen on a written page, a poem can appear to be an intimidatingly odd creature that seems strange to the child unaccustomed to exploring the delights of poetry. However, to the child who has been introduced orally to poetry from different cultures and eras, the poem on the page will be seen as a new challenge well worth the effort. Young children begin their formal education with a sense of joy about language; the oral performance of poetry can strengthen that joy and open up a rich legacy of emotional and intellectual understanding and satisfaction.

Group Performance

Group performance is an exciting option for involving more than one person in the oral sharing of literature. In its most basic form, group performance means assigning the narrative lines to one performer and having other performers deliver the lines of characters in the story. Props, scenery, costuming, makeup, and lighting can all be imaginary or mimed, as can be actions (such as turning on a light or climbing up a mountain). Performers can become chairs to sit on, horses to ride, doors to open. Because each performer has the support of others, group performance can be an invaluable tool for encouraging children to participate in the performance of literature.[10]

Group performance can also be done with a compiled script. Such scripts typically utilize a number of literary selections connected by some common theme – how a holiday is celebrated in different lands, growing from childhood to adulthood, an exploration of the works of an individual author. Compiled presentations typically feature solo and group performances and may be used for in-class exercises or for public assemblies.[11]

The most complicated of the group approaches to the performance of literature is Chamber Theatre, originated by Robert Breen of Northwestern University as a means of dramatizing narrative point of view. Utilizing many techniques of traditional theater, Chamber Theatre performances range from inexpensive group demonstrations of literature to elaborately staged productions complete with costumes, lights, props, etc.

Chamber Theatre is an exciting medium because of the potential it offers for exploring a piece of literature. Because the narrator of a story is featured, the staging in Chamber Theatre allows us to see the here and now of the storytelling as well as the there and then of the action. Chamber Theatre allows us to show simultaneously the "real" action of a story and anything happening in an imaginary world. The staging of Chamber Theatre allows us to see both conscious and unconscious messages; we can dramatize both what a character is saying aloud to others and what a character is really thinking. Because Chamber Theatre allows for the use of dance, song, and multi-media tools such as video and slides, we can both tell a story and make ironic comments on it, if such seems appropriate.

In short, Chamber Theatre is a type of group performance that allows us to be imaginative and still focus on the literature being performed. In dramatizing the narrator, the script will redefine the position of the narrator in theatrical and social terms. The narrator's psychological relationship with the story will be translated into a social reality. For example, if the narrator seems to be a very controlled person who clearly controls our view of the characters and the action, we might choose to embody the narrator as a doctor or a play director. If the narrator seems to be chatty and interested in gossipy details about the characters, you might choose to embody the narrator as a servant. If the narrator gives us access to the mind of one of the characters, we might choose to embody the narrator as a confidante of that character. If the narrator seems to be a highly manipulative person, you might embody the narrator as a puppeteer controlling the characters and their actions. Additionally, Chamber Theatre translates into social terms the narrator's relationship to the characters and action. As appropriate, we see the narrator interact with characters back in the action, or remain aloof, or spy on them. Finally, the narrator's stylistic traits are also translated into social terms. If the narrator is animated or flamboyant or clinical or stilted or melodramatic or poetic or descriptive, these psychological stylistic traits will be embodied in the narrator's dress and physical appearance, gestures, and general demeanor.

The next step in the process is to make decisions concerning other script features such as the number of actors to be used and line assignments. If a narrator or character has a particularly complex personality, we might choose to assign an actor to embody each facet of the personality. If there are several characters in the story that serve similar functions, we might choose to have one actor play all of these characters, to underscore the similarity of roles. Narrative lines can be reserved for the narrator or characters may say narrative lines about themselves, depending on the character's level of self-awareness. Dialogue tags can be retained, not only as an identification of who is talking but as a means for either the narrator or character to comment on action or character. Lines may be repeated by several characters, showing contradictory points of view or as a means of underscoring what is being said or as a way of creating a choral effect.

In this short essay, it is not possible to fully explore the possibilities of Chamber Theatre.[12] Suffice it to say that Chamber Theatre is an exciting medium. It can simultaneously show us narrator and characters, as well as different levels of reality and a character's actions as well as her thoughts and feelings. However, in inexpereienced hands, Chamber Theatre is a medium with potential drawbacks. Because the medium is so rich, with so many options and possibilities, some novice directors lose the text in the midst of all of the extras. Despite its potential drawbacks, however, Chamber Theatre, as well as other forms of group performance, offers exciting possibilities for exploring literature and presenting it to an audience in novel and stimulating ways.

Conclusion

In this essay we have taken a brief look at some of the possibilities open to the person wanting to share orally literature with an audience. Oral interpretation can be used in a variety of contexts – as a probe for writing assignments, as a way of sharing a literary selection that illuminates an era in history, as a means of studying another culture, or merely as a means of enjoyment. However it is used, oral interpretation is a skill and an art that can create in an audience a lifelong love for reading and literature.

Notes

[1]Wallace A. Bacon, "A Sense of Being: Interpretation and the Humanities," *Southern Speech Communication Journal* 11 (1976): 135-141.

[2]Wallace A. Bacon and Robert S. Breen, *Literature as Experience.* (New York: McGraw-Hill, 1959).

[3]For general background on oral interpretation, as well as genres and styles of performance, consult such texts as Charlotte Lee and Timothy Gura, *Oral Interpretation,* 6th Edition (Boston: Houghton Mifflin Company, 1982) and Beverly Whitaker Long and Mary Frances Hopkins, *Performing Literature* (Englewood Cliffs: Prentice-Hall, Inc., 1982).

[4]For further information on the history of oral interpretation, see David W. Thompson's edited book entitled *Performance of Literature in Historical Perspective* (Lanham, Md.: University Press of America, 1983).

[5]Mary Lascelles, *Jane Austin and Her Art* (London: Oxford University Press, 1939): 20.

[6]Two concise books that further explicate the concept of point of view as well as other important ideas relevant to oral interpretation are Charlotte Lee's *Speaking of Interpretation* (Glenview, Illinois: Scott Foresman and Company, 1975) and K.B. Valentine's *Interlocking Pieces* (Dubuque: Kendall/Hunt Publishing Company,

1977).

[7]For further information about narrators, consult any basic oral interpretation text and/or Wayne C. Booth's *The Rhetoric of Fiction* (Chicago: University of Chicago Press, 1961).

[8]Zena Sutherland, Dianne L. Monson, and May Hill Arbuthnot, "Understanding Children," *Children & Books*. Sixth Edition (Glenview, Illinois: Scott, Foresman and Company, 1981): 19-38.

[9]William Bascom, "The Forms of Folklore: Prose Narrative," *Journal of American Folklore* 78 (1965): 3-20.

[10]For more reading about group performance, see Beverly Whitaker Long, Lee Hudson and Phillis Rienstra Jeffrey's *Group Performance of Literature* (Englewood Cliffs: Prentice-Hall, Inc., 1977) and Marion L. Kleinau and Janet Larsen McHughes's *Theatres for Literature* (Sherman Oaks, Ca.: Alfred Publishing Col, Inc., 1980).

[11]Any literature used for a public performance is subject to restrictions as enumerated in copyright law. For further details see Madeline M. Keaveney, "Issues in Interpretation," *Literature in Performance* 1 (1980): 108-111.

[12]For further information see Joanna Hawkins Maclay, *Readers Theatre: Toward a Grammar of Practice* (New York: Random House, 1971) or Robert S. Breen, *Chamber Theatre* (Englewood Cliffs: Prentice-Hall, Inc., 1978).

20

Speech Anxiety in the Classroom

Joe Ayres

"I have to give a speech tonight, but I can't think of anything to say. I don't know why the boss asked me to do this anyway. Look at me, I'm shaking like a leaf. I'll never be able to give this speech."

Given the way this person is thinking, it is not surprising he or she is nervous. Feelings of anxiety emerge when we think we have nothing going for us. This chapter is premised on the notion that positive, not negative, thinking enables us to cope with speech anxiety. In order to encourage positive thinking about public speaking four specific exercises are presented. The first exercise is designed to identify your public speaking strengths and suggests how you can use your strengths to overcome your weaknesses. The second exercise is designed to help you identify irrational, negative thoughts you may have about public speaking and to help you learn how to counter those thoughts. The third exercise helps you associate positive, relaxed feelings with public speaking, and the last exercise helps you visualize yourself in a positive and constructive manner during a public speech. Working through this set of exercises will help you develop positive thoughts about public speaking.

Exercise 1: Assessing Your Strengths and Weaknesses as a Speaker

Every speaking situation involves a speaker, an audience, the speech and the setting. Any or all of these elements can contribute to speech anxiety.1 This portion of this chapter discusses how you can determine which of these areas are contributing to the anxiety you experience during a speech.

The Speech

Every speech can be considered in terms of its purpose, complexity, familiarity, and importance to the speaker.

Purpose. Speech purposes range from descriptive in nature to persuasive in nature. Most people experience less fear when they have to describe something (vis. a recent vacation) than they do when they are trying to persuade (vis. convincing others to purchase a specific vacation package).

Complexity. In general the less complex a topic is the less fear it will provoke. Discussing the availability of word processing programs should produce less anxiety than explaining how such programs are constructed.

Familiarity. Talking about something you know very well is usually much less fear provoking than talking about something you know very little about.

Importance to the Speaker. Presenting a speech that concerns things that are near and dear to your heart is likely to produce more fear than talking about something you do not particularly care about. If you are a women's rights advocate and have been asked to make a presentation about those issues, you will probably be more fearful than you would be if you were asked to talk about restaurants you had visited recently.

Audience

The audience is a central part of the speaking situation. Several aspects of the audience are related to stage fright including knowledge level, size, and disposition.

Knowledge Level. If the audience knows more than you do about a topic, fear potential is high.

Size. Generally speaking, talking to a group of ten is much less fear provoking than addressing a group of five hundred. This reaction to the size of the group is due in large part to how conspicuous the speaker feels and how impersonal the audience seems to be.

Disposition. There are a number of ways to consider audience disposition but one important way is to consider whether the audience is in favor of, neutral toward, or against the position you are taking. Talking to audiences that do not like your views is more fear provoking than talking to people who agree with you.

Speaker

From the standpoint of stage fright there are at least three characteristics of speakers that need to be considered – motivation, experience, and credibility.

Motivation. Motivation involves the desire to do well. The more highly motivated you are the more potential there is that you will experience speech anxiety. Let us assume you are interviewing for a job and have to make a formal presentation at a Board of Directors' meeting. The stakes are high because you really want the job. Being fearful in this situation is much more likely than if you were visiting the plant and the Board of Directors invited you to attend their meeting to share your impressions.

Experience. Generally speaking, the more experience you have in giving speeches the less fearful you will be when asked to deliver a speech.

Credibility. Credibility concerns how trustworthy and competent others perceive you to be. If you feel you have a high degree of credibility, you are not likely to experience fear from this source.

Setting

Speeches are given in a variety of settings that differ in their fear provoking potential. Two aspects of settings are related to speech anxiety – formality and lead time.

Formality. The degree to which you control your presentation is related to fear. If you have little control, as in the case in very formal settings, the potential for fear is high.

Lead Time. Let us assume you are attending a dinner held in honor of a friend when the host drops by to tell you you are going to be asked to say a few words. You will be much more likely to experience fear in this situation than if you had been asked to make this presentation three months in advance.

Interaction of Speaking Elements

While each of the things above are important in their own right, they tend to take on added impact when considered together. Imagine the person who has a Pro-Choice stand, has little experience in giving speeches and is asked with very little lead time to talk to a group of 250 Pro-Life advocates. This person will probably be pretty fearful about this speech. Of course, things are seldom this difficult, but it does illustrate how these factors can interact to create speech anxiety.

Rating Your Strengths and Weaknesses

Now that we have discussed the various aspects of the speaking situation that are important contributors to stage fright, it should be possible for you to consider your relative strengths and weaknesses. Think about a speech you have to deliver (or might have to deliver) and then rate how fear provoking this aspect of the situation might be for you on the following scale. Circle one if you have little fear associated with the item, two if it is slightly fearful, and so on.

	Not fear provoking	1	2	3	4	5	extremely fear provoking
The Speech							
Purpose							
descriptive		1	2	3	4	5	
instructive		1	2	3	4	5	
persuasive		1	2	3	4	5	
Complexity							
not very		1	2	3	4	5	
somewhat		1	2	3	4	5	
very		1	2	3	4	5	
Familiarity							
not very		1	2	3	4	5	
somewhat		1	2	3	4	5	
very		1	2	3	4	5	
Personal Importance							
not very		1	2	3	4	5	
somewhat		1	2	3	4	5	
very		1	2	3	4	5	
Audience							
Knowledge Level							
low		1	2	3	4	5	
moderate		1	2	3	4	5	
high		1	2	3	4	5	
Disposition							
for		1	2	3	4	5	
neutral		1	2	3	4	5	
against		1	2	3	4	5	
Size							
small		1	2	3	4	5	
moderate		1	2	3	4	5	
large		1	2	3	4	5	
Speaker							
Motivation							
low		1	2	3	4	5	
moderate		1	2	3	4	5	
high		1	2	3	4	5	
Experience							
low		1	2	3	4	5	
moderate		1	2	3	4	5	
high		1	2	3	4	5	

Credibility					
low	1	2	3	4	5
moderate	1	2	3	4	5
high	1	2	3	4	5
Setting					
Formality					
low	1	2	3	4	5
moderate	1	2	3	4	5
high	1	2	3	4	5
Lead Time					
short	1	2	3	4	5
moderate	1	2	3	4	5
lengthy	1	2	3	4	5

For any given speech your fear levels will differ depending on the factors and the combination of the factors listed above.

Strategies for Overcoming Specific Weaknesses

A basic strategy for overcoming the fear provoking potential of a speech is to stress ingredients that are less fear provoking. In this section we describe basic strategies to cope with fear that arises from the various aspects of a speaking situation. As each strategy is reviewed consider whether that strategy might be used to cope with the sources of stage fright you identified above.

The Speech

Purpose. If possible, your initial speeches ought to be descriptive in nature. In that way you will have some experience before you deliver speeches that are more persuasive in nature. Interestingly, most basic public speaking courses are structured in precisely this fashion. The initial assignments include things like informative speeches and describing a process, with persuasive speeches being assigned toward the end of the course.

Complexity. It is usually less fear provoking to present less complex material. Let us assume you want to talk about timing in automobiles. Providing all the details about engine construction (for example how the position of the valves, pistons, distributor, and crankshaft coordinate) so that people can really understand the principle behind timing is probably too complex unless you are talking to a group of mechanics. For most audiences, discussing how to set the timing on a car would be more suitable and much less complicated.

Familiarity. If you do not know the material, you would be wise to decline an invitation to speak. As a general rule, if you feel you know the basic information and only need to look up a few details, then you are probably familiar enough with the topic to accept a speaking engagement. For instance, let us assume that someone wants you to talk about dieting, that you have tried a number of diets yourself, and that you regularly read information about dieting.

It seems you would have little trouble pulling a speech together on this topic. On the other hand, if you are an enthusiast for one particular diet and do not know much about others, you probably are not familiar enough with the general material to give a speech on this topic.

Personal Importance. If you find that you are really committed to a topic and the prospect of talking about the issue creates a great deal of fear, perhaps you can reduce the risk by revealing less of your committment than you might if you were less fearful. For instance, let us assume you passionately believe pornography laws should be stricter. Rather than presenting a speech that strongly advocates the passage of such laws, you might be more descriptive and present an overview of the laws that exist (perhaps through a comparison with laws in other communities) and let the audience draw their own conclusions about the adequacy of those laws.

Audience

Expertise. It is very fear provoking to talk to groups who are better informed than you are. If you must speak in this situation, a convincing approach is to acknowledge the audiences' superior knowledge by using phrases like, "as you are aware," "yesterday when I was talking to Dr. Smith, he pointed out. . . .," and so on.

Disposition. Normally people are more anxious when the audience disagrees with the position they are advocating than when the audience is in agreement. One way to cope with anxiety in this situation is to begin your speech by discussing the things you and the audience agree upon. This approach tends to reduce hostility and also gives you a chance to calm down. Another thing you can do is to begin your speech in a way that acknowledges differences but sets a receptive tone (such as acknowledging everyone's legitimate concerns and pointing out that differences of opinion foster a more thorough consideration of the problem).

Size. One way to make a large audience seem smaller is through your eye contact pattern. Rather than scanning the entire group, focus on particular individuals as you look at each section of the audience (do not look at just one individual for the whole speech but focus on one person as you shift your eyes from one part of the audience to another). It is much easier to talk to this one person than a mass of five hundred.

Speaker

Motivation. If your anxiety is related to your motivation, you probably are concerned in part due to your desire to be effective but thinking you will be unable to do so. At one point in my career, I was apprehensive because I was to appear before a committee to convince them that public speaking ought to be a required course at the university. I really felt this was important and was worried that others would not agree. Instead of preparing a sound case I kept thinking about how awful it would be if I failed. I finally realized that I could not control what action the committee took. I only controlled the effort I put into developing the speech. In reality my job was to find evidence for and against public speaking as a requirement and to let the evidence speak for itself. That is, I defined "a good job" in terms of my activities, not in terms of something I could not control.

Experience. The only real way to gain experience is through experience. You can gain experience by taking a public speaking class or joining a group that stresses public speaking activities like Toastmasters.

Credibility. The best way to gain others trust is to earn it. Work hard on preparing your speeches and let that work show by citing the sources you consulted and by carefully developing the points of your speech. Also, try to think about "what is in it" for the audience and talk from their point of view as much as possible (vis. "Fill out a donor card, that way you will have the satisfaction now of knowing you did the right thing.").

Situation

Formality. If you are in a very formal situation, find out the rules and use them to your advantage. Try visualizing yourself being formal and doing it well.

Timing. If you do not have much time to prepare, tell yourself, and mean it, that you are not going to worry about how little time you have, how terrible this is going to be, and the like. Those things are negative comparisons and only enhance your problem. Instead of engaging in negative thinking, use the time to focus on your presentation. I know that is more easily said than done. Consequently, the next three sections of this chapter present ways to help you overcome such negative thinking.

Exercise 1: Rational Thinking

Some people assess their speaking strengths and weaknesses in a very irrational manner. No matter what their strengths are, they feel they are failures. Albert Ellis[2] has spent a lifetime exploring such irrational thought processes. He believes that the anxiety associated with irrational thinking can be overcome if we develop rational counters to our irrational thoughts. For example, how likely is it that everyone is going to be convinced by your speech? Highly unlikely. What would it matter if no one was convinced? Would the world come to an end? Would you be fired? Would your husband/wife divorce you? More than likely, none of these things would happen. All that would happen, in almost all cases, is that your opinion would differ from that held by the audience.

If you think that great speakers and speeches convince everyone, think again. Lincoln's Gettysburg Address is considered to be one of the finest speeches ever delivered. However, most of the people attending the speech did not think much of it. The domestic papers criticized Lincoln for doing a miserable job.

Ellis and Harper[3] developed the ABC technique to help you identify and challenge irrational beliefs. The ABC method contains the following steps:

1. Situation or Event (A)
2. Anxiety (C)
3. Irrational Thinking (B)
4. Statements challenging your irrational thinking
5. Restatement of irrational thoughts into rational statements

The following example points out how you could use rational thinking to cope with a situation in which you think you lack credibility, in particular you think the group thinks you are dishonest.

Let us assume you are a business person about to give a speech to eighty police officers and you are very worried about it because police officers think all business people are "crooks." The irrational thinking here seems obvious but let us put it into the above five steps and see how it works out.

1. The situation (A) is a forthcoming speech to eighty police officers.
2. The person is worrying (C) about the police officers.
3. The person thinks police officers believe that business people are crooks (B).
4. Are all business people crooks? How many police officers believe business people are crooks? Don't business people rely on police officers to protect them from crooks? How often do police officers arrest business people compared to other types of people? What rational basis is there for this belief about police officers?
5. Police officers are no different than other groups of people vis-a-vis their beliefs about business people. There is no reason to think these police officers will think you are a crook. Why would they ask a crook to talk to them? What would be so bad if they did think so? Is there any reason they could arrest you? The worst that could happen is they would not appreciate the speech.

As you can see, examining an anxiety producing situation exposes some of the irrational thinking we do to make ourselves anxious. You could profit enormously by examining whether the weaknesses you identified in the previous section are grounded in irrational thinking.

Exercise 2: Systematic Desensitization

Wolpe[4] points out that people cannot experience relaxed and tense states at the same time. Wolpe developed a technique called systematic desensitization for helping a person learn to feel relaxed in anxiety producing situations like public speaking. The technique involves learning deep muscle relaxation and then thinking of fear provoking scenes while remaining relaxed. The following general procedures are basic elements in systematic desensitization.

The first thing you need to do is find a setting away from everyone else where you can be comfortable – perhaps a living room couch or your bedroom. Next, you will need relaxing music of the instrumental variety. Once you have settled into a comfortable position with the music you have selected playing softly in the background do the following:

1. Inhale slowly and deeply. Hold that breath while you count to eight. Then exhale slowly and completely. Repeat this process several times.
2. Tightly clench your left fist. Hold these muscles in the tense position for ten seconds, then relax the muscles completely. Repeat.
3. Tightly clench your right fist. Hold these muscles in the tense position for ten seconds, then release. Repeat.
4. Flex your bicep muscles by bringing your hands upward towards your shoulders. Hold this position for ten seconds, then release. Repeat.
5. Shrug both shoulders. Feel the tension. Hold this position for ten seconds, then release. Relax. Repeat procedure.
6. Wrinkle up your forehead. Hold these face muscles in the tense position for ten seconds, then release completely. Repeat.
7. Close your eyes tightly. Feel the tension around your eyes. Hold this position for ten seconds. Relax. Repeat.
8. Press your tongue to the roof of your mouth. Feel the tension. Hold that position for ten seconds. Relax. Repeat.
9. Press your lips together. Feel the tension around your mouth. Hold that position for ten seconds. Relax. Repeat.
10. Push the back of your head against the chair (or back as far as possible without bending your head back). Feel the tension. Hold that position for ten seconds. Relax. Repeat.
11. Arch your back. Feel the tension in your back. Hold that position for ten seconds. Relax. Repeat.
12. Suck in your stomach. Hold that position for ten seconds. Relax. Notice the difference between tension and relaxation. Repeat.
13. Tense your buttocks by pushing yourself into the seat of a chair. Relax. Repeat.
14. Tightly tense the thigh muscles in both of your legs. Hold these muscles in the tense position for ten seconds, then release. Relax. Repeat.
15. Point your toes upward, toward your face, tensing the muscles in the calves of your legs. Hold that position for ten seconds. Relax. Repeat.
16. Turn the toes of both your feet downward. Hold this position for ten seconds. Relax. Repeat.

Some people can achieve a relaxed state by tensing and relaxing larger groups of muscles. One way to do this is to tense the face and neck muscles – relax; tense the arm and trunk muscles – relax; and then tense the lower body –

relax. In general, you should tense the muscles for 5-15 seconds and then relax them for at least 5 seconds. Repeat the tensing and relaxing until you feel completely at ease.

Once you feel completely relaxed, almost drowsy, the next step is to think about delivering a variety of speeches while remaining relaxed. You are to imagine being the speaker in the scenes suggested below. If you start to feel tense while thinking about the scene, stop thinking about it and do some muscle relaxation exercises until you feel comfortable again. Then think about the scene again. Repeat this process until you can thoroughly imagine all aspects of the scene while remaining relaxed. Start with the first scene and work your way through all ten.

Scene One

You are at a grade school class and are about to talk to the class about something you know a great deal about.

Scene Two

You are about to describe the equipment your committee purchased for a local group.

Scene Three

At a club meeting you are about to deliver a report detailing the organizations' activities for the past summer.

Scene Four

At a formal dinner you are about to praise the president of your living group.

Scene Five

You are about to introduce the main speaker at your old high school's commencement and are not sure how to pronounce his or her name.

Scene Six

You are presenting a speech to a small group of voters urging them to vote for a particular candidate.

Scene Seven

You are addressing a large group, but those in attendance are very supportive.

Scene Eight

You are talking to a small group of people you feel are more knowledgeable than you are – but it is important you convince them to take the action you are advocating.

Scene Nine

You are talking to a large group in an auditorium. The group is unfamiliar to you and you have never been in this auditorium. You do know this group opposes your position.

Scene Ten

You are presenting your case to an ethics committee. You have been accused of unethical conduct. Your accuser is present and has packed the room with his/her supporters.

Once you have worked through these scenes, try working through scenes that revolve around the weaknesses you identified earlier in this chapter.

Exercise 3: Visualization

Anxious people usually feel their speeches are going to be poorly done. By imagining a poor speech performance, you often create a poor performance. We can overcome this source of performance anxiety by learning to envision ourselves making a good presentation. Visualization[5], i.e. imagining yourself doing well, is one way to develop such positive thinking. The visualization script below will help you imagine a positive outcome for an informative speech.

Visualization Script

Close your eyes and allow your body to get comfortable in the chair in which you are sitting. Move around until you feel that you are in a position that will continue to be relaxing for you for the next ten to fifteen minutes. Take a deep, comfortable breath and hold it . . . now slowly release it through your nose (if possible). That is right . . . now take another deep breath and make certain that you are breathing from the diaphragm (from your belly) . . . hold it . . . now slowly release it and note how you feel while doing this . . . feel the relaxation fluidly flow throughout your body. And now, one more REALLY deep breath . . . hold it . . . and now release it slowly . . . and begin your normal breathing pattern. (Shift around if you need to get comfortable again.)

I now want you to begin to visualize the beginning of a day in which you are going to give an informative speech. See yourself getting up in the morning, full of energy, full of confidence, looking forward to the day's challenges. You are putting on just the right clothes for the task at hand that day. Dressing well makes you look and feel good about yourself, so you have on JUST what you want to wear which clearly expresses your sense of inner well-being. As you are driving, riding, or walking to the speech setting, note how clear and confident you feel, and others around you – as you arrive – comment positively to you regarding your fine appearance and general demeanor. You feel thoroughly prepared for the task at hand. Your preparation has been exceptionally thorough, and you have really researched the target issue you will be presenting today. Now you see yourself standing or sitting in the room where you will present your speech, talking very comfortably and confidentially with others in the room. The people to whom you will be presenting your speech appear to be quite friendly, and are very cordial in their greetings and subsequent conversations prior to the presentation. You feel ABSOLUTELY sure of your material and of your ability to present the information in a forceful, convincing, positive manner. Now you see yourself approaching the area from which you will present. You are feeling very good about this presentation and see yourself move forward eagerly. All of your audio visual materials are well organized, well planned, and are clearly an aid to your presentation.

Now you see yourself presenting your talk. It is really quite brilliant (if I do say so myself) and it has all the finesse of a polished, professional speaker. You are also aware that your audience is giving you head nods, smiles, and other positive responses that clearly give you the message that you are truly "on target." You are now through the introduction and body of the speech, and are heading into an absolutely brilliant summarization of your position on the topic. You now see yourself fielding audience questions with equal brilliance, confidence, and energy that you exhibited in the presentation itself. You see yourself receiving the congratulations of your classmates. See yourself as relaxed, pleased with your talk, and ready for the next task you need to accomplish that day; filled with energy, purpose, and a sense of general well-being. Congratulate yourself on a job well done!

Now . . . I want you to begin to return to this time and place in which we are working today. Take a deep breath . . . hold it . . . and let it go. Do this several times and move slowly back into the room. Take as much time as you need to make the transition back.

Although this script concerns informative speaking, you should easily be able to adapt it to other situations. The important aspect of visualizing is positive thinking. DO NOT ALLOW NEGATIVE THOUGHTS TO CREEP IN. Practice visualizing until you are thinking positively about every aspect of a speech.

Summary

The opening portion of this chapter discusses aspects of speaking situations and considers how each aspect is linked to stage fright. Strategies for overcoming anxiety related to each aspect of the speech situation are presented. The next section of the chapter points out how rational thinking can help you cope with stage fright. Then an exercise is presented to help you learn to feel more relaxed in speaking situations. Finally, an exercise is included to help you visualize public speaking in a positive manner.

Notes

[1]Nelson, R.B., *Louder and Funnier: A Practical Guide for Overcoming Stage Fright* (St. Paul: Pragmatic Publications, 1984), pp. 29-45.

[2]Ellis, A., *Reason and Emotion in Psychotherapy* (New York: Lyle Stuart, 1962).

Ellis, A. and Harper, R.A., *A New Guide to Rational Living* (Englewood Cliffs, New Jersey: Prentice-Hall, 1975).

[4]Wolpe, J. and Lazarus, A.A., *Behavior Therapy Techniques* (New York: Pergamon Press, 1966).

[5]Ayres, J. and Hopf, T.S., Visualization: A Means of Reducing Speech Anxiety, *Communication Education, 34*, 1985, 318-323.

21

Nonverbal Communication in the Classroom

John S. Leipzig

Beginning Considerations: Sarah's First Day

This was Sarah's first day in her new position as a fourth grade teacher at Lake Elementary. She was replacing a teacher who had retired after twenty-five years of service; ten of those years were spent in the classroom that Sarah was now to occupy. Sarah walked into a room with student desks in five rows facing the teacher's desk which was twelve feet away from the middle row. The desks were arranged so that the students faced the teacher and the chalkboard instead of the windows or the door. The room was freshly painted in the pale yellow color that was typical of all of the rooms at Lake Elementary. Sarah had learned in her methods courses that it was especially important to be prepared for that first encounter with students so she had spent countless hours writing her lesson plans, organizing the materials for the lessons, and decorating the two bulletin boards in the room with purchased materials since she put more time into her lesson plans and didn't have the time to develop her own bulletin board materials. That morning she put on a tailored blue skirted suit and had applied her typical amount of makeup and perfume, no more or no less than she did for any other initial meeting. She was confident that she was ready that morning when the bell rang and in came 28 mostly beaming anticipatory faces.

She met the children at the door and shook their hands briefly and then she directed them to their assigned seats. Sarah could not help but notice that some students were dressed better than others and that some appeared more energetic than others while some carried the odor of woodsmoke. Though she didn't notice it at the time, she would stand closer to some children than others as she directed them to their seats. She also noticed that some children seemed to change the position of their bodies in their desks when assigned to sit by specific children. When all were seated she began with the phrase "Good morning boys and girls. We will begin the year with introductions. To help us

273

get to know each other I have placed each of you in rows alphabetically." At that very moment Sarah noticed that the students began to appear restless and a worried look came over some of their faces. Sarah continued, "Today we will work on the solar system. Would you all pick up your science texts that I have placed on your desks and turn to page 1." At the end of the day an exhausted Sarah went home with an unsettled feeling, something just was not right about the day. She knew she had thoroughly prepared her lessons but somehow it didn't seem to be enough.

Sarah was correct in feeling that there is much more to classroom preparation and teaching than the preparation of the class content. Sarah had invested most of her effort in being ready for the verbal aspects of teaching without preparing for the nonverbal aspects. Recently, a number of writers have been discussing teachers' concentration of classroom effort upon verbal versus nonverbal processes even though research confirms the belief that the major and central concern of classroom communication is nonverbal by nature.[2,3] The example of Sarah can be used as a springboard into a discussion of classroom nonverbal communication. Sarah, like many teachers, needs to be aware of a number of dimensions of nonverbal communication that were at work in the classroom.

Time was the first crucial concern that confronted Sarah. It was her first day and her students started in the fourth grade. She had just replaced a teacher who had given a quarter century to teaching and a decade in that particular classroom. Our system of education is full of formal examples of the use of time. We use age and levels to indicate student readiness for placement. The same is true for teachers who have spent the requisite amount of formal time becoming ready for this first day. But informally, when is the right time to begin introductions and when is it time to begin science? What does it say about the tangibility of time when we devote more time to some activities than to others? The beginning class activities occurred in the morning and some of the children were more awake than others; it was autumn, and it was the very first day of school. All of these temporal considerations, called *chronemics*, are vital classroom concerns, but seldom are these concerns explicitly included in the education of teachers.

A second concern was the environment that Sarah and the students shared. The colors were muted at best in the technicolor world of the students. The arrangement of the desks in the room and the lack of stimulating materials also contributed to the feel of the room. The fact that students were seated by their names indicated the assignment of territory by an external source. Two major dimensions of nonverbal communication, *proxemics* (space, territory, and environment) and *artifactual* (objects) are involved in this portion of the example. Artifacts are also present in Sarah's and the students' dress and appearances that affected the distancing of the interactions in the classroom.

A third area of nonverbal concern is expressional. Some students came in with beaming faces and later were seen to be restless with their gestures. The worried feeling Sarah had most likely was present in her mannerisms throughout the course of the day. This area of nonverbal study, known as *kinesics* involves the perception of facial, gestural, and postural communication cues.

Sarah's bubbling voice when she welcomed the students changed to a businesslike manner when she introduced science and changed yet again to one that became thin by the end of the day. These changes affected her interactions with her pupils. When she worked through the introductions of the students, her vocal qualities varied in pitch with appropriate pausing to let each student know it was their turn to speak. The students responded appropriately to the cues by telling stories about themselves. *Vocalics* is the name that is given to the vocal but nonverbal cues shared with others through the voice.

The fact that Sarah chose to meet each child at the door with a handshake could indicate to each student a formal businesslike climate from the first, since few teachers would feel comfortable touching students at all during the initial formation of a class. *Haptics* is the name given to the study of tactile aspect of communication.

Two final areas of concern often not discussed are the *olfactory* and *gustatory* dimensions of nonverbal communication. There are a multitude of smells present in schools and in the classrooms. Some of the smells are quite pleasant and others are not, but all affect the ambiance of the environment. Gustatory areas are often tied to the food smells present, and research has concentrated upon the tie between nutrition and student performance which has also linked this performance to specific types of foods consumed.[25]

With the mysterious myriad of nonverbal cues present in the classroom it is a small wonder that many teachers choose to invest their effort preparing content for verbal instruction and leave the nonverbal aspects of communication to take care of themselves naturally. Unfortunately, such decisions cause the time and effort that teachers put into course preparation to be negated by nonverbal factors such as the classroom environment, a hurtful look or intonation they exhibit, the way they distance themselves from their students, a firm touch given to correct, the length of the lesson, or the time of day a lesson is presented. If a student smells something that is reminiscent of another more pleasant experience or one that indicates that it is time for lunch, that student may not attend well to other messages.

Sarah is to be complimented for her diligence in the preparation of her lessons but fell into the same trap that many teachers fall into by thinking that the verbal channels of communication are the primary channels in which the teacher can exhibit some degree of situational control while the nonverbal channels are somehow mysterious and take care of themselves. Nonverbal communication is not only misunderstood by many but it is systematically ignored due to this misunderstanding. Unfortunately, the failure to take into account the nonverbal implications of human communication often can be linked to teacher success or failure in the classroom.

The Need For Teacher Training In Nonverbal Communication And Why It Is Often Missing

Scholars in both the disciplines of communication and education have become concerned with the lack of specific teacher preparation in nonverbal communication,[4,28] and many professionals have developed resource booklets and bibliographies on the nonverbal aspects of classroom instruction. One booklet entitled *Nonverbal Communication* is in its third edition[27] and outlines what educational research says to the teacher. The 34 page booklet is available either through ERIC or from the NEA professional Library. Two particularly helpful bibliographies on classroom uses of nonverbal communication are also available through ERIC.[8,31] The existence of such materials not only highlights the increasing and continuing concern by both education and communication disciplines for the training of teachers in nonverbal communication but provides teachers with easily accessible and useful references to help facilitate explanation of the impact of nonverbal communication in the classroom.

The increasing respectability of the study of nonverbal communication is evidenced not only by the existence of increasing volumes of material on the subject, but by scholars who are bringing cohesion to its study.[5] Still a number of myths surrounding the study of nonverbal communication seem to surface from time to time when the subject is mentioned, and these need to be explored before tying the research in nonverbal communication to the classroom and its relationships.

Myth #1: Nonverbal communication stems from a natural process.

The major argument is whether or not nonverbal communication is a learned activity or not. The problem is actually one of the approach taken to explain nonverbal behavior.[15] While some scholars take a more biological approach, others take a sociological approach. Some claim that much of nonverbal behavior is innate while others claim it is learned. Most scholars do agree that both sociological and biological factors need to be considered but seem to lean heavily toward learned behavior as the predominant mode.[20] What causes the myth to be so prevalent is that nonverbal behaviors are not explicitly taught like verbal behaviors.[25] What happens is that nonverbal behaviors are learned and then communicated through the observation of significant others' nonverbal behaviors. While some research, especially in facial expressions, seems to indicate culturally shared origins of basic facial expressions, other cultural data points to the conclusion that most nonverbal behaviors are learned behaviors. Current work in hemispheric style indicates that much nonverbal communication comes from right brain processing, while verbal communication comes from left brain processing, (though the left deals with the interpretation of nonverbal as well as verbal behavior).[15] What seems to be most important is that nonverbal communication tends to be more analogical than verbal communication and thus is learned more through induction versus deduction. Nonverbal behaviors are as open to explanation as verbal behaviors, and methods for teacher instruction through analogical methods can be incorporated into education programs. Through the use of examples, teachers could add to their repertoire of communication behaviors to be applied in their classrooms.

> Myth #2: Nonverbal communication is more believable than verbal communication because it is not as prone to manipulation.

People express the belief that when they are confronted with contradictory nonverbal and verbal messages that they are more likely to believe the nonverbal because it is less prone to deception. Deception is not only possible by skillful use of nonverbal cues but much recent research has identified nonverbal cues that indicate deception by communicators.[5] Many of these cues have been found to be situationally specific and thus are often open to misinterpretation.[19] The environmental manipulation of many nonverbal cues in the marketing of services and goods surrounds us. Grocery stores are arranged to direct one to certain items that have been intentionally packaged to gain one's attention. Open-space classrooms are designed with the goal of increasing communication among teachers and among students and teachers.[5] Many fast food chains have designed their facilities to get one in and out quickly by making the chairs minimally comfortable and so close to the next person to encourage one to eat and leave so that the next person can take the same space. The point is that nonverbal symbols are manipulated all of the time and the belief that the cues are somehow more believable makes many receivers of nonverbal messages quite susceptible to their influence and prone to situational deception. Educators need to be very aware of those situationally specific behaviors that make deception possible in the day to day interactions that they have with all of the members of the educational community.

> Myth #3: When nonverbal behaviors are not intended for another, they should not be considered as communicative.

This issue affects all aspects of communication and the controversy revolves around the issue as to whether cues must be intended for another to be considered communication. Many have expressed the belief that while most verbal communication is explicitly constructed to be communicated to another, many nonverbal cues seem to be more implicit. While a student may not intend to send specific messages by the clothing that she or he wears or by averting his or her gaze when asked a question, the point seems to be if the recipient of the cue ascribes meaning to the act, then a communicative activity has occurred whether it is intended or not.[15] While much interpersonal work concentrates its effort upon the shared nature of communication, it is important to note that many shared nonverbal messages may not have been intentionally constructed for that particular communicative event. The student dress code may be more tied to normative dress expectations that may not be the same as the teacher's and that dress might unintentionally affect the interactions between the student and the teacher, whereas the aversion of gaze might be specifically communicating a cue to the teacher and is an intended response to a query. Nonverbal communication in the classroom is a relational process shared by teachers and students. A useful working conception of the process of nonverbal communication is:

Nonverbal communication involves the manipulation of nonlinguistic symbolic cues which affect the relationship of the persons involved.

Nonverbal communication cues often work in concert with verbal cues to assist participants to better understand the nature of the relationship that they share. Nonverbal cues are neither more or less important than verbal cues but are coequal in importance. Certainly in some communicative events nonverbal cues or verbal cues may take precedence in the construction of meaning, but both influence relationship quality and both should be considered in the teacher-student relationship and as such deserve more attention in the teacher training process.

Dimensions Of Nonverbal Communication: What The Research Can Mean To The Teacher

While most writers of nonverbal communication emphasize the integrative nature of a variety of communicative cues, it is easier at this juncture to discuss the individual dimensions of nonverbal communication keeping in mind that many of the dimensions work together in the construction of meaning. In the effect of any one given dimension of nonverbal communication on student performance is variable due to a wide range of factors.[30] Changing just the room color or seating arrangement may not be enough to alter student performance. However, a color change with a new room arrangement tied to a specific learning activity which is scheduled just before Winter break and is accompanied by supportive teacher gestures, facial expressions, touch, and vocal qualities might as a whole have the desired effect. Mindful of this need for integration, the following section will tie current research in the nonverbal dimensions of chronemics, proxemics, artifacts, kinesics, vocalics, haptics, and olfactory/gustatory to the teacher-student relationship.

Chronemics

Few dimensions of nonverbal communication have received less attention than has time, yet for classroom communication time is one of the most vital concerns. Andersen, Andersen, and Mayton studied the effects of chronemics in the classroom and concluded that a child's understanding of time increases as the child ages. Specifically, the authors discovered that synchrony and duration are tied to age which means that younger children perceive time as passing more slowly and therefore demand more activity in a shorter period of time due to the fact that their brain responses are faster than older children and adults.[1]

The nonverbal study of time is divided into the study of psychological, biological, and cultural time orientations. Psychological studies refer to the work of Meerloo and Cottle suggests that each person adopts a personal orientation to time which can be past, present, future, or time-line. People are characterized by whether they project future events, dwell in the past, think about the here and now, or analyze time as a sequence of events from past to future.[26] Of interest would be a comparison of the time orientations of teachers and students. One might suspect that younger students would be more present-oriented than many of their teachers. Cottle extended Meerloo's work studying the difference between people that view time as a whole or in its parts. Cottle discovered that males view time as a continuous event in which they are losing time while females learn to view time more acceptingly as a moment to moment type of process.[7] The impact on the teacher-student relationship due to these differing time perspectives bears further investigation.

Biological time orientations are represented by the cyclic features of biological rhythms tied to physical cycles (23 days), emotional cycles (28 days), and intellectual cycles (33 days) which have also been linked to orality.[21] Luce suggests that children have variable rhythms that may predispose them to be morning or evening people which could affect student performance (and perhaps even teacher performance).[23]

Cultural time systems also have profound effects in the classroom. Hall notes the existence of technical time, formal time, and informal time systems.[12] Technical time is the way of measuring time in precise scientific units which, while important to scientific discovery, has limited utility in the discussion of classroom relationships. Formal time is the particular way that cultures conceptualize time, such as in decades or generations. Formal time systems are ordered (Monday comes after Sunday but before Tuesday), are cyclical (Autumn follows Summer and precedes Winter), have duration which is tied to the depth of an event (the American school year is seen as short by other cultures that spend more time each day and year in educating their young), and are viewed in terms of tangibility (we trade time for money). Informal time is the personalized approach we take toward using time in our everyday lives. Duration also plays a part in terms of how long a lecture seems versus a hands-on exercise. Activity refers to what needs to be done in a given period. The concept of punctuality is another aspect. Do teachers begin their lessons precisely as scheduled or do they wait for a few minutes or so?

Another element is whether the person comes from a culture that views time monchronistically or polychronistically. Monochronistic time cultures view time as scheduled and discrete while polychronistic time cultures view time in terms of activities to be done. Many Native American cultures are polychronistic and express this by conducting activities differently than monochronistic cultures. As a professor, I expect that students will on occasion schedule meetings for individual advice. With monochronistic students I find that we schedule a time and they show up usually within fifteen minutes of that time but with polychronistic students I am never sure. I have found that appointment times do not always run the lives of polychronistic students. What happens is one day the student appears at the door for assistance and says "you and I are here now so it must be time to work together": quite a different approach from "it is 10:30, the time we previously scheduled, so it must be time to work together." Some problems teachers run into when working with differing time systems is that they find it hard to understand that other events take precedence over school, such as it is time to hunt because the whales are in or it is time to harvest the crops because they are ready. Crops and whales apparently have no respect for teachers' schedules.

Recently, some authors have been concerned with the pace of life and how this affects children. Elkind has written two thought provoking books which examine how modern society hurries children into growing up and then they have no place to go. He contends that often one finds overscheduled children and harried parents trying to fit too much activity into too little time. As a result we see stressed out children who don't have time to be children but who instead become mini-adults in dress, appearance, and manner.[9,10] Listen to your students as they talk about all of their activities and view their manner and dress, and you might be able to predict those children in a time bind. Certainly try not to schedule your class so tightly that the schedule becomes more important than the people who are there at that time relating to one another.

One last area of chronemic concern to teachers is wait-time. Different students have different cultural predispositions for the amount of time they expect between conversations. As a result the time may vary from less than a second to over five seconds. This simple difference can cause massive problems in the classroom. Greenbaum found a lengthening of wait time with his research with the Choctaw tribe, and this finding has been reconfirmed with a variety of native cultures.[11] Being aware of wait-time differences can often be the difference between a student being perceived as reticent or overtalkative by persons with differing time perspectives.

Teachers can become more aware of time and time systems that students employ through explicit practice with the systems. Teachers can run an exercise in which they ask students to communicate about events in their life that have (past), are (present), or will be important; and, from the information explore differing time predispositions. Turn-switching can also be controlled by practice with silence. Too often teachers feel that if they do not fill in the pauses they are somehow out of control. If teachers wait 5 to 6 seconds before providing answers to their own questions they will talk less and their students will talk more in the classroom. Schedules and activities have always played a major role in educational systems, and many are just now trying to tie those schedules and activities more realistically to the way children and their teachers view time.

Proxemics

Much research on proxemics has focused on the effect of the environment, territory, and space on people. In an excellent review of the literature, Hickson and Stacks provide the reader with a number of conclusions that would be applicable to the classroom situation. Studies indicate that communication frequency increases as the surrounding colors become more exciting, interpersonal attraction goes up in attractive rooms, attraction decreases as the temperature increases with the motivation to work being better in temperatures below 70 degrees Fahrenheit, student activity goes up when classrooms are lit with full spectrum lights versus blue spectrum lights, students located in the front of the class participate more frequently, and participation is as a function of the size of the class.[15]

In a review of the effects of space on instruction, Miller worked with the concept of the three types of space: fixed-feature (not changeable), semi-fixed-feature (large hard to move objects), and informal space (dynamic personal space). He felt that the mood created by the classroom has profound effects on student/teacher relationships and advocates that classrooms be seen as adaptable so that they stimulate students while still ensuring their privacy in a secure and comfortable place for learning.[27]

The work on human territoriality also has implications for the classroom. Lyman and Scott indicate the existence of four types of territory: Public, interactional, home, and body. Public territory is characterized by open access. Schools and other public buildings fall into this category. Interactional territory is more mobile and is defined by more limited access into areas that are occupied for discrete periods of time. A classroom within the school is often viewed in interactional terms. Home is the territory you claim as being under one's direct control. One's private bedroom in the house is an example. Body territory is defined as yourself including that which is covering you.[24]

Since humans defend territory, it is not unusual to find conflict situations in which people have defined the same space differently. For example, when a teacher defines a classroom as home territory, the student as interactional, and the parent as public, all could be in for a series of very heated arguments. Territoriality can also be tied to students taking possession of the space surrounding their desks. Given the fact that people establish territories quickly, the effect produced by altering that territory can be profound upon the feelings of the students. This is not to say that teachers should not alter desks, but that they need to be cognizant of the ensuing disruption and the anger that might be associated with the change. With territorial disputes comes resentment and overt fighting which can alter the learning that will be taking place in the classroom.

Personal space perceptions also have been tied to education. Miller notes the distancing categories of intimate (up to 1 1/2 feet), personal (1 1/2 to 4 feet), social (4-12 feet), and public (12 to 25 feet) that characterize specific communicative activities in American culture. Teachers' and students' desks are typically 12 feet or more away which would place much of their interactions in the public distance category which would have a strong effect on the interpersonal relationship between the students and the teacher.[27]

Teachers can affect the classroom climate by being aware of the environment, the territorial expectations, and the personal spacing that exist in the classroom. If the teacher allows the students to participate in the creation of the learning environment, students will also take greater ownership of the learning that takes place in that space. The territory that teachers and students occupy for the year should be viewed as shared interactional space. Just imagine the effect upon students who walking into a room with lots of materials from paint to desks are told that they and the teacher will redefine the appearance of the space. Of course, the teacher has to be the prime facilitator during construction, taking into account particular classroom learning objectives. How wonderful it would be to see brightly colored rooms in which the students and teacher selected the room color and arranged and rearranged the objects in the room based upon the activities that were to occur in that classroom! The teacher's desk might not always be 12 feet away but might be in the middle of the room surrounded by student desks or the teacher might not use a desk at all. The real point is to experiment with the students in the construction of an environment that is the most conducive to the tasks that will be jointly undertaken. If teachers and students spent the first week of school working together as a team to construct the learning environment and then began formal instruction, a supportive cooperative beginning might provide the model for continuing behavior for the entire year.

Artifacts

Tied closely to proxemics is the dimension of artifacts (objects). Desks, pencils, books, and other classroom materials are artifacts as are student and teacher dress and physical appearance. Relational concerns often dictate our personal choices of artifacts. People tend to chose objects that tie us to others in our peer groups.[18] The choice of certain literary materials for the schools and classrooms has sometimes been the subject of embittered battles over what the inclusion of certain types of literature symbolizes to the learner, and some court cases have also focused on the dress and grooming habits of students.

Much of the work on artifacts has dealt with dress. Roach and Musa discuss the two dress functions: protection from the environment and a means of communication. People living in the far north understand the importance of protection. Northerners own a variety of winter clothes ranging from down coats to layers of undergarments that are worn to class and then partially removed for the day. The stories of hardships encountered by trying to put a down parka over an evening gown are legend in this country. While it is very important that teachers be aware of the physical dangers encountered when children are improperly dressed for the environment (such as tennis shoes in –40 weather), the social messages associated with dress carry even more significance for classroom communication. While the popular literature is replete with dress prescriptions which claim that men should wear darker solid colors in suits with white shirts and a dark tie while women should wear gray or blue skirted suits with a white blouse and never wear a sweater,[15] the real point is that an implicit dress code exists in most professions and at school. People identify with others through conformity to the code. When I was in junior high the dress code was Levi's (with the belt loops and back pocket stitching removed), a white undershirt covered by an open Pendleton plaid shirt, and tan J-C sandals. Most of the students followed the norm. How big of a leap is it to consider Mohawks and purple hair as another cultural artifact?

While dress is easily changed, body appearance is another matter. Physical attractiveness is directly tied to the quantity of social interaction.[15] Clifford and Walster found that teachers tied attractiveness to achievement potential, intelligence, and the perception of parental involvement.[6] Perceptions of personality characteristics being associated by certain body shapes suggests that endomorphs (fat body) are associated with dependency, sluggishness, and warmth. Mesomorphs (athletic body) are associated with dominance, confidence, and talkativeness. Ectomorphs (thin body) are associated with shyness, meticulousness, and coolness.[15] While the research does not indicate valid ties of these personality characteristics, some believe the relationships exist and treat people accordingly.

Teachers need to be cognizant of the dress norms that drive student behaviors, of the effects of the school's dress code, and of their own personal expectations for dress. While individuality can easily be expressed through dress, it can be at the cost of group identification. Teachers can also work with students and parents to select appropriate classroom artifacts. While consensus may not always be reached, the reasons for all of the choices can be aired. Teachers must realize that personal dress preferences they express and the way they personalize a room make strong statements as to what they believe is important.

Kinesics

Gestures and facial expressions have been studied extensively by nonverbal researchers, because much of our emotional feelings are expressed through facial and other bodily gestures. Children learn early in life that the face provides important information about the emotional state of the communicator. I remember my own daughter at a very young age grasping my chin and turning it toward her to better "see" what I meant when I talked. While most people are fairly accurate in the identification of basic emotions (happiness, sadness, surprise, anger, fear, contempt, disgust, interest, determination, and bewilderment), they are less accurate when attempting to classify a set of emotions such as amazement and astonishment. Specific tests for facial sensitivity are available which gauge teachers' and students' sensitivity to facial cues. One of the best is the FMST (Facial Meaning Sensitivity Test).[22] linking expressions and teaching suggests that women are better decoders of facial expression than men but that both male and female teachers are not very accurate in rating student facial cues when it comes to the comprehension of material.[28]

Special attention in kinesics is paid to eye gaze behavior since the eyes are used to regulate interaction, to exercise control, to facilitate goal attainment, to give additional information, and to express relationship. Students learn quickly what gaze means to an individual teacher and how to use that information to determine if they need to answer a teacher's question or not. On the other side, teachers use student gaze behavior as an index of interest and attentiveness.[28]

Teachers have long used gaze to correct student behavior and to reward those who perform. Making explicit the looks that one uses to symbolize actions and testing the sensitivity of students and the teacher to specific cues can be an exciting and rewarding classroom activity.

Vocalics

The vocalized nonverbal aspects of communication also have received a great deal of research attention. Often how we say something carries as much meaning as the words we actually select. Paravocal and paralinguistic studies indicate that student participation is highly affected by vocalic cues.[28]

Teachers' and students' perceptions associated with voice qualities and vocalizations have applicability to the classroom. Voice qualities are those aspects of the voice like pitch range (highness or lowness of the voice), articulation (precision of speech), tempo (rate of delivery), and rhythm (smoothness of presentation). Vocalizations deal with vocal characterizers (laughing, crying, yelling), voice qualifiers (such as duration of the speech) and vocal segregates (voiced pauses such as uh-hum).[15] Some research findings discussed by Malandro and Barker (1983, 287-90) indicate that the positive use of vocal cues facilitates student learning, that fast rates of delivery are seen as more persuasive, and that vocal qualities are used to judge a person's credibility.[25]

Much of the work in vocalics has attempted to determine the effects of dialects on communication. Native born speakers are rated more pleasing and dynamic by members of their own dialect community. Americans rate general American speech (Midwestern) as the most credible. They do not profess a preference for their own dialect and do not consistently rate it the highest. Any judgments they make on the basis of dialect are not lasting. Of particular importance to the teacher is the use of vocalics for the regulation of interaction. Sequencing of student and teacher talk is a major component of the classroom. Hickson and Stacks review the turn-taking sequence in terms of a variety of cues. Turn-maintaining cues such as audible breaths and vocalized pauses in addition to the lack of variance in pitch at ends of sentences allow one to retain conversational control. Turn-supressing cues by the use of vocalized pauses also allow one to indicate that one does not desire a turn. Turn-yielding cues such as the raising or dropping of pitch at ends of sentences and by the cessation of speech give the other the cue to begin. Finally, turn-taking cues tied to interrupting others are recognized vocalic cues.[15]

By experimenting with turn-sequencing, teachers will be better able to judge the conversational requirements that will allow for all students in the class to have the opportunity to participate. Additionally, the teacher can use turn cues to ensure greater student involvement in the question-answer process.

Haptic

Touch has received more negative attention than many of the other areas of nonverbal communication. We are bombarded with literature indicating that there are OK and not OK touches, and intimate touches have been under assault due to the fear of disease and death. This dimension of haptics and the importance of touch norms have profound implications for teaching. People have a basic physiological need to be touched but the type, location, and duration of that touch is very much culturally manifested and interpreted. Research in cultural differences in touch frequency discovered that couples in cafes had vastly differing amounts of contacts per hour. The couples were observed in cafes in four different countries. In San Juan, Puerto Rico the couples touched on average 180 times per hour, 110 contacts in Paris, 2 touches in Gainesville, Florida, and 0 contact in London.[16,17] Teachers in multi-cultural classrooms need to consider variations in touch expectations that exist for different cultural groupings. Other work has gone into the types of touch tied to specific categories in which they function. Heslin classified touch as Functional/Professional (doing something for you – like a doctor's examination), Social/Polite (handshakes), Friendship/Warmth (arm-in-arm), Love/Intimacy (arm-in-arm, hand in other's back pocket), and Sexual Arousal.[13,14] The most important consideration is that the persons in the relationship agree on the meanings of the touch being shared. Major problems arise when there is disagreement as to intent of particular touches.

Much work has gone into discussing the effects of violations of touch norms such as holding onto a handshake too long or by using your position to show dominance over another by touch. Teachers are aware that when grasping a student the violation of the personal space is a control gesture that carries with it power and control implications. Teachers also realize that positive pats can provide reinforcement to students.[27]

While touch is vital to human communication, the possible misinterpretations of the intents of touch especially to those from cultures with low frequencies of touch should warn the teacher to take into consideration the social implications associated with any touch. The best guide is to make any touch norms between the teacher and student explicit.

Olfactory-Gustatory

The sense of smell is directly tied to the brain. This means that unlike other senses that are connected to the opposite side of the brain, the sense of smell is wired into the same side in which it resides making for the quick and direct translation of the odor. 1989, 200). The importance of smell in identification of people has been well researched by the perfume industry. What we don't take into account is how influenced we are by odors that trigger memories (pleasant and unpleasant) directly. Many products have been specifically scented to trigger brand identification.[15] A Classroom and a school are filled with odors of books, plants, and other items that can trigger memory. Some teachers may wish to experiment with different odor provoking objects to check student reactions and the subsequent impact of various odors on learning. Teachers may also wish to see how students rate one another and form preferences for one another based on smells liked and disliked in common.

Taste is often tied to olfaction since the two senses work in tandem. People taste in different regions of the mouth from the palates, to the tongue, to the back of the throat. Most regions are studded with taste buds which are the tiny bumps on the tongue that can be seen in the mirror. As people age they lose taste buds and regions which would explain in part how tastes change. Young children are very sensitive to tastes which might explain why they are often more discriminating as to their food preferences. A Department of Defense study tied personality to taste. Red meat eaters were linked to action, fish and veggie eaters to recreation, starchy food eaters to complacency, salad eaters to fast-moving types, and dessert eaters to dominance.[25] While the correlational results are open to misinterpretation, the fact remains that governmental agencies are looking into the relationship between how we act and what we eat. The teacher is often one of the few people who see the day to day effects of nutrition upon student performance.

In addition to exploring different tastes with students, the teacher can make other professionals in the system as well as parents aware of any drops in student performance tied to possible eating deficiencies. Furthermore, the teacher can see how students rank one another in terms of their taste preferences for food and drinks. Do some students reject other students because of eating and drinking preferences that are different than their own?

Concluding Observations: Sarah's Second Year

This review of some of the ties between nonverbal communication and classroom relationships should reinforce the conclusion that the nonverbal dimensions of communication are connected to perceptions that we have of others which can affect performance and evaluation in the classroom. While classroom communication activities need to be viewed as a whole, it is important to realize that each of the nonverbal dimensions can and do have an impact upon the whole.

When Sarah returned to Lake Elementary after completing a course in nonverbal communication for teachers, she decided to apply some of the findings to her own grade four classroom. She began by bringing lots of posters and other materials for the students to use in decorating the room. She tentatively arranged the desks in a semicircle with her desk facing students only four feet away. She dressed in a comfortable matching pants outfit in keeping with the dress custom set by the faculty in the school and used limited accessories and makeup. She chose not to use perfume on the first day.

When the children arrived for their first day of school, Sarah greeted them with a voice full of excitement and joyful anticipation for the year they were to share. She asked the students to select a desk they would like and told them that as the week progressed that they would be able to rearrange the seats in the room. Sarah decided to reserve touch for a later date if it seemed appropriate, but she did escort each of the children into the classroom mindful that she stayed in close proximity to each student and that she gave each one direct eye contact.

Sarah also had selected a number of live plants for the classroom and had persuaded the custodians to change her cool blue ceiling lights to full spectrum lights. She also had called some of the parents and had asked them to bring in some freshly baked snacks for the children so that the room would smell like freshly baked goods. She was mindful of the fact the snacks would also ensure that all of the children would begin the day with a nutritious snack. After the children had finished with the snack and had been given a few minutes to talk with their new neighbors in the classroom, Sarah began with "today let's talk about the year's activities. We need to decide how we want to change this room so that it will be comfortable during the activities that we will be doing. If you do not see something here that you think would help us, just let me know and I will see if I can find it." Sarah sensed that the students were quite excited about the possibilities but were a little tentative since this was really a new approach to education for them.

The first content area dealt with the solar system and the students began talking about the changes they could make. The students decided that the class would drape black construction paper around the room and would paint closeby stars and galaxies on the paper. The students would take care to calculate relative distances of objects before placing them on the paper. The desks were to be grouped as if they were the planetary systems within the solar system and each group was assigned the task of finding out all they could about their particular planetary system for a report back to the class. Sarah's desk was designated as the sun and she had to give the first report with the Mercury planet group being next.

Sarah was just as exhausted as the first year when she returned home that day, but her time was even more constrained because now she had to spend even more time working on the lessons for the next few days given the decisions she and the students had made. Sarah knew that the time invested was worth a few late nights given the excitement that she and the students felt during that first day of her second year at Lake Elementary. Sarah knew that her actions affected the learning that occurred in her classroom and she was willing to take some time to consider the impact of the nonverbal dimensions upon classroom instruction.

Nonverbal communication should be included as a vital portion of teacher training and certification programs so that the unspoken means of communication are fully incorporated into the teaching-learning process. Only after all the aspects of communication are included in learning decisions can we truly say that we are consciously educating the whole child.

Noted References

[1]Andersen, P.A., J.F. Andersen, and S.M. Mayton. "The Acquisition of Nonverbal Attitudes and Behaviors in School children, Grades K-12." Paper presented at the annual meeting of the Speech Communication Association, Louisville, November 1982. ED 221 896.

[2]Andersen, P.A., J.F. Andersen, and S.M. Mayton. "The Development of Nonverbal Communication in the Classroom: Teachers' Perceptions of Students in Grades K-12." The *Western Journal of Speech Communication 49* (Summer, 1985): 188-203.

[3]Andersen, J.F., R.W. Norton, and J.F. Nussbaum. "Three Investigations Exploring Relationships Between Perceived Teacher Communication Behaviors and Student Learning." *Communication Education 30*(October 1981): 377-392.

[4]Boileau, D.M. "Nonverbal Communication: Classroom Influence and Topic." *Communication Education 30* (July 1981): 305-310. Brooks, D. M. and A. E. Woolfolk. "The Effects of Students' Nonverbal Behavior on *Teachers." The Elementary School Journal 88* (September 1987): 51-63.

[5]Burgoon K., J.K, D.B. Buller, and W.G. Woodall. *Nonverbal Communication: The Unspoken Dialogue.* New York: Harper and Row, 1989.

Clifford, M.M. and E.H. Walster. "The Effect of Physical Attractiveness in Teacher Expectation." *Sociological Education 46* (1973): 248-258.

[7]Cottle, T.J. *Perceiving Time: A Psychological Investigation With Men and Women.* New York: John Wiley & Sons, 1976.

[8]Darling, A.L. and Staton-Spicer, A.Q. *Teacher-Student Interaction in the Classroom: An Annotated Basic Bibliography.* Annandale, VA: Speech Communication Association, 1987. ED 289 217.

[9]Elkind, D. *All Grown Up No Place to Go: Teenagers in Crisis.* Reading, MA: Addison Wesley, 1984.

[10]Elkind, D. *The Hurried Child: Growing Up Too Fast Too Soon.* Rev. Ed. Reading, MA: Addison Wesley, 1988.

[11]Greenbaum, P.E., "Nonverbal Communications Between American Indian Children and Their Teachers." Final report of grant NIE-G-81-0117 funded by the National Institute of Education, Washington, D.C., 1983. ED 239 804.

[12]Hall, E.T. *Beyond Culture.* Garden City, NY: Doubleday, 1976.

[13]Hall, E.T. *The Hidden Dimension.* Garden City, NY: Doubleday, 1969.

[14]Heslin, R. "Steps Toward a Taxonomy of Touching." Paper presented at the Western Psychological Association Convention, Chicago, 1974.

[15]Hickson, M.I. and Stacks, D.W. *NVC Nonverbal Communication: Studies and Applications.* 2d ed. Dubuque, IA: Wm. C. Brown, 1989. 9-96 and 151-207.

[16]Jourard. S.M. "An Empirical Study of Body Accessibility." *British Journal of Social and Clinical Psychology.* 5(1966): 221-231.

[17]Jourard. S.M. *Disclosing Man to Himself.* Princeton, NJ: Van Nostrand, 1968.

[18]Katz, A.M. and Katz, V.T. eds. *Foundations of Nonverbal Communication.*

Carbondale, IL: Southern Illinois University Press, 1983.

[19]Knapp, M.L., M.J. Cody, and K.K. Reardon. "Nonverbal Signals." *Handbook of Communication Science.* C.R. Berger & S.H. Chaffee eds. Newbury Park, CA: Sage, 1987: 385-418.

Knapp, M.L., J.M. Wiemann, and J.A. Daly. "Nonverbal Communication Issues and Appraisal." *Foundations of Nonverbal Communication.* A.M. Katz & V.T. Katz eds. Carbondale, IL: Southern Illinois University Press, 1983: XIX-XXXI.

[21]Lane, L.L. "Communicative Behavior and Biological Rhythms." *The Speech Teacher* 20(1971): 16-19.

[22]Leathers, D.G. *Successful Nonverbal Communication.* New York: Macmillan, 1986.

[23]Luce, G.G. *Body Time: Physiological Rhythms and Social Stress.* New York: Random House, 1971.

[24]Lyman, S.M. and M.B. Scott. "Territoriality: A Neglected Sociological Dimension." *Social Problems* 15(1967): 237-241.

[25]Malandro, L.A. and L.L. Barker. *Nonverbal Communication.* Reading, MA: Addison-Wesley, 1983.

[26]Meerloo, J. "The Time Sense in Psychiatry." *The Voice of Time.* J.T. Fraser ed. New York: Braziller, 1966.

[27]Miller, P.W. *Nonverbal Communication.* 3rd ed. West Haven, CN: National Educational Association Professional Library, 1988. 17-30. ED 293 190.

[28]Miller, P.W. "Silent Messages." *Childhood Education.* 58 (September/October 1981): 20-24.

[29]Roach, M.E. and M.E. Musa. "Functions of Dress." *Foundations of Nonverbal Communication.* A.M. Katz and V.T. Katz eds. Carbondale, IL: Southern Illinois University Press, 1983: 169-176.

[30]Smith, H.A. "Nonverbal Behavior and Student Achievement in the Elementary Classroom." Paper presented at the meeting of the Canadian Society for the Study of Education, Saskatoon, Saskatchewan, June 1979. ED 181 000.

[31]Stacks, D.W. Nonverbal Communication: Theory, Assessment, and Instruction. A Selected Annotated Bibliography. Annandale, VA: Speech Communication Association, 1985. ED 289 211.

Section Six

Educational Communications Technology

22

Communication Technology in the Classroom

Erv Schieman

Definitions and Terminology

The field of educational technology suffers from the ambiguity of its definition. Over its history, educational technology has had many definitions put forward but no single definition has been universally accepted. Perhaps this is an indication that the field still has not reached maturity and is still in its evolutionary phase. As a result of this the term education technology has meant and will probably continue to mean, different things to different people. Most definitions of educational technology can be categorized into two distinctive classes: the view of educational technology as devices (or AV when referring to various types of instructional media) and the view of educational technology as a process. This process is very often referred to as the systems approach. The most comprehensive definition then should contain the notions of both of the above categories.

Perhaps the most comprehensive definition is that suggested by the Commission on Instructional Technology:[1]

> Instructional technology can be defined in two ways. In its more familiar sense, it means the media born of the communications revolution which can be used for instructional purposes alongside the teacher, a blackboard . . . The pieces that make up instructional technology include: television, films, overhead projectors, computers, and other items of "hardware" and "software" to use the convenient jargon that distinquishes machines from programs . . .
>
> The second and less familiar definition of instructional technology goes beyond any particular medium or device. In this sense, instructional technology is more than the sum of its parts. It is a systematic way of designing, carrying out, and evaluating the total process of learning and teaching in terms of specific objectives, based on research in human learning and communication, and employing a combination of human and non-human resources to bring

more effective instruction.[2]

Another definition of the field is provided by Galbraith who sees that technology as the systematic application of scientific or other organized knowledge to practical tasks.[4] A third important idea linked with the educational technology field is that of individualized instruction. The Association of Educational Communication and Technology[3] has provided a definition which is useful for our purpose. It is as follows:

> The educational technology approach has been directed towards expanding the range of resources used for learning, emphasizing the individual learner and his unique needs, and using a systemic approach to the development of learning resources.[1]

The task of understanding the field is further complicated by the use of varying terms which may or may not always have the same meaning for readers and listeners. The partial list includes

audio visual,
audio visual communication,
A-V media,
educational media,
instructional media,
instructional technology,
educational communication and technology,
instructional development,
instructional design,
educational media and communication, and
learning technology.

Regardless of the term being dealt with, it is suggested consideration be given to define the field as follows:

> A teaching/learning pattern designed to provide reliable, effective instruction to each learner through the application of scientific principles to human learning.[5]

To reduce the field of educational technology to mere machines, television, film or computers is to misrepresnt the facts. Since instructional media and learning materials surround us, they are part of the student's total learning environment and experience. Instructional media provides the means for teachers to teach and make possible the appropriate conditions for learning to occur. Therefore, the operation of equipment must be viewed as a small portion of the much larger concept of educational technology.[6]

The Concrete – Abstract Experience Continuum

The understanding of the implication for use of instructional materials in the teaching process can be illustrated by thinking of experience as a range with the concrete ones at one extreme and the abstract ones at the opposite end. Suppose a teacher places this definition from Funk & Wagnall's Standard College

Dictionary on the overhead projector or blackboard:

glockenspiel – a portable musical instrument consisting of a series of chromatically tuned metal bars and played by striking with small light hammers.

What is it? Not many students would recognize it from its abstract verbal description. If the teacher then produced an example of a glockenspiel, there would now be a concrete object to make the abstract image more understandable. This is one task of the teacher – to take that which is abstract and difficult to understand and make it more concrete, teachable and understandable. The teacher can employ instructional media and materials – the tools – to facilitate the learning process. Instructional media and materials can provide a wide range of experience for learners. These experiences are graphically shown on the "Cone of Experience" and move the learner from the actual experience of touching and handling a glockenspiel (for example) to the experience of observing a mediated event of the device and ultimately to the recognition of symbolic representations (flat pictures, diagrams or words) of the devices.

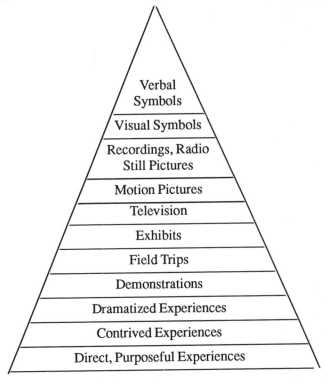

Dale's Cone of Experience. From *Audio Visual Methods in Teaching,* Third Edition, by Edgar Dale, Copyright 1954.

The base of the cone represents experiences that are direct, live and meaningful. At the apex of the cone are the most abstract – and the principle tool of instruction as well the most difficult teaching tool of all experiences – words.

Communication and the Learning Process

It has been suggested that the shift from an unidirectional to a systems concept in education is an outgrowth of society's new sophistication with technology generally and instructional media and materials specifically. As well, the attention given to the development process whereby fresh and innovative curriculum materials are made available to learners, referred to in the educational technology literature as instructional design, has fostered a whole new look at how messages, using the media, have affected the learning process. With the much greater emphasis on the learner resulting from a systems approach, the "receiver" of instructional messages communicated through media has the same importance as the "message" and the "medium" (delivery system). Much of the recent research in the educational psychology field has moved us in this direction. One has only to visit a school to see the nature of this shift. No longer does the teacher rely solely on verbal communication, though it is still heavily used and very important, but verbal messages are complemented by various auditory and visual messages.

Communication Competence

Perception and communication lead to understanding and learning: the goal of all instruction. What skills must a teacher possess in order to teach effectively? Part of the answer to this comlex question lies in part to the teacher having an understanding of the communication process. Though there are many models of communication described and used in teacher training programs, most have a similar generic structure. One of the simplest models if the example employed by Kemp and Smellie:

> This model (originally developed by Shannon and Weaver) illustrates that a message (at the mental level), generally in the form of information, originated by a source or sender (the brain of an individual), is encoded and converted into transmittable form (a thought verbalized, as for conversation, by being turned into sound waves, or words written for a script). The message then passes through a transmitter (print, slides, film, videotape) via a suitable channel (air, wire, paper, light) to the receiver, (a person's senses-eyes,ears,other sensory nerve endings), then to the destination (brain of the receiver) where the message is decoded (converted into mental symbols).[7]

Sender		Message	Transmission Channel	Receiver		Destination
	→		→		→	
Source of Message		Encoded		Message Received		Message Decoded
			Feedback			

The Shannon – Weaver model of communication adapted from Kemp and Smellie (1989).

A goal of all education is to teach students various communication skills. Teachers select concepts and materials to teach the basic communication skills: voice and speaking improvement, reading, writing, listening and viewing skills. When introducing new concepts and ideas, teachers often use symbols which are meaningful for the learners. This is an assumption every teacher, every artist, every after dinner speaker and every T.V. news reader makes. Signs are part of every individual's means of communication and such examples as &, $, #, =, icons on a computer screen and mathematic formulas all come with a certain meaning. Anyone not familiar with these meanings is surely lost as one would be when confronted with a strange foreign language. When meanings are not shared between "sender" and "receiver" (or writer and reader) , then a situation exists where the communication will be poor or non-existent.

Modern educational psychologists tell us that understanding is a developmental process and exists on three successive levels. Level one is the experience level where the meanings being communicated are usually accurate and not subject to gross misunderstanding. Unfortunately not all learning can be presented or can occur at this level because conceptualization and generalization do not always occur in experience but can be inferred from it.

The second level is that of vicarious experience. Much of what we learn of the world around us comes from this level. These replacements for the real thing are used extensively by teachers to bring the "outside" world into the classroom. Therefore, the detonation of a nuclear bomb and its effects can be experienced without the deleterious, "real life" ramifications. These experiences can be gained through reading good literature, biographies and plays. Vicarious experiences are available through exposure to still pictures, television, resource people, artifacts, models, dioramas, educational games and computer simulations. As the Dale Cone of Experience illustrates, the more concrete and realistic the vicarious experience, the more closely allied it will be to the first level (actual experience.) Teachers must be aware that misunderstandings can occur in dealing with vicarious experiences. Young children can easily mistake relative sizes when, for example, they are shown equal size pictures of a mouse and a horse. Distracted impressions can occur as a result of close-up shots, unreal colors, out-of-date shots, and animation. These can all convey misunderstandings.

Understanding abstractions is the third general level of communication. It likely represents the most complex level of communication and can therefore lead to the most likely areas for misunderstanding. This level of communication is characterized by words spoken and written, by scientific and other formulas, and symbolization.

Most cultures use forms of abstractions as communication shortcuts, allowing for the condensing of ideas, thinking and experiences. If one were to consider, for example, a term such as "blueattached which all convey something quite different. There are the various shadings of color, the term when it is a name for a dog or a brand of beer and the depicting of feelings of lonesomeness and nostalgia. When the term then is used in various contexts, (i.e. scientific, artistic etc.), a variety of understandings can result. While these three levels of understanding are obviously an oversimplification of the concept (because there really are many more levels), they are useful in attempting to delineate what is meant when we are discussing the concept of understanding.

The Values of Instructional Media

Teachers, in the not so distant past, had to rely almost entirely on the chalkboard, a few dated political/geographical wall maps and atlases and probably a few text books which served as the only reference material. Modern teachers, by contrast, have access to a wide range and variety of resources to choose from, ranging from those materials housed in the classroom or learning resource center to those resources located elsewhere but accessible immediately (or nearly so), by electronic means.

Such basic values in instructional media as concreteness, enrichment and strong motivational interest are apparent to modern teachers. Instructional media can also show processes which would not ordinarily be accessible, such as the opening of a flower blossom or the dividing of an animal cell. Events occurring far away can be brought into the classroom through media such as television or film. Feelings, attitudes, exotic animals, or far away exotic places can be readily communicated to learners in group or individual settings through a variety of media. The voices of famous people can be brought into the learning environment to make an occasion more realistic with the actual voice and face serving to motivate learners. The media help teachers to convey changes in time, location and speed. The media can speed up or slow down events and processes to make them more understandable to viewers. Above all, the media provide for the sharing of opportunities for all learners. The experiences, no matter how esoteric and unusual, can be made available to learners regardless of economics, geography and culture. The media also provide integrated experiences with examples and illustrations ranging from the concrete to the abstract, with objects, events and people shown pictorially with text and graphics. The media can bring experts on most subjects into the classroom and supply multiple resources for learning which might otherwise be unavailable.

Attitude and behavior changes are possible (though sometimes inadvertently) through the use of instructional media. An important application of media is for the purpose of getting and holding the attention of learners. Without this attention learning cannot take place. Through the use of instructional media, it has been shown, learners will experience greater acquisition of information and will retain that factual knowledge longer. It has also been demonstrated that the media can stimulate voluntary reading on the part of learners. The media constitute a method for introducing and dealing with controversial or delicate subjects which many teachers might feel uncomfortable with as a discussion topic. The media can be employed to present alternative perspectives on these controversial or delicate issues. The media also put students in contact with the realities of their social and physical environment. Last but not least, another benefit of using instructional media is that the media can be used for all age and ability groups.

Viewed another way, instructional media can depict and clarify non-verbal symbols and images, complex relationships, temporal and spacial relationships, quantitative relationships, macro views of organisms and processes, abstract relationships and contrasting relationships of occurrences and people. All of this is possible when the materials are well designed and employed appropriately in well planned instructional environments and under conditions where specific learner objectives have been identified.

Recognition of the many benefits that instructional media hold for learners has increased the amounts of attention and effort given to the development of resources for teachers. These supplementary materials include reference and bibliographic lists, film and videographic resource lists, kits, games and simulations, listening skills, materials lists and a range of computer software to provide for drill and practice, tutorial, problem solving and gaming activities.

As we approach the end of the twentieth century and begin the planning for the early twenty-first century , the technological innovations being introduced into education will become even more desirable and inevitable. With this wide-spread proliferation of technology also come problems. These problems are ones of finances, teacher training, administrative organization and its integration with our foundational theories of learning. Secondary technological problems related to factors such as standardization of formats, inadequate techniques for bibliographic control, the cataloging, housing and distribution of resources also contribute to slow and sometimes poor use of instructional media.

The conditions of teaching have changed and the contributions of educational technology have provided the impetus, at least in part, for the recent rapid developments. At one time teaching was a one-dimensional art and teacher competence was directly related to the teacher's knowledge of content. The role of the teacher changed when emphasis on skills in organizing and presenting content, usually referred to as method, was introduced. Another window was opened for the classroom teacher, when knowledge of the learner became important. The things that motivate individuals, change behavior, and knowledge of how the environment interacts with learners became important skills to be acquired by professional teachers. A fourth aspect which has recently influenced on the roles and responsibilities of teachers is that of the learning environment. The recognition that humans learn through synthesis of content, method, motivation and "systems" designed learning materials is a relatively recent approach. It is currently thought to be important that learners be taught how to learn (metacognition) rather than be guided through content. Clearly, teaching has changed, but the above discussion of conditions illustrates a progression to more complex involvement in the teaching process.

How to Use Instructional Media Effectively

There can clearly be many ways to integrate instructional materials into lesson plans. Teachers should be encouraged to use media and materials in innovative ways by employing strategies which are appropriate for their learners, their teaching environment and the teaching style. It should be recognized that due to the nature of the profession, where highly trained teachers have skills to employ media in a variety of ways for a variety of purposes, no universally accepted strategies exist. However it is appropriate, especially for new teachers, to have suggested guidelines for media utilization where the guidelines have been accepted by the profession.

It must be pointed out that the guidelines which follow are suggestive only and are not meant to be definitive. The list is not exhaustive since there are many and space precludes the listing of all constructive uses. These guidelines are broad and the reader should be aware that not all suggestions are appropriate for all situations, but nevertheless they are derived from formal research conducted as far back as the 1940's and 50's as well as the practical experiences of several generations of educators. Briefly stated, the accepted processes for effective media utilization includes the preview of all materials, the practicing of the presentation, careful preparation of the learning environment and the preparation of the audience.

Guideline 1: Choose instructional materials which are appropriate for your audience and which fit specific objectives of the lesson or unit of instruction. The first step is to list your objectives and then select media and materials which best meet these objectives. This avoids the situation where media are employed merely for the sake of using materials.

Guideline 2: Plan in advance. Locate as many suitable materials as possible using resource center catalogs, study guides, published reviews, media distributors' information brochures, and colleagues' appraisals. Once the materials have been identified, it is incumbent upon teachers to familiarize themselves with the materials by previewing them. Only then can a teacher wrap the lesson around the instructional materials. Integrate these materials into a lesson plan, considering the sequence, timing and coordination of all learning activities. It is at this stage of the planning process that sensitive materials can be accommodated or eliminated.

Guideline 3: Practice the presentation before attempting it before an audience. This is advisable for all presentations a teacher may undertake, not only those in a classroom. It is advisable to practice the presentation at least once before a mirror with an outline or notes. Others use audio or video recorders to record and playback the practice session for critiquing later. The familiarity of the material, and the amount of time available determines how often the presentation should be practiced.

Guideline 4: Prepare the environment. Utilization may require a darkened room, an adequate power supply, and access to light switches and possibly a public address system. These must be planned for and checked out in advance. The teacher should always check out the equipment to prevent embarrassing problems, and have the materials installed on the equipment and properly cued to the section to be used. The volume controls should be adjusted to a comfortable listening level.

Guideline 5: Prepare the audience in advance. Learners must be ready for what you are about to present. Discuss with the group the materials to be used, by name, by type, the source and other pertinent information. Learners should be aware of the reasons for using certain materials. They should be made aware of important things: associations to be made and considered; new or complex vocabulary, symbols and events; negative features and controversial issues should all be pointed out in advance. Therefore, directing attention, initiating motivation and providing a suitable rationale are all critically important when using media materials for instruction.

Guideline 6: Plan for audience participation. This participation can occur before, during, after or in a combination of places. The amount of participation will be determined by the topic, the materials, the lesson objectives, the age and the maturity level of the audience. It has long been known that participation by learners in the learning process improves learning. Researchers and writers such as Dewey, Skinner, and more recently the cognitive psychologists, have supported the notion that active manipulation of information by participants leads to learning. The implications for teachers are clear. The situation most conducive to effective learning is one where there is participation by learners of learning activities which are objective-based.

Guideline 7: Evaluate the materials and the learners. Assessment of how well the materials have met the criteria will determine whether they can be used again, either with some modifications or in their entirety. Judge whether the learners reacted positively to their use and whether the content was accurate, objective and comprehensive. Ultimately too, the question of whether the students have learned what was intended must be determined. To what degree does the learner's new skill and/or knowledge meet the criteria identified in the predetermined lesson objectives? The method of evaluation depends on the objectives. Depending on whether simple recall/ recognition is required or whether process-type behaviors are required, such as operating a wood lathe, will determine how evaluation is to occur. For simple recall information, simple written or oral examinations are appropriate. In other instances performance will be assessed by other means. It is very important to keep in mind that the methods of evaluation are directly related to the stated objectives and wherever possible should be specified in the objectives.

Integrating Pictorial Media into Instructional Plans

The emphasis accorded the visual sense in the teaching process (the audio element will be discussed later) is due to the fact that so much of what we interact with and learn from is visual. One must be aware of the danger, though, of associating too much learning from this communication channel when in fact more complex processes are involved. For example, our perception of an image may be triggered by a single visual stimulus, the lead singer of a heavy metal rock band, for example, but the understanding of the complete image is a series of both physiological and psychological functions. Visual sensory perception cannot be thought of as a single discreet process and, therefore, caution must be exercised since we deal with media communication as separate visual and audio entities.

Visual Media

A simplified means of classifying visual materials would be to consider them as projected versus non-projected media. Though this is a very crude means of analyzing instructional materials, it can be useful. Therefore, such media materials as filmstrips, 16mm film, 35mm slides, overhead transparencies and in some cases, television and computer screens are projected media. While the non-projected media would include materials such as posters, flat pictures, printed materials (including maps and the like). One may also consider video images and computer graphics, when viewed on a monitor to be of this sort.

The advantages of using projected images include: enlargement of images(with the attending benefits), bright colors which are attention getting when the room is darkened), and suitability for viewing by large groups. When projecting images from 16mm or video, the teacher has the advantage of displaying both motion and sound. While projecting stills (slides) does not have the attributes of film or video, it is very useful for controlling the pacing and sequence. As well, slides along with transparencies can be locally produced and will therefore be inexpensive and available in a short time. The disadvantages when employing projection include the fact that usually the room is dark and precludes learners from making notes. The other major disadvantages are those associated with management of young learners viewing learning materials in a darkened room. Other disadvantages of using projected learning materials are related to expensive projection equipment (both film and video) which the school may not be able to afford, problems of scheduling space and equipment, ordering the films or video and the mechanics of setting up the equipment and possibly the environment for viewing.

Non-projected visuals have the advantage of permanence. They seldom wear out, they can be left out for continuous use and can be locally produced at low expense or purchased at a low expense. These materials may not possess the glamour of some projected learning materials, but they can be effective instructional resources nevertheless.

It is useful for the beginning teacher to remember that all visuals have their appropriate applications and the knowledge of each material's unique contribution can make instruction more effective. The effective teacher will employ a variety of these materials in different ways which will result in the increased benefits for learners.

Planning for Audio Media

The magnetic tape recorder in the cassette format comprises the bulk of audio use in classrooms. Radio in North America no longer is widely used for instruction and reel-to-reel tape machines are quickly going the way of the Edsel. The phonograph or record player still has instructional uses but appears to be diminishing. The niche for compact discs still has to be determined.

Tape recorders enjoy some popularity with teachers as recorded material can be manipulated to control pacing and sequencing. One can have the advantage of radio (except immediacy) where voices of famous people, experts and interesting events can be shared by groups. It also has the advantages over record players in that the recording can be played multiple times without serious deterioration. The obvious advantage of tape over records is, of course, the recording capability.

All audio devices and materials suffer from the fact that when used inappropriately become one-way communication channels. Only when teachers are familiar with the recorded content can they stop the tape,carry on discussion, raise questions to make the audio medium more interactive and effective.

Due to this problem of using a single sensory approach, audio becomes significantly more difficult to use compared to multi-sensory materials. If the teacher involves the other senses with the content being presented, the chance of learning occurring is enhanced.

As with other media materials, audio needs to be introduced to alert the learners as to the "why" of the resource. By discussing the medium and its content beforehand, the learner is guided and informed to the point that the content becomes much more meaningful. The learner can anticipate, in this way, what is going to occur and in what order it will occur. Certainly questions related to the objectives improve the understanding of the content and the inquiry approach teaches the students learning strategies.

The uses of tape recordings are varied and limited only by the imagination of the teacher. Foreign language instruction is one important application in both the record and playback mode. Learners recording their own voices specking in a foreign language can be most useful in correcting pronunciation.

Another interesting application for audio is in the joint use situation where slides and sound are combined. This slide-tape format can be easily produced, can be a format for student-produced media (and therefore be highly motivating), and can be effective, quite inexpensive and involves relatively simple skills for local production.

Less Frequently Used Communication Channels in Instruction – Smell, Taste and Touch

When dealing with learning and learners, there is considerable evidence which suggests that a direct relationship exists between the sensory involvement and more effective and permanent learning. This relationship also makes intuitive sense when one considers what is commonly remembered or forgotten with regard to experiences. Certainly remember a gorgeous sunset over a lake, the first visit to a zoo where the sights and smells have a profound effect, a visit aboard an aircraft carrier or our first airplane ride. The experiences we are prone to forget are those which have little sensory involvment. Conversely, those things which can be easily recalled involve total sensory stimulation. Therefore, learning opportunities involving smell, taste, touch and sight and hearing are probably critical and should be brought into the instructional planning picture by teachers. For young learners to experience the contact with a pineapple by touch, smell and taste rather than by just seeing a picture is a most valuable direct, first hand experience.

These above experiences are made possible by stimulation of our sensory mechanisms: the taste buds, the nose, the eyes and ears, and the nerve endings embedded in our skin. The perceptors are our contact with the world of things and events. These are tools by means of which we come to know our environment. Awareness of the importance of these tools is crucial for teachers; however, they are merely a means of information gathering. The information gathered is transmitted to the brain where impressions and thoughts are formulated through a process known as cognition. Our knowledge gained through perceptions is then a joint effort between our sensory apparatus and our brain's cognitive mechanism.

Fleming and Levie[3], through years of research have identified, from behavioral science, principles which can be used in the design and development of learning materials. In a summary of the major conclusions concerning perception and the involvement of the senses, the researchers have generated these useful points:

1. Since perception is relative (rather than absolute), provide reference points to which unknown objects or events can be related and difficult concepts through steps.

2. Since perception is selective, present essential factors one step at a time.

3. Since perception is organized, use number and verbal (next, either) cues to order a message.

4. Since expectation influences perception, give directions for finding an answer in an illustration.

5. Draw attention to changes in how relevant ideas in a message are presented (by means of brightness, movement, novelty, asking questions, posing problems).

6. Characteristics (brightness, color, texture, form, and size) should be selected

and arranged carefully because they have a positive influence on perception.

7. Use the visual channel for presenting spatial concepts and the auditory channel for presenting temporal concepts.

8. For difficult material presented aurally, use short sentences, redundancy, and excellent technical quality.

9. The most compatible modes that permit the highest information level are simultaneous auditory and visual presentation of a subject provided by slides and tape, sound film, and video recordings.

10. Use lines around, under, and between to cue groupings; accentuate and relate elements in a visual.

11. Facilitate recognition of similarities and differences by presenting several related objects together.

13. Make the organizational outline of a message apparent (subtitles, transitional statements).

14. The better an object or event is perceived (by means of applying the above-stated and other perception principles), the more feasible and reliable will be memory, concept formation, problem solving, creativity, and attitude change.

As a teacher you must be aware that when you are developing instructional media you must plan to provide desirable perceptual experiences taking into consideration the backgrounds of your learners and the environment in which the instruction is to occur. Factors such as the treatment of the topic using a dramatic approach as opposed to an inquiry approach, the nature and type of examples to be used, the vocabulary, the grammar, the pacing and the sequencing, the visuals and the graphics to be used and the possible use of narration all are determining factors which can influence perception. Careful attention to the design process helps to ensure that learning can be interesting as well as effective for the learners.

Using a Systems Approach to Teaching with Instructional Media

All too often the beginning teacher is faced with situations in the classroom where every event appears to be a crisis. When this persists the teacher becomes more concerned with survival than with devising and using instructional strategies which are effective. This often results in the situation where the question "What do I have to do?" becomes the central instructional solution. By adopting a systems approach to educational technology, the more appropriate question then asked is, "What do the learners need to do to achieve the stated objectives?."

A systems approach is nothing more than a method of organizing the curriculum, the instructional procedures and the learning environment in such a way as to optimize the learning that is to take place. Everything that concerns the educational program in a classroom is viewed as an integral component of a larger system. These closely interrelated elements are carefully planned and

orchestrated by the teacher with the assistance of other educational professionals to provide a stimulating learning environment and to prepare the students
for instruction and ultimately learning. Heinich, Molenda and Russell[6] provide
a useful model for teachers to follow which very much simplifies the process.
They have devised the ASSURE model to ensure that learning takes place and
to ensure that effectual use of media in the classroom occurs. The model
includes the elements of:

> Analyzing learners
> Stating objectives
> Selecting media and materials
> Utilizing materials
> Requiring learner performance
> Evaluating and revising the material's effectiveness

Analyzing Learners

A knowledge of the learners is essential for any instructional event so that
appropriate planning can be carried out. The theory is that you must know your
learners so that the best instruction can be selected and presented, thereby aid-
ing in the achievement of the objectives of the instruction. Included in the
analysis are the (1) general characteristics of the learners and (2) their entry
level knowledge. Also of use would be information about skills they already
possess and their attitude towards the topic.

Stating Objectives

While goals are usually broad statements of the terminal learning, objectives are more specific, identifying, with some precision, what the results of
instruction are to be. Objectives are often derived from an assessment of needs,
(from the curriculum guide) or identified by the teacher using several sources of
information.

Selecting Media and Materials

With information about your audience of learners and what the result of
instruction is to be, you have the beginning and the end portions of the instructional plan. Now you must determine how to overcome the knowledge
deficiency of the learners. To "bridge" the gap the teacher must choose from
one of the following three selections: (1)select and use available learning
materials, (2) modify these already available materials or (3) design fresh
materials.

Utilizing Materials

When the materials are in hand, the teacher must decide how to best deploy them, whether to use them in small groups or individualized ways and to determine how much time is to be spent using the media materials. Previous to this the teacher must schedule equipment and facilities. Reference materials must be identified, located and reviewed. At this point the teacher must preview any films or videos to determine their appropriateness and accuracy. Other aspects related to showmanship must be considered using presentation techniques described previously in the "How to Use Instructional Media Effectively," section.

Requiring Learner Performance

For learning to be effective, it must be active rather than passive and participatory rather that solely demonstrative. To the greatest extent possible, practice should be an integral part of the lesson, and correct responses should be acknowledged and reinforced. This suggests that examinations should not directly follow the instructional session but suggests that the learners have had opportunities to respond and to receive feedback. The instruction should be learner-centered, as well as interesting, dynamic and stimulating, and this suggests variety. Variety in the way learner responses are encouraged will not only get the attention of the learners, but variety will also hold their attention.

Evaluating and Revising the Materials Effectiveness

Following the period of instruction, including practice, it is important to conduct an assessment of the learning. The evaluation of the impact of the media materials is important to the teacher as well as to the learner knowledge of the material's effectiveness is important. Clearly then, the whole instructional process must be assessed to determine whether objectives are being met, whether the organization, pacing, sequencing, and environment are appropriate and whether the learners understood the instructions and use of materials in the correct fashion. When there are differences detected, as a result of the evaluation, between the intended objectives and what actually was attained, the time has arrived for revisions to be made. The more specific the results of the evaluation, the easier it is to determine where revisions are to occur.

Innovations in Instructional Technology

Of the many changes in educational technology experienced over the past quarter century, four appear to have great promise for the improvement of learning, for the productivity of our schools and for the improvement of educational opportunities for all learners regardless of their economic, geographic or cultural status. The first innovation which is on-going is the miniaturization of the communications media. This trend has resulted in several changes occurring in the way technology is used. Miniaturization has tended to lower costs, has resulted in easier-to-use equipment and has made media and media systems much more portable. These factors have made media and media materials more accessible to all learners in both formal and informal ways. This development has done a great deal to address many inequalities in our school systems.

Media such as video recorders (VCR's), videodiscs, CD-ROM (Compact Disc - Read Only Memory) technology, micro-processors and microcomputers are all examples of technology that has undergone the changes identified above. Even 16mm projectors have become more portable and easier to operate as have audio recording devices. Great changes have and are occurring in the information storage formats. An area currently experiencing an upsurge in interest is the learning network. A learning network can be as simple as two distant schools maintaining computer contact or as complex as world-wide linkages with many institutions sharing information. The most common application of learning networks are linkages using electronic mail (E – mail). In these applications, students in their respective schools compose messages on their microcomputers and transmit them to their desired locale through a modem and a combination of land and satellite lines. E-mail has the benefits of:

(1) linking students with each other,
(2) offering educational experiences outside the classroom,
(3) linking students with distant resources (e.g., databases), and
(4) offering in-service, teleconferencing and credit course opportunities.

Other innovations which could have important impacts on instruction in schools of the future are such concepts as artificial intelligence, expert systems, psycho-technology and bio-technology. Ongoing work in the area of learning styles and teaching styles could also advance the field of instructional media and materials. Electronic systems used to deliver instruction (distance education) are also sure to benefit education. Open and closed T.V. broadcasting, cable systems and satellite receiving dishes and mode linkages mean that small group, large group and individual instruction can be transmitted from where the instructor is to where the learner is. Computer conferencing and audiographic systems are being developed making it possible to deliver instruction which can include any combination of voice and sound, pictures, graphics and text. The mechanics and electronics of transmitting smell, taste, and touch have yet to be developed. happening. Remember that before the telephone was invented, the transmission of the human voice, electro-magnetically, was not thought possible.

Noted References

[1]Association for Educational Technology and Communication(1977). *Educational Technology: Definitions and Glossary of Terms*. Washington,D.C: AECT, p. 36.

[2]Commission of Instructional Technology (1970). *To Improve Learning: An Evaluation of Instructional Technology.* (Vol.1). New York: Bowker, p. 21.

[3]Fleming, M. and Levie, H. (1978). *Instructional Message Design: Principles From the Behavioral Sciences.* Englewood Cliffs, N.J: Educational Technology Publications.

[4]Galbraith, J.K. (1967). *The New Industrial State.* Boston: Houghton Miffen, p.12.

[5]Heinich, R., Molenda, M. and Russell, J. (1985). *Instructional Media and the New Technologies of Instruction.* Second edition. New York: John Wiley and Sons, p. 284.

[6]Heinich, R., Molenda, M. and Russell, J. (1989). *Instructional Media and the New Technologies of Instruction.* Third edition. New York: MacMillan Publishing.

[7]Kemp, J. and Smellie, D. (1989). *Planning, Producing and Using Instructional Media.* Sixth edition. New York: Harper & Rowe Publishers.

23

High-Tech Talk:
Computers in Classroom Communication

William J. Hunter and *John Beames*

Some educators might cringe at any mention of the word "technology" in the context of interpersonal communication, thinking that there was something inhumane, anti-human or unhumanistic about technological devices. We hope to put that view to rest by discussing the ways in which "communications technology" can contribute to humanistic interpersonal communication.

Technology makes it possible for us to deliver education over greater distances, a practice that is known as "distance education" and which is increasingly occupying a place of importance in higher education – for example, through Alberta's Athabasca University – and in secondary level public education – for example, through Alberta's Correspondence School in Barrhead. But delivering the "same old education" at greater distances is only part of what the technologies could do. They could reduce the psychological distances between children and what they need to learn by creating a sense of excitement about communication and learning. For example, who would ask the relevance of learning to write if they were frequently greeted with requests for information from interested people at the other end of the province, the country, the world? The new technologies could also expand our horizons. For example, they can help us to come to know about people whom we would otherwise never meet and can let us see how those people are like us so that we may come to value them as thinking, feeling beings even though we may never see them. Communications technologies could also let us see how those people differ from us so that we might come to value the diversity that makes the world more like an exotic salad than a thin gruel.

The Alberta Teachers' Association magazine recently devoted an entire issue to the theme "Global Education" in which the articles stressed the importance of helping children to perceive the interrelationship of people the world over and our dependence on a common environment. It is clear in all of the articles that those interested in global education are driven by humanitarian concern for the welfare of all the world's people; but it is striking that in 14 articles, the only reference we saw to the telecommunications technologies that are helping to create the "global village" was this:

> Through the study of technological systems, our students will come to understand how much of the interconnected-ness of peoples and nations in the modern world is due to rapid technological advances, particularly in communications and transportation – the two primary means of human contact. Ultimately, the study of technological systems will enable the students to understand the transformation of the world toward a global society; to explore the ramifications of that transformation on the world's peoples, cultures and nations; and to develop knowledge and skills for living in and coping with an increasingly complex world.[1]

We believe that the *study* of technological systems will not be sufficient to bring about these objectives. Changes of this magnitude will require the active involvement of teachers and students in *using* communications technology to improve the quality of the classroom experiences of all children by expanding their access to information and by bringing them into closer proximity to one another – a kind of anti-distance education. One model for achieving this kind of change is the Scandinavian "telecottage" – a community centre (often a school or library) equipped with microcomputers, fax machines or other telecommunications equipment for use by the people of the community. Originated in Sweden, telecottages are becoming common in Finland and are beginning to appear in developing nations.[2]

If we are to use modern communications technologies in ways that bring people closer together, then we must understand what technical possibilities exist and how we can use those possibilities in humanistic ways. It should be useful, then, to describe some of the current innovations in the technology of educational communication and suggest ways in which those innovations might become constructive and exciting components of the classroom learning environment. Our comments will focus on: (1) technologies that may enhance communications within a classroom, (2) technologies for communication with the world outside the classroom, and (3) possible future directions.

Technology and Communication in the Classroom

Although the rationale we have given above applies chiefly to the use of technology to bridge great distances, we are also concerned about increasing the quality and quantity of communication within classrooms, since interpersonal distances are not always correlated with physical distances. Moreover, many of the long distance applications we will discuss also depend to some extent on familiarity with such applications as word processing and databases. It is therefore worth our while to examine applications that can serve to enhance in-class communications. For those to whom this material is unfamiliar, the following definitions may be useful:

Word processor. A word processor is a computer program that assists in the typing and formatting of documents. Since the words being typed are not immediately printed, but are stored in the computer's memory chips, the writer has the freedom to go back and change any part of the work easily. Most word processors also have options that simplify the addition and deletion of sentences or paragraphs, that increase the writer's flexibility in setting and changing margins and other formatting features, and that allow whole blocks of text to be moved or copied easily. Some also include extra features that check the spelling of a document, automatically re-paginate after changes, alphabetize bibliographies, allow multi-column printing or any of a great variety of other options.

Database. A database is an organized body of information. A simple example of a database is a telephone book. The information about any one person (or company) in the phone book would be called a record; the kinds, or categories, of information (e.g., name, address, phone number) are called fields. Database software makes it possible to retrieve information from a database in a variety of ways, e.g., you could use a telephone directory database to find all of the people whose last name was Brown and whose phone number starts with 287- or you could have it list everyone whose address includes the initials "NW" and the word "Varsity." Databases also allow flexible sorting of information, so that you might decide to put your phone directory in order of phone number (highest to lowest) instead of alphabetically by name.

Spreadsheet. Spreadsheets are similar to databases but they have the additional feature of allowing the inclusion of formulas that will automatically recalculate answers every time new information is added to the spreadsheet. In spreadsheet terminology, information is stored in "cells." Each cell may contain text, numbers or formulas. The overall organization of the spreadsheet is a type of grid in which each cell is the intersection of a row and column. When a cell (or cells) contain a formula, the spreadsheet will automatically carry out the calculations stated in the formula each time new data are entered anywhere in the spreadsheet. Spreadsheets were originally developed for accounting applications which require a lot of repeated calculations. In educational settings, spreadsheets allow teachers to engage students in explorations of the effects of changing some parts of a formula ("what-if" applications), for example, what happens to the class average (on height or whatever) when a new student is added? What happens to monthly mortgage payments when the interest rates drop a point? How does the volume of a gas change when its temperature is increased? The instant feedback from these calculations and the opportunity to to quickly many different examples provides the student with an environment in which important concepts are available for self discovery.

It is probably safe to say that the greatest impact that computers have had on education so far has been in the use of word processors as a writing tool. There has been speculation about the potential benefits of using word processors to teach writing skills.[3] Many teachers and writers have told of the successes they have had in using word processors, but it is not yet clear whether the use of word processors in teaching writing is having a noticeable effect on the quality of students' writing.[4] There is some indication that the situation may be changing as some students are now using their word processors to make more substantial revisions in their writing, but we are unlikely to see major improvements until teachers are prepared to teach more about the processes of writing and revision (for a description of the writing process and its relation to word processing.[5] Nevertheless, we can still ask the question: "How may the use of word processors be expected to improve classroom communication?" Part of the answer lies in the consistent research finding that students write more often and they write longer papers when they use word processors.[6] Writing more is not the same as writing better, but it's a start. And since students can easily revise and change what they have written, their written work becomes the basis for discussion of the techniques and methods of writing. This constitutes a form of peer teaching and may require that teachers help students develop skills in constructive questioning and constructive criticism but these should be part of the humane communication that we are seeking.[7]

This view is not restricted to the use of word processors in teaching writing, but it applies to the whole range of writing activities that are subsumed in the phrase "writing across the curriculum.[8] discussion of their own written lab reports may be as useful in biology class as would discussion of student-written sports news in physical education. An extension of the use of word processors is the use of desktop publishing systems that allow students to incorporate graphics, borders, columnar organization, and variations in font styles and sizes into their written work. This may involve the use of a fairly simple newspaper simulation like Newsroom, a somewhat more complicated student-oriented desk top publishing package like Publish It! or The Children's Writing Workshop, or full scale professional desk top publishing software like PageMaker or Ready, Set, Go. Whatever the technology used, the idea is to allow the students to experience the responsibility of preparing a final, publishable copy of a collaborative writing effort like a school newsletter or a class research report. Of course, to achieve the full benefit of such an activity, it is expected that the final product would be "published," at least insofar as it would be distributed beyond the classroom. While there is little research available on the educational use of desk top publishing, it seems evident that the magnitude and complexity of the task would engage students in frequent, task-oriented communication as they seek agreement about the materials to be included, the revisions necessary, the formats used, the nature of individual's responsibilities, and the very process of making the decisions.[9] Of course, none of this *requires* publishing (or even word processing), but the availability of the technology increases the attractiveness of the task and puts more of the decision-making within reach of the students themselves.

Attention to the role of technology in the process of writing serves to remind us of the nature of our overall educational goals, one of which might well be "to enable students to become intelligent consumers of knowledge," that is, to help them acquire skills in obtaining, organizing, analyzing, interpreting, and reporting information. Each of these steps is likely to involve considerable interpersonal communication even if the students are working on individual projects. For example, the student may need to request assistance from a librarian in locating information sources or to have a parent proofread a report. However, we can increase the students' opportunities to participate in constructive classroom communication if we encourage the development of group projects that extend our goal to the production of knowledge. Creating new knowledge is a most scholarly activity and a worthy goal for education at every level. By having students share the responsibilities involved in gathering new information, organizing it, and analyzing it, we may save sufficient time to allow them to learn to use computer software to facilitate these tasks. Both database software and spreadsheets offer the students a framework for organizing information and tools for easily conducting analyses that would hitherto have been too time consuming or too complex for them to attempt. In this context, increasing the quantity and quality of student-to-student communication is being viewed as both an intended outcome of instruction and as a principal instructional method.

This dual function of students' classroom communication was evident in an English as a Second Language project carried out at the Alberta Vocational Centre.[10] In this project, a network of computers equipped with word processing, database, and spreadsheet software became the impetus for adult immigrants to use the English language to carry out assigned classroom tasks. Here again, computer technology has the potential to add both to the quality and quantity of classroom communication. In particular, "paint" software and animation programs make it possible for students who lack the manual dexterity necessary for artistic production in many other media to achieve a sense of accomplishment and to become better consumers of artistic communication by developing a better understanding of artistic production. Likewise, music generation software, with or without the possibility of input from musical instruments, can provide students with an environment in which the exploration of musical concepts and relationships is not dependent on the long, slow process of acquiring skill with an instrument. This is another example of using computer technology to provide students with opportunities for creative production and, in the process, to build their critical awareness as consumers.

All this activity can serve as a basis for generating classroom conversation and writing that will help students to formulate and organize their own thinking about the topics they have explored. Communication within the classroom may also benefit from the use of technologies associated with communication with the outside world. For example, in the absence of any access to electronic mail, teachers could use word processors to simulate an electronic mail environment by providing students "mail boxes" in the form of shared diskettes. Such a technique would not only provide a basis for discussing the technology that exists outside the classroom but also would capitalize on students' fondness for sending one another notes by making this a legitimate writing activity. An even closer approximation can be obtained using the public domain program Kid-Mail which simulates electronic mail and bulletin boards by storing student-written messages in individual "accounts" on a class disk. Some of the benefits of anti-distance education might also be obtained by mailing these disks from one class to another. With imagination, the reader should be able to turn almost all of the suggestions in the following section into such useful in-class activities.

A still closer approximation to the benefits of anti-distance education may be obtained through the use of local area networks. Local area networks enable several computers to share such resources as printers, disk drives, and software. They consist of two or more machines connected directly to one another by special cables and allow the transmission of a wide variety of types of information including text, graphics, and video if a video disc player is one of the connected machines. With appropriate software, such as the CoCo program used with the ICON computers in many Ontario classrooms, local area networks allow students to use electronic mail for in-school communication with one another and their teachers. At the Calgary Board of Education's University Elementary School, a local area network is used to give students access to word processing software and to make it possible for students to share files and work together on projects.

Technology and Communication with the World Outside

We have shown that teachers can use communication technologies as a means of increasing the amount and variety of communication that takes place *within* their classrooms. Such applications might be regarded as luxuries, but when education must span great distances, it becomes necessary to consider other ways of transmitting information – other communications media. For instance, though it is seldom done, we could arrange for a fifth grade class in Yellowknife, Northwest Territories, to have a telephone conversation with a fifth grade class in Ecum Secum, Nova Scotia. Likewise, a high school drama class in Goose Bay, Newfoundland, could send a videotape of their performance of *Hamlet* to a comparable class in Brandon, Manitoba. When our method of transmitting information involves sending signals electronically, as in a phone call, the activity is referred to as *telecommunication*. Clark has suggested that we define types of telecommunication in terms of the machine used (telephone, computer, fax machine, etc.), the medium of transfer (over air waves or over some form of wire or cable), and the mode of presentation (voice, text, video, etc.).[11] Since many forms of telecommunication use more than one machine and may require different transfer media, it is not possible to clearly classify types of telecommunication according to these categories; but it is possible to use these terms as a basis for describing some of the common forms of telecommunication. Of course, the real challenge lies in turning these forms of distance communication into appropriate educational activities. That is, how can we use these technologies to bring the world into the classroom?

Some possible answers to that question follow our attempts to describe various forms of telecommunication using Clark's terminology.

Teleconferences involve the use of telephones to transmit voice messages over telephone lines. Several parties may participate in teleconferences from different locations and arrangements at each location may allow for several different people to participate in the conversation. Teleconferences are often used in business and in distance education to reduce the need for expensive travel, but they have not been widely used for what we have called anti-distance education. University researchers sometimes arrange teleconferences to plan research or to share results of their investigations. Sometimes the thesis or dissertation defenses of graduate students are conducted with one or more of the examining faculty calling in from a distance. Many universities, particularly in Australia, where great distances and a small population have led to a heavy reliance on distance education, offer some of their courses to distant students using tele-conferences as part of the communication between instructors and students.

Teleconferences can be expensive, so it is unlikely that schools will be able to make a lot of use of this technology unless special rates are made available to them. However, a simple telephone call from one classroom to another is no more expensive than any other phone call and a speaker phone is all that is needed to share the call with a whole class. Moreover, enterprising teachers should have little difficulty in persuading telephone companies of the promotional value of having children learn about teleconferencing, providing that their demands are not unreasonable. One useful strategy may be to arrange a 30 minute teleconference involving two or three locations within a single province or state as a sort of culminating experience in the study of local history or geography. Selected students at each cite could give two-minute reports on the results of group investigations (e.g., a study of headstones in local cemeteries, interviews with retirees, etc.) via the teleconference, leaving a little time for general discussion. Such an activity would require that the students be well prepared and would afford opportunities for interesting follow up activities (e.g., comparing trends in local development or tracking the impact of an epidemic). The impact of a teleconference might be greatest if students had had previous communication through letters or electronic mail.

Videoconferences are similar to teleconferences except that both voice and video images are transmitted and the medium of transfer is likely to include air waves and possibly satellite relays (international telephone conversations may also involve the use of these media). Carl and Densmore have described the use of videoconference techniques to deliver university courses through interactive instructional television.[12] In research conducted at Mount Saint Vincent University in Halifax, they found that students who were 15 connected to an on-campus class through videoconferencing did not differ from on-campus students in their levels of achievement in the course. In this setting, the students at a distance saw the course on television (via a satellite connection) and contributed to the class discussion using standard telephone connections. An expanded version of the educational use of videoconferences is developing in the United States under the name of the Star Schools Network, which has as its objective to increase the quality of education available to students in remote rural areas and under-privileged inner-city communities by giving them access to highly skilled teachers through video transmission. In some cases, these programs work like the Carl and Densmore set-up; in others, the student may see a videotape and have telephone access to advice and assistance from the instructor at a different time. Clark has described four other satellite-based educational services available to U.S. educators.[13]

Equipping a classroom for sending video signals is an expensive proposition, even equipping a receiving station is likely to be out of the question for many school jurisdictions. The educational benefits, particularly for isolated schools that have difficulty hiring specialists in all areas of the curriculum, may well justify the expense. To be successful, a program of video conferences would require professional video technicians, special training for instructors, and coordination at the provincial level or higher. If the project were properly managed, students might also have the opportunity to become involved in video production and to engage in serious study of the methods of the mass media.

Electronic Mail refers to the practice os using a computer to send printed messages or text over telephone lines to a "host" computer which either stores the message until the intended recipient calls in (with his/her computer) to read it or forwards the message to some other computer that the recipient will call. Making such connections requires that all of the computers involved be connected to telephone lines through a device called a modem which translates computer signals to a form that can be transmitted on a telephone line (and translates incoming messages from the phone line to signals the computers can work with). Special programs are also required to insure that the computers are (sending and receiving) information according to common standards. A difficulty with electronic mail, as with many other forms of computer-based telecommunication is the need for typing skills. While this is a genuine concern, it is clear that people interested in doing so can acquire reasonable typing skills in a short period of time.[14] And once a message has been entered into a computer, it can be sent to several people without retyping or copying. This also means that people can easily forward or copy messages that have been received from others, a possibility that has some potential for abuse.[15] A big advantage to electronic mail is that messages can be exchanged in a matter of hours, even minutes, rather than days. People who use electronic mail say that this immediacy of response leads them to communicate more often and to derive more pleasure from their exchanges. And, as Jason Ohler recently said of electronic mail in Alaska: "To many, electronic mail is an end to isolation."[16]

In teaching an undergraduate class recently, one of the writers used electronic mail to give the students an opportunity to engage in a discussion with the author of their textbook. This exchange let the students get a second opinion on some issues and provided the textbook author with valuable feedback about his work. To make this connection, the instructor used an academic and research network called NetNorth. NetNorth is a system of connections of 88

Canadian academic and research computers (using telephone lines reserved for this purpose), including a computer in the education faculty at The University of Calgary. However, the textbook author works at Northern Illinois University which is not part of NetNorth. Nevertheless, NetNorth is connected to a similar Network in the United States, BITNET, which connects about 400 universities and research centres in that country. BITNET, and therefore NetNorth, is also connected to other networks in Europe, Asia, and Australia, giving university scholars access to a global academic community through electronic mail on a combined total of over 2 000 computers.[17]

The authors of this chapter receive electronic mail daily from students and faculty in North America and Europe who share their interests in educational technology and telecommunications. Recently, Robert Carlitz, an astronomer and physicist at the University of Pittsburgh, has proposed the development of a similar global network for use by teachers and students, a proposal which is gathering support in the academic electronic mail community.[18] In the absence of such a global network, however, many teachers have found other networks that can provide their students with opportunities to engage in long distance electronic mail communication. For example, for those working with IBM or IBM compatible computers, there is an international electronic mail and conferencing network called FidoNet which has been established by individual computer enthusiasts who are willing to have their computers serve as hosts through which others can communicate. Each FidoNet host computer forwards the mail received to other computers in the network so that most messages are delivered the following day. Although there is sometimes a charge for using FidoNet, the costs are usually quite small. Systems operators in the network report that their personal charges range up to ten dollars per month. There is rarely a charge made to actual users of systems belonging to FidoNet; however, where charges are levied, they are commonly around twenty dollars per year. FidoNet allows for shared, public conference areas. Any person reading messages in a conference area is free (and encouraged) to contribute to discussions in progress.

Conference areas include education, disabled persons, Viet Nam veterans, Greenpeace, Kidnet, Writer's Conference, AIDS/ARC, astronomy, physics, home and garden as well as over a hundred other topics. It is interesting to note that the International FidoNet Association (IFNA) forecasts that, within two years, FidoNet will be the largest computer-mediated telecommunications network in the world. For teachers using Apple II computers, the corresponding system is FredMail. Some software designed for other purposes (e.g., The Newsroom) will also enable teachers to send messages via phone lines from one classroom computer to another. An obvious application of electronic mail is having students write to penpals (keyboard pals?), but our experience has shown that communication apprehension ("What will I talk about?") may result in little communication and even less education if students are not given a *reason* to communicate. However, Crowley obtained high levels of involvement by providing technical support to both teachers and students and allowing a period of exploration during which students were encouraged to write freely "about anything, to anyone, without evaluating what they wrote.[19] In a four-month-long project that began with messages between two classrooms in the same city and grew to involve 200 students in seven different schools from Nova Scotia, Alberta, and Oregon, over 1 000 messages were exchanged. Messages ranged in length from one-liners to chapters in a student-authored book. According to Crowley, "What emerged as most significant about the messaging activities was that the students began to see themselves as readers, writers, and researchers." The geographic distance and cultural diversity of the groups seemed to the researchers to be major sources of motivation to write. Two Calgary teachers have recently reported taking advantage of the fact that most communications software also allows the possibility of a "chat" mode – direct and immediate communication between two people using different computers at the same time.[20] It might be regarded as a computer based simulation of a telephone call. One might expect that the typing demands of such a system and the availability of an easier alternative (telephone) would make this an impractical tool for school use, but Bahniuk and Ponting report considerable success in using the chat mode to enhance instruction in both elementary language arts and elementary social studies. Lange has described a variety of current and projected uses of telecommunications in business education.[21] Other innovative projects are under way all across North America and around the world.

Once students and teachers are comfortable with electronic mail, it can become a means of importing information either from other students or from people with special expertise. In this way, it may serve to enrich the students' investigations into every subject in the curriculum. With experience, it is highly likely that this activity will expand to include the use of information retrieval services and bulletin boards.

Information Retrieval refers to the practice of searching remote or distant databases using local computers and telephone connections. Although many of the databases available at present are likely to be too expensive for many schools, the resourceful teacher will find that there are some free or low-cost alternatives available, e.g., NASA has a large database of astronomy and other space science information which anyone may search free of charge. Similarly a meteorological information database is available from the U.S. Weather Service. The only costs involved in using these databases are the long distance telephone charges. Within Alberta, the Suicide Information and Education Centre offers free public access to its database of information about suicide and suicidal behavior. Since database searching requires some practice, it would be wise to learn to use database software before calling a remote database.

In a previous section, we indicated that database software provides students with tools that will help them to organize and analyze information. We believe this to be a most useful instructional activity, but we also recognize that vast quantities of information already exist in useful organizations and that they are available for our use. University librarians are usually familiar with the major databases available in specific subject areas, but Canadian teachers will find that a great many useful databases are available to them through the services of iNet 2000, a service provided through regional telephone company offices. Those with particular interests in computer-based teaching will find several software evaluation databases already in existence. As we approach the year 2000, we should expect that the ability to locate information stored in electronic databases will become as integral to scholarly activity in many subject areas as using the card catalogue or the *Reader's Guide to Periodical Literature* have been in the past. It is already the case that a major portion of the requests for information from Alberta's Suicide Information and Education Centre are made by high school students. At present, most of these students do not conduct the searches themselves; but as the use of such databases increases, we can not reasonably expect that governments and non-profit organizations will continue to pay for sufficient professional staff to respond to all of the requests that will be forthcoming. As with so many other things, skill in the use of databases will be added to the curriculum requirements. Because of the nature of much of the information currently stored in electronic databases, it is most likely that social studies will be most directly affected. Teachers who welcome the opportunity to have their students working with up-to-date information now have at their disposal the means to insure that classroom discussions are focused on some of the best knowledge available.

Bulletin Board Systems (BBS's) offer a variety of services including electronic mail and electronic conferences in which people "post" messages on the bulletin board so that anyone who signs on to the host computer may read the messages. You might think of it as a kind of electronic graffiti. BBS's also allow users to "upload and download" files, that is to send or receive copies of documents or programs. An advantage of BBS's is that they offer the possibility of getting in touch with new people. They are frequently used as a way of getting help with finding information, especially information about computers and software. Bulletin boards often focus on some theme of common interest to the people who regularly contact the board, for example, education, electronics, or war-gaming. Some BBS's offer such additional services as database access, on-line games, and on-line text editing (to enable subscribers to cut and paste information from database searches).

In the Calgary area alone, over 100 bulletin board services are now in operation. Since most of these services depend on the willingness and interest of one person who makes his/her computer available as a host, the number tends to fluctuate as individuals' interests change. Some of these bulletin boards exist primarily to serve the game-playing interests of many computer enthusiasts. For example, Trade Wars is a popular game at the time of this writing. The object of this game is to gain control of the universe through interplanetary trade. Part of the game is the "Cabal," a group of "bad guys" controlled by the computer program. The Cabal may attack the holdings of any player at any time (to introduce the operations of chance into the game). Teachers might wish to judge for themselves whether any educational benefits might be derived from this game or others available on local bulletin boards. In many communities there is a local bulletin board dedicated to the interests of teachers. The McGraw-Hill Publishing Company operates two bulletin boards called MIX and BIX which are international forums for the discussion of issues in education and technology, respectively.

Bulletin boards may also operate on larger computer systems. For example, the Disability Information System of Canada (DISC) operates an electronic mail and conferencing (bulletin board) service for handicapped Canadians. DISC uses the University of Calgary's education faculty computer and the Net-North network as a means of providing communication services to disabled people. For some of DISC's clientele, the use of this computer, (aided by special translation devices suited to their disability), is their major source of communication with other people. In some communities, local universities will provide teachers with access to the NetNorth/BITNET system so that they may communicate with other teachers and/or participate in electronic conferences focused on education. One such arrangement is provided to teachers in British Columbia (and others) by the *FORUM program available at Simon Fraser University. At present, the NetNorth system has hundreds of conferences and newsletters available including an educational technology conference (EDTECH), a communications newsletter (CRTNET), and a psychology newsletter (BITNET Psychology Newsletter). There are also general news services and special news services available; for example, at the time of this writing, there is a newsletter containing information about developments from the Chinese students' demonstrations. One interesting variation on a bulletin board has resulted in hundreds of people sending messages of support and encouragement to the volunteers involved in cleaning up the Alaska oil spill.

With this variety of information services available, teachers can easily find some bulletin boards that would contribute to their professional development and others that would provide opportunities to enrich the classroom experiences of their students.

Telex and Facsimile are additional means of sending printed information over telegraph or telephone lines. Telex also requires the use of a keyboard, but is less versatile than electronic mail because the system does not allow for computer storage of messages; they simply come in to the terminal one after another. Facsimile (or fax) machines do not depend on keyboards (and are therefore very popular with a lot of business people who cannot type); rather, they send a picture of a page from one machine to a distant machine over phone lines. A handy way of thinking about this is to imagine that you are putting a page into a photocopying machine and that the copy is coming out somewhere else.

The writers are not aware of any school programs that use Telex, but some university commerce programs receive stock market information in this manner, just as brokers do. Fax machines have recently been used extensively in a distance education project in Southern Alberta. In this project, students in remote rural high schools were given the opportunity to take courses not offered in their schools through a distance education program that used mail, phone, and fax as ways of delivering instruction to students and getting papers, comments, and questions from students. The speed with which fax machines could make distant teachers' evaluations of tests and papers available was one of the features that led to the use of this technology in the project, which is currently being evaluated.

Telewriter is a unique hardware and software package that enables students in a distant classroom to "share" a computer screen with an instructor. Instructors use the screen much like a blackboard to make notes, sketch ideas, or illustrate concepts using a graphics tablet to input information. Students in the distant classroom not only see the information on their screen as it is being written, but also have the opportunity to use the same screen to send messages back or raise questions during instruction. Telewriter is designed for use as an integral part of a videoconference or teleconference.

With so many communications options available to them, it may seem surprising that these technologies have not already become a significant element in elementary and secondary school teaching. Unfortunately, the costs of telecommunications are not generally included in the price of education. Indeed, few teachers are even likely to have direct control over any instructional expenses, so the decision to spend money on telecommunications ordinarily will be in the hands of an administrator.

Given the information provided thus far, a teacher should be well prepared to make a case for spending money on telecommunications, but still may not be able to choose from among the options available. If the principal objective is to inform students about telecommunications, then a variety of techniques should be employed; but if students are to develop a genuine understanding of this technology, they will need to see it used (and use it) as a general tool for learning. That is, it will have to be integrated into their instruction in other subjects. In that case, the teacher will need to decide which of the various technologies will best achieve the content area objectives. Such decisions are seldom susceptible to unequivocal decision rules.

How do students actually respond to the use of these new technologies? It is still early in the game, but comparative studies of students learning with standard in-class methods versus those using some form of telecommunication seem to suggest that the use of telecommunications poses no big problems and may offer advantages resulting from increased student-to-student communication.[22]

Future Directions in Educational Telecommunications

It should now be clear that the use of telecommunications is a fast-growing area of educational innovation. Government-sponsored communications networks for school use already exist in some jurisdictions (e.g., MYNETin Manitoba and ASPEN for special educators in Alberta) and are developing in others (e.g., EDNET in Oregon). In other places, teachers have been given access to telecommunications through connections to university computers (Alaska, British Columbia, Calgary). The BITNET network started with only six universities participating in 1981 and has grown to include 2 000 computers worldwide in just eight years.[23] Technologies which had seemed not to be of much interest to educators are beginning to generate new interest – as, for example, the growth of interest in educational television evident in the Star Schools project and other satellite based services. As always, the question arises: "Where do we go from here?" Based on the kinds of innovations in existence today, it seems reasonable to predict:

1. increased access to information retrieval services of particular interest to teachers, like lesson plan databases, test item banks, job listings, software evaluation databases, bulletin boards devoted to the results of action research and program evaluations, etc.;

2. development of child-oriented communications systems that work from simple, intuitive menus and allow for easy error correction. This will likely include kid-friendly databases on subjects of interest to children (superheroes, children's literature, computer games, etc.);

3. improved access to the sending of graphic images, including animated sequences;

4. capability of sending video signals over telephone lines, including the ever-imminent videophone;

5. widespread development of telecommunications-ready classrooms and strong expectations (perhaps even curriculum requirements) that telecommunications will be part of the instructional method in at least some subject areas;

6. use of telecommunications to provide easy access to education from outside the classroom. Remote access will be provided for adult learners, the physically disabled, the geographically remote, people with contagious illnesses, in general, anyone who cannot be, or who prefers not to be, physically present in the classroom. Some parents may choose to capitalize on such access to develop alternative schools in their homes or communities;

7. continued emphasis on the development of independent learning skills. With ready access to so many sources of information, teachers and students will gradually cease to view the teacher's role in terms of information transmission. Teachers will organize study groups and research teams, propose challenges, suggest information resources, provide social and motivational support, evaluate student work, and arrange special broadcasts, lectures, discussions and so forth.

If all goes well, what will be the consequences of anti-distance education? Consider what you might have done instead of reading this chapter. Suppose you had spent two or three hours reading bulletin board notices concerned with the educational uses of telecommunications and participated in a videoconference discussing uses of telecommunications in education with students and scholars in four countries. Then suppose you wrote a four page paper summarizing your thoughts on the value of this educational innovation and submitted it to a bulletin board which resulted in your receiving comments from seven people, including two renowned experts with whom you subsequently exchanged electronic mail messages. Which way would you learn more? Which way would you enjoy more?

Notes

[1]W. Kniep, "Essentials of Global Education," *The ATA Magazine, 69* (1980), 12-15.

[2]J. Oksman, "Telecottages in Finland," *Online Journal of Distance Education and Communication, 2* (1989), 4-8.

[3]C. Daiute, *Writing and Computers* (Reading MA: Addison Wesley, 1985). Bruce, "How Computers can Change the Writing Process," *Language Arts, 62* (1985), 143-149.

[4]K. Branan, "Moving the Writing Process Along," *Learning 1984*, (October). Reprinted in W.J. Hunter, ed., *Creative Teaching with Microcomputers* (Lexington, MA: Ginn Press, 1986). "Creative Writing with Computers: What do Elementary Students Have to Say?," *Computers, Reading and Language Arts*, (Summer/Fall, 1984). Reprinted in W.J. Hunter, ed., *Creative Teaching with Microcomputers*, (Lexington, MA: Ginn Press, 1986). B. Collis, "Research retrospective: 1984-1989," *The Computing Teacher, 16* (1989), 5-7. Hunter, J. Begoray, G.Benedict, B. Bilan, G. Jardine, P. Rilstone, and R. Weisgerber, *Word Processing and the Writing Process*, (Calgary: Education Technology Unit, The University of Calgary, 1988).

[5]J. Willinsky, "When University Students word Process Their Assignments," *Computers in Schools*, (1989a), (in press). Hunter, "Concerns re: Reposting of Messages," Note on EDTECH forum in BITNET, 7 July, 1989. Daiute, 1985.

[6]C. Etchison, "A Comparative Study of the Quality of Syntax of Compositions of First Year College Students Using Handwriting and Word Processing," ERIC Document 282215, (1985). J. Willinsky, "Remedial Language Arts Instruction and Desktop Publishing," (The University of Calgary, 1989b), (in preparation).

[7]C. Copp, "The Use of Classroom Analysis of Taped Peer Tutorial as Feedback Mechanism for Improvement in Tutoring Behaviours," Master's thesis, (Mt. St. Vincent University, Halifax, N.S., Canada, 1985).

[8]D. Barnes, *Language, the Learner and the School* (Harmondsworth: Penguin, 1971).

[9]Willinsky, 1989b. I. Warkenton, "Student Newspapers and Desktop Publishing," *ATACC Journal, 7* (1989), 25-30.

[10]I. Simpson, and V. Larsen, "Ariel: A Networked Computer Simulation," (Calgary: Alberta Vocational Centre, 1988). W. Ayers and B. Winge, "KidMail V5.0," (Cue/Sofswap).

[11]C. Clark, "Telecommunications is Here and Now," *The Computing Teacher, 15* (1988a), 24-25.

[12]D. Carl and B. Densmore, "Introductory Accounting on Distance University

Education Via Television (DUET): A Comparative Evaluation," *Canadian Journal of Educational Communication, 17* (1988), 81-94.

[13]C. Clark, "What Goes Up Must Come Down: Learning by Satellite," *The Computing Teacher, 16* (1988b), 13-15.

[14]Hunter et al., 1988.

[15]L. Hunter, 1983. "Basic Writers and the Computer," ERIC Document 237975, (1983).

[16]J. Ohler, "What Electronic Mail Offers Educators: Reflection of an Online Teacher," *Online Journal of Distance Education and Communication, 2* (1989), 22-25.

[17]H. Isakson and T. McInish, The Electronic Journal: A New Era. *Online Journal of Distance Education and Communication, 2* (1989), 13.

[18]R. Carlitz, "A Proposal for a Global Network for Children," *Online Journal of Distance Education and Communication, 2* (1989), 3-4.

[19]M. Crowley, "Organizing for Electronic Messaging in the Schools," *The Computing Teacher, 16* (1989), 23-26.

[20]R. Bahniuk and P. Ponting, "The Chat Mode in the Elementary Classroom," *Computers in Education, 5* (1988), 30-31.

[21]B. Lange, "Telecomputing in the Classroom," *ATACC Journal, 7* (1989), 8-10.

[22]L. Smeltzer, "An Analysis of Receiver's Reactions to Electronically Mediated Communication," *The Journal of Business Communication, 23* (1986), 37-55. Carl & Densmore, 81-94.

[23]Isakson & McInish, 9-13.

Part B

Selected Readings

. . . and
can't we say, and saying
                    comprehend
its magnanimity:

To whisper
across this frozen country
certain possible words.

From "Poem: The Distances," Douglas Barbour

24

Improving Communication and
Teacher-Supervision Relationships
Through Cooperative Teacher Evaluation

Ray Fenton and *Doug Nancarrow*

Introduction

Good evaluation practices have the potential to encourage teachers to improve their instructional skills. Bad evaluation practices have the potential for alienating and demoralizing both teachers and their supervisors. The development and implementation of cooperative and goal driven evaluation in a large public school system provided an opportunity to demonstrate how the modification of the communication context can effect instructional behavior and improve the professional and personal relationships between teachers and their supervisors.

Recent literature in the field of supervision has stressed the need for effective communication between teachers and supervisors. Specific factors have been identified which can improve the teacher-supervisor relationship and focus the evaluation process on improving instruction.[1] The role of collegial behavior has been stressed and peer review suggested as a way of focusing on instruction and improving the competence of evaluation.[2] The idea of cooperative evaluation has been suggested as a possibility.[3] However, there has been no full scale demonstration of a system which would bring supervisors and teachers together through the process of cooperative evaluation to improve instruction.

The Problem

The search for an improved system of evaluation grew out of a feeling that the approach which had been in place for more than a dozen years in the Anchorage School District had become a mere formality. At best, the completion of an annual 12 item behavioral checklist seemed to provide an occasion

329

when a supervisor could give a teacher some praise and recognition for a year of effective teaching. At worst, it was a demonstration of the unilateral authority of the principal which resulted in an alienation of the teacher without any useful improvement in instruction. Leaders of the Anchorage teachers collective bargaining group, the Anchorage Education Association, and the school administration felt that the evaluation process should do more than fulfill the law requiring annual evaluation of teachers and could provide an opportunity to improve instruction and strengthen the personal relationship between teachers and their supervisors.

The old supervisor controlled checklist system sometimes resulted in an evaluation being placed into a teacher's mailbox without comment. Many principals discussed evaluations with teachers and provided written elaborations of the checklist but even the best of principals had little time to give to the process. Most principals tried to use the evaluation to guide teachers who they felt needed assistance.

In cases where the teacher was rated as being in need of improvement, the principal was admonished to provide the teacher with assistance. However, no provision was made for any follow up on performance. It was only in cases where a teacher was identified as a case for dismissal that principals were told to document the performance of the teacher, to closely monitor the teacher's behavior, and to make regular and repeated observations of activities in the classroom.

Teachers were dissatisfied with the system because they felt that they were not being given the chance to be evaluated on their teaching. Many teachers felt that the checklist items were not defined and not appropriate for a professional evaluation. Supervisors were dissatisfied with the system because they felt the sterile checklist provided them with little opportunity for acting as leaders who could have a positive effect on instruction. Both teachers and supervisors felt that the supervisor controlled evaluation process limited communication and that there was a substantial opportunity for conflict and personal dissatisfaction with a minimal opportunity for interpersonal support and professional development.

The Solution

A school system wide committee was formed from a cross section of principals, teachers, and other professional staff to explore alternative evaluation systems and produce a new approach to evaluation. Elementary and secondary teachers composed more than half of the thirty person group. The remainder included an educational researcher, a special education supervisor, a representative of the principal's union, the head of the teacher's union, the staff development specialist, and a member of the personnel department. All of the participants except the staff development specialist and educational researcher were volunteers who felt that the evaluation system needed change.

The group started with a venting of negative feelings about the checklist evaluation system and then turned to a review of current supervision systems. After a year of considering such varied topics as clinical supervision, collegial supervision, peer supervision, developmental supervision, supervision cycles, accountability, models of teaching, and the various factors that had been reported by McGreal and others to effect successful evaluation, the group was hopeful.[1] A feeling emerged that good evaluation was based on a positive, trusting, communicative relationship between a supervisor and teacher involved in working toward the common goal of improved instruction.

The process of evaluation was initially thought to be less important than the outcome of developing a supportive relationship in which a teacher and supervisor could work together. However, it was not long until the process was identified as the communication context which could bring together the teacher and supervisor into a positive and cooperative relationship. The development of a systematic process became the major effort of the committee.

The checklist approach was done away with by the committee in favor of a specified series of conferences and observations. The heart of the new system was that evaluation would be limited to a cooperative effort to assess the progress of the teacher toward fulfillment of some instructional goal jointly specified by the teacher and principal. So long as the general performance of the teacher was satisfactory, evaluation would take place relative to the goals specified and the principal would for the most part act as a facilitator.

The usual course of the new annual evaluation would be a goal setting conference or conferences early in the school year which would result in a written goal statement prepared by the teacher and accepted by the principal. The teacher would then work toward the goal with the principal providing assistance and support. During the course of the year, the principal would make at least three observations of the teacher at least two of which would be jointly planned and scheduled.

The usual sequence of observation activities would start with a meeting prior to the actual observation to discuss the instructional activity the teacher planned and the type of observation and record keeping which would be done by the supervisor. This meeting would be followed by the observation which would last through an entire lesson or class period. Finally, there would be a debriefing conference where the principal would report what was observed and a joint assessment of the instructional effort would be made.

Toward the end of the school year, the principal and teacher would get together to assess the progress made toward the goal or goals specified at the start of the year. Goals and observations would be reviewed as well as a general discussion of progress and what might happen in the future to further the goals of the teacher. The product of this final conference or conferences was specified by the committee as a joint statement which would be signed by both teacher and principal and forwarded to the personnel office.

The chief obstacles to the plan were identified as the cost in time for teachers and supervisors and the inexperience of supervisors in cooperative goal setting and evaluation methods. The checklist system resulted in brief meetings or observations, usually at the convenience and under the direction of the principal. The new system required one or more lengthy conferences for goal setting and the end of year appraisal as well as time consuming conference and observation sequences. Insisting that the scheduling of the evaluation activities would be cooperative with planning, goal setting and even the content of the final evaluation being a product of mutual agreement was a substantial change to which supervisors had to adjust.

Phase I: An Experimental Implementation of Cooperative Evaluation

A small scale initial test of the cooperative evaluation approach was undertaken with a dozen volunteer supervisors who asked a few tenured teachers to join in the year long experiment. Supervisors kept time logs and observation records. An evaluator experienced in collaborative assessment was asked to review the system and meet with the volunteers prior to and after the completion of the evaluation process. Structured interviews were conducted separately with supervisors and teachers to probe the fairness of the system, the efficacy of the system, and attitudes of the participants toward cooperative, goal oriented evaluation.

All indications were positive. The experienced teachers and principals felt the approach resulted in better performance in the classroom by teachers, a more collegial relationship between teachers and supervisors, and instructional innovation on the part of teachers. Teachers said they felt encouraged to try new content and instructional techniques. Both teachers and principals reported that they had spent about twice as much time involved in evaluation under the cooperative model. The estimated time involvement was substantiated by the time logs kept by supervisors.

The one major caution of the evaluator was that this first year long test had been done under the best of conditions. The principals and volunteers were all experienced and tenured staff who felt little or no threat from the evaluation process. There was a general understanding that this might be a one time experiment where any failure would be attributed to the system rather than the individual participant. The evaluator characterized it as success in a "green house" but also felt that it showed that the system could work.[5]

Phase II: A Large Scale Implementation of Cooperative Evaluation

The school board approved the full scale implementation of the new process for the next year. Principals were admonished to start the process of conferences and observations early in the year. A brief training session for principals and supervisors was scheduled just prior to the start of the school year.

A set of formal directions and forms were prepared for support of the cooperative evaluation system for a large scale second year test. The directions included the specific requirement that at least one goal be related to observable instructional behavior which would serve as a basis for conferences and observations. A form which might be used for recording observations was developed at the request of principals who were uncertain of observation methods. A set of "instructional competencies" was developed as a guide for areas of potential improvement. And, the semantics of the directions were discussed until time required that the package be prepared and distributed.[5]

The time problem was ameliorated for supervisors through the acceptance of an evaluation sequence where tenured teachers, more than 80% of the teaching staff, would be formally evaluated only every other year. In years in which they did not participate in a cooperative evaluation, tenured teachers would have a less focused evaluation without formal goal setting and without any required observation. This minimal evaluation required only that the principal make a statement at the end of the year that the performance of the teacher had been satisfactory and to indicate the basis for that judgement in order to fulfill the minimum state reporting requirements.

The second year implementation took place in more than 100 elementary and secondary schools with approximately 225 administrators and 2400 teachers. Administrators and staff members were given training in the evaluation system at the start of the school year. Participants from the small scale test, members of the committee which developed the evaluation system, and other teachers and principals who had been initiated into the system participated in introducing the new evaluation model. Principals were provided with the opportunity to participate in advanced training sessions on goal setting, conducting conferences, and methods of classroom observation. Short in-services were held on goal setting, observation methods, and record keeping for teachers at most schools. Where possible, in-services were conducted by teachers who had participated in the system.

For the first year of full district-wide implementation of cooperative evaluation, principals were required to use the cooperative approach with a minimum of 5 teachers and to allow a corresponding number of teachers to participate in a minimal evaluation. This resulted in teachers being evaluated with the older checklist and minimal observation system, the new goal setting, conference-observation, and cooperative assessment system, or the minimal evaluation system with no required conferences or observation.

A comparison of the effects of the three approaches to evaluation was planned based on the responses of teachers and principals to questionnaires concerning their experience. District program evaluation staff also made regular visits to schools and met with teachers and principals for discussions of the evaluation process. A sample of teachers were asked to complete the Survey of Supervisory Practices developed by Lee Goldsberry, Paulette Harvey, and Nancy E. Hoffman for their research on supervision and the relationship between supervision and teachers perception of their supervisors.[4]

What is the effect of evaluation in a cooperative communication context?

The implementation of the cooperative evaluation system provided an opportunity for the comparison of three very different evaluation contexts. The new cooperative goal setting model was to be used in all schools with five or more teachers. A minimal evaluation without required observation or goal setting was to be used with some tenured teachers. A checklist rating system was used with some teachers in most schools. This implementation allowed the comparison of the effects of the cooperative system which called for relatively high levels of interaction, cooperation, and communication with a supervisor oriented checklist system and a minimal evaluation without specified criteria or activities.

Since the participants had some choice about the evaluation in which they participated, there must be some caution in the interpretation of the findings. Conversations with principals and teachers suggested that principals and supervisors tended to use the cooperative evaluation with teachers whom they felt needed the most supervision and the minimal evaluation with experienced teachers who had proven their ability. There were also a few teachers who were less than trustful of the new evaluation system and opted for the older supervisor directed evaluation with which they were comfortable. However, there was a generally positive feeling about the new system as it was being introduced and few teachers or principals voiced any substantial concerns or reservations during the course of the year.

A brief district questionnaire and the Survey of Supervisory Practices Teacher's Form were sent to a sample of 1,000 teachers at the end of the school year. Usable returns came from 512 teachers or 51% of the sample. The district questionnaire asked teachers which type of evaluation they experienced and if they considered their evaluation to have been fair. More than 92% of those reporting each type of evaluation felt that their own evaluation had been fair. The Statistical Package for the Social Sciences was used in the analysis of all survey data.

Among other things, the Survey of Supervisory Practices asks teachers to select from a list of adjectives those terms which they felt characterized the supervision which they received during the school year. Most of the terms directly relate to the quality of the communication between the supervisor and teacher within the evaluation context. Examination of the pattern of responses for the teachers under each of the three evaluation systems suggests that there were some notable differences in the relationship between teachers and supervisors as a result of manipulating the communication context.

Table 1 indicates the frequency with which teachers participating in cooperative evaluation, supervisor directed evaluation, and minimal evaluation selected the various adjectives. Each descriptor is listed, the total number of teachers selecting the descriptor is indicated, and the percent selecting the descriptor is indicated for each of the three groups. The pattern of responses is consistent with the comments made by teachers when they were interviewed by evaluators during the year.

Some of the descriptors seem to stand out as more important for all three of the groups and reflect the positive aspects of any teacher-supervisor relationship. Those that differentiate the cooperative, minimal, and checklist approaches to evaluation generally favor the cooperative approach. It was more often identified as organized, productive, systematic, and collaborative. The supervisor directed approach was chosen by a larger proportion of that group as supportive. The minimal evaluation approach without specified goals, conferences, or observations had fewer descriptors chosen and in no case had a larger positive proportion than either one of the other two approaches.

Teachers were asked to indicate which descriptor was most important to them in their characterization of the evaluation they had received. The descriptor identified as the best descriptor for all three types of evaluation was supportive. Supportive was selected as best by 42% of those evaluated under the supervisor directed evaluation, 24% of those participating in collaborative evaluations, and 21% of those receiving minimal evaluations. The second most often selected descriptor was collaborative which was selected as important by 6% of the teachers under the supervisor directed system, 25% participating in collaborative evaluations, and 12% of those with minimal evaluations.

When asked which descriptors would best describe evaluation as the teachers would like it to be, the most often chosen descriptors were supportive, meaningful, and constructive. Cooperative evaluation was more often found meaningful and constructive than the other two types. It was felt that the checklist system was more often described as supportive because supervisors opted to use the checklist only as an opportunity for reinforcement rather than as a real evaluation or instrument useful in staff development.

Other Survey of Supervisory Practices items revealed interesting differences:

- Cooperative evaluation teachers were more likely to see the purpose of evaluation as "to assist me to improve my teaching" (51%), than those in the supervisor directed or minimal evaluations who most often selected the response" to comply with legal requirements that I be observed."
- Cooperative evaluation teachers were more likely to initiate observations by asking their supervisors to schedule an observation with fully 45% initiating observations as opposed to 22% for the minimal observation group and 29% for supervisor directed evaluation teachers.
- When teachers who had the supervisor directed evaluations were observed teaching, they were much more likely to report that the supervisor was unaware of the purpose of the lesson observed (58%), than either cooperative evaluation (13%), or minimal evaluation (40%), teachers.

There were also notable differences among the groups in relation to the

Table 1

Effect of Cooperative Evaluation Teacher Assessment

Descripton	Total Selecting	Percent Selecting Checklist N = 54	Percent Selecting Cooperative N = 54	Percent Selecting Minimal N = 173
Continuous	229	40.7	47.6	38.7
Collaborative	260	38.9	57.5	40.5
Threatening	30	5.6	6.1	1.7
Rational	198	27.8	40.8	36.4
Arbitrary	41	9.3	6.8	9.2
Meaningful	268	50.0	58.5	39.9
Constructive	316	64.8	68.4	46.2
Supportive	406	87.0	79.3	72.8
Discouraging	37	5.6	7.5	6.9
Disorganized	45	5.6	7.8	11.0
Stimulating	127	27.8	27.9	17.7
Useless	44	7.4	6.8	11.6
Intuitive	68	18.5	13.6	10.4
Encouraging	330	64.8	69.0	53.2
Systematic	153	25.9	35.4	20.2
Destructive	13	1.9	2.4	2.9
Uniform	104	18.5	20.7	19.1
Productive	259	44.4	57.8	37.6
Sporadic	78	13.0	15.0	15.6
Boring	19	1.9	4.4	2.9
Directive	125	29.6	27.6	16.2
Varied	91	16.7	17.0	18.5
Organized	232	33.3	50.0	38.7
Trivial	40	5.6	8.2	7.5

evaluation process and the exploration of instructional innovations in the classroom. The teachers reported that the supervisor identified possible changes in instruction or that the teacher and supervisor jointly came up with innovations for 64% of the cooperative evaluation group as opposed to 44% of the supervisor directed evaluation group and 51% of the minimal evaluation group. The changes in instruction which were discussed with supervisors were tried out and found worthwhile by 62% of the cooperative group, 40% of the supervisor directed group, and 41% of the minimal evaluation group.

Table 2
Effect of Cooperative Evaluation
Teacher Assessment of Supervisor Behavior

Question	Average Checklist N = 48	Average Cooperative N = 287	Average Minimal N = 155	Value of F	Level of Significance
Supervisor was knowledgeable	1.97	1.78	1.85	1.026	.359
Supervisor had a grasp of my goals	1.91	1.70	1.98	5.059	.007
Supervisor was *not* helpful to me	4.02	4.24	3.96	3.800	.023
Supervisor got me to think about new methods	2.64	2.35	2.56	3.656	.027
Supervisor did *not* observe me enough to make a good judgment	3.25	3.80	3.19	13.625	.000
Supervisor helped me to grow as a professional	2.83	2.71	2.79	.423	.655
Supervisor monitored my student's achievement	2.87	2.70	2.82	.883	.413
Supervisor emphasized my student's achievement	2.51	2.48	2.85	5.695	.003
Supervisor did *not* make clear comments.	3.91	4.02	3.75	3.288	.038
Supervisor did *not* identify weakness areas	3.62	3.70	3.62	.332	.717
Supervisor did give me helpful comments	2.52	2.42	2.67	1.618	.201
Supervision was helpful to me	2.40	2.26	2.67	7.501	.001
In-services were *not* related to evaluation	3.06	3.41	3.14	4.390	.012
I welcome observations by other teachers	2.02	1.69	1.88	4.284	.014

Teachers were also asked to rate the accuracy of a series of specific statements about their relationship with their supervisor. Table 2 shows that the three systems result in some significant differences in how supervisors are perceived. *Generally, the most positive responses are from the teachers who participated in the cooperative system and the least positive responses are from the teachers who had minimal evaluation.*

Teachers participating in the *cooperative model* on the average *found their supervisors to be more helpful, to give clearer comments, to be be more helpful to their personal growth and to be most interested in the achievement of students.* Teachers under the older checklist evaluation system found their supervisors to be the least helpful, the least likely to encourage innovation, and less likely to encourage their personal growth.

The most serious question raised by the results shown in Table 2 is about the effects of the minimal evaluation.condition. The average ratings by teachers showed that this group, not surprisingly, found supervisors to have less knowledge of their goals, the achievement of their students, and also to be generally less helpful to their professional growth and development.

Phase III: Complete Implementation of a Cooperative Evaluation System

The following year teachers and principals were not given the option of selecting the supervisor directed evaluation approach. All evaluations were to be either cooperative or minimal. Non-tenured teachers and teachers who had minimal evaluations the prior year were assigned to cooperative evaluations. Tenured teachers who had supervisor directed evaluations had either minimal or cooperative evaluations. Those who had cooperative evaluations in Phase II were assigned to minimal evaluations.

At the end of the year a sample of 500 teachers were sent a questionnaire concerning evaluation. Usable questionnaires were returned by 248 teachers, 49% of those surveyed. One hundred and forty-one surveys were returned by teachers who participated in cooperative evaluations, 57% of the return, and 101 were returned by teachers who participated in minimal evaluations.

This questionnaire focused on the differences in the two types of evaluation: cooperative and minimal. The responses of the teachers participating in cooperative and minimal evaluations again showed some notable differences. Most of those participating in cooperative evaluations reported three or more conferences with supervisors (77%), and three or more classroom observations by supervisors (66%), as opposed to 64% of the minimal evaluation teachers reporting two or fewer observations and 74% reporting two or fewer conferences. Seventy six percent of the group with cooperative evaluations and 60% of the minimal evaluation groups reported that they had tried new teaching methods. Sixty five percent of the cooperative group and 54% of the minimal group felt that they had made worthwhile changes in their teaching.

No real difference was found in the feelings of teachers about the fairness of their evaluations. Ninety one percent of the cooperative group felt that their evaluations had been fair and accurate while 4% felt that their evaluations were overly positive. This compares with 89% of the minimal group who felt their evaluations were fair and accurate and another 1% which felt their evaluation to be overly positive.

Again, *the cooperative evaluation was found to be the more positive choice.* However, it was evident that supervisors had not given up on the evaluation of the minimal evaluation group. Substantial numbers of teachers who had participated in minimal evaluations were reporting an amount of evaluation contact which was close to that under the supervisor directed evaluation reported during the prior year.

An end-of-year questionnaire was sent to a sample of 50 supervisors with a series of questions about their reaction to the cooperative and minimal appraisal alternatives. Questionnaires were returned by 47 supervisors, 94 % of the sample. The supervisors included 4 senior high school principals, 9 junior high school principals, and 33 elementary school principals. The average principal supervised a staff of 44 and reported 10 to 15 cooperative and another 10 to 15 minimal evaluations for the year.

Principals reported fewer observations than teachers with 2 or 3 observations for 98% of the cooperative evaluations and 1 observation for 63% of the minimal evaluations. Principals estimated that 75% of the observations for cooperative evaluations were 45 minutes or more and 77% of the minimal observations were 30 minutes or less. A final evaluation conference time of less than 30 minutes was reported for 53% of the cooperative evaluation group and 82% of the minimal evaluation group. This indicated that the perceptions differed somewhat about the amount of supervision which was taking place. It may be that teachers consider some contacts as evaluative which supervisors see as non-evaluative.

Principals and other supervisors were asked to rate the overall cooperative evaluation system. It was rated as excellent by 23% of the supervisors, good by 47% of the supervisors. Only eight principals (16%), rated the new system as fair or poor.

A follow up open ended question showed that those who were most positive about the system liked it because they felt it improved their ability to influence instruction. Many supervisors also reported that they enjoyed the collegial role they were encouraged to play when working with teachers. Those who rated the system as fair or poor indicated that they felt there was not enough time for true cooperative evaluations, that all teachers should be fully evaluated each year, that there should be some rating system based on specific minimum performance criteria, or that it was unrealistic to expect principals knowledgeable enough of instructional methods across grades and subjects to play a useful role in instructional improvement. Even some of the principals who were most positive about the system felt that they needed help in providing assistance to teachers who wished to work on instructional programs in which the principal had no training.

Three years of trial and development has provided ample evidence that *the cooperative approach to evaluation is preferred by most of the supervisors and teachers*. Survey results and interviews provide ample support for the cooperative approach in spite of the increased time commitment reported by principals and a continuing concern for the evaluation of teachers on a regular basis. However, the results did not fully reflect the positive nature of comments made by teachers and supervisors about the system. Even those who were negative about the system as implemented were more likely to identify a desire for an elaboration of the cooperative system than to suggest a return to the basic checklist approach.

Conclusion

Changing the communication context had a substantial effect on teachers and principals. The change from an evaluation system without much required interpersonal communication to one which required a variety of joint activities resulted in positive changes.

Supervisors and teachers quickly came to favor the cooperative evaluation model. They both reported that it resulted in increased instructional innovation. The teachers who participated in cooperative evaluations were more likely to describe their evaluation as organized, productive, systematic, and collaborative than teachers who participated in either supervisor directed or minimal evaluations. However, teachers who participated in the supervisor directed evaluation process were more likely to characterize their evaluation as supportive.

Teachers felt that supervisors whom they worked with in cooperative evaluations were more likely to participate in the evaluation process because of a desire to help improve teaching than to simply fulfill a legal requirement. This positive orientation was also reflected by other survey items which showed that teachers in the cooperative relationships not only came up with more instructional innovations but that they were also more often successful implementing those innovations than the teachers who participated in either minimal or supervisor directed evaluations.

Teachers in the cooperative relationship were more likely to feel that their supervisor was knowledgeable about their goals, were more helpful, made enough observations to make a good judgement of instruction, and placed a greater emphasis on student achievement. When the average ratings of teachers of the practices of their supervisor in 12 areas were compared, the ratings of those who had participated in cooperative evaluations were the highest.

There is no guarantee that the change to the communication context imposed through the adoption of a cooperative evaluation system will result in an ongoing cycle of improvement through the years. However, it is expected that this is just what will happen because the change is self reinforcing. That is, the more support that supervisors and teachers give each other, the more they will be willing to explore and to try new innovations resulting in continued improvement in instruction.

Noted References

[1]T.L. McGreal, *Successful Teacher Evaluation*. Alexandria, Va.: Association for Supervision and Curriculum Development, 1983.

[2]R.J. Alfonso, G.R. Firth and R.F. Neville, *Instructional Supervision: A Behavior System*. Boston: Allyn and Bacon, 1981. See also, R.J. Alfonso and L. Goldsberry, "Colleagueship in Supervision" in T.J. Sergiovanni ed., *Supervision of Teaching*. Alexandria, Va.: Association for Supervision and Curriculum Development, 1982. See also, L.F. Goldsberry, "The Realities of Clinical Supervision." In *Educational Leadership*. Alexandria, Va.: Association for Supervision and Curriculum Development, April 1984.

[3]D. Johnson and R. Johnson, "On Cooperation in Schools: A Conversation with David and Roger Johnson." In Educational Leadership. pp 14-19. Alexandria, Va.: Association for Supervision and Curriculum Development, November 1987.

[4]L.F. Goldsberry, "Evaluation of the Anchorage Cooperative Teacher Evaluation for 1984-85." Anchorage, Ak.: Anchorage School District, 1985.

[5]R.J. Fenton et al. "The Effects of Three Models of Teacher Supervision: Cooperative, Supervisor Crontolled, and Minimal." A paper presented to the American Educational Research Association Convention at San Francisco, California; 1989.

25

Developments in Child-Computer Communication

Tom Jones

The human computer interface is easy to find in a gross way – just follow a data path outward from the computer's central processor until you stumble across a human being.[1]

I think the very best computer systems will be ones where you don't know there's a computer. When I go to use the refrigerator or grind some coffee beans, I don't say 'I am going to the kitchen to use my electric motor'.[2]

Introduction

The next time that you have an opportunity to spend time in a classroom in which children are using microcomputers, pick a spot away from the activity and observe how the children are interacting with these machines. Try to focus on the ease (or dis-ease) that the children are experiencing while they carry out their activities. Perhaps you may want to make some mental notes about the behaviors that you observe. Then, at some point in your observations, suspend reality for a moment and imagine that each of the children is, in fact, working with a common-place, readily-available classroom tool – something traditional like a pencil, a pair of scissors or a piece of chalk – and not with a microcomputer. Do they appear to you to be working as they would with any of the non-computer tools? Do you notice any hesitation on the part of the children? Do they appear relaxed and satisfied that they are accomplishing their goal? Or do they seem confused? Are they making a number of futile attempts to do something and, as a result, calling on their neighbor for help? Do you sense any frustration on their part?

The point of the exercise suggested above is to provide you a viewpoint or "lens" through which a prospective (or practicing) teacher might assess classroom activities which involve microcomputers. The central question is this: are children able to use the microcomputer to carry out some pertinent educational activity with as little – and hopefully less – effort as they would with tools that have long been a part of the classroom environment? Like it or not, a large number of such machines are in Alberta schools today and they will undoubtedly be part of the classroom scene in the future. There has been a decade or so of hyperbole surrounding their use and effectiveness in the teaching-learning process. Critics have cited the fact that, although there is now strong evidence that the microcomputer does have a beneficial effect on children's learning for particular applications[3], educators must balance these small but significant gains against the other uses to which the funds which were spent to purchase the computers might have been put (e.g., lowering the pupil-teacher ratio, hiring specialists, acquiring other supplies).

This chapter will address these questions by (1) focusing on some general concerns about how people communicate with computers, (2) describing a theoretical basis for the design of educational microcomputers, (3) reporting on research findings in the area of child-computer interaction or communication and (4) providing suggestions for how teachers might deal with classroom-based situations. We begin with a discussion of some of the issues in human-computer communication.

Is communicating with a computer difficult?

It can be – and it quite often is – but it doesn' t have to be. At one time, as one wag has put it, you had to be a member of the "information priesthood" in order to gain access to the enigmatic and obscure commands which give the user the power to make the computer do something. The "code" was the key to unlocking this power and it took many months or even years to master how the commands were strung together in a form that was palatable to the machine. It was not a pleasant business and there existed a wide gap between those who knew the code and those who simply wanted something done.

Today, however, the scenario is quite different and many computer manufacturers and software developers are couching advertisements for their products in terms such as "user-friendly" to allay customer fears about the difficulty in using personal computers. In many instances, these same manufacturers also include installation or set-up programs, readable and well-prepared documentation, on-disk training modules (a form of computer-assisted instruction) and technical hot-lines all of which are intended to make the process of getting things up-to-speed easier for the novice. With respect to the computers themselves, most manufacturers (including IBM) and software production companies (e.g., Microsoft) are moving toward a computer "look" or "feel" that reflects the work done at XEROX's Palo Alto Research Center in the late 1970s and which has had a significant impact on the "friendliness" of computers. The most ubiquitous example of this new "look" and "feel"computer is the Apple Macintosh. Features such as scrolling windows, pop-down/tear-off menus, pointing devices (mouse, trackball), icons and dialogue boxes have become the standard for interaction. These interfaces are commonly-referred to as GUIs (graphical user interface) and WYSIWYGs (what you see is what you get).

These features have only recently made their way into the educational arena as evidenced by the writing of a Macintosh-like version of the Apple II GS operating system and the introduction of the ICON microcomputer in Ontario. More on these features and the ICON later.

Human-Computer Interaction. Underlying these developments has been a concern about and an interest in how human beings communicate with the computer and this has resulted in the formation of an area of interest which cuts across the two domains of cognitive science and computing science. Questions about human-computer dialogue and how it can best take place has moved to the forefront of hardware and software development and has become a focal point for much research. This new discipline, human-computer interaction (a.k.a. human-factors, ergonomics, software engineering), has, as its focus, the design and implementation of computer systems (microprocessor, input/output devices, storage media, software) which lend themselves to efficient and productive use by human beings. Put another way, the designers of computer systems are attempting to push the technical obstacles into the background so that the user (sophisticated or not) can accomplish his or her goal quickly and easily. A strong emphasis in this discipline is on the establishment of theoretically-based and generalizable guidelines which will aid in the design of systems while they are on the drawing-board (i.e., before they are manufactured) and which ultimately result in providing users with tools to do whatever it is they wish to do with a computer without having to draw on limited attentional resources in order to determine *how* to get the computer to do it.

Two terms come to mind when speaking of the science of human-computer interaction: transparency and mediation. In the eyes of the HCI designer, a computer should be transparent to the user and should serve as a mediating device to the attainment of some goal. To put it negatively, the computer should not in any way hinder the carrying out of the intended task. If this occurs, then the computer has not been properly designed. What we are talking about, then, is communication or dialogue. Diagrammatically, we can depict this communication or interaction as follows (Figure 1):

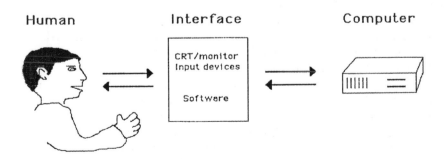

Figure 1. Human-Computer Communication

On the left side of the dialogue, we have the human being who wishes to perform some task which requires or is facilitated by a computer. On the right side, we have the computer which has been configured or set-up for the task. Examples of the task are the generation of text (word processing), the production of a graphic (draw/paint program), the manipulation of data (database management), the sending of electronic messages (telecommunications) or the writing of a customized or personalized program (programming). Between these two lies the interface which may be defined as those components to which both parties in the dialogue have access. The dialogue or communication takes place primarily as a result of the exchange of symbols (text, sound, graphics). The questions of interest to us are two: what form should the symbols take and by what means should they be exchanged?

To make clear why such an area of interest has surfaced, consider the following example. Historically, users of computers have communicated with these systems by way of the keyboard. Typically, a user would type in a series of text commands (the "code") following a prompt (e.g., >, %, $) on a display screen. Such symbol-sharing continues to this day. For example, if one wished to draw a rectangle on the screen, the following series of commands would be input:

line (10,15) – (10,150)
line (10,150) – (200,150)
line (200,150) – (200,15)
line (200,15) – (10,15)

The values in brackets represent the x-y co-ordinates on the screen grid. Note that each of text characters in the example would have to be typed exactly as indicated or the system would respond with an error message and the user would have to try again.

Compare this with how a user indicates to a system which employs a GUI interface – in this case, the Macintosh environment – to draw a rectangle (Figure 2):

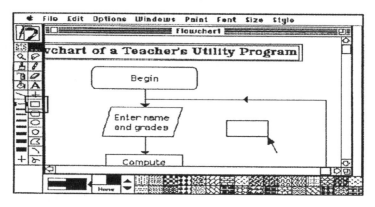

Figure 2. Graphical User Interface

The user would first move the cursor (large arrow) to the rectangle icon (indicated by the black box at the left of the screen), select the rectangle by depressing and releasing a button on the pointing device, move to the desired location and then depress, drag and release a button again (more on this later). Presto! – a rectangle. Obviously, the GUI provides the user with a far more intuitive and "real-world"-like feel for the steps that one follows when drawing a geometric figure such as a rectangle. For the other shapes, the reader should note that all of the basic drawing options are visible on the screen at all times and that the user literally "gets what he sees."

A story (perhaps apocryphal) of just how far matters can go awry in text-based command systems goes like this. A user wished to modify some existing text (a word-processing document, for example). Normally, the way to proceed would be for the user to type the word "edit," wait for the file to be opened and then go about making the desired changes. However, for some reason, the user had forgotten that the file was already opened and that the same sequence of letters – e-d-i-t – would result in the selection of all the information contained in the file "e" for everything), the deletion of the text ("d"for delete) and the insertion "i" for insertion) of the letter "t" at the beginning of the file. This was obviously not what the user intended and, to make matters worse, the last input from the keyboard, the letter "t," did not permit the system to undo the previous commands and consequently the entire original file was lost. This is unlikely to happen today given the state of text-based command systems but the moral, if you will, of the story should not be lost. The user did not remember what "mode" the system was in (operating system or application) and keyed in a series of letters which were logical and appropriate but gave rise to an unexpected and annoying result. The human and the computer were not communicating.

Dynabook. Interestingly, many of the GUI interface features which have been described above arose out of a project in which the goal was to develop a type of dream machine for educational use. During the 1970s, researchers at the Xerox Learning Research Group in Palo Alto, California, set out to construct a new communication tool for children based on the idea that information should be able to be retrieved dynamically. This tool, which was known as the Dynabook, was the brainchild of two visionaries, Adele Goldberg and Alan Kay, and was originally intended to be a moldable – i.e., easily modifiable by the user – medium for handling information. As Goldberg states,

> We set out to build a system that people themselves, both children and adults, could mold into the kinds of tools that they required, including designs for some basic ones that would be generally useful yet indeterminately modifiable.[4]

The Dynabook – in today's terminology, a personal computer – was seen as a medium whose design would emphasize the communication and classification of information. The Dynabook would be applied in the delivery of instructional vignettes (CAI – computer assisted instruction), including the presentation of simulations or games; in the knowledgeable interaction of a tutor or "coach" for directing a task (ICAI – intelligent computer assisted instruction), or in the possible forms of controlling the medium itself – i.e., programming. The Dynabook would be a transparent tool for children in that ideas could be "discovered," many different types of information could be manipulated (text, graphics, sounds) and all this could be done with a minimal amount of effort. The Dynabook was intended to present little or no obstacle to the child with respect to ease of use.

Summary. The perception that computers are difficult to use persists and for good reason. The means by which a computer user and the computer communicate – i.e., the interface – has been cited as the weakest link in that dialogue. Two trends, one in the marketplace and the other in cognitive science/computing science, suggest that this state of affairs is rapidly changing and that children will be among the recipients of these advances.

Theoretical foundations

In the educational computing arena (as in many others), there is a great deal of speculation and debate as to what constitutes the "best system." Much of the time, the promotion of one system over another is done on rather shaky grounds. Advocates of one particular computing system may be working out of past experience, personal bias or some measure of product loyalty (IBM versus Apple). It is quite clear that little is to be gained by floundering around in a sea of the latest (and perhaps already dated) microtechnology. Having recognized this dilemma, experts in the area of human-computer interaction have for many years been calling for the establishment of an applied psychology that is theory-based in which decisions about the inclusion or exclusion of various components in a system would be well-grounded in advances in cognitive psychology.

One approach to system design that has been shown to be very fruitful is information processing theory. Two very powerful premises in this attempt to describe human behavior in general and human-computer interaction in particular are the ideas that the activities that go on inside people's heads take a certain amount of time (usually milliseconds) and that a sequence of processes (serial or parallel) is brought to bear on the incoming or existing information. By using such a model in which human beings are viewed as processors of information, information processing theory provides a common framework in which sub-models of memory, problem solving, perception and behavior can be integrated with one another and in which formulations (i.e., quantitative predictions) for human-computer interaction can be grounded. A depiction of a generic information processing model is given in Figure 3:

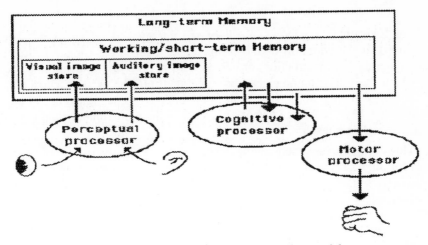

Figure 3. Human information processing model

For each of the three processors (perceptual, cognitive, motor), psychologists have determined as a result of numerous empirical studies that a cycle of approximately 1/10 of a second is the minimum amount of time required for the processor to encode or to operate on items or chunks of information. An item might be a number, a word, a concept or a step in a complex skill. Similarly, values for the storage capacity of the various memory constructs and the decay time of the items stored in these memories have been determined. In Figure 3, the arrows indicate the manner by which the processors and the various memories and stores work on each other. Note that, in terms of temporal sequence, events generally occur from left-to-right although there are situations that do not follow exactly these steps (e.g., the recollection of a past event may trigger some action). By breaking down tasks into very small steps and calculating the time required by the human processing system to execute these steps, one can predict within reasonable limits how long it will take someone to act.

Of course, we, as educators, are interested in the human component in the performance model and particularly interested in the factors that describe children's attributes (intellectual abilities, cognitive style, experience, knowledge, perceptual-motor skills). With performance models, the designer of a computer system can *predict* the utility (or lack of utility) of the system that he is designing. In other words, by taking into account descriptions and data about the factors delineated above, a system which is better than others can be designed and then put into the hands of children.

Educational Computing – Latest Developments

Given the above description of the trends in the marketplace, of the early investigations into a technological tool for children and of the utility of a specific theoretical approach to human-computer interaction, are there signs that something similar is being undertaken in the design of a child-computer interface? The answer is "some but not a great deal." With respect to computer use in Education in general, much of the energy and resources has been expended in the adoption of the computer as a substitute for the instructor (computer-assisted instruction) or has been spent on trying to determine ways in which the microcomputer can be integrated into the existing curriculum. Although both approaches can result in the effective pedagogical use of computers, they have, to a large extent, side-stepped the more fundamental issue of "ease of use" or transparency.

However, there are encouraging developments. The Government of Ontario has, for the past 6 years, funded the development of a sophisticated computer system for school use. In addition, research on how children communicate with the computer is being carried out at the University of Calgary. In both instances, the goal is to provide school-aged children with an easy-to-use, productive and efficient tool and one which matches their stage of development. From a number of perspectives, these activities have grown out of the introduction and popularity of graphical user interfaces and the innovative work done by the Dynabook group. Let's take a closer look at both of these developments.

The ICON. In Ontario, the Ministry of Education has been instrumental in supporting the design and development of an educational microcomputer (the ICON) which reflects the trends reported earlier. With respect to child-computer communication, McLean[5] has used the term, "enhanced user interface," to describe the framework and features of the means by which children in Ontario will interact with microcomputers. However, the Ministry has gone even further by laying out hardware and software specifications that must be met by developers and manufacturers if they intend to produce products that are to be purchased by Ontario schools. These functional specifications include two items of interest to us.

In terms of hardware features, the Ministry has given significant emphasis to how the child will interact with the computer. Specifically, hardware must be provided which allows the child to point on the monitor or display screen. Three of the more popular devices are depicted in Figure 4:

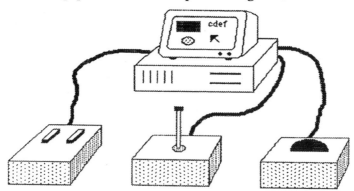

Figure 4. Pointing Devices

These devices are deemed an effective way of pointing since they provide direct information to the computer about the two-dimensional motion of the hand (the original pointing device!). They can accommodate both rapid motion to the vicinity of a target location (usually an icon) and fine motion near it by means of a software-selectable gear ratio.

For *software,* an enhanced user interface consists of screen displays which provide for a graphics-based or visual (as opposed to textual) interaction. Thus, children would communicate with the system by moving a cursor (usually an arrow or small rectangle) about the screen, by setting it on an icon or graphic (see Figure 2) which stands for some option (e.g., open, copy) and by pressing a button or key. Interfaces of this genre are said to be more "user-friendly" and less prone to misinterpretation in that the user is working in a visual environment in which the onus is put on the microcomputer and not on the child to "remember" all the options.

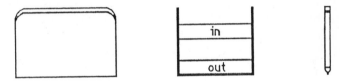

Figure 5. Typical icons

Objects available for manipulation such as folders, files, telephones and the processes that the child might apply to those objects (open, move, etc.) are to be represented by iconic images or pictures (Figure 5). Essentially, this means that the child will always have in full-view exactly what process is taking place and what is being acted on.

Research. Although the success of the ICON as an educational microcomputer is debatable, there is no denying that its implementation has caused many in the educational computing field to attend to its unique features. More pointedly, the attention that was paid to the ergonomic features (read "interface") by the ICON developers has put at center-stage the fact that a microcomputer which is intended to be used by children in schools must mirror the idiosyncracies of that population.

To this end, three facets of child-computer interaction have recently been investigated at the University of Calgary: (1) the prediction of pointing time when young children are using input devices; (2) the effect of the use of these input devices on their motoric processing rate; and (3) the content, recognizability and preference for animated icons as an interface feature. The remainder of this section will report the findings.

Prediction of Pointing Time. The amount of time required to move a cursor to a particular location on a display screen or monitor by means of an input device is a crucial factor in an interface. Obviously, a component in a computer system which has been shown to be more efficient than another should be given serious consideration if the goal is to provide a transparent, efficient system.

Keeping in mind for the moment the call for a system design which is theoretically-based (i.e., a design which would allow for the prediction of users' behavior before the production of the system), a question might be asked about the differences among children with respect to one feature in an enhanced interface – input devices other than the keyboard. This class of alternative input devices would include the mouse, trackball, joystick and lightpen among others. There are a number of ways to go about addressing this question.

A more productive way would be to determine whether or not a law or rule which could be applied to some or all of these pointing devices and which could be incorporated into a large-scale design equation for educational microcomputers could be applied. Fitts' law can be used to predict movement or pointing time for targets of a reasonable size. Fitts' law states that the time to move to a target of width W and distance D is a linear function of the ratio between W and D. Thus, according to Fitts' law, one can predict how long it will take to point to a target if the width of the target and its distance from the starting location of the pointing movement are known. For computer interfaces, the target might be a text character, an icon or a portion of a graphic. But does this law apply to children when they are using pointing devices?

Jones[6], in a study to determine the applicability of Fitts' law to children, found that equation 2 above does indeed apply to three input devices (mouse, joystick, trackball). From the standpoint of the interface design, this is valuable information. Essentially it means that, if one intended to build a model of a computer system for use by children and wanted to predict how much time it would take children to carry out a task (e.g., point to an icon on a screen), then the designer of such a system could include the prediction equation (Fitts' law) as part of the overall estimation of the time necessary to complete a broader task. That is, one has gained some measure of generalizability as a result of incorporating the results of information-processing-based research.

Processing Rate. A second set of studies has looked at children's processing rate, the amount or quantity of information (expressed in bits) which a child can act on over a period of time. With respect to the motor behavior of pointing, a typical processing rate for children is in the range of 7-10 bits per second. Studies which have looked at such rates for pointing with pencils and fingers (even feet) consistently give these results. If one were to ask, "does using a pointing input device in an enhanced interface place more load (i.e., decrease the processing rate) on children when compared to pointing in non-computer environments?" one would hope that the answer would be "no." It would be unwise to incorporate into an educational tool a feature which hinders children's ability to carry out some task regardless of how small the difference might be. A series of studies by Jones[6,7] suggests that this is exactly what happens. A first study[6] looked at the how young children (6, 8, 10 years-old) manipulated three pointing devices (mouse, joystick, trackball) in tasks that required them to point to targets of various sizes. Two tasks were involved: a discrete task in which the children executed a single pointing movement and a continuous task in which the children carried out multiple pointings. The results were as follows:

		Discrete	Continuous
Age	6	1.98	1.36
	8	1.53	1.73
	10	1.56	1.96
Peripheral	mouse	1.59	1.65
	joystick	1.87	1.73
	trackball	2.18	1.57

Table 1. Processing Rates for Age and Computer Pointing Peripheral[6]

Note that the values in table 1 are lower by approximately a factor of 4 than the typical processing rates of 7-10 bits/sec. – i.e., when children are not using computer pointing devices. What this suggests is that the use of these devices places an extra load on the children's already limited processing resources. Perhaps, then, these types of input devices should *not* be used by young children although one might argue that the ability to predict their pointing time (via Fitts' law) is worth the trade-off.

In a second study, Jones[7] looked at the effect of children using two pointing devices (mouse, trackball) under two conditions: "viewing" or "not viewing" their hands while pointing. This was an attempt to shed some light on the low processing rates obtained in the first study. In addition, the subjects were presented with pencil and paper and asked to tap at two targets in a reciprocal or alternating fashion as fast as they could for 15 seconds. The targets on paper were the same width and distance apart as those displayed on the computer screen. The results are given in Table 2.

Leaving aside for the moment the differences as a result of the "view"/"not view" treatment, note that the children's processing rates for the computer devices are for the most part much lower than those obtained when they pointed with a pencil. Although the data is not clear-cut (the processing rates for the 6 and 8 year-olds using a pencil are out of the expected range), it again appears that computer pointing peripherals place a more exacting load on the children's motor system.

Animated Icons. What should the icons look like in this child-centered world of "seeing and pointing" given that graphical icons (as part of a more general metaphor) comprise one-half of a GUI (graphical user interface)? In the commercial arena, virtually all software today uses static icons to represent options or objects. Townsend recommends that icons which are designed for use by children should "clearly depict, indicate and distinguish a program's commands and operations,"[8] yet the iconic component in existing interfaces for child-computer interaction merely mirrors what is available in the business or general-purpose application software – i.e., the icons are static.

With respect to iconic configuration, one possibility is to look at the nature of the icon itself. What should be the content of the icon and what particular features should it possess? To determine the former, one might simply rely on

Age	View*	Device	Bits/sec.
	1	mouse	3.68
	1	trackball	1.06
6	2	mouse	14.29
	2	trackball	1.03
		pencil	15.38
	1	mouse	1.81
	1	trackball	1.42
8	2	mouse	3.06
	2	trackball	1.04
		pencil	28.57
	1	mouse	3.11
	1	trackball	2.67
10	2	mouse	4.78
	2	trackball	22.22
		pencil	10.00

*1 = view hands   2 = no view hands

Table 2. Bits Processed Per Second for Computer Peripherals
and Pencil/Paper Pointing Movements

an adult notion of what these various icons might look like; however, a more productive approach would be to solicit suggestions from the children themselves and to develop and to test the effectiveness of these configurations on other children of the same age. A preliminary step in this investigation was carried out to pinpoint how young children conceive actions which are typical of what occurs when communicating with a computer (see Table 3 for a list of those actions).

With respect to features, the use of animation was seen to have potential. The rationale was two-fold. First, films, videotapes and other communicative means of the dynamic representation of some process or activity have long been available to teachers. Second, in the area of reading instruction for young children, an innovative approach (Bridge Reading Program) has been developed by Dewsbury in which the instructor employs written words, logographs (pictures) and physical gestures to teach initial skills. Dewsbury contends that the teaching of reading should harness the familiarity and impact of pictures (logographs) and physical actions (gestures) both of which are an integral part of a young child's world.[9]

In order to test these ideas, suggestions made by an initial group of elementary-aged children about the gestural content of typical computer-related tasks were used to develop animated (see Figure 5 for an example) and static icons (actually, the static version was simply one "frame" or step taken from the animated version) which were then shown to another group of children to ascertain whether or not the second group could correctly identify what the suggestions of the first group represented and which of the two formats they preferred.[10] Sixty children (6, 8 and 10 year-olds) comprised the second group.

a)   b)   c)   d)   e)

Figure 6. Example of Animated Sequence for "Draw."

The results for the validation segment of the study were as follows:

Action	Animated	Static	Action	Animated	Static
1. Put away	16.7	6.7	8. Point	80.0	76.7
2. Get	3.3	6.7	9. Move	70.0	20.0
3. Send	66.7	60.0	10. Erase	40.0	20.0
4. Open	43.3	30.0	11. Drag	60.0	56.7
5. Close	20.0	16.7	12. Copy	83.7	76.7
6. Write	96.7	90.0	13. Cut	80.0	66.7
7. Draw	83.3	60.0	14. Paste	63.7	63.3

Table 3. Correct Response for Animated Versus Static Treatment (%)

For 13 of the 14 computer tasks listed in Table 3, the percentage of children who were asked to describe the computer action depicted by the animated icons out-performed those who were exposed to the static format. However, the spread between the percentage scores was not high. For 4 of the animated actions and 6 of the static actions, less than 50% of the children correctly indicated the action involved. This was not surprising given that the subjects in the second group were simply asked to state in one or two words what the moving or static drawing on the computer screen represented – i.e., they were not provided a context in which to respond.

The results for which format the subjects preferred were more clear-cut. In each instance, more than 50% of the children selected the animated icon as the one which best captured the designated action. Table 4 lists the results across all three age levels.

It is clear that elementary-aged children can identify the content of animated and static icons which have been, in effect, generated by their peers and that they prefer the animated format. In the first case, it appears that the animated icons contained more relevant or meaningful information in that a gestural (to use the Bridge Reading program's term) component was inherent in the task's representation and thus provided an additional clue as to what it stood for.

Action	Animated	Static	Action	Animated	Static
1. Put away	75.0	25.0	8. Point	51.7	48.3
2. Get	65.0	35.0	9. Move	85.0	15.0
3. Send	81.7	18.3	10. Erase	91.7	8.3
4. Open	51.7	48.3	11. Drag	76.7	23.3
5. Close	51.7	48.3	12. Copy	70.0	30.0
6. Write	78.3	21.7	13. Cut	86.7	13.3
7. Draw	78.3	21.7	14. Paste	78.3	21.7

Table 4. Preferences for Icon Format (%)

Summary The fact that children move through various stages of cognitive and motor development and therefore require computer systems which are markedly different from those that are presently available in schools has only recently been addressed. Hardware/software development and research grounded in information processing theory are being carried out in which the goal is to provide a sophisticated and child-centred interface for educational use. The introduction of the ICON microcomputer in Ontario and studies at the University of Calgary are a response to the practical and theoretical issues that must be addressed.

Classroom applications

What are the implications of these developments for teachers and students who wish to use computers as part of the communication that goes on in the classroom? Can microcomputers be put to productive use even though a dedicated educational microcomputer which has been designed specifically for children is not widely available? Most assuredly. But, at the same time, educators should be demanding that microcomputers whose interface captures the most recent advancements in both hardware and software and which are built to adapt to children's cognitive and motoric idiosyncracies be provided as a resource for the classroom.

For the moment, however, a teacher can do much to mitigate the problems that the children will face because of the state of existing interface design. The following suggestions should be helpful in setting up an environment in which the children can still make good use of the resources:

First, look for software that, at least on the surface, has a similar look and feel. If a teacher is using MS-DOS machines, procuring a "shell" program from a local user's group which allows students to choose from menus as opposed to typing commands should reduce the difficulty of dealing with the operating system. Other utilities of a similar nature for both IBM and Apple microcomputers are available;

Second, provide maps of the system or program that is being used. Don't, however, simply list a tree-like breakdown of all the options of the program but rather draw a flowchart of the steps that are required to carry out the most important and often-used tasks (e.g., save a file, print a file);

Third, during the initial stages of the instruction in interface use, choose a series of steps that are concise and which will immediately result in some tangible output. For very young children, this will be especially helpful and will remove a number of abstractions which lie between what they do and what results;

Fourth, as soon as the teacher can pick out students who are more proficient than others, initiate a "buddy system" so that these students can help the slower ones. Peer tutoring is a very powerful instructional strategy;

Fifth, generalize, if possible, from one application to another although this may be very difficult given the many differing interfaces which are included in educational software. This would mean grouping programs at least according to function and then choosing those that resemble each other in some way. Programs which run on the ICON and Macintosh will make this a great deal easier as the interface for these computers has been standardized.

Notes

[1]Card, S.K., Moran, T.P., & Newell, A. (1983). *The Psychology of Human-computer Interaction.* New Jersey: Lawrence Erlbaum Associates.

[2]Norman, D.A. (1989). Interface critic considers visual cues, ease of use. *MacWeek,* 3(12), 19-20.

[3]Roblyer, M.D. (1988). The effectiveness of microcomputers in Education: a review of the research from 1980-1987. *T.H.E. Journal,* 16(2), 85-89.

[4]Goldberg, A. (1979). Educational uses of a Dynabook. *Computers and Education, 3,* 247-266.

[5]McLean, R.S. (1983). Ontario Ministry of Education specifies its microcomputer. In *Proceedings of the Fourth Canadian Symposium on Instructional Technology,* (pp. 436-441). Winnipeg, Manitoba: National Research Council of Canada.

[6]Jones, T. (1989). An empirical study of children's use of computer pointing devices. Manuscript submitted for publication.

[7]Jones, T. (1989). The effect of computer pointing peripherals on children's processing rate. In press.

[8]Townsend, B.M. (1986). Iconic commands and command systems. Unpublished manuscript, Sheridan College, Software Evaluation Unit, Toronto, Ontario.

[9]Dewsbury, A. (1983). *Bridge Reading Handbook.* Toronto: O.I.S.E. Press.

[10]Jones, T. (1989). Children and animated computer icons. In press.

26

Sexism and Communication

Ronald E. Sept

Successful teaching, like many other professional activities, relies very heavily on the quality of the relationship between teacher and student. Without genuine trust and respect, it is doubtful whether any significant amount of learning can take place. Even the most captivating curriculum and delivery will collapse if we fail to establish this essential bond.

Forming quality relationships with students is, of course, one of the delicate tasks which makes good teaching a true art; even experienced teachers find this one of the most perplexing aspects of their work. Despite its difficulty, however, quality relationships with students is a learnable skill that can be developed through proper training and practice.

This chapter discusses several ideas about human communication which may be helpful in improving student/teacher relationships. We begin by reviewing a number of basic principles of communication which have important implications for the development of human relationships in general. In outlining these implications, I will point out how communication can damage and benefit relationships.

To help illustrate some of these impacts, I will focus on a particular aspect of human relationships – the issue of sexism - as a way of demonstrating some basic problems that can get in the way of developing effective relationships. Besides being an area of considerable debate amongst teachers and other professionals, sexism is important because it reflects a number of more deeply-rooted problems in human communication. By examining the nature of sexism, I hope to shed light on these basic problems, by examining sexism from a less conventional point of view. We usually think of sexism as something which occurs only in cross-gender (i.e. male/female) relationships, and more importantly, as something done exclusively to women by men. In this respect, we are often misled by the assumptions that sexist attitudes and behavior belong exclusively to men and that the experience of being subjected to sexism belongs exclusively to women. With a little thought, of course, most of us will admit that this is not necessarily true; women can also behave in stereotyped ways toward men, and men can experience the impact of such behavior as well as women. In our everyday understanding of the term "sexism," we almost always view it from the woman's point of view. A man's perspective on sexism affords us an opportunity to illustrate some of the less obvious ways – beyond strictly gender-based ones – in which human relationships can become biased and unbalanced. Throughout this discussion, I will use sexism as an example to illustrate how various kinds of inequalities come to be reflected in human relationships through ineffective communication.

Communication and Human Relationships

Whenever we talk about human relationships, the issue of communication is never far away. In fact, it is useful to think about communication as the very process by which these relationships are created and maintained over time.

To some extent this goes against everyday notions about communication. Most of us think of communication as a process of moving information from one place to another, or simply as a means of expressing ourselves to others. Both of these, of course, are true in a narrow sense; but communication is also much more than this.

We've all heard the phrase "no man is an island" (note the sexist bias?). The significance of this comment is that because we are human, everything we do is either directed towards or affected by other people. It's as if we are all part of a huge telephone network into which each of us has a number of direct connections. We constantly get information about the world through these connections, and we constantly send information out into this network whenever we say or do anything. Being human means that you can't disconnect ourselves from the network, nor can you prevent other people from receiving information about your actions. We are all permanently and irrevocably linked.

Communication plays a key role in this "human network." In a very obvious way we use communication to send specific messages to people or to get particular things done within our own corner of the world. However, the real importance of communication is not just that it helps to move information about within the network, but that it actually creates the linkages on which the whole network is based. We do not communicate because we are inter-connected; we communicate in order to become connected in the first place.

The idea that communication creates human relationships suggests a very different way of thinking about communication. Communication scholars[1] have attempted to formulate general principles which describe this different way of thinking about how and why we communicate. Several of these principles are outlined as follows.

(1) *You cannot NOT communicate* – The first principle suggests that no matter

how hard you might try, you cannot stop communicating. You often hear people say that so-and-so has "stopped communicating," that someone "won't communicate", or that some people just "can't communicate." Comments like this often suggest that people define communication as something that only happens when someone speaks. In truth, communication is underway well before people speak, and continues well after they finish.

The reason we can say this is related to the fact that people generally use their entire range of sensory abilities when they interact with other people. When we communicate we take in information through the senses of vision, touch, smell and taste, as well as through what we hear in the form of speech. Because we use all of this information in making sense of what other people are doing, the entire range of human behavior has the potential to be interpreted as expressing or communicating specific pieces of information. In other words, all behavior has this potential to convey information; and since it is impossible to not behave,[2] it is also impossible to stop conveying information to others. Thus, you cannot NOT communicate.

(2) *Communication is both verbal and non-verbal* – When you hear people say that someone has "stopped communicating," what they usually mean is that the person has stopped speaking; but there are still a number of ways in which information about the person can be conveyed, interpreted, and acted upon by others. When we meet people, we use a number of sources of information beyond what they say to create initial impressions about who they are and what they're up to: we notice how they're dressed, how they stand or walk, the kinds of gestures and facial expressions they use, and a host of other non-verbal cues. Moreover, when people do speak, we use other cues like vocal rate, volume and pitch of their voice to help interpret what they are saying. We use the entire range of non-verbal cues to assist us in obtaining information about people and to help interpret what they convey verbally.

In everyday experience, we tend to emphasize the verbal components of communication and to dismiss the non-verbal. In reality, communication is always a combination of verbal and non-verbal elements, each of which adds its own pieces of information to the overall message. In order to understand what someone "means," we must recognize that considerable amounts of information are conveyed non-verbally and that verbal and non-verbal messages interact together in complex ways to convey meaning.

(3) *Communication is not always intentional* – Because a great deal of what we communicate is conveyed non-verbally, our ability intentionally to plan and control certain parts of our messages is limited in important ways. While we may carefully choose our words, and perhaps even some of our gestures, significant parts of our communication are conveyed through means over which we have only minimal control.

For example, overall facial expressions are often difficult to "manufacture," and some features of the face like blushing, eye movements, and so on, are often entirely out of our control. The same is true of overall body postures, as well as some finer body movements which convey a great deal about our attitudes and emotional state. Thus, while we may control certain parts of our communication intentionally to convey specific messages, a great deal of the information we convey about ourselves is communicated quite unintentionally and not under conscious control.

(4) *Meaning is created by people, not contained in words* – When we talk with others, most of us tend to assume that our words act as if they were containers for the ideas and experiences we want to express. We select words which have particular meanings and we string them together in such a way that others will get the meaning that we intended to send, like putting something on a conveyor belt and sending it physically over to the other person.

In actual fact, meanings are not "transported" in this way. Meaning do not exist within the words themselves, they occur within the minds of the individuals who interpret the words. Rather than being containers of meaning, words act as symbols which we use to re-present (literally, to present again) our ideas to others. When others receive our message, they use our symbols to make inferences about the kind of experience we might be having, based on their own understanding of the events and ideas you are talking about. Although the rules of language give some common basis for interpreting these meanings, in the end we have our own ways of "making sense" of the symbols others send.

In this sense, communication is not simply a matter of "packaging" meanings into words and "sending" them out for another person to "unpack." Instead, it is a much more complex process of assembling and presenting sets of symbols which others will later use to interpret your meaning. The meanings we communicate are not sent by us, but are created by the receivers through their interpretation of our symbols.

(5) *Communication involves a process of creating shared meanings* – As we have seen, meaning lies ultimately within individuals. We can never know directly what other people mean: we can only interpret their meanings from the words and other symbols they use. In order for us to live and work together in society, the meanings which each of us attach to our experiences must somehow be similar enough for us to coordinate our actions toward common ends. Communication makes this possible by allowing us to test our interpretations and gradually move toward a shared understanding of our experience.

When I communicate a specific message to you, I wait for your response in order to obtain some indication of how you've interpreted that message. If your response indicates that you have interpreted the message differently than what I had intended, I may send a second message to try and alter that interpretation. Similarly, when you receive another person's message, you cannot be sure whether you have interpreted that message correctly; but you can test the validity of your interpretation by responding a certain way and waiting to see how the other person responds in turn. We use this back-and-forth process of proposing and counter-proposing meanings in order to negotiate what appears to be a common meaning for the message at hand.

In this way again, communication is not simply a matter of sending information, but is an active negotiation of meaning between two or more people. It is interesting to note here that we may never be able to say in an absolute sense whether or not these two people actually share the same meaning. In normal interaction all that seems necessary is that our meanings be similar enough that our work together goes more-or-less smoothly. While it may appear that we understand one another, we may actually be working with meanings that are just similar enough to make our actions appear consistent.

(6) *All communication conveys "content" as well as "relationship" information* – Whenever two people communicate, meanings are negotiated on at least two important levels. On the surface, we reach agreement on the meanings of the symbols and other information which convey the content of the message. At the same time, we also engage in a less obvious negotiation concerning the relationship between communicators. The reason for this is that the meaning of specific messages can vary considerably depending on the kind of relationship in which they are communicated. When you laughingly call your best friend a "jerk," for example, it has an entirely different meaning from what it might have if said to a stranger!

Because meanings can vary depending on the relationship in which they are communicated, we rely heavily on an initial definition of the relationship between communicators to determine the meaning of subsequent messages. In most cases, this relational definition is never expressed openly, but remains a largely implicit part of the conversation. For example, when a boss asks a secretary to go and get coffee, the request indicates a specific content message – that he or she wants a drink - but also implicitly contains, or at least proposes, a specific relationship between the boss and the secretary - that the boss has the power to ask the secretary for coffee. In responding to this request, the secretary can either get the coffee, and thereby accept the relational definition proposed by the boss, or the secretary might challenge the implicit relational message by refusing to get coffee.

The important point here is that in every instance of communication there are at least two levels of meaning being negotiated: a content level which conveys information about the subject matter at hand, and a relational level which defines the relationship between communicators. While the latter often remains only implicit in the interaction, it is a critical element in determining how the remainder of the message will be interpreted.

The principles outlined above portray human communication as a complex process in which the "conveyance" of meaning, if we can actually use this term, is accomplished through a series of interpretive stages, eventually leading to a negotiation of shared meanings among the individuals involved. This negotiation takes place on the basis of several sources of information, some of which are intentionally produced to convey specific messages, but many of which occur unintentionally as part of the personal and situational context of communication. In making sense of their situation, individuals use the entire array of available information to create their own sense of meaning and significance. Interaction consists of the sharing of individual meanings in an ongoing effort to establish common meanings, which ultimately form the basis for joint action.

Critical to this process is the establishment of a shared definition of the relationship between individuals. Relational definitions provide participants with a common basis for interpreting messages, and thus form an important basis for ongoing communication. In this respect, communication plays the fundamental role of initially creating the relationships around which virtually all of our lives revolve.

Despite their importance, relational aspects of communication are usually only an implicit part of the messages we send – often being expressed unintentionally and non-verbally.[3] As a result, unless we are trained to recognize these aspects of communication, most of us remain unaware of how our own patterns of interaction affect our relationships with others. Often, we may not be aware how even very common patterns of speech can have deep and lasting impacts on others with whom we communicate. In what follows, I will examine a personal example which illustrates how a seemingly un-remarkable comment can have a disturbing impact on the formation of a relationship, as well as on at least one of the individuals involved.

Being Handy: The Male Equivalent of Sexism

I indicated earlier that sexism was an important area of concern for teachers and other professionals, both in its own right, and as a reflection of more deeply-seated problems in human communication. Women are often thrust into degrading stereotypes by patterns of speech and behavior which reflect underlying inequities within the fabric of our society. What I hope to show in the following example is that these inequities, as much as they may be evident for women, are by no means restricted to the female gender. I also want to show by this example not only that sexism can be experienced equally by a man, but that there is an underlying commonality between male and female versions of sexism which reflect even more basic problems in human communication. I turn now to my example.

For several years I have been designing and building furniture of various kinds as a hobby. I never considered myself very good at it; I just enjoyed the physical effort as a diversion from my academic work. Eventually, however, my home came to be furnished largely with pieces which I had built myself.

Most people, it seems, find it unusual for a twentieth-century city dweller to have any kind of practical skill; that, at least, was the impression I got from acquaintances who marveled at the "home made" articles that populated my house. I became quite accustomed, and eventually quite un-impressed, by comments about how nice it must be to make your own furniture.

One day however, a new acquaintance was visiting my wife and I happened to overhear a conversation in which comments were being made about our home. At one point I heard the friend say to my wife "My, he sure is handy!" Although I had heard that phrase many times before and had never paid any particular attention to it, for some reason I heard it on this occasion in a very different way. For some reason not yet apparent, being called "handy" suddenly had a very odd and disturbing ring to it.

For several days this comment kept forcing itself back into my mind. The comment had left me intellectually puzzled as well as strangely insulted, though there seemed to be no logical reason why it should have such an effect. Eventually, I came to understand that, at a very basic level, I was feeling personally degraded by the remark. Rather than feeling that the comment had been a compliment (as I'm sure it had been intended), being called "handy" had left me feeling put-down and somehow cheapened. All of a sudden, it was very undesirable to be called "handy." As I thought further about this, I also came to understand why this was true: to be "handy" meant that I was seen as valuable primarily because of what I could produce, not for what I was. When our friend called me "handy", she was not seeing me as a person; she was referring to my ability to do particular things. I felt insulted because she was, in a sense, looking right through me as a person and only seeing that part of me that was useful for a particular task. With one word I had been reduced to a mere tool.

This sense of having someone look right through you, reminded me of something I had often heard women talk about in discussing experiences of being treated in a sexist or chauvinistic manner. Sexist comments focus on limited features. Typically, for example, women feel that men only see the physical exterior and ignore anything that might be going on inside. This is, I believe, what it means to treat someone as a "sex object."

Interestingly, my own feeling of being called "handy" was very close to this; only in this case I was not being treated as a object of sex, but as an object of work. Being called "handy" in a very subtle way focuses attention away from my human characteristics and puts me in a category with other things which have particular uses. Focusing in on my handiness, in other words, was essentially de-humanizing because it suggests my value as a person rests mainly in my ability to perform specific kinds of work.

Now, I am quite sure that the woman who made this remark had no intention of saying this. Indeed, she is probably a very "liberated" and egalitarian individual who would balk at the thought of being considered sexist. But good intentions notwithstanding, her pattern of communication had the effect of proposing a relationship between her and I in which my role was defined in terms of my practical utility. Such a relationship is consistent with social stereotypes which place men in the role of worker and provider to women; indeed, this relationship is simply the flip side of stereotypes which cast women into the role of the helpless and dependent housewife. In this sense, I believe my experience in being called "handy" is directly parallel to what many women must feel as the recipient of other sexist remarks. If this is true, I now have a much clearer understanding of what that experience is really like.

The Essential Elements of Sexism

The example above is in many ways a very simple (some might even say overly simplistic) one. Feminists in particular might argue that my experience cannot fairly represent the kind of experience which a female might have, since this was only an isolated incident and not part of a systematic pattern of role stereotyping. I accept this critique without question – there undoubtedly are several dimensions of sexism which my example does not reflect.

The example is, nonetheless, an instructive one. In its simplicity it can help us to discover some of the basic elements of the experience of sexism; and because it offers an unusual perspective on such experiences, it also allows us to see these elements apart from their typical setting. In what follows then, I want to highlight four main points which the present example illustrates with particular clarity.

(1) *Sexism Goes Both Ways* – If it wasn't already obvious, this example should demonstrate quite clearly that sexism is not restricted just to females. While its true that women may be far more commonly the target of sexist remarks and behavior, there can be no doubt that both genders are equally susceptible to this kind of interpersonal put-down.

The basic structure of sexist experience appears to be that one person treats the other, either through speech or other action, in a stereotypical manner. This means that the "victim" of sexism is not seen as a complex, multi-faceted individual, but rather as a reflection of some static, one-dimensional role or pattern. Within society we learn to recognize patterns of behavior and to associate them with specific social roles. These stereotyped patterns help to make the world a little easier to understand by making it seem more orderly and predictable; but they also portray people as if they were one-dimensional cut-outs. When we view people as a reflection of stereotypical roles, we lose sight of the unique qualities which make each of us an individual and see only the qualities which our stereotype leads us to expect.

Sexist forms of speech and behavior arise whenever we view another person through the distorting lens of gender-based roles. Our society is full of stereotypes which place both men and women into awkwardly one-dimensional categories – men are hard and women soft, women are nurturing and men are productive, men are decisive and assertive, women are flexible and compliant. All of these characterizations are obviously so limited in their application that one wonders how they have come to be accepted. Yet we see these same compartments used again and again to distinguish male and female behavior.

The important point here is that any time we use a gender-based stereotype, regardless of our gender, we engage in potentially sexist behavior. In this respect, it is just as easy for a woman to treat a man in a stereotyped fashion as the other way around. Interestingly, it is also just as easy for a man to treat another man in a sexist manner, and for one woman to treat another the same way. It is the use of gender-based stereotypes which makes something sexist, and this is entirely independent of the speaker's gender.

(2) *Sexism Treats People As Objects* – A second and far more important lesson which the present example provides is insight into the actual experience of being treated in a sexist fashion. When we use stereotypical roles to characterize an individual we focus in on only a limited range of who that person actually is. The stereotype selects out only a limited set of characteristics and highlights these as the most important, sometimes the only, aspects worth noting. As I suggested in the example, we come to see the individual as valuable only in terms of the qualities highlighted by the stereotype. Stereotypes thus degrade the individual by suggesting that they are only important in very limited ways.

The problem does not stop there however. Not only do stereotypes cast individuals into restrictive roles, they also tend to accentuate the instrumental value of the person's behavior, and not the person in his or her own right. In other words, stereotyped roles focus our attention toward behaviors which have a specific use or application, and then define the value of the individual in those terms. In my example, being seen as "handy" meant that I was valuable only in so far as I was "useful" or capable of doing specific kinds of things; I was being recognized primarily because of my value as a tool or instrument.

To the extent that we see others in an instrumental way, we treat them as objects and not as people. The personal disturbance I felt as a result of my experience was the product of being reduced from being a complex, thinking and feeling individual to a mere object – an object of work. In the same way, I believe women often feel a profound sense of de-personalization when they are treated as objects of sex, housework, et cetera. What is important here is not what kind of role is being assigned, but the extent to which that role characterizes the individual as an object.

The essential nature of sexism is, in this respect, fundamentally the same for both men and women. To be on the receiving end of a sexist remark is to be equated with an object and to be recognized only for your value as a means toward specific ends. Such treatment is profoundly de-personalizing in the sense that it discounts the essential individuality of the person and diminishes their value as a person in and of themselves. I do not mean to deny here that important differences exist between men and women in terms of how persistent and systematic such treatment may be; there clearly are social barriers which make women more susceptible to sexist experience. In its essential form however, the nature of that experience and its impact on the individual is common to all kinds of stereotypical behavior.

(3) *Sexism Reflects Imbalances Of Interpersonal Power* – There is yet another dimension of sexism which the present example allows us to explore: its relation to issues of power in interpersonal relationships. I have described the sense of personal de-valuation I experienced as a product of being treated like some kind of tool. Although bad enough in itself, there is another component of the experience which was even more profoundly disturbing. Not only had I felt

used, I also felt that there was no way of going back and changing what had happened. I felt powerless to correct what had been done or to change how I felt. In a word, I felt victimized.

What this illustrates is that the experience of sexism is closely related to issues of interpersonal power. Power is a basic element of every human relationship, and each of us has the ability to influence others in the course of our interactions. The way in which power is distributed varies considerably from relationship to relationship. Sometimes relationships can be so overwhelmingly unbalanced that one individual ends up with virtually no influence at all, resulting in feelings of victimization and powerlessness.

Treating people instrumentally is one of the ways people use to exercise power within their relationships with others. When we define people in terms of an isolated quality like gender, it is easier to view them as an entity over which one can have a certain degree of control or power. When we assign people to stereotypical categories, we make the world appear orderly and predictable; we also gain a sense of control over that world by defining those individuals, and our relationships with them, as something over which we can exercise power to our advantage.

This "political" aspect of sexism is well-recognized by feminists.[4] As they suggest, the frequency of sexist behavior and attitudes in everyday interaction reveals an immense imbalance of power within society as a whole which systematically leaves women feeling victimized and powerless to change their situation. While we need to be especially wary when these problems occur systematically to a particular social group, I believe it is important to realize that the experience of being dis-empowered is a problem which can equally affect any human being. We need to be aware of its occurrence in all kinds of relationships, and to recognize the impact it may have for all of the individuals involved.

(4) *Sexist Communication: A Subtle Denial Of Humanity* – One of the most curious aspects of the example outlined above was the fact that such a strong response could result from what appeared to be a very casual remark. I might not even be surprised if you were to suggest that my response was an irrational over- reaction. This is, after all, precisely what women are frequently told when they articulate their experiences with sexist behavior. The strength of the reaction to sexist behavior illustrates the fact that being treated in this manner, even if it is done very subtly, has important repercussions for an individual's sense of personhood and humanity.

Earlier we discussed how the relational components of communication – those aspects that define the relationship between people – are often conveyed quite unintentionally and implicitly alongside more obvious messages. The relationships created at this level of communication are seldom defined openly, yet they are important in helping people orient themselves within the interaction. The entire meaning of the exchange, including the person's own role and position within the interaction, can vary depending on how the relationship is initially defined. Thus, even though they may be a very subtle part of communication, relational components strongly influence how people view themselves and their status within the relationship. In the case of sexist communication, the relational components convey to the "victim" the message they that are not seen as people, that they are valuable only as means to ends, and that they have no real power within the relationship.

In sum, the example above allows us to suggest four major conclusions regarding "sexist" behavior: (1) sexism is not restricted to any specific group but can occur equally in all kinds of relationships, (2) the essential character of sexism is that it involves an attempt to treat another individual in an instrumental fashion – that is, as an object which has specific uses, (3) underlying sexist behavior is a more deeply-seated attempt to gain control of the relationship by dis-empowering the other individual, and (4) sexist attitudes are frequently communicated unintentionally by patterns of speech and behavior which reflect underlying social biases.

Our analysis of the example also portrays the impact which sexist behavior can have on the individuals involved. Sexism, like other examples of stereotypical behavior, defines individuals in terms which force them into uni-dimensional categories and which de-value unique personal qualities. At the same time it also denies the individual the power to alter that definition. In both of these ways, sexism de-personalizes the individual.

Overcoming Sexist Communication: Suggestions for Teachers

Given how strongly sexism can affect a person, it is important that we take whatever steps are necessary to increase our understanding and awareness of sexism (as well as other forms of stereotyped behavior). For example, each of us could become more aware of the social stereotypes which run rampant in our society, and of the ways that these are reflected in everyday language. The way we typically speak about genders, racial, or ethnic groups, often reveals systematic inequities within our society as a whole. It is also important that we come to better understand our own personal stereotypes. While society as a whole reflects numerous biases and mis-perceptions of people, each of us has our own individual set of beliefs and values which reflect the biases of our own communities and families. Examining personal beliefs about specific social groups can be helpful in developing tolerance and understanding.

As we have seen, sexist and other stereotypical behaviors are the product of attitudes which deny peoples' individuality. No matter how much a person may represent membership in a specific social category, it is wise to remember that each person is a complex individual with a wide variety of abilities, qualities, and areas of strength and weakness. While we all fall into specific roles or groups from time to time, none of us is just a role occupant or group member. We are all unique and valuable as individuals in our own right. We all recognize this about ourselves, but we sometimes forget that this also applies to other people.

These general attitudes will carry directly over into the teaching context. A respect for individuals will be evident in the way that you address and communicate with each of your students. If you have an understanding and an appreciation for diversity, you will be able to recognize students as unique individuals, not just as members of social groups. Your knowledge of how social stereotypes are embedded in language will help you to identify instances of sexist and related behavior; and prevent these from recurring, both in yourself and in your students.

There are also a number of practical suggestions to be made in relation to the teaching process itself. Some of these concern the actual curriculum and its delivery, while others have to do with your general presentation of the material and your communication with individual students. As far as curriculum issues are concerned, I believe the same kind of personal learning about social stereotypes that I suggested above should be part of the ongoing learning process. Learning about sexual, racial and ethnic stereotypes within society (including how particular groups are portrayed within society) should be a basic part of the material we teach. In the elementary grades we can begin to introduce these ideas within modules on world geography, history and social studies, by including basic information on cultural and social variations into the existing curriculum. For more mature students, a more explicit presentation of alternative perspectives, including feminist points of view, should be openly explored in classes in which social issues are directly addressed. Students of all ages should be encouraged to explore gender and racial differences as a regular part of their education.

In addition to than the actual materials of education, the teaching process itself should reflect a consistent attempt to remove stereotypic views from the classroom environment. In many ways, the classroom represents one of the most powerful environments for the learning of social attitudes and behaviors. Several avenues may be open for making that environment as free of all kinds of social prejudice as possible.

Careful selection of textbooks is one strategy which can do a great deal to reduce the presence of stereotyped representations of gender and ethnic differences. Textbooks vary considerably in the degree to which they promote such stereotypes, and it is the responsibility of teachers to choose texts which represent an appropriate balance of individual differences.

Similar selectivity can also be applied to the teacher's own use of examples in teaching. Without careful consideration of one's own attitudes, it is easy for a teacher to communicate his or her own social biases to the students through examples which reflect social stereotypes. Consistently using male characters in discussing professional or working people and female characters in discussing child-rearing and homemaking, for example, can actively promote gender stereotypes as examples of appropriate behavior. A balanced selection of examples can remove systematic biases from your presentation of materials in class.

It is also possible for teachers to promote gender stereotypes in other kinds of classroom behavior. For example, if a teacher consistently reflects gender stereotypes in asking students to do various tasks around the classroom, these can also be unconsciously promoted as acceptable. Always asking girls to help clean up and asking boys to do heavier work, for example, can easily convey traditional sex-role stereotypes to students. Teachers concerned about eliminating such views should carefully monitor their own behavior in such cases.

In general, teachers should strive to become more aware of their own use of language within the classroom setting. As we have seen in this chapter, sexist or other stereotypical attitudes can sometimes be conveyed even through language which appears otherwise very innocuous. Because the meaning of specific terms and phrases can vary depending on the relational context of communication, teachers need to become aware of how their verbal and nonverbal communication can create particular relationships with students. If those relationships bear any hint of sexist bias, seemingly innocent words can often convey very harsh and disturbing meanings. Under these conditions, it would not be surprising that students' academic performance might be affected. If we want all students to gain equally from the educational process, we must strive to eliminate this kind of relational pollution from the learning environment.

Because the classroom is a situation in which students learn a great deal of their social behavior, teachers have a great responsibility to ensure that it offers as positive a learning environment as possible. Part of this responsibility can be met through the teacher's own behavior as a role model. By carefully monitoring their beliefs and patterns of speech, teachers can provide a living example of communication which does not promote social stereotypes. The teacher can also help students to adopt similar communication patterns by noting and correcting examples of sexist speech in the classroom. By creating a social environment which promotes the value of individual differences, teachers can lesson the prejudicial the attitudes which the coming generation will bring with them into the adult world.

Notes

[1]See for example, P. Watzlawick, et al, *Pragmatics of Human Communication* (New York: Norton, 1967).

[2]Even standing perfectly still and refusing to talk or even blink is itself a behavior which can convey the impression that you are refusing to engage in any interaction. This is not a lack of communication, but rather an act of communicating the desire to withdraw from interaction.

[3]This is often exemplified in discussions of the concept of "Metacommunication." See, for example, P.Watzlawick, et al, *Pragmatics of Human Communication* New York: Norton, 1967).

[4]See for example, C.Kramarae, *Women and Men Speaking,* Rowley, MA: Newbury House, 1981; and McConnell-Ginet, et al, *Women and Language in Literature and Society,* New York: Plenum, 1980.

27

Communication and Students at Risk

Vic Grossi

Preamble

Everything we learn is filtered through our feelings. Although we may be strongly motivated about why we want to learn, what we learn is highly influenced by the affective viewpoint; that is, as being pleasant or unpleasant, and its meaning to us. This relationship between learning and our feelings about learning continues to be an important area of further investigation.[1] Teachers are in a unique position as having regular contact with students and by default become trained observers of the student's behaviors. Consequently, they are frequently the first adults to become aware of situations which may be indicative of children at risk.

For the purposes of the present discussion we will identify "at risk" to mean students who may in the near future exhibit behaviors or make verbalizations to strongly suggest a degree of emotional instability. This may be in conjunction with labels such as identifying a student as sad, moody, depressed, weepy, angry, out of control or who may be at risk to self destructive behaviors. We might also want to discuss the self-esteem of the student and what precautions teachers can take to ensure a positive self-concept throughout the school years. While not all learning has to be pleasurable, it would seem that learning must be regarded as having sufficient worth for an individual to invest in it. This worth might involve fresh insight, a feeling of self-sufficiency, the means towards reaching a desired career goal or simply a more comfortable life.[2]

As for this chapter, its aim is to alert teachers to verbal and nonverbal communication that is indicative of students at risk.

373

Students at Risk to Running Away

Researchers in recent time have identified running away behavior or typically referred as A. W. O. L. behavior as increasing cross all grade levels and costing not only dollars to track these students down but also questioning the quality of the learning.[3]

Beginning in the 1960s and continuing through the '70s and into the 1980s, running away continues to be seen as an ever increasing action or reaction among our youth. It has been reported that in 1975, 10% of all boys and almost 9% of all girls reported running away at least once and interesting enough running from school at least once.[3] What can the teacher do to identify or at least help identify children that may be at risk to running away. Much has been written on the subject of runaways and in reviewing the professional literature it becomes apparent that observations may reflect differences in how the data was gathered.[4] Runaways are seen and studied in the offices of private clinicians, in school guidance clinics, social service agencies, protective social agencies, involuntary runaway shelters and juvenile police units. Some are long distance runners, some are gone for months, some only stay away overnight, and some never return.

According to Jenkins, the runaway reaction child is seen as emotionally immature, apathetic and seclusive. Here he/she is unwanted, rejected and comes from a small family. The unsocialized aggressive child shows the most psychopathology of the three groups.[5] Wolk and Brandon,[4] in studying a solicited sample of adolescents from run away homes and schools found that:

- runaway adolescents report more punishment and less support from their parents;
- runaway girls report the most and runaway boys the least degree of parental control;
- runaways hold a less favorable self-concept, specifically on the dimensions of anxiety, self-doubt, poor inter-personal relationships, and self-defensiveness; and
- runaways also manifest as an aspect of self, a readiness for counselling.[4]

The authors further state runaway adolescents, compared to non-runaways, manifest a self-concept that is more defensiveness, more self-doubting and less trusting. It is a self-concept that damages interpersonal relationships. The runaway act is an extreme form of response to what is perceived by the student, as a lack of validation of the struggle for autonomy and perhaps that runaway boys may be responding to the absence of sufficient control while runaways girls are repelled by too much control.

What then, can be summarized that may be helpful to teachers in the classroom? Perhaps some limited generalizations may be made about the complex phenomenon which seem to lead to running away from both home and school:

running away from home and school is easier today and is seen as a socially acceptable or at least common place form of protest in older children and adolescents;

– there seems to be a greater prevalence of oppressive home situations today, either in terms of serious neglect or abuse, or in terms of increased tendencies for the direct or indirect externalization of emotional conflicts within families;

– there is a greater number of incomplete and inadequately structured families which are unable to provide the emotional supports necessary to accomplishing the tasks of adolescent development;

– most runaways do manifest signs of immature or incomplete ego development in relation to themselves, their parents and society, some few are emotionally disturbed;

– there are many self-harming implications in running away, but running can also be seen as a protective defense against hurt feelings with parental relationships or school relationships.[6]

Clearly, more research is required to further elucidate specific issues within young people who run away.

Helping Teachers Identify Types of Child Abuse

There appears to be have been a drastic increase of media and research attention to this ever increasing and quite serious problem of child abuse.[7] The media has continued to report allegations of teachers and parents or other caregivers engaging in various form of abusive behavior towards young people. By understanding what constitutes incidences of child abuse, researchers in general have recognized at least four forms in which the survival, security or development of children may be seen to be in danger.

1. Child Neglect

Physical neglect occurs when a parent fails to provide supervision, guidance, medical care, food, clothing or shelter that might reasonably be expected of any parent. This inadequate provision is associated with:

– unreasonable and unnecessary danger to the child's safety;

– unreasonable and unnecessary discomfort to the child;

– severe or chronic health problems including the failure to thrive syndrome;

– childhood behaviors that may threaten the safety of the child or the other person; and

– social ostracization of the child which is significant because of its severity or duration.

2. Physical Abuse

Any non-accidental physical injury inflicted upon a child under 18 years of age by a parent, caregiver, teacher, babysitter or any other adult is considered to be physical abuse. Abuse could be rated as mild (a few bruised, welts, scratch, cuts), moderate (numerous bruises, minor bruises, and single fracture), severe (large burns, central nervous system injury, multiple fractures, or any life threatening abuse), extreme (abuse resulting in very severe injury or death). It also includes the feeding of poisonous, corrosive or non-medical mind altering substances to a child. Chronic bruising or repeated injuries of adolescents by a parent is considered to constitute physical abuse.

3. Emotional Abuse

Emotional maltreatment may include emotional abuse (the use of threats, terrorism or other chronic parental behaviors), emotional deprivation (the chronic withholding of affection) or verbal assault (the focusing of negative feelings such as anger or rage on a child). It may include the continual scape-goating and rejection of a specific child in the family. The parental behavior is considered abusive if it causes a measurable impairment of a child's capacity to view himself/herself as a separate individual with dignity and self-worth.

4. Sexual Abuse

Sexual exploitation is any parental behavior or behavior of others (usually adults) permitted or condoned by the parents, teachers or guardian which involves erotic gratification of the caregiver or other person, performed with or without resistance on the part of the child and with or without accompanying physical abuse. This may range from exposure and fondling to intercourse, incest and rape. Sexual acts between consenting peers are generally excluded from this definition.[8]

Indicators of Child Abuse

It is important to be mindful of the fact that observation of one or two of the behaviors in any age group does not necessarily mean abuse. However, some of the factors included may indicative of other problems. Documentation of unusual behaviors may help school personnel become aware of an abusive or neglectful pattern.[9]

Physical neglect indicators include the following:

- Unattended medical or dental problems (such as infected sores, decayed teeth, glasses not provided when needed);
- Child always seems hungry, (is seen begging, stealing or hoarding food, and comes to school with little food of his own);

– Poor hygiene; inadequate and inappropriate or soiled clothing;
– May be emaciated or may have distended stomach (indicative of malnutrition).

In addition the teacher may note that the child:

– is frequently late or absent from school without explanation;
– informs the teacher that there is no caregiver in the home;
– exhibits stealing, vandalism or other delinquent behaviors;
– has poor peer relationships, perhaps because of hygienic problems or a depressed negative attitude because of low self – esteem;
– is fatigued, listless or sleepy;
– craves affection;
– shows destructive type behaviors; and
– indicates behaviors that pose a threat to his or her safety.

Teachers should also be alerted to physical abuse indicators in their students which might include:

– unexplained bruises and welts on face, lips, mouth, torso, back, or sides; or numerous bruises of different colors (reflecting shape of articles used – cord, rope, belt buckle, clothes hanger);
– bald spots.
– human bite marks;
– unexplained burns;
– cigarette diameter on soles of feet or palms of hands;
– immersion burns;
– electric burner or iron shaped burns;
– unexplained fractures, lacerations or abrasions;
– injuries regularly appearing after absences or weekends;
– defensiveness in regards to injuries;
– consumption of poisonous, corrosive or non medical mind altering substances.

The behavioral symptoms may include:

– exhibition of low self-esteem;
– wariness of physical contact with adults;
– apprehension when other children cry;
– reporting of injury by parent;
– resists changing clothing for school activities;
– early arrival, stay late at school and appears reluctant to go home;
– wearing clothing that covers body and maybe inappropriate for warm months;

– cannot tolerate physical contact or touch;
– extremes in behavior, aggression or withdrawal.
– being a chronic runaway.
– being unable to form good peer relationships (abused children are some-times forgiven by their parents for making friends or bringing them home; and
– being fearful (the child may assume that all adults hurt children and is con-stantly on guard).

Teachers should be aware that abused children typically explain injuries by attributing them to accidents in play or sibling conflict. It is generally recom-mended that no staff member should attempt to press a child on the subject of parental or guardian abuse. Any doubt about reporting a suspected situation is to be resolved in favor of the child and the report made immediately.

Teachers are in an excellent position to recognize possible sexual abuse indicators. These might include:

– difficulty in walking or sitting,
– pain or itching in the genital area,
– frequent urinary or yeast infections,
– sudden onset of enuresis and encopresis, and
– frequent unexplained sore throats.

Behavioral symptoms associated with sexual abuse include:
– shows unusual interest in sexual matters and seems to have more sexual knowledge than is appropriate for child's age,
– does drawings which are sexually explicit, beyond developmental level,
– shows an inordinate fear of males or seductiveness towards males,
– has large number of gifts, or money from a questionable source,
– is exceptionally secretive,
– has bouts of crying with no provocation,
– is not permitted to participate in extra curricular or community activities,
– is unwilling to participate in physical activity,
– talks about or attempts suicide,
– is a chronic runaway,
– masturbates publicly and excessively,
– reports sexual approaches by an adult,
– involved in adolescent prostitution.[8]

Emotional indicators may include:
– speech disorders,
– severe allergies or ulcers, and

– physical development.

Teachers may be alerted to behavioral indicators of emotional abuse or neglect which include:

– indicating poor self-esteem by way of body language, facial expression or other non verbal communication patterns,
– constant apologizing, even when not at fault,
– inappropriate emotional response to situation,
– behavioral extremes, in other words compliant, and passive or aggressive and demanding,
– sleep disorders, inhibition of play,
– cruelty, vandalism, stealing, cheating,
– rocking, thumb sucking, biting,
– enuresis,
– fearing failure, gives up and won't try again,
– setting high standards for own performance in order to gain approval, then can't cope,

Emotional abuse is often difficult to pinpoint and it is not as visibly specific as is physical and sexual abuse or neglect, nor is it easy to substantiate. Nevertheless, its effects on children are dramatic.

According to the latest provincial Child Welfare Legislation, it is not necessary that the reporting teacher observe any external physical signs of injury to the child. It is sufficient merely to presume that abuse has occurred when a child complains of having been sexually molested or of pain which he/she says has resulted from an inflicted injury. In such cases the report should be made. It is not the teacher's responsibility to substantiate the abuse. It is the teacher's responsibility to report his/her concerns or suspicions.[8]

What then is the role of the teacher in possible child abuse situations?[11]

A child who discloses a situation involving abuse or neglect to a teacher requires a sensitive and understanding response. In these instances communication skills, both verbal and non verbal, are of utmost importance. It is important to believe the student; it is also very important to alleviate guilt, in other words reassure the student that he/she is not to blame and many others have had similar experiences. The teacher might also communicate support by thanking the student for showing trust and commending the student for having the courage to disclose what might be a very serious incident.

The teacher should be careful not to react with horror, alarm or disgust, as this may further traumatize the child. It's important that the teacher not criticize the offender in any way because the student may still care deeply for this individual.

Avoid the temptation of promising the child that you will not tell anyone. This, in a way, removes your ability to take control of the situation. Remember that the purpose of reporting the maltreatment of the child is to get help for the troubled child and his/her family. One final note might be to re-emphasize that it is important that the teacher not ask a student why he/she let it go on for so long, as this might imply that the student had the ability to stop it from happening.[11]

In summary when dealing with the ongoing support of an abused child, the teacher should know the resources in the community and cooperate with Child Welfare workers. The teacher should also let the student know that he/she is there to help and listen if needed, and to try and give the child the additional attention whenever possible. In addition it is important that the warmth loving reassurance be attributed to the child on a regular basis for a period of time. Teachers should also work with allied professionals who will likely be called in to counsel the child. Teachers should be concerned about the rights of the child, the rights to life, food, clothing, shelter and security. The parents also have a right to receive help and support.

Teachers should keep aware of their own feelings and perceptions through the investigative. They should not be adverse to reaching out and asking for counselling, as this process may affect all concerned.[8]

Child abuse is a serious and complex problem. In many cases school personnel are the only resources available to a child. By detecting and reporting expected cases of child abuse and neglect, the school can play a critical role in protecting the interests and well-being of the child. Teachers are especially important in the process of communication at all levels to ensure that the relationship between the teacher and the child is supportive and positive throughout this investigative process which might occur.

Self-Destruction Behavior in Schools

Self destructive behavior of students is a very complex syndrome that is influenced by the interactive effects of environmental, developmental and intrapsychic factors. Suicide among our youth is increasing. According to the Bureau of Vital Statistics for the years 1979 to 1982, in the 15 to 24 year old category, the number of suicides has risen 12.4% per 100,000. This figure represents an increase of over 300% since 1950. This rate places suicide third to accidents and homicides as causes of death in this age group.[14]

John Davis in a recent article dealing with suicidal crisis in schools stated that, given a high school population of 2000 students, one would expect suicidal thoughts in perhaps as high as 25 to 30% of the student body. There could be as many as 50 suicide attempts each year and about one successfully completed suicide every 2 to 4 years.[12]

These self-destructive behaviors have become a major concern and the understanding of the nature and dynamics of suicidal behavior is crucial for the prevention of such action as well as for effective therapeutic outcome. The literature throughout the last decade is clear. More and more children and adolescents think about suicide, more and more are attempting suicide and unfortunately more are committing suicide.[13] We can only guess as to the actual number of threats or attempts since the accuracy of these statistics leaves a lot to be desired. Statistics can be inaccurate owing to over or under-reporting. It is safe to assume that suicides are not over reported because of the denial and social stigma associated with suicide, particularly with children and adolescents. Often information from suicide attempters is distorted and may be very different from data obtained, if possible shortly before the attempt.

Dispelling Common Myths

In schools part of the difficulty in obtaining accurate information concerning suicide and other self-destructive behaviors is perhaps a number of prevailing myths which may be directly or indirectly adhered to by our educators.[14]

One commonly held myth is that children who talk about killing themselves rarely do it. In recent years there have been a number of articles to suggest that most young people who commit suicide have in fact given some clue or warning of their intent. The implication is that all suicidal threats, gestures and attempts should always be treated seriously.[15] There is some initial data to indicate that they mere notion of idolizing about death and other fantasies are a part of the personality make-up of someone who is contemplating a serious suicidal threat.

Another myth is the claim that suicide is inherited and passed from one generation to another. Although suicide may have associated variables which are common within families, what is passed on to the young person is the style and manner of coping with problems. The adult represents the most significant other to that young person, therefore how the adult responds to stress and problems of everyday living will quite readily be passed on to the children.

It is held by some people that the suicidal person wants to die and feels there is no turning back. In fact with the younger population, in most cases there is ambivalence about dying. The person will call for aid immediately following an attempt at suicide and this type of attempt has been labeled "a cry for help."[14]

The myth that all suicidal children and adolescents are depressed at the time of their attempt has received considerable press.[12] Although the impression is often associated with suicidal feelings, not all young people who want to kill themselves are depressed. In fact some people who attempt suicide appear to be happier than they have been in quite a while, because they have decided to resolve all of their problems at the same time. Related to this myth is that of a depression lifting and there be no longer any danger of suicide. It has been reported in several investigations that the greatest danger of suicide exists during the first three months after a person recovers from a depression.[16,15,10]

This holds even more true with the adult population, but there is not sufficient evidence that it is also true for suicidal young people. Perhaps the myth that receives the most attention is that if you ask a suicidal person about his or her intentions, you will encourage the person to commit suicide.[14] Recent research suggests the opposite is true. Talking about the suicide will often lower he anxiety level provided there is established rapport, trust and honesty between the person asking the questions and the person answering.[16]

The final myth that prevails is that suicide is a spontaneous activity which occurs without warning, especially in young people. There are the impulsive spur of the moment personalities that use self-destruction as a means to achieving attention or manipulating or getting out of responsibilities. However most young people who are suicidal plan their self-destructiveness in advance and then present communication both verbal and non verbal that indicates they are becoming more and more suicidal.[16]

Identifying Possible Risk Factors in Students

Having stated the aforementioned, the concern for teachers is that sometimes they cannot identify who in their class are at risk for to self destructive behaviors and who are not. In general, some red flags for teachers include:[16]

- a reduction in weight,
- loss of motivation,
- reduced grade levels,
- inability to concentrate at school,
- a shift in extreme forms of behavior (in other words a moody student who has been happy or a very happy student being very sad and angry),
- a quiet spoken individual suddenly becoming rambunctious and little tyrant "a child that has been typically out of control, overly active and generally into mischief suddenly showing signs of withdrawal."
- lack of spontaneity,
- decrease in general activity,
- giving away of prized possessions to friends and relatives (this is a way of putting their life in order and parting with materialistic things),
- writing poems about death, the afterlife,
- drawings about death, the afterlife,
- bringing to school knives or guns or ropes and showing them to peers,
- skipping classes,
- incomplete assignments,

It is most unfortunate that myths have permeated the public educational sector. It is critical that myths concerning young suicide people be dismissed and replaced with facts. Therefore, systematic research of a long-term nature is required. It's interesting that articles or research on suicide are seldom found in school psychology journals. This is further complicated by political and financial risks in allowing research to be conducted within school systems.[14] However no amount of political, financial or other administrative risks can ever match the potential risk of a suicidal school age child or adolescent going unnoticed.

For the teacher who reads the paper and hears the radio or watches T.V. there ultimately has been an increase of sensitivity towards young suicides. We have often heard the statement that the children are our most precious resources. However to a suicidal young person this statement has lost meaning; for this person has no purpose in living any longer. Society, parents and teachers in part share the blame that a young person addresses in rationalizing the intent to die.

Conclusion

The intent of this brief paper was to highlight verbal and non-verbal signs which could alert the teacher to possible at risk students. Running behaviors, abuse behaviors and self-destructive behaviors were discussed. A major problem confronting the teacher is the possible anxiety aroused when dealing with such a student. This anxiety may be due to training and experience. The implication is that more inservices and/or workshops are needed. Indeed, the task of saving lives recognizes no status or jurisdictional boundaries. The teacher continues to be the major gate keeper to screening, filtering, detecting and confirming at "risk students." Teachers, however, must be supported internally by administrative staff and externally by society to help students "at risk."

Notes

[1]D. Kronick, "Exceptional Treatment," *Alberta Teacher's Magazine,* March/April, 1988.

[2]A.J. Yates, *Behavior Therapy,* New York: Wiley, 1970.

[3]D.A. Russell,*On Running Away,* London: Van Nostrand Reinholt, 1981.

[4]S. Wolk and J. Brandon, "The Runaway Adolexcent's Perception of Parents and Self," *Adolescence, 12,* 46-52, 1977.

[5]R. Jenkins, "The Runaway Reaction," *American Journal of Psychiatry, 128,* 21-28, 1971.

[6]C. Zastrow and R. Navarre, "Help for Runaways and Their Parents," *Social Casework,* February, 1975.

[7]Alberta Social Services and Community Health, "Program Manual – Child Welfare Act," July 1985.

[8]S. Goodman, "Child Protection: A School's Responsibility," Media Services Group, Calgary Board of Education, 1986.

[9]I. Kaufman and L. Heims, "The Body Image of the Juvenile Delinquent," *American Journal of Orthopsychiatry, 28,* 146-159, 1988.

[10]J.M. Toolin, "Therapy of Depressed and Suicidal Children," *American Journal of Psychotherapy, 32,* 243-251, 1978.

[11]R.E. Helfer and C.H. Kempe, *The Battered Child.* University of Chicago Press, 1974.

[12]J. Davis, "The Prediction of High School Suicidal Behavior," *School Psychology, 29,* 312-316, 1985.

[13]J. Barter, D. Todd and D. Swaback, "Adolescent Suicide Attempts: A Follow-up Study of Hospitalized Patients," *Archives General Psychiatry, 19,* 523-527, 1968.

[14]V. Grossi, "Suicidal Behavior in Schools: Dispelling Common Myths," *Alberta Teacher's Association Magazine,* March/April, 1986.

[15]P. Paulson, D. Stone and R. Sposto, "Suicide Potential and Behavior in Children," *Suicide and Life-Threatening Behavior, 8,* 225-242, 1978.

[16]C.F. Wells and I.R. Stuart, "Self-Destructive Behavior in Children and Adolescents," Van Nostrand Company: New York, 1981.

28

Noisy Communication and Imagination in Education

LeRoy D. Travis

To see a World in a Grain of Sand
And Heaven in a Wild Flower
Hold Infinity in the palm of your hand
And Eternity in an Hour.

(William Blake)

Comingling Contraries and Imagination

Many of you know that there are two kinds of people in this world. There are those who think there are two kinds of people and those who don't. Those of us who think there are two kinds of people are very tolerant of those who don't. *Even though we know that there are others who are contrary to us, we comingle with them.* Indeed we need them to be right.

I'm not sure that those who don't think there are two kinds of people are so very tolerant. To this I will return later. Meanwhile, let me indicate why I think there are two kinds of people and why I think failure to realize this basic fact is important.

A failure of imagination is demonstrated when one fails to realize there are two kinds of people. Moreover, this failure of imagination is a condition which generalizes noise that interferes with learning, with the capacity of teachers to teach, with education and cultivation. Imagination is an expression of our intelligence. We fall short when we don't cherish, protect, cultivate and employ it. Life without intelligence, without imagination, is a noisy, unpleasant condition.[6,7]

So let us remember there are two kinds of people whenever we undertake endeavors that entail other people. We should remember the dead while we mingle with the living. When we refuse to see that we die as we live; when we repress the truth of death's presence; we act as if death doesn't matter. Well remember that the world is populated by the ugly as well as non-ugly people. Again, this is an important truth. If one forgets that there are ugly as well as non-ugly people one might become engaged in a fight with ugly people – and they have nothing to lose. And, educators should remember that there are the motivated and the unmotivated. When this is forgotten trouble arises – no matter which of the two groups is forgotten. When a teacher fails to imagine the possible presence, and comingling of those who are motivated (or disposed to grapple with matters at hand and those who are not so disposed) both the teacher and the members of the unimagined group will make noise that inter-feres with the educational endeavors of the others. This noisy state of affairs can incite antagonisms, strife and fights between people, and it interferes with education and cultivation.

Accordingly, we have reason for concern about imagination and its well-being in culture and education. This concern is shared with others in the com-munication trades. Contemporary writers and scholars like V.S. Naipaul, Oliver Sacks and Northrop Frye express a tradition of concern with these same matters that received attention from venerable poets such as William Blake, W.H. Auden, and Matthew Arnold.

An Imaginative Idea: Sedation by Film

Naipaul says the camera makes the world we inhabit seem ordinary; and that sense of familiarity or ordinariness sedates or subdues wonder, imagina-tion, and meditation on a world that is always both old and new.[14] While the camera can be used with artistry to stimulate wonder, thought and imagination, such artistry like all artistry, is uncommon. Commonplace camera work is ubi-quitous, cliche and monotonous. So, *the tranquilized imagination which exag-gerates the ordinariness in everything, fails to take note of the contraries,* or what the poet Blake called the "comingling of contraries," that an alert imagi-nation finds everywhere.

We are all used to the association of imagination with childhood fantasy, art, and creation generally. However, we may be unduly primitive in our psychol-ogy if we suppose imagination is just a faculty which is sometimes at work and then only in special circumstances. Naipaul makes the entirely reasonable assumption that imagination is implicated as a regular feature of all attempts to make sense of the world we inhabit, in all we do to examine the particulars of experience.

If he is correct, we in the communication trades have reason to pause and reflect on these matters. Let us consider the world of teaching as an illustrative domain wherein the velleity of imagination is standard if not universal.

Imagination and the Occupation of Teaching

Teaching, something I've been doing for nearly thirty years, is, in my view, many things. One of the first things we need to remember is that teaching is an occupation. Occupation holds a person in place; place fixes a person in time. A person in place and time lives according to the rhythms of sleeping, eating, working and communing. So teaching occupies particular social, cultural, economic and biological as well as temporal and spatial, niches.

In this pedagogic world – as it is commonly, even usually, organized - one finds little that fires the imagination. Granted, one does notice a monotonous fervor; and there is no lack of pseudo-seriousness. Indeed solemn frivolity is rampant in education. Much in the occupation is stupifying for bright adults. Even people of middling abilities and modest personal strength, those who happen to be the vast majority of teachers, don't stand up well to the monotony of tool thinking which seems to prevail among those who have the power to structure the work world of teachers.

Tool-Thinking, Teaching and Imagination

The comingling of contraries complicates (and this is why Blake said that without contraries there is no progression). When the prevailing impulse is to simplify, tool thinking tends to triumph over imagination, understanding and indeed knowledgeability. An examination of tool thinking reveals its appeal to the beseiged, the semi-educated as well as the dull and unimaginative. Tool thinking, as Bettelheim describes it, emphasizes utility. "Skills" is the watchword.

When reading, for example, is not regarded first and foremost, as a source of stimulation and knowledge under the volitional control of the reader, it becomes merely a tool one masters to attain some other end. Says, Bettelheim:

> Tool thinking is concerned with tools: how best to master and perfect the use of them. The point is that one masters use of a tool for a reason – to attain some other end; mastery of the tool itself means nothing. . .
> Such tool thinking applied to learning, though it has its place. . . will not lead to scholarship.[2]

If one is urged to learn "reading skills" for some solemn and remote prospect like the preparation of one's income tax forms or gaining acceptance in employment that requires the "processing" of printed information, the noise of such urging diverts attention away from the genuine goals of reading which are connected directly to "the independent acquisition of knowledge through one's own efforts, motivated by one's own curiosity.". Too often nowadays, one senses that "concentration on efficiency in developing a skill at the expense of emphasis on its deeper purpose makes the skill itself seem unimportant." Thus teachers are encouraged to make learning easy, pleasant and amusing; and so they "often end up creating vacuous images of life and people" and reading "seems pointless because the reading matter is so empty."[2] If content doesn't matter, why learn to read?

Sweetness and Light Versus Noise of Mechanism and Method

Tool thinking, while emphasizing skills and utility, deemphasizes facts and knowledge, trivializes understanding and knowledgeability. The venerable poet, critic and educator, Mathew Arnold, warned us against this more than a century ago when, in *Culture and Anarchy,* he identified as "our besetting danger," the over-valuation of and faith in "machinery". Arnold stressed the significance of content in his embrace of culture as the source of the "sweetness and light" that forestalls anarchy. He recommended culture

> as the great help out of our . . . difficulties; culture being a pursuit of our total perfection by means of getting to know, on all matters which most concern us, the best which has been thought and said in the world; and through this knowledge, turning a stream of fresh and free thought upon our stock notions and habits, which we now follow staunchly but mechanically, vainly imagining that there is virtue in following them staunchly which makes up for the mischief of following them mechanically.[1]

While observation, thinking and reading were identified by Arnold as the principal means by which a person comes to what is reasonable, good and beautiful, of "far more" importance is the content of his thoughts, the objects of his observations, the particulars of *"what* he reads."[1]

More recently, the distinguished neurologist, Sacks reiterated Arnold's distress about the over-valuation of "machinery" and under-valuation of particular content. Addressing the "folly" of translating all manner of terms to mechanical categories, Sacks wrote:

> This is the madness of the last three centuries, the madness which many of us . . . go through, and by which all of us are tempted. It is this . . . view – variously paraphrased in medicine, biology, politics, . . . etc. – which reduces men to machines, automata, formulae . . . systems and reflexes. It is this in particular, which has rendered so much of our . . . current . . . medical literature unfruitful, unreadable, inhuman and unreal.
> There is nothing alive which is not individual; our health is ours; our diseases are ours; our reactions are ours – no less than our minds or our faces. Our health . . . and reactions cannot be understood . . . in themselves; they can only be understood with reference to us . . . Yet [the prevailing impulse] dismisses our existence, either reducing us to identical replicas reacting to fixed stimuli in equally fixed ways . . . seeing our diseases [or ignorance] as purely alien and bad, without organic relation to the person . . .[18]

Tool thinking shifts emphasis away from content and the efforts of the learner. In the bargain, a mystique is created around special metaphors: "skills," "processes" and techniques or "methods" that are putatively critical factors in school learning. Accordingly, the organizational emphasis and talk mislead everyone about what matters. In spite of the fact that research on the promotion of general skills indicates that this tool emphasis is misguided at best.[5,8,15] and general developmental formulations are of little worth as guides to practice.[4,11,12,13,17] textbook writers[21] persist in the "folly" of prescribing tools to teachers. All the while, says Bettleheim.

> ... the problem of all teaching is essentially that of stimulating curiosity in the students while at the same time giving them the conviction that they are able to satisfy parts of it through reading and study. The problem of teaching to read, then, is primarily one of convincing pupils that the printed word holds the answers to important questions abut which they are curious.[2]

When this is not understood the educational system and the children within it are inundated with so much worthless content and noise only an active and well-stocked imagination can ignore and thereby transcend the clap-trap and educate itself.

Surface and Depth in Teaching

This returns us to what is involved in teaching. Above all, that is on the surface, teaching entails talk. Talk expresses and forms impressions. But talk is only one of the various symbolic forms of communication which are called on to fill the place and time that teaching occupies. Language, myth, art and ritual are all public communications of a communal sensibility. These, in mixtures of one or another degree of richness or poverty, are found where the teaching occupation is seen. However, if on the surface, teaching entails talk and the other means of expressing a communal sensibility, at the depths it entails repression.

Consider that life entails death. Here is a stark example of the comingling of contraries. If one wishes to reflect intelligently on life, understand it somewhat, come to terms with it so to speak, one needs to take account of the facts of death. As Camus says: "The order of the world is shaped by death."[3] But this is rough stuff. the attentive observer knows that in the flux of memories, anticipations, wishes, fears, schemes, cares, concerns, emotions, perceptions, interpretations, judgments, defenses, and manoeuvers; in the flux of social-psychological interplay, no single "reality" is sovereign. *Within and between individuals and groups, trust and suspicion, hostility and sympathy, cooperation and resistance comingle.* In the classroom, teachers are wise who manage to maintain a tension between freedom and necessity: between structure and spontaneity; between the palpable and the abstract. As pupils and teachers interact with one another and grapple with texts, impulse and reflection comingle as do sharpness and dullness, puerility and maturity, acceptance and rejection, interest and estrangement. What is banal here is mysterious there; and what seems sensible there is nonsense here.

The flux of experience is fixed by our nature and condition. We cannot escape from the comingling of good and evil, beauty and ugliness, truth and falseness. Each category calls forth the null category which defines its limits, its boundaries, and the contrasts upon which its meaning depends. So while teachers may group children to reduce the complexities that arise when sharpness and dullness (or when helplessness and self-sufficiency comingle), they cannot separate singularity from generality since only thought makes the particulars of life's experience general.

Accordingly, the tacit coexists with the explicit in even the most punctiliously planned and meticulously monitored precision teaching. So too timidity and boldness dwell in every soul just as do innocence and corruption. We are all both tough and fragile, courageous and cowardly, resolute and self-doubting; and while few teachers have not sensed vulnerability in children more should see a remarkable resiliency in them too. In the face of the multitude of antinomies, many teachers fall silent and manifest velleity as their principal public quality.

This velleity (this condition of suspended wish, thought, feeling and action; this paralysis of will and character), reflects an incapacity to ignore the incessant demands, the meddling, the inconstancy of official direction and the fickleness of commitment that characterize the world of teaching. It also reflects a consequence of the common, absurd refusal on the part of thinkers, the theoreticians in education, to call things by their right names; and, in particular, it shows the result of an avoidance by educators to admit that teaching is not a singular, coherent activity; that rather, it donates a multitude of very different activities and conditions whose variety, whose particularity, precludes the development of a coherent teaching technology.

So the velleity of so many teachers reflects a condition of unresolved conflict and repression that arises from the fact that teaching of almost any sort is an evolving emotional situation with indeterminate thoughts, feelings, reactions, expectations, conflicts and more. Meanwhile, the discourse about teaching virtually always ignores this and strives toward formulae, methods and prescriptions. In the absence of a tradition which strives to articulate the tacit knowledge upon which teachers depend and in the absence of a psychology of tact which is the psychology of practice, many teachers are beset with doubts, conflicts, and guilt. Their velleity reflects these doubts, conflicts, guilt and the repression which such can evoke.

Others, in numbers that decline somewhat as experience increases, manifest that monotonous fervor that I mentioned, which expresses faith in the fashion of the moment. This is essentially a manifestation of the ideological heavy breathing one hears elsewhere – especially in the business world. The scope of the imagination is truncated severely by ideological hyperventilation. So we get the exaggerations that betray defenses at work, that signal the presence of repression, guilt, conflict and sensed inadequacy. So we hear much talk of strategies, methods, technologies, analysis; and we see little resistance to (or criticism of) such talk inappropriateness of exaggerating cool rationality in teaching.

If widespread velleity and ideological heavy breathing are comingled for long in the body of schooling, teaching becomes a decultured trade; and the man with a teaching license is too often well described by that line of Yeats: " . .

A man full of the secret spite of dullness . . . "

Both the fervent booster and the timid spirit are ready to hide in the folds of familiarity. According to the well-known British educational philosopher Henry Wilt, who, in Sharpe's apocraphal story, attempted to teach humanities to those in Pipefitters I and Meatcutters II

> "All you have to do is tell people what they want to hear and they will believe you no matter how implausible your account may be.[20]

Obviously, the two last decades are not unlike the one Auden p. 458) described as "a low dishonest decade." In such times, the dull pedagogue who needs no further stupification is hussled by the prophets of tool thinking and does what he is told. In so doing, his imagination is diverted or put to sleep and his "noise" interferes with the wits of his pupils.

The Sense of the Ordinary, the Camera and Subdued Imagination

So, Naipaul says that the camera makes everything seem ordinary and that the sense of ordinariness sedates and subdues the imagination. Since a tranquilized imagination is short of energy, edge and powers of penetration, it tends to exaggeration. It follows the easy course. It refuses to serve volition. It fails to take notice of subtlety, of the comingling contraries, the contradictions in life that make living or teaching by recipe the absurdity it is. So we may owe something to the camera for the over-abundance of dull, inarticulate picture-people – those dominated by simple images and shallow thought – those who make so much noise in the name of education.

Naipaul is a splendid writer of novels and essays. His works please this reader for more than one reason. However, for present purposes I'll mention just one reason which is that his works are infused with evidence of an alert or restless imagination. He shares his sense of the comingling of contraries in all he portrays for the reader. He is a great wordsmith, as was William Blake, who, we remember, said that without contraries there is no progress. Great wordsmiths know how words can force us to notice things. Naipaul wants us to notice how the ubiquitousness of the camera's pictures puts words out of work.

We all know that the camera photographs anything that reflects light. We can even get photographs of phenomena that don't reflect light if their energy characteristics are transformed to light variance. In other words, just about everything in the world that stimulates, delights or excites us can be and is aimed at by somebody's camera. We know this because everywhere we see pictures from settled or frozen stills to unsettled or moving images. Nearly everything is given camera treatment. That is, nearly everything is simplified and made to seem ordinary; and what seems ordinary can be taken as is, and invites no further thought: we have seen it before.

The extraordinary becomes, in a sense, like everything else when given camera treatment. We are shown pictures and suppose we know all about the depicted subject; and we don't have to be told "that's the way it is" by an avuncular voice once we have seen the pictures. Many tend to suppose that they *know* that is the way it is.

Now Naipaul may be saying something quite important when he says the camera tranquilizes the imagination by making everything seem ordinary. All who have known disappointment upon viewing a filmed treatment of a cherished book or play or short story from radio will tend to resonate with Naipaul's alarm. So might textbook writers who have had their prose exposition savaged by editors who insist that lightening up or thinness be given priority with picture appeal.

Other Possibilities

So few of us will not have some measure of sympathy for Naipaul's idea. Furthermore, other forces may be at work, and may be just as effective or more effective than the camera in tranquilizing imagination. For example, maybe the contemplation of or noticing of comingled contraries lacks appeal for some. When they encounter complexity they short circuit.

This last suggestion brings me back to teaching because teaching, some might suppose, is undertaken to help those taught become familiar with some topic. It is charged, in a sense, with *the burden of exaggerating the ordinariness of everything*. That is, it is undertaken *to make plain and simple what is obscure and difficult*. At least it can be, and is often, regarded that way.

However, I have noticed that whether or not it is regarded that way, teaching can make a fascinating subject seem banal and uninteresting. Oddly enough, this can be accomplished by striving to make the subject seem important or interesting. Exaggerated seriousness or the monotony one sees in those who find everything exciting or who enthuse over all children in general – even the repulsive ones, can transport the imagination of anyone in earshot into the arms of Morpheus.

Of Tact and Possibility: The Liberation of Imagination in Education

One must grant that there are real, unavoidable constraints and forces which urge teachers to look for managerial routines, organizational gambits, procedures and patterns that reduce the complexity or simplify lives interacting in school rooms. Since rigid adherence to hard and fact rules produces folly and nonsense, what does not respect the unpredictable nature of routes taken by imagination inevitably interferes with imagination.

The critical task of keeping the paths clear requires of the teacher the same refusal of hard and fast rules as was recommended by the poet Housman to those who would undertake textual criticism. Said Housman,

If a dog hunted for fleas on mathematical principles, basing his researches on statistics of area and population, he would never catch a flea except by accident.[23]

The teacher, like the dog, must have a timely sense of what and where to scratch; and like the dog and critic, the teacher is not well-guided by the statistics of area and population. Unfortunately this is not widely understood; and the consequence is that much "noise" is generated in and around schooling sites by those who suppose they know how to teach best when in fact such knowledge is possessed by nobody. This unpleasant truth is too seldom expressed – perhaps because, as Bernard Shaw once said, a temptation to tell the truth should be just as carefully considered as a temptation to lie.

In saying this, Shaw drew our attention to the complexities of social interactions. He pointed to a social standard beyond the intellectual standards of truth and falsehood. Northrop Frye's discussion of such matters clarifies the significance of Shaw's point for analyses of teaching and learning. Frye says that when we interact, the imagination is at play; and the imagination uses words to express a certain kind of social vision. Whatever is said may represent the actual meaning of a speaker or the words may be just a disguised expression of the speaker's emotional state. Often, we assume the latter but pretend to be assuming the former: we act as if people are what they seem to want us to believe about them. This social vision, says Frye, is that of society dressed up in its Sunday clothes.[6]

So much of the time we meet one another at the level of thought clichés the pat formulae of advertising, Tory talk (of the good old days) or liberal myths (about progress or promise). The clichés of the day signal the presence in the user's mind of an outlook which insulates him from genuine thought, and gives him the illusion that he thinks. The pat formulae of clichéd thought thought signify the presence of automatic, mechanical reactions – and the debasement of language and human relations arising from the commercial wish for a "nice day" or the indiscriminate declaration "that's great." Accordingly, ordinary speech serves to cover situations just as do the clothes we wear. In this way, says Frye, the imagination is left untried, unalert, uninformed and uninspired.[6]

Now, some might object to this criticism of conventionalism. Like Shaw, the objector might sense a need to keep social interactions from getting too rough. He might resort to smooth talk. After all, can we do without tact? Can we not imagine the strife we would face in a world without that tact which Cocteau said consists in knowing how far to go in going too far?

This is a serious objection for we teachers who, at once, wish to be honest and truthful but also wish to live in harmony. If we suppose that general education is concerned with the development of essential meanings – meanings which enable a person to be cultivated in speech and in the appreciation of symbols, gestures and the aesthetic dimensions of experience; which permit informed perception and reflection in matters of fact and confer a capacity for discipline in one's endeavors and relations with others; which enable one to chart an ethical course of conduct and which give one possession of a civilized outlook – if we accept this, we have need of an informed sense of tact.

What, then, is tact and how does it bear on our psychology as teachers and on the imagination of those we would teach? Since Jean-Paul Sartre was both an experienced teacher and a reflective, articulate observer who recorded his thoughts on tact, a review of his views seems appropriate for present purposes.

What we call tact, said Sartre is connected with "subtlety of spirit":

> To act with tact is to appreciate a situation at a glance, to embrace it as a whole, to feel it rather than to analyze it, but it is at the same time, to direct one's conduct by reference to a multitude of indistinct principles of which some concern vital values [e.g. grace, nobility, vivacity, biological style, life plan] and others express ceremonies and traditions of politeness that are altogether irrational. Thus to act 'with tact' implies that the doer of the act has adopted a certain conception of the world, one that is traditional, ritual and synthetic; one for which *he can give no reason*. It implies also a particular sense of psychological ensembles, it is in no sense critical, and . . . it takes on its whole meaning only in a strictly defined community with common ideas, mores and customs.[19]

Accordingly, Sartre regarded tact as a basic comprehension of others and adaptation of oneself to them in the spirit of that "sense of their particularity which precludes a general or universal human nature that calls for universal treatment."[19] Tact, then, is not merely the intelligence of the heart. While it entails a sympathetic or empathic sense, it also requires a knowledgeability born of direct experience that yields the knowledge that allows us to recognize something (in a facial expression, posture, vocalization or general appearance) by integrating awareness of particulars which we are unable to identify.[16]

Such knowledge seems necessary for the immediate appreciation of the possibilities and limitations that inhere in a social situation; it also seems to be entailed in the practical adjustments, upon which teachers rely as they address the flux of particulars in a teaching situation. Herbert Simon has called such acts of adjustments in the flow of events "satisficing.". Such acts "make sense" in the press of time, but they do so without recourse to deductive logic. Rather, their worth depends more on mutual trust, tact and good will as well as the teacher's thorough knowledge of the content of matters at hand and the people involved in his or her situation.

In the End

In closing, I want to underscore the significance of the foregoing considerations for those who would suppose, (a) that "a teacher must be a . . . craftsperson, applying trustworthy tools and procedures . . . with skill . . . "[21] (b) that teaching is a general name for a broad range of activities (not a simple concept that refers to a clear, and closed set of phenomena), (c) that teaching is undertaken with no explicit or preconceived purpose (Socrates had no behavioral objectives or lesson plan books), and (d) teachers should embrace (rather than fear) contrariety.

Noted References

[1]Arnold, M. (1960). *Culture and Anarchy*. London: Cambridge University Press (first published in 1869), 6 and 49.

[2]Bettelheim, B. (1980). *Surviving and Other Essays*. New York: Vintage, 142-168.

[3]Camus, A. (1960). *The Plague*. Harmondsworth, Middlesex, U.K.: Penguin Books, 107-108.

[4]Carey, S. (1985). Are children fundamentally different kinds of thinkers and learners than adults? In S. Chipman, J. Segal & R. Glaser (Eds.). *Thinking and Learning Skills, Volume 2: Research and Open Questions*. Hillsdale, N.J.: Erlbaum, pp. 485-517.

[5]Chipman, S., J. Segal & R. Glaser (Ed.) (1985). *Thinking and Learning Skills, Volume 2: Research and Open Questions*. Hillsdale, N.J.: Erlbaum.

[6]Frye, N. (1963). *The Educated Imagination* Toronto: CBC Publications.

[7]Frye, N. (1988). *On Education*. Toronto: Fitzhenry and Whiteside.

[8]Hayes, J. (1985). Three problems in teaching general skills.

[9]S. Chipman, J. Segal & R. Glaser (Eds.). *Thinking and Learning Skills, Volume 2: Research and Open Questions* Hillsdale, N.J.: Erlbaum, pp. 391-405.

[10]Hirsch, E. (1989). The primal scene of education. *The New York Review of Books, 36*, 3, 29-35.

[11]Kessen, W. (1988). Introduction: The end of the age of development. In R. Sternberg (Ed.). *Mechanisms of Cognitive Development*. Prospect Heights Illinois: Waveland Press. pp. 1-18.

[12]Leven, I. (Ed.) (1986). *Stage and Structure: Reopening the Debate*. Norwood, N.J.: Ablex.

[13]Murray, F. (1984). The application of theories of cognitive development. In B. Gholson & I. Rosenthal (Eds.) (1984). *Applications of Cognitive-Development Theory*. New York: Academic Press. pp. 3-18.

[14]Naipaul, V.S. (1981). *The Return of Eva Peron*. Harmondsworth, Middlesex, U.K.: Penguin Books.

[15]Nickerson, R. (1988). On improving thinking through instruction. In E. Rothkopf (Ed.) *Review of Research in Education*. Vol. 15, 1988-89. Washington, D.C.: American Educational Research Association. pp. 3-57.

[16]Polanyi, M. (1966). *The Tacit Dimension*. Garden City, N.Y.: Doubleday.

[17]Resnick, L. (1984). Toward an applied developmental theory. In B. Gholson & T. Rosenthal (Eds.). *Applications of Cognitive-Developmental Theory*. New York: academic Press. pp. 263-280.

[18]Sacks, O. (1983). *Awakenings*. New York: Dutton/Obelisk.

[19]Sartre, J.P. (1965) *Anti-Semite and Jew* (Translated by G. Becker). New York: Schocken Books (First Edition, 1946).

[20]Sharpe, T. (1978). *Wilt*. London: Pan Books.

[21]Slavin, R. (1986). *Educational Psychology: Theory into Practice*. Toronto: Prentice-Hall.

[22]Tierney, P. (1983). Herbert Simon's simple economics. *Science 83. 4,* 9 (November) 82-86, 88.

[23]Wells, R. (1988, July 15-21) Holding out alone. *The Times Literary Supplement* No 4450, 723-724.

29

Whole Language: A Problem

Robert D. Chester

Whole language, a relatively recent grass-roots movement in Reading and Language Arts instruction, has become a topic of growing interest and concern for many North American parents and educators. The movement has captured the attention of both the general public and the educational community. This is not surprising when one considers that it is led by such prominent educators as Goodman and Goodman, Smith, Harste, and Edelsky. It is equally not surprising that many of those involved in the movement have come to view whole language as some sort of educational panacea. We might ask: "What is it?" "From where did it come?" and, "Where is it going?" There appear to be many unanswered questions about whole language and, quite curiously, few critics to ask them. Indeed, judging from the paucity of criticism that has made it to print, one is left with the impression that there are no problems. It is from this observation that the present chapter takes its focus. It will identify and explore the obvious problems facing the movement, and address them.

Whole Language: What is it?

The first problem lies with the definition of whole language. The problem is not in the lack of a definition; rather, it lies with the proliferation of definitions that is emerging from the literature. As expressed by Gunderson and Shapiro, "The term whole language has nearly as many definitions as it has advocates."[13] Each proponent, according to his or her own assumptions about education, communication and learning, appears ready to offer a definition and an explanation of whole language which matches those assumptions. For example, Rich defines whole language as " . . . an attitude of mind which provides a shape for a classroom," and whole language instruction as " . . . a political activity since a true whole language notion returns power where it belongs – to the children and the teacher in the classroom."[23] For Edelsky, Draper, and Smith,

(1983) whole language appears to be a movement away from skills instruction, basals, and traditional methods and materials towards a more eclectic, but undefined, philosophical approach to instruction across the entire curriculum. Paulet on the other hand, sees whole language as an approach to teaching language arts which integrates listening, speaking, reading and writing centered in experiential learning.[20] Wangberg and Reutten use the term as a synonym for the language experience approach to teaching. According to them, "Through a whole language, or language experience approach, learners are encouraged to express their thoughts, feelings and experiences."[27] Fox (1986), who attributes its development to Kenneth and Yetta Goodman, refers to whole language as a program "in which literacy is seen as a natural extension of the child's language development."[11] Others have suggested using whole language with behavioral objectives,[18] or even as a vehicle for teaching spelling[16] and basic skills.[4,22] Ironically enough, even publishers such as Nelson, McGraw-Hill Ryerson, and Holt Reinhart are now producing basal reading series with a whole language orientation.

So one returns to the original question, "What is Whole Language?" Is it a philosophy, a modification of existing practices, or a specific approach? And the answer is, of course, yes. As currently offered in the literature and in educational and public forums, whole language may be any one or a combination of all of the above, depending upon who is defining it.

Whole Language: From Where Did It Come?

Many of the problems in defining whole language lie with its evolution and the influences of those individuals who have contributed directly or indirectly to its growth and development. Depending on whose contributions one includes, and how heavily those influences are weighed, differing descriptions and definitions of whole language emerge. Thus the term whole language becomes a superordinate covering a multitude of language and communication theories and practices. For example, ideas about the importance of integrating reading, writing, speaking, and listening are far from new. Thus, the influences of language experience proponents such as Allen[1], Stauffer[25], Lamoreaux and Lee,[17] and Hall[14] have done much to shape current understanding of an integrated approach to teaching language and communications arts. And, if one examines carefully Allen's model for a Language Experience Approach in Communication, one is hard pressed to see any differences between it and whole language as it is frequently presented. If there is a difference, as argued by Altweger, Edelsky, and Flores,[2] it would appear to lie more in conceptualization than in practice, i.e., why such an integration is important, not how it is implemented.

Two other major contributors influential in shaping our present conception of whole language are Sylvia Ashton-Warner and Holdaway. Ashton-Warner's organic reading, an experience centered approach to reading instruction, bears a striking similarity to the whole language emphasis on the use of the student's own language and concepts.[2] Holdaway, using many of the same procedures and working with a similar population, did much to explain and extend Ashton-Warner's work.[15] Since so much of what these two educators advocated, particularly in terms of children's rights to decision making in their own learning, has been adopted by the whole language movement, their influence should not be underestimated.

Depending on which definition one chooses for whole language, one can see other significant contributors, e.g., Grace Fernald and her work with the kinesthetic approach and early writing,[10] or Marie Clay and her work with the integration of reading and writing.[5] Without doubt, the best known proponents of the whole language movement are psycholinguists Kenneth and Yetta Goodman[12] and Frank Smith.[29] With their emphasis on reading as a meaningful act only when processing meaningful text, and their view that what the reader brings to the reading experience is equally as important as the text itself, they have added much to whole language proponents' argument for experience based reading instruction.

The list goes on as to who contributed what, when, and what it means. Whole language appears to have evolved from language experience, psycholinguistics, process writing, and a myriad of other educational developments occurring over past decades. Because it is still developing, it is impossible to say what other influences may yet come to bear on it.

Whole Language: What About Research Credibility

A second problem lies in the research credibility of the whole language movement. As with most grass-roots movements, the complexities of the evolutionary process frequently mask the real concerns and intentions of their proponents. This appears to be what is happening in whole language. Identifying problem areas and finding solutions become even more difficult when the definition of purpose and intent is too general and the focus is too broad. It would appear that what is most needed at this point is a more exact definition of whole language. Without such a definition and consensus of agreement by those both within and outside the movement, whole language is open to any interpretation. As it now stands, to those outside the movement, anyone implementing any program labeled 'whole language" is in fact providing a whole language program. No matter how poor or ill conceived, if that program fails, whole language has failed.

This lack of definition makes it difficult, if not impossible, to determine the nature and substance of any contributions being made by whole language. To date, most of the research on whole language has been qualitative in nature. As noted by Page, "Small samples, introspection, and disregard for revered statistical procedures are characteristic of many of these qualitative studies."[19]

However, having said this, he then goes on to defend the use of qualitative research as being the most appropriate tool for accessing the types of information needed by whole language investigators. While one must agree that qualitative research is important, it is equally true that it is limited in terms of producing results and recommendations appropriate for generalization to other populations. For the latter, one needs empirical research, and this appears to be in short supply where whole language is concerned. With few exceptions, most of the whole language research that has emerged has failed to define whole language in terms of specific investigations, has provided only vague information about procedures, populations, controls, and measures and has produced little in way of empirical evidence. Even the exceptions, e.g., Gunderson & Shapiro,[13] Edelsky et al.,[8] and DeFord[7] have not produced results which can be replicated in other situations. In view of the confusion presently surrounding the whole language concept, this is not surprising. However, it would appear that one major obstacle could be overcome through the use of an operational definition of whole language. By using such a definition, the researcher could describe whole language in terms of the methodology and materials employed in the investigation and provide results based on that definition. Such a procedure would allow for replication, comparison, and generalization to other appropriate settings. This approach appears to be far superior to glowing testimonials from individuals who tell us how well whole language succeeded, without telling us how they defined it or what took place. As Emans so appropriately puts it, "Hypotheses unchecked by objective evidence are no more than superstitions and unfounded personal opinion."[9]

Whole Language: Communication problems

A third problem, no less serious than the first two, is the tendency of whole language proponents to present themselves as keepers of the whole truth, or at least to appear to do so. Much too often the literature concerned with whole language is saturated with statements such as "Negative comments from uninformed teachers make me realize that I have a responsibility to educate and support my fellow teachers as they move towards a whole language philosophy."[21] If whole language teachers are more informed, more sensitive to the needs of the children, more aware of how to address those needs, more dedicated etc., then it follows that teachers who are not whole language teachers must be less informed, less sensitive, less dedicated, and so on. Without following the analogy further, it appears that the debate over whole language has set people into two camps: those for whole language and those unenlightened masses who, for one reason or another prefer more traditional approaches. As Suher states " . . . pro-phonic extremists tend to reduce the complex views of advocates of whole language instruction to simple phrases like "look-say." Conversely, true believers in whole language instruction brand phonics advocates as heartless Skinnerians . . .."[26] This division is unfortunate since one would assume that most educators are in education to assist children by making the most of the knowledge, skills, and resources available to them. And while some of the differences between the proponents of whole language and proponents of other approaches may be based on genuine philosophical conviction, it would appear that an even greater amount of the difference may be attributable to a lack of communication. The present ambiguity about the purpose and intent of whole language, and its lack of a clear definition, seem to have generated a great deal of confusion for parents and educators on both sides of the issue.

Whole Language and the Future

One can only speculate about where whole language will go from here. If it is to become a credible, viable alternative to other instructional programs already in place in the classrooms, it must examine its goals and objectives as they relate to the existing educational community. High among the priorities here is the recognition of contributions by other educators who are equally dedicated to excellence, but who prefer other approaches to instruction. More success can be gained by demonstrating what whole language can accomplish than by basal bashing and denigrating the contributions of other approaches.

Resolutions to some of the problems facing whole language would seem to revolve around better communication about the purpose and focus of whole language and better criteria for determining when, where, and under what circumstances it can be most appropriately implemented. For example, one suspects that some of the confusion and anxiety generated by the movement could be allayed if it were better understood in terms of its implications for those educators expected to implement it. In fact, many may justifiably ask what it is that they are supposed to implement. According to Rich, whole language cannot be described as a formula or as a set of published materials.[23] Altwerger et al. adds that is not a whole language approach, not teaching skills in context, not a method, not a basal approach, not an approach, not language experience, and not a new term for open education.[2] Information regarding what whole language "is not" appears readily available; identifying a consensus of information about what whole language "is" appears more elusive. Furthermore, even if one accepts the philosophical gestalt behind whole language, how can this be translated into meaningful, educational classroom activities for young children?

Concern over this lack of understanding is not limited to teachers and other educators; it is also shared by parents of those children involved. No doubt, committed proponents of whole language have gained satisfactory answers to these questions and are comfortable with those answers. However, until those answers are brought forward and explained to teachers expected to implement whole language and to parents of those children involved, much of the anxiety and confusion is likely to persist. It is not sufficient to claim a better understanding and knowledge of a better way; rhetoric and personal conviction are only sufficient for those already converted.

Finally, determining when, where, and under what circumstances an educational institution should commit to whole language is a decision that should be made in consultation with all members of the educational community. Before committing every teacher in the district or even every teacher in a school to this approach, it should be field-tested with those administrators and teachers who understand and support its philosophy. Indeed, there are instruments such as the Theoretical Orientation to Reading Profile which have been reasonably successful in identifying teachers suited to the whole language approach.[6]

In conclusion, if the amount of enthusiasm and interest generated by whole language is any indication, the movement created an atmosphere in which many parents and educators are forced to re-examine their fundamental beliefs about communication teaching, language acquisition, and the classroom environment. Unfortunately, while creating a lot of interest and excitement in some quarters, it has caused a great deal of anxiety and frustration in others. There appear to be a lot of unanswered questions, and unless these are addressed, whole language may well go the way of other innovations such as i.t.a. and the open area classroom. Paramount at this time is the need for a better definition of whole language, more and better research, and better communication about the movement's aims and goals. These questions are matters of substance; they will not go away.

Noted References

[1]Allen, R.V. (1976). *Language experiences in communication.* Boston: Houghton Mifflin.

[2]Altwerger, B., Edelsky, C., & Flores, B. (1987). Whole language: What's new? *The Reading Teacher* 144-156.

[3]Ashton-Warner, S. (1963). *Teacher.* New York: Simon and Schuster.

[4]Botel, M., & Seaver, J. (Nov. 1984). *Phonics revisited: Toward an integrated methodology.* (ERIC Document Reproduction Service No. ED 252-819).

[5]Clay, M. (1975). *What did I write?* Auckland: International Reading Association.

[6]DeFord, D.E. (1979). *A validation study of an instrument to determine a teacher's theoretical orientation to reading instruction.* Dissertation, Indiana University.

[7]DeFord, D.E. (1981). Literacy: Reading, writing,, and other essentials. *Language Arts,* 58, 652-658.

[8]Edelsky, C., Draper, K. & Smith, K. (1983). Hookin'em in at the start of school in a 'whole language' classroom. *Anthropology and Education Quarterly,* 14, 257-81.

[9]Emans, R. (1986). Theory, practice, and research in literacy learning. In D. Tovey and J. Kerber (Eds.), *Roles in Literacy Learning.* Newark, DE: International Reading Association, Inc.

[10]Fernald, G. (1943). *Remedial techniques in basic school subjects.* New York: McGraw-Hill.

[11]Fox, D. (1986). The debate goes on: Systematic phonics vs. whole language. *Journal of Reading,* 29, 678-680.

[12]Goodman, K., & Goodman, Y. (1981). A whole-language, comprehension centered reading program. Program in Language and Literacy Occasional Paper Number 1. Tucson, Ariz.: College of Education, Arizona University [ED 310 630].

[13]Gunderson, L. & Shapiro, J. (1987). Some findings on whole language instruction. Reading-Canada-Lecture, 5, 22-26.

[14]Hall, M. (1976). *Teaching reading as a language experience.* Columbus, OH: Merrill.

[15]Holdaway, D. (1979). *The foundations of literacy.* New York: Ashton Scholastic.

[16]James, M. (1986). Self-selected spelling. *Academic Therapy,* 21, 557-563.

[17]Lamoreaux, L. & *Lee, D.M. (1943). Learning to read through experiences.* New York: Appleton-Century-Crofts.

[18]Osburn, B. (1983). *Lesson plans, behavioral objectives and "whole language" can they work together?* (ERIC Document Reproduction Service No. ED 262-376).

[19]Page, D. (1986). The researcher, whole language, and reading. In D. Tovey and J. Kerber (Eds.), *Roles in Literacy Learning.* Newark, DE: International Reading Association Inc.

[20]Paulet, R.O. (1984). The whole language approach: Will it be used in Quebec and Manitoba? *English Quarterly,* 17, 30-36.

[21]Powell, L. (1987). Following the Children. *Classroom,* March/April, 20-21.

[22]Ramsey, W. (1985). Infusing clinical reading instruction with whole language. (ERIC Document Reproduction Service No. ED 266-411)

[23]Rich, S.J. (1985). Restoring power to teachers: The impact of "whole language." *Language Arts,* 62, 7, 717-724.

[24]Smith, F. (1978). *Understanding reading,* 2nd ed. New York: Holt, Rinehart and Winston.

[25]Stauffer, R.G. (1970). *The language-experience approach to the teaching of reading.* New York: Harper and Row.

[26]Shuher, C. (1987). ERIC/RCs report: Orthodoxies in language arts instruction. *Language Arts,* 64, 4, 416-419.

[27]Wangberb, E. & Reuten, M. (1986). Whole language approaches for developing and evaluating basic writing ability. *Lifelong Learning,* 9, 13-15, 24-25.